Conditions of work digest

Volume 14   1995

WORKING TIME AROUND THE WORLD

International Labour Office   Geneva

ISBN 92-2-109510-X

ISSN 0257-3512

Price for individual issues: 50 Swiss francs

Editor: Michele B. Jankanish

The International Programme for the Improvement of Working Conditions and Environment (PIACT) was launched by the International Labour Organization in 1976 at the request of the International Labour Conference and after extensive consultations with member States.

PIACT is designed to promote or support action by member States to set and attain definite objectives aiming at "making work more human". The Programme is thus concerned with improving the quality of working life in all its aspects: for example, the prevention of occupational accidents and diseases, a wider application of the principles of ergonomics, the arrangement of working time, the improvement of the content and organization of work and of conditions of work in general, and a greater concern for the human element in the transfer of technology. To achieve these aims, PIACT makes use of and coordinates the traditional means of ILO action, including:

- the preparation and revision of international labour standards;
- operational activities, including the dispatch of multidisciplinary teams to assist member States on request;
- tripartite meetings between representatives of governments, employers and workers, including industrial committees to study the problems facing major industries, regional meetings and meetings of experts;
- action-oriented studies and research; and
- clearing-house activities, especially through the International Occupational Safety and Health Information Centre (CIS) and the Clearing-house for the Dissemination of Information on Conditions of Work.

Printed in France

SAD

Table of contents

About this publication

The *Conditions of Work Digest* is a serial publication of the International Labour Office. Prepared by the Conditions of Work and Welfare Facilities Branch, Working Conditions and Environment Department, it is a reference source for all who are interested in working conditions and the quality of working life. Each issue is devoted to a subject of topical interest. The *Digest* includes information drawn from laws, regulations, collective agreements and other important texts. Additional features are included as appropriate, such as annotated bibliographies, relevant international standards, special sources of information and specialized glossaries.

Topics on conditions of work and quality of working life, such as the following, are covered:

- working time issues, including hours of work, shift work, part-time work and flexible hours;

- work organization and job content;

- the impact of new technologies on quality of working life;

- working conditions of specific groups, such as women workers, older workers, homeworkers and clandestine workers, and the subject of child labour;

- work-related welfare facilities and services.

Titles in the *Digest* series are as follows:

— Special issue on visual display units (Vol. 5, 1/1986);

— Flexibility in working time (Vol. 5, 2/1986);

— Alcohol and drugs: Programmes of assistance for workers (Vol. 6, 1/1987);

— Women workers: Protection or equality? (Vol. 6, 2/1987);

— The emerging response to child labour (Vol. 7, 1/1988) [out of print];

— Work and family: The child care challenge (Vol. 7, 2/1988);

— Part-time work (Vol. 8, 1/1989);

— Home work (Vol. 8, 2/1989);

— Telework (Vol. 9, 1/1990);

— The hours we work: New work schedules in policy and practice (Vol. 9, 2/1990);

— Child labour: Law and practice (Vol. 10, 1/1991);

— Workers' privacy, Part I: Protection of personal data (Vol. 10, 2/1991);

— Combating sexual harassment at work (Vol. 11, 1/1992);

— Preventing stress at work (Vol. 11, 2/1992);

— Workers' privacy, Part II: Monitoring and surveillance in the workplace (Vol. 12, 1/1993);

— Workers' privacy, Part III: Testing in the workplace (Vol. 12, 2/1993);

— Maternity and work (Vol. 13, 1994).

Other ILO serial publications of interest to users of the *Digest* include:

— *Safety and health at work: ILO/CIS Bulletin*. References and abstracts covering books, articles, laws and regulations on all aspects of occupational safety and health (produced by the International Occupational Safety and Health Information Centre of the ILO);

— *International Labour Review*. Articles on economic and social topics affecting labour, research notes and book reviews; news briefs on events in countries and regions; and news features probing into recent developments;

— *Labour Law Documents* (from 1919-1989 called *Legislative Series*).[1] Reprints and translations of selected labour and social security legislation recently adopted in countries throughout the world.

Individual issues of the *Digest* and above ILO serial publications can be ordered from the Publications Branch, International Labour Office, CH-1211 Geneva 22, Switzerland.

This publication may be cited as follows:

ILO: *Conditions of Work Digest* (Geneva), Volume 14, 1995, on *Working time around the world*.

---

[1] Discontinued from 1996; last issue 1995/3.

Acknowledgements

This issue of the *Conditions of Work Digest* was prepared by Robert Husbands, Gisela Schneider and Shengjie Li. Thanks are due to all those who contributed to different parts of this *Digest*, in particular Maria Aparicio, Dirk Belau, Gerardo Gúnera-Lazzaroni, Catherine Bråkenhielm Hansell, Juan Carlos Hiba, Chantal Paoli-Pelvey, Marie-Claire Séguret and Linda Wirth. Special appreciation is due to Kristine Falciola for the processing of the manuscript.

The Office would like to thank the many individuals, governments, employers, trade unions, research institutes and other organizations that provided information for this issue of the *Digest*.

Introduction

Introduction

This issue of the *Conditions of Work Digest* provides an overview of working time legislation throughout the world, and focuses on trends in regulation and practice in a selected number of countries.[1]

Part I presents a review of working time, employment and protection, which discusses the relationship between the length and arrangement of working time and employment preservation or creation. It emphasizes that social protection, especially in a time of uncertainty and flexibility, is paramount and that employment is not the sole reason to advocate changes in working time.

Part II contains a short summary of current trends in working time and 16 country studies from the different regions of the world. The studies illustrate how working time issues have evolved over the years, and how current law and practice determine hours of work for different categories of workers in the countries concerned. They also include information on normal hours of work, overtime and absolute maximum hours, rest periods, shop-opening hours, public holidays, paid annual leave and other types of leave, and, in some cases, shift and night work.

Part III consists of four sets of tables containing the basic legal provisions of 151 countries, which are preceded by a summary of the main findings. The first table covers normal hours of work, paid annual leave and public holidays. The second table focuses on overtime restrictions, premium pay and compensatory time off. The third table gives the provisions for rest periods during the working day, between working days and between working weeks. The fourth table mentions those countries that provide for special types of leave, be it for personal reasons, civic duties, religious reasons or others. A complete list of the legal sources containing the provisions cited is also provided.

---

[1] Previous issues of the *Conditions of Work Digest* focused on specific aspects of working time arrangements ("Flexibility in working time", Vol. 5, No. 2, 1986; "Part-time work", Vol. 8, No. 1, 1989; and "The hours we work: New work schedules in policy and practice", Vol. 9, No. 2, 1990).

Part I:
Working time, employment and protection

Working time, employment and protection

Introduction

The evolution and revolution in working time continues. In principle, the diversity in working time arrangements could provide for a much closer match between personal preferences and working time, but this often does not appear to be the case: some people are overburdened by their hours of work with no time left for leisure, family and community, while others have more time than they know what to do with. There remains a serious mismatch between the hours people want to work and those available to them.

The debate on working time and employment is not new. Since the Industrial Revolution, there have been those who repeatedly predicted that reductions in hours would be damaging for business. At the same time, there have been those who continually held out the promise of shorter working hours as a cure for unemployment. At least since the 1930s, arguments for worksharing have appeared periodically when unemployment was substantial during economic recession or depression. But, as always in history, things are not so clear-cut and the problem is what lessons to draw.

Clearly, the issues today are more complex. It is obvious that working time is in the forefront of social and economic debate because of the employment problem — the "common" affliction of many countries. The latest OECD data show unemployment declining only in Canada, the United Kingdom and the United States. Advances in technology, re-engineering and new ways of organizing work are allowing companies to have global reach without global size. The distribution and allocation of time, for men and women, is at the heart of powerful concerns about gender, family and production. As people join the labour market much later than before and can expect to retire earlier, the contraction of working life has implications not only for different forms of leave and flexible working time arrangements, but also for training and social security. Further, while the trend towards the "24-hour, 365-day" society might promote jobs, it also gives rise to working "unsocial hours", increased overtime, and "atypical" forms of work and precarious employment, which are usually characterized by low pay and inferior benefits.

Greater flexibility in determining the duration and organization or arrangement of working time to respond to economic pressures and workers' needs and preferences raises issues concerning protection. The "standard" work-week is disappearing, and there is a change in emphasis towards annual working hours and longer intervals for the average calculation of maximum hours per week, which may have repercussions on safety and health. The possibility of derogating legislation through collective bargaining is also happening in some countries. The increasing significance of enterprise- or plant-level bargaining and the weakening of union power, in some cases, have enabled workers to negotiate individual contracts allowing for greater flexibility, but at the same time have enabled employers to seize the opportunity to minimize fixed costs. With increasing flexibility in working time, what should be the basic safeguards? At what level should they be? How do we ensure in a policy of general deregulation that working time does not become the flexible resource to compensate for inadequate planning, poor organization of work and chaotic market structures?

This Part of the *Digest* describes how the length and arrangement of working time can contribute to employment preservation or creation. But it also emphasises that social protection, especially in a time of uncertainty and flexibility, is paramount and that employment is not the **sole** reason to advocate changes in working time. Specifically, the issues of worksharing, working time flexibility, social protection in a changing environment, and a vision of the future of working time are discussed. Considering that numerous other influences are involved and that situations in the countries vary, certain issues are simply raised to enlarge the vision of the problem and to assist in finding common ground where worker protection and time "sovereignty" can be reconciled or combined with enterprise and business requirements.

Worksharing: Is it just a matter of arithmetic?

Explaining arguments in favour of worksharing in simple terms, it is claimed that increases in productivity and output have led to "jobless growth", that it is unfair for some workers to be employed and others not, and that existing work should be shared or redistributed between the "haves" and the "have-nots". By reducing hours of work, available employment could be divided more equitably. Worksharing, however, is controversial because it puts into question the traditional thinking that new technology and increases in productivity and output create more jobs than they eliminate in the context of a growing economy. Moreover, worksharing is rejected by some because, they argue, the skill levels of the unemployed may not match those needed in the economy. In addition, unemployed skilled workers may not be available in the locations where work may be created, and there may be family or personal reasons restricting their willingness to relocate quickly. While unskilled work, in principle, could more easily be distributed, unskilled workers are among the lowest paid workers and can scarcely afford to share their already low wages. Moreover, unskilled work is generally decreasing and skilled work increasing in the industrialized countries.[1]

Also, there are questions relating to how work should be shared. Should income as well as work be shared, or should work be shared without a reduction in wages? If wages are not reduced proportionately, will it affect enterprise competitivity? Should worksharing be undertaken only at the enterprise level and be voluntary, or should it take place at the national level and be required by law? Should it take place in terms of reductions in daily or weekly hours; limits on overtime; additional paid leave or long-term leave; or limits on lifetime hours of work through, for example, early retirement? Also, tactically, should worksharing be used as a temporary measure to respond to an economic crisis, or should it be a long-term strategic choice to create jobs? These issues are reviewed below.

---

[1] See generally V. Di Martino: "Megatrends in working time", in *Journal of European Social Policy*, Vol. 5, No. 3, 1995, pp. 235-249; "A case for work-sharing?", in *Employment Policy Institute Economic Report*, Vol. 7, No. 15, December 1993, pp. 1-5; P. Dörsam: *The employment effects of a reduction and flexibilization of working time in selected European Union countries*, unpublished working paper prepared for the ILO, 1995; "One lump or two?", in *The Economist*, 25 November 1995, pp. 21-22.

Voluntary worksharing at the enterprise level:
An approach to preserve jobs?

Worksharing may have a limited role to play in employment preservation, or a more orderly rationalization of labour in a period of economic difficulty, if it is undertaken voluntarily at the enterprise level. In a period of economic recession, for example, the economy is by definition not growing, and the sharing of work may be a satisfactory means of limiting layoffs and retaining skilled workers, particularly if the employer estimates that the downturn is temporary. It may be that wages may have to be reduced in part or proportionally to any hour reductions to maintain competitivity and not increase unit labour costs, but there is evidence — essentially from the richer countries in Western Europe — that workers are willing to have slightly reduced incomes to save the jobs or limit the job losses of their colleagues, at least in a short-term perspective.[2]

Such an attitude towards worksharing, however, is more likely to be expressed by workers with relatively good incomes than by workers in low-income jobs. Worksharing which involves income-sharing would be scarcely acceptable to low-income workers who already have difficulty making ends meet. In the case of the worksharing agreement involving Volkswagen in 1993, which covered some 113,000 workers and involved a 20 per cent reduction of the normal working week to 28.8 hours averaged over the year as well as a pay cut of around 10 per cent, 30,000 jobs cuts were avoided in large part because the German auto workers concerned were relatively well paid to begin with.[3]

Other worksharing agreements at the enterprise or sectoral level have also managed to preserve jobs by reducing hours of work and, in most cases, income as well. For example, a sectoral agreement in western Germany in the coalmining industry, which ran until the end of 1995, covered 87,000 workers and avoided dismissals of 10,000 workers. This agreement provided for an extra 30 days of leave and a pay cut of around 10 per cent with special compensatory arrangements made for the workers with the lowest wages. Other worksharing agreements designed to protect employment at the industry level were concluded as well in Germany, but made actual hours and wage reductions subject to the signature of an enterprise agreement. As of mid-1994, worksharing agreements in Germany that guaranteed employment through hours reductions were estimated to cover some 700,000 workers and to have preserved approximately 80,000 jobs.[4]

In France, a number of agreements at the enterprise level to preserve or create jobs have also been concluded. According to one study of 208 agreements by the Confédération française démocratique du Travail (CFDT — French Democratic Confederation of Labour), around 50 per cent of the agreements were aimed at saving jobs, 40 per cent at creating jobs, and 10 per cent at reorganizing working hours. It was reported that 11,000 jobs were preserved and 4,500 jobs were created. Sixty per cent of these agreements, however, provided for a number

[2] "A case for work-sharing?", op. cit.; Dörsam, op. cit.

[3] "Perspectives — Working time and employment: New arrangements", in *International Labour Review*, Vol. 134, No. 2, 1995, pp. 264-265.

[4] ibid., pp. 265-266.

of measures other than reductions in hours of work and included part-time work (26 per cent), general reductions in hours of work (20 per cent), phased early retirement (20 per cent), early termination of employment (8 per cent), compensatory leave for overtime (7 per cent), long-term leave (5 per cent) and other measures (14 per cent). In 15 agreements, a "time saving" provision was included, which allowed workers to accumulate part of their leave or bonus payments and have them converted into accumulated paid leave for a period of several months, during which time a temporary worker could be hired. In 70 per cent of the agreements which provided for hours of work reductions, proportional or partial wage offsets were also negotiated.[5]

In another French study of 131 agreements, it was found that job preservation agreements were most common in industry, and that reduction of the wage bill was the determining factor. In 70 per cent of the cases, the reductions in wages were compensated by reduced working hours. Typically, the hard-pressed companies had envisioned dismissing a number of workers to cut costs, and the trade unions had made a counter-proposal to reduce hours of work and wages.[6] Similar worksharing agreements have also been reported in other industrialized countries, such as Canada and Italy.[7]

Worksharing schemes adopted by private companies during periods of economic difficulty appear generally to have had a temporary character. More normal working hours and higher incomes have been restored relatively quickly during subsequent periods of economic expansion.

Mandatory worksharing at national level: An offensive strategy to create jobs?

In contrast to voluntary agreements entered into between workers and their employer at the enterprise level, mandatory worksharing at the national, macro-economic level is imposed by law. It can take the form, for example, of laws which require reductions in hours of work per day or per week, reductions in overtime through strict quantitative limits on its use, increases in paid annual leave or long-term leave, and incentives for early retirement.

Examples of attempts to legally mandate reductions in working time to create jobs have been attempted in some countries, most notably in France in 1982, when the work-week was reduced by law from 40 to 39 hours with no reduction in pay, and when legally required paid annual leave was increased from four to five weeks. An analysis of the results of this experience indicates that there was only a small amount of job creation as a result. Employers reacted in a variety of ways to increase labour productivity, with the consequence that only

---

[5] CFDT: *Réduire le temps de travail: Du temps pour soi, du travail pour tous* (Paris, February 1995).

[6] G. Aznar (ed.): *Répertoire 1994 des "innovations temps de travail": 131 cas d'entreprises* (Paris, Guy Aznar Conseil, 1995).

[7] Human Resources Canada: *Report of the Advisory Group on working time and the distribution of work* (Ottawa, December 1994), pp. 40-41; information provided to the ILO by the Confederazione Generale Italiana del Lavoro (CGIL — Italian General Confederation of Labour), November 1995.

a small number of new jobs were created.[8] Evidence shows — and not simply in the French case — that employers have historically reacted in a dynamic way to limitations of working time and, frequently, this has been in the form of increased labour productivity which dampens the employment generation effect anticipated.[9]

Economists who have constructed econometric models of the effects of working time reductions on employment generation have reached contradictory results, in large part due to the different assumptions used. The use of some econometric models has resulted in predictions of some job creation as a result of general reductions in hours of work, while others have found that forced reductions in hours of work could actually decrease employment. Models which find negative effects tend to assume that wages are held constant when reductions in working time are made, and assume a decrease in competitiveness as a result.[10]

Similar problems emerge with respect to the idea that quantitative limits should be placed on overtime to encourage such a redistribution. The evidence, however, does not equivocally support the notion that such restrictions on overtime will result in substantial job creation. One view, typically advanced by employers' organizations, is that skilled workers — who perform the bulk of overtime work — may not be readily available for a given occupation from the pool of unemployed, and that recruitment and training may be too expensive or lengthy if the need for additional personnel is only of a temporary and immediate character. Thus, restrictions on overtime may lead employers to limit their output rather than hire additional workers. The other position, traditionally supported by trade unions, is that quantitative limits on overtime, or a requirement of compensation in lieu of overtime after a certain amount of paid overtime, should be imposed so that employers will be encouraged to hire new workers.[11]

Overtime tends to be cyclical, rising in the initial stages of economic recovery when employers are unsure of the strength of economic expansion and being supplemented by the hiring of new workers as the economic recovery continues. Similarly, overtime tends to fall in times of economic recession. This also allows the wage rate and wage bill to vary according to the economic cycle without the employer openly conceding a wage increase during periods of expansion (increased overtime) and workers not openly conceding a wage decrease (reduction or elimination of overtime) during an economic downturn. Severe limitations on its use with the goal of generating new employment may be counterproductive, in some circumstances, if it inhibits the ability of an enterprise to respond rapidly to fluctuations in

[8] Dörsam, op. cit.; "Perspectives — Working time and employment", op. cit., p. 271.

[9] M. White: *Working hours: Assessing the potential for reduction* (Geneva, ILO, 1987), pp. 1-22; Commission of the European Communities: "Working time, employment and production capacity", in *Social Europe*, Supplement 4/91, 1991, pp. 81-86.

[10] W. van Ginneken: "Employment and the reduction of the work week: A comparison of seven European macro-economic models", in *International Labour Review*, Vol. 123, No. 1, January-February 1984, pp. 35-52. See also Dörsam, op. cit. Compare H. Seifert: "Employment effects of working time reductions in the former Federal Republic of Germany", in *International Labour Review*, Vol. 130, No. 4, 1991, pp. 495-510, with E. Neifer-Dichmann: "Working time reductions in the former Federal Republic of Germany: A dead end for employment policy", in *International Labour Review*, Vol. 130, No. 4, 1991, pp. 511-522.

[11] G. Bosch and S. Lehndorff: *Annual working hours in Germany*, CONDI/T/WP.2/1995 (Geneva, ILO, 1995).

demand. The question, however, remains open whether unrestricted use of overtime dampens the attraction of hiring new workers. Some governments have imposed such quantitative restrictions on overtime, while others have traditionally mandated that premium payments should be made, but without any quantitative limits.

Another worksharing argument advances that older workers should be granted financial incentives from public sources to leave the labour market so that unemployed younger job seekers can have their places. A number of economists dispute the entire logic of such schemes, arguing that skills of different workers are not necessarily interchangeable, and that efforts to reduce the labour force participation rate or to limit the general volume of hours worked will result in lower output and fewer jobs, and may have little impact on the unemployment rate.[12] Publicly financed schemes to encourage early retirement, however, have been found to be too expensive in a number of countries, and a trend to earlier retirement appears to be taking place in any event.[13]

Working time flexibility: Consequences for job creation

Flexible forms of work tend to enhance labour market efficiency and productivity by better matching the demand for labour with the supply. Although there are a wide variety of flexibility alternatives (see Table 1), some of the more recent developments in flexible working time arrangements, and their employment implications, are discussed below.

---

[12] Dörsam, op. cit. See also Economic Policy Committee, OECD: *The role of structural policies in reducing unemployment*, document no. ECO/CEP/WP1 (Paris, 1993).

[13] G. Bosch, P. Dawkins and F. Michon (eds.): *Times are changing: Working time in 14 industrialized countries* (Geneva, International Institute for Labour Studies, 1994), pp. 22-23; ILO: "Ageing societies: Problems and prospects for older workers", in *World Labour Report 1995* (Geneva, 1995), pp. 31-54.

Table 1. Characteristics of selected working time models[14]

Model	Characteristics
Flexitime	Allows workers to schedule their own hours of work within specific limits; during core periods workers must be present.
Shift work	Workers succeed one another at the workplace so that operation hours exceed the hours of work of individual workers. The main types are: (a) continuous shift work (establishment operates 24 hours a day, seven days a week); (b) semi-continuous shift work [like (a), but with weekend break]; (c) discontinuous shift work ([like (b) but with operating hours less than 24 per day and at least one daily break]. The length of shifts can vary considerably, the most common being eight-hour shifts. There are also short or part-time shifts, and long shifts, which may involve up to 12 hours of work a day. Fixed and rotating shifts are possible.
Compressed work-weeks	Normal weekly hours of work are scheduled over fewer days. If week-end work is required, average weekly hours might be shortened to compensate for the inconvenience. To cover extra days of work, rotation schedules might be adapted or part-time workers hired.
Annual hours and hours averaging schemes	Workers' hours are defined on an annual, rather than a traditional, weekly basis. As long as minimum and maximum limits on normal daily and weekly hours are respected, no overtime premium is payable. Permits the adaptation of working time to seasonal or other variations in supply or demand. Wages are often paid on an average basis throughout the year. Schemes can be introduced in connection with shift work.
Staggered hours	Workers or groups of workers start and finish work at slightly different, but fixed, times.
Overtime	All hours worked in excess of normal hours or work, unless taken into account in fixing remuneration.
Time-autonomous work groups	Groups are oriented to work at a certain task with variations in weekly hours of work within the period fixed to fulfil a certain task.

[14] ILO: *Conditions of Work Digest* on "Flexibility in working time", Vol. 5, No. 2, 1986; ILO: *Future ILO action on working time*, working paper presented to the Meeting of Experts on Working Time, Geneva, 11-19 October 1993, MEWT/1993/2.

Model	Characteristics
Part-time work	Work of less than a normal full-time schedule. Special forms include jobsharing, progressive retirement, parental part-time work, and part-time work combined with shift work and/or flexitime.
"On-call" work	Work on an as-needed basis. Arrangements vary, e.g. the German on-call (KAPOVAZ) refers to an employee's status during a particular shift or period of work where the employee does not have to report to work, but must be available if needed. An on-call employee may work during periods of heavy workload and, during others, be on a non-pay status. The employee is thus subject to periodic release and recall.
Sabbatical leave	Period of leave (for renewal, extended research, etc.) with pay sometimes granted to workers, usually those with professional or academic positions, or at least a guarantee of returning to the same position.
Parental leave	Authorized leave, either with or without pay, which applies either to a mother, a father or both for the purpose of caring for children.
Educational leave	Leave for educational purposes during a working period. May be provided for formal education, vocational training, training for union activities, etc. May or may not be paid.
Phased retirement	A system in which part-time employment is used to provide a gradual transition from working life to total retirement. Alternative terms: gradual or progressive retirement.

Reduced hours of work and extended operating time

In some recent collective bargaining agreements, normal operating hours have been extended while, at the same time, hours of work have been reduced. For example, an agreement concluded in September 1995 between Volkswagen and its employees focused more on the issue of working time flexibility than on worksharing. In exchange for increases in pay, flexible working time arrangements were agreed to, which included a provision that workers could be called to work up to 12 Saturdays per year.[15] In a somewhat similar agreement involving Chrysler Canada, which was negotiated in September 1993, a night shift was introduced and hours of work reduced, with the result that 800 additional workers were hired.[16] Another example, in France, concerns the Bouhyer Foundry, where employees had been working three shifts, nine hours a day, four days a week. In May 1994, working hours were reduced, while operating time was expanded to include Saturday with the creation of

---

[15] "Germany: Settlement reached in Volkswagen dispute", in *European Industrial Relations Review*, No. 261, October 1995, p. 6.

[16] Human Resources Canada, *Report of the Advisory Group on working time ...*, op. cit., pp. 40-41.

additional employment.[17] Reduction in hours of work often appears to be the price to be paid by employers for increased flexibility, particularly the extension of operating time and the scheduling of more hours of work during unsocial hours, such as the evenings, nights or weekends. From an economic point of view, longer operating hours mean that production equipment can be used more intensively, thereby bringing unit costs down and making hours reductions more feasible for employers.[18]

Longer operating time is also a trend in the service sector. For example, the trend has been to expand opening hours in the retail sector in some countries, such as Canada, France, Germany and the United Kingdom.[19] Although this may not always result in shorter working hours, it does have an immediate employment effect as new workers and, in many cases, part-time or weekend workers are engaged as a result. The employment effect may, however, be dampened, as small stores may not be able to adapt as efficiently. The result, therefore, may be a measure of job displacement taking place from smaller to larger establishments.[20]

Hours averaging and use of a reference period in excess of a week

In some agreements, reduced hours of work are compensated by acceptance by the workers of a longer reference period for balancing long working hours in periods of peak demand, against short hours of work in periods of slack demand, for the determination of overtime payment. These longer reference periods allow employers to reduce or eliminate overtime by balancing out weeks with a high volume of work against weeks where there is less need for labour. Reductions in hours of work in exchange for longer reference periods also increases productivity, because unit costs are less given the elimination or substantial reduction of overtime payments.[21]

The use of a reference period of longer than one week, which does not apply overtime rates to long hours worked during one week if they are balanced out by shorter hours in another week, is a common characteristic of several flexibility options. For example, time off in lieu of overtime payment, flexitime, and hours averaging schemes where the reference period is one month, three months or one year all have a common feature of calculating weekly working time on an average of hours worked during a given reference period. Hence, the average weekly hours worked becomes only an abstract notion as one may never work this amount, but work more or less than this amount in all weeks.[22] In a number of countries, such as Germany, Italy, Japan and the United Kingdom, the social partners in some sectors or large

---

[17] Aznar, op. cit., p. 117.

[18] Commission of the European Community, "Working time, employment and production capacity", op. cit., pp. 81-86.

[19] See country studies in Part II of this issue of the *Conditions of Work Digest.*

[20] Dörsam, op. cit.

[21] Bosch and Lehndorff, op. cit.

[22] ibid.

enterprises conduct their negotiations on the basis of annual, rather than weekly, hours.[23] Hours averaging schemes are also practised in France, where weekly hours may be averaged over 12 weeks, and in the United States, where the use of a reference period of more than one week is permitted for calculating overtime for certain occupations.[24] There appears to be no immediate employment creation effects from hours averaging schemes, and some have argued that the immediate employment effects may be negative if there is sufficient improvement in productivity. However, these measures also reinforce an enterprise's competitiveness, which may help to create jobs in the medium and long term.[25]

Although flexibility has often been characterized by extension of operating time or hours averaging schemes in various forms, the other major face of flexibility which has important employment implications concerns atypical forms of work and, in particular, part-time work.

Part-time work

Part-time work as a percentage of total employment has grown significantly between 1973 and 1994 in all industrialized countries, except Italy. It is predominantly a female phenomenon and appears to be directly related to the substantial increases in labour participation rates of women in the workforce and their efforts, in many cases, to balance work and family responsibilities.[26]

Increases in part-time work have also gone hand-in-hand with the fact that women's employment growth has outpaced employment growth for men in all industrialized countries, with the exception of Japan, which experienced almost equal employment growth for both men and women. Increases in part-time employment have also taken place in the context of decreased labour force participation rates by older men and a general decrease in male labour force participation rates.[27] Between 1973 and 1993, growth in part-time work has outpaced growth in full-time jobs in all industrialized countries, with the exception of Italy. During this same period in France and the United Kingdom, overall employment rose exclusively from increases in part-time employment, and almost all of Germany's increase in employment was attributable to an increase in part-time jobs.[28]

---

[23] ibid. See also M. Agostinelli: *Annualization of working hours in Italy*, unpublished working paper prepared for the ILO, 1995; P. Blyton: *The development of annual working hours in the United Kingdom*, CONDI/T/WP.4/ 1995 (Geneva, ILO, 1995); S. Hutchinson: *Annual working hours in the United Kingdom* (London, Institute of Personnel Management, 1993).

[24] See the United States country study in Part II of this issue of the *Conditions of Work Digest*.

[25] Dörsam, op. cit.

[26] Parental leave policies in a number of countries apply equally to men and women, and such leave can be taken in such a way as to allow part-time work. See generally ILO: *Conditions of Work Digest* on "Maternity and work", Vol. 13, 1994. Family responsibilities may also refer to care for aging parents or a disabled person.

[27] ibid., pp. 16 and 215. See also ILO, "Ageing societies ...", op. cit.; US Department of Labor, Bureau of Labor Statistics: *International comparisons among the G-7 countries: A chartbook*, Report No. 890 (Washington, May 1995), pp. 6-7 and 18-19.

[28] Bureau of Labor Statistics, US Department of Labor, op. cit., pp. 20-21.

Table 2. Size and composition of part-time work, 1973-94 (percentage)[29]

Country	Part-time employment as a proportion of total employment						Women's share in part-time employment					
	1973	1979	1983	1992	1993	1994	1973	1979	1983	1992	1993	1994
Australia	11.9	15.9	17.5	24.5	23.9	24.4	79.4	78.7	78.0	75.0	75.3	74.2
Austria	6.4	7.6	8.4	9.0	10.1	---	85.8	87.8	88.4	89.6	89.7	---
Belgium	3.8	6.0	8.1	12.4	12.8	12.8	82.4	88.9	84.0	89.7	89.3	88.1
Canada	9.7	12.5	15.4	16.7	17.2	17.0	68.4	72.1	71.3	69.7	68.9	69.4
Denmark	---	22.7	23.8	22.5	23.3	---	---	86.9	84.7	75.8	74.9	---
Finland	---	6.7	8.3	7.9	8.6	8.5	---	74.7	71.7	64.3	63.1	63.6
France	5.9	8.1	9.6	12.5	13.7	14.9	82.3	82.1	84.3	83.7	83.3	82.7
Germany	10.1	11.4	12.6	14.4	15.1	---	89.0	91.6	91.9	89.3	88.6	---
Italy	6.4	5.3	4.6	5.8	5.4	6.2	58.3	61.4	64.8	68.8	70.5	71.1
Japan	13.9	15.4	16.2	20.5	21.1	21.4	70.0	70.1	72.9	69.3	67.7	67.5
Neth.	---	16.6	21.4	32.5	33.4	35.0	---	76.4	77.3	75.2	75.7	75.1
New Zea.	11.2	13.9	15.3	21.6	21.2	21.6	72.3	77.7	79.8	73.3	74.2	74.9
Norway	23.0	27.3	29.6	26.9	27.1	26.5	76.4	77.0	77.3	80.1	80.5	80.6
Sweden	---	23.6	24.8	24.3	24.9	24.9	---	87.5	86.6	82.3	81.3	80.1
UK	16.0	16.4	19.4	22.8	23.3	23.8	90.9	92.8	89.8	84.9	84.5	83.6
USA	15.6	16.4	18.4	17.5	17.5	18.9	66.0	68.0	66.8	66.4	66.2	67.3

Part-time work may be undertaken by those who would prefer to have less income and more leisure time. Part-time work is also performed by students, whose average period of education has been lengthening in industrialized countries, and by older persons — in some cases, in the form of phased retirement.[30]

There is evidence that some part-time work is involuntary, that is to say that the person concerned would prefer to have a full-time job but cannot find one. While it appears that this

[29] OECD: "Recent labour market developments and prospects", in *Employment Outlook*, July 1995, p. 210.

[30] See generally ILO: *Conditions of Work Digest* on "Part-time work", Vol. 8, No. 1, 1989; Dörsam, op. cit.

concerns a relatively small percentage of part-time workers, involuntary part-time work is increasing in several countries.[31]

In the United States, around 6 million workers out of 20 million part-timers are involuntary ones, and the total increase in the ratio of part-time to total employment since the early 1970s has been among workers who usually work part time but would prefer full-time work.[32]

In Canada, involuntary part-time work has doubled in the last 20 years.[33] An attitudinal survey by the Commission of the European Communities found that 37 per cent of all part-time workers would prefer to work full time.[34]

Studies also have found that involuntary part-time work is more common among men than women. Part-time work — like overtime — also appears to be more prevalent during the initial stages of economic recovery and, at least in some countries, appears to be followed by more substantial creation of full-time jobs as the recovery is confirmed. Under this hypothesis, part-time work could be a means of eventually obtaining a full-time job in some situations.

The development of part-time work as a percentage of total employment in industrialized countries has occurred with the broad shift away from manufacturing to services.[35] The service sector has traditionally used a significantly larger share of part-time workers than the manufacturing sector, which historically has used the fewest number of part-time workers.[36] Longer operating hours in some sectors of economic activity have led to a decoupling of operating hours and individual employees' hours of work. In some cases, this has resulted in the hiring of part-time workers to ensure coverage of total operating time. The hiring of part-time workers can entail, as a consequence, a reduction in overtime pay to full-time workers who might otherwise be required to work. Some commentators have characterized this type of part-time work as a new form of shift work which frequently is not accompanied by premium pay for working unsocial hours, in particular for evening or weekend work in some service sectors.[37]

---

[31] OECD, op. cit., pp. 78 and 90-96; OECD: *Employment Outlook*, July 1990, pp. 179-192.

[32] Bureau of Labor Statistics, US Department of Labor: *An overview of BLS data on part-time work, temporary and self-employment* (Washington, 1993), p. 4.

[33] M. Bedard et al.: *Employment in the service economy* (Ottawa, Economic Council of Canada, 1991), p. 75.

[34] Commission of the European Communities, "Working time, employment and production capacity", op. cit., p. 22.

[35] OECD, *Employment Outlook*, July 1995, op. cit., p. 18; Bureau of Labor Statistics, US Department of Labor, *International comparisons among the G-7 countries*, op. cit., pp. 22-23.

[36] See, for example, Eurostat: "Working time in the European Union — The average working week from 1983 to 1992", in *Statistics in focus: Population and social conditions*, No. 1, 1995, p. 9.

[37] B.A. Hepple and C. Hakim: *Legal and contractual limitations to working time: United Kingdom*, Working Paper No. WP/94/46/EN (Dublin, European Foundation for the Improvement of Living and Working Conditions, 1994), pp. 21 and 28; "Shift pay survey 1994", in *Bargaining Report*, No. 143, October 1994, p. 6.

Social protection in a time of uncertainty and flexibility

The well-being of workers is directly linked to the level of hours and how those hours are organized. Working time is one of the aspects of working conditions, perhaps after remuneration, that has the most direct, most perceptible, impact on the day-to-day lives of workers.[38]

Social protection is paramount today for several reasons. First, "destandardizing" the duration and arrangement of working time could have detrimental effects on safety, health and well-being. Second, some forms of "flexibilization" have resulted in the development of "atypical" forms of work and precarious employment, which are frequently characterized by low pay and inferior conditions. Third, an increasing concern of workers is to have time "sovereignty", namely that they can have control over some of their time.

Protecting workers' health and safety

The most basic and most important argument for adapting regulation of working time to flexible working practices is its contribution to workers' safety, health and well-being. Modifications in legislation, or the decentralization of negotiations to the enterprise or individual level, should not lead to the dismantling of basic standards. Flexible working time measures which allow long hours in a day or during one or two weeks (through, for example, hours averaging schemes, overtime and compressed work-weeks), could endanger the health and safety of workers and of others as well. Compressed work-weeks can, in some countries, allow up to 12 hours of work per day, and this may have adverse effects on some workers and is generally inadvisable for certain occupations and industries. Similarly, the extension of operating time both in the service and industrial sectors implies that more shift work will be performed. Studies have demonstrated that certain shift systems can cause disruption of sleep, increased fatigue and nutritional problems, and adverse effects on family and social life.[39]

The physiological effects of the long duration of work on performance show that there is an absolute ceiling to the energy which an individual can convert for the tasks of production, after which the counter-productive effects of fatigue set in. Hectic and inappropriate schedules also contribute to stress and undermine productivity. However, it has been argued that the shortening of working hours could lead to an increase in work intensity and thus to more, rather than less, fatigue and stress. It is essential, therefore, if reductions in hours of work or changes in work schedules are pursued that the full context of the organization of work and the content of jobs, rather than hours alone, should be considered.[40]

---

[38] J.M. Clerc (ed.): *Introduction to working conditions and environment* (Geneva, ILO, 1985).

[39] Office of Technology Assessment, Congress of the United States: *Biological rhythms: Implications for the worker* (Washington, 1991).

[40] ILO: *New forms of work organisation*, 2 volumes (Geneva, 1979).

Extending protection to "atypical" employees

Extension of operating hours, the desire to limit overtime and the scheduling of work during periods of peak demand have led to the expansion of atypical forms of work, such as part-time work and temporary work. Workers in these types of jobs "generally receive lower hourly wages than full-time employees and no health or other benefits ... require more public assistance, have less money to spend and save, and pay less taxes. Moreover, they are routinely denied the full protection of their country's labour and employment laws. They are likely to experience considerably more job turnover, and receive much less job training. All in all, the contingent workforce bodes very poorly for a long-term economic strategy that seeks to create a competitive, productive, stable, well-trained and decently compensated workforce".[41]

In many industrialized countries, laws and regulations have been adapted, or are in the process of being revised, to extend protection to such workers, particularly to part-time workers. The ILO has acted recently in this field with the adoption of both a Convention and Recommendation on part-time work. While there are many factors and interests concerning controlling or promoting flexibility, governments can create "a level playing field" so that everyone at work — whatever their hours and patterns of work — can expect at least the same basic standards of protection.

Controlling time — working time "sovereignty"

The diversity in working time arrangements should not result in workers losing control over their scheduling of work and the arrangement of their free time. A step from "just-in-time" production to "just-in-time" workers would have significant social implications. Workers need a basis for planning their personal lives and to be able to spend adequate and common time with family and friends. Advance notice to workers of the scheduling of shifts and overtime is critical, and the employer can often anticipate to a reasonable degree staffing requirements for peak periods in seasonal or cyclical work. In some cases, where extra shifts are planned which can be cancelled if orders fall unexpectedly, experience shows that it is less acceptable to workers to be called on short notice than to have unexpected free time. Flexible work practices should not become a substitute for adequate manpower planning.

In some cases, there may be a range of flexibility options available to employers to satisfy their goals. Taking into consideration the preferences of workers may be in the mutual interest of employers and workers alike.

A related issue is that reductions in working time, the implementation of working time reductions in the form of more paid annual leave, compensatory time off for overtime worked, sick leave and other types of leave have all led to considerable increases in the need for workers to cover for absent colleagues. In some cases, this constraint could translate into workers actually having less leeway in controlling their working time.

---

[41] Intervention of the Honorable Howard Metzenbaum, Chair, Committee on Labor and Human Resources, United States Senate, February 1994.

Table 3. Working time preferences of employees[42]

Question: Would you be willing to work different hours if you were offered higher wages or additional leisure time, if the schedules implied ...

Country	Early or midday shift		Night shift		Saturday shift		Sunday work		Variable working time	
	Yes	No	Yes	No	Yes	No	Yes	No	Yes	No
Belgium	51	34	19	67	42	44	24	62	52	34
Denmark	63	29	24	70	41	52	31	63	34	58
Germany	45	51	10	85	33	62	10	85	34	61
Greece	61	39	4	96	8	91	2	98	24	76
Spain	72	20	28	64	40	52	19	73	47	42
France	68	25	30	62	56	40	30	66	74	21
Ireland	67	25	32	62	58	35	30	63	61	31
Italy	57	43	10	90	51	49	12	88	66	34
Netherlands	60	35	10	90	9	91	1	99	17	88
Portugal	56	31	3	84	2	85	0	87	26	61
UK	69	31	39	61	56	44	39	61	55	45
Total	61	35	22	74	44	54	21	75	52	44

Note: Percentages under "yes" and "no" do not add up to 100 per cent due to workers giving no response.

Policies to cut hours of work are in line with an overriding interest by workers to find a satisfactory balance between work and their other, often diverse, personal interests, such as caring for their family, the desire to learn new skills, the desire to enjoy leisure activities and community participation. Workers may wish to change the balance many times as their lives change and, therefore, change their working time schedules as well.

[42] Directorate-General for Economic and Financial Affairs, Commission of the European Communities: *European Economy*, No. 47, March 1991, p. 148.

The changing mechanics of social protection

An interesting question which arises from increased diversity in working time arrangements is how flexible working time can be controlled and regulated by labour inspectors. Previously, most workers started work and finished work at the same time, and the day and week were the standard reference periods for calculating the legal hours of work, overtime and rest requirements. Such uniformity eased the task of labour inspectors considerably who could, by showing up at certain times of the day and by looking at fairly straightforward bookkeeping records, establish whether violations had taken place or not. In workplaces with standard workdays or weeks which go beyond legal minimum requirements and reference periods ranging from two weeks to one year for balancing out surplus and deficit hours to determine the right to overtime payment, the task of enforcing legal working time regulation has increasingly become more complex.[43]

This difficult enforcement of legal standards also comes at the same time that union participation rates are decreasing in most industrialized countries. Although the number of workers covered by agreements negotiated by organized workers appears to be greater than the actual union membership rates, the trend in some countries does appear to be towards a less-organized and less collectively represented workforce than before.[44] As measures regarding enterprise flexibility are typically decided at the enterprise level and workers' organizations or workers' representatives are decreasingly able to ensure that legal standards on working time are respected, the balance of power may be shifting in favour of the employer unilaterally taking decisions on working time arrangements.[45]

These developments may lead to a workplace where the worker may be the primary source of information about violations of legal regulation, and suggest that workers in all enterprises will therefore have to be informed in detail of their rights. Given the complexity of working time scheduling in some enterprises, it is far from clear that workers may fully understand when an employer is violating the law or not. Possibly other worker participatory structures will evolve at the enterprise or plant level for this purpose.[46]

With working time flexibility increasing, regulation faces a two-fold task. On the one hand, the regulatory framework has to become more flexible while, on the other hand, regulations guaranteeing minimum conditions of work have to ensure that the trend towards more flexibility also translates into advantages for the workers. To influence the future regulation of working time in such a way, an effective interaction between legislation and collective agreements seems desirable.

Similarly, regulation also has a role to play in assuring a minimum level of benefits for all workers, including those who have regular, full-time employment. For example, in the United Kingdom, the Directive of the European Union on the organization of working time mandates

---

[43] Bosch and Lehndorff, op. cit.

[44] OECD: "Collective bargaining: Levels and coverage", in *Employment Outlook*, 1994, pp. 167-188.

[45] Bosch and Lehndorff, op. cit.

[46] ibid.

that workers shall have certain rest breaks and a minimum period of paid annual leave. Although the great majority of British workers already benefit from similar or superior benefits, a small minority of workers in workplaces which are not unionized have long hours with no rest breaks and little or no entitlement to paid annual leave. Compliance with the Directive should benefit these workers and remove any incentive to cut costs in this area, as it will be legally required for all employers covered by the Directive.[47]

The future of working time: Current trends and likely developments

Broad reductions in working time have been viewed by the labour movement as a central goal to increase the general well-being of workers and their families. Hours of work per worker have decreased considerably in this century. This decrease has been characterized by shorter working weeks, more paid public holidays, increased paid annual leave, the evolution of paid sick leave, earlier retirement, delayed entry into the workforce and, more recently, extended long-term paid leave for maternity, paternity and educational purposes, among others. This evolution has also been characterized by a general reduction in the number of working hours one performs in a lifetime.[48] Although reductions in working time in the developed countries have slowed considerably in the 1980s and 1990s relative to previous decades in this century, it is likely that the broad trend towards further working time reductions will continue, subject to some important qualifications.[49]

The first point is that the massive entry of women into the workforce has changed the situation considerably. It is likely that women entering the workforce today will actually work more, not less, hours in their lifetimes relative to the experience of previous generations of women. This suggests that continued and increased attention to women's needs in the duration and arrangement of working time will have to be taken into account.

The second point is that while working time reductions will probably continue to occur at the aggregate level, the working hours of individuals and sectors may become more disaggregated, with some workers employed for short hours and others for long hours. According to Eurostat, actual hours of work in France, Germany, Italy and the United Kingdom were broadly stable or decreased slightly for employees in the time period 1983-93. These figures include both full-time and part-time employees.[50] However, if one counts only the actual annual hours of full-time workers, the data show both decreasing and increasing actual hours of work. For example, in France and the United Kingdom, actual annual hours for full-time workers increased slightly between 1983 and 1993, while they declined in Germany and Italy.[51] Changes in technology, competition at the national and international

---

[47] See United Kingdom country study in Part II of this issue of the *Conditions of Work Digest*.

[48] Bosch, Dawkins and Michon, op. cit., p. 15.

[49] E. Fontela: "The long-term outlook for growth and employment", in OECD: *OECD societies in transition: The future of work and leisure* (Paris, 1994), pp. 25-45.

[50] Eurostat, "Working time in the European Union", op. cit., p. 3.

[51] ibid., p. 5.

levels, and employee preferences will increasingly influence a broader diversification of working time arrangements.[52]

The manufacturing sector also shows a variety of developments.[53] For example, in the period 1980-94, actual annual hours of work increased in Canada, Italy and the United States, but decreased in France, Germany, Japan and the United Kingdom. Between these countries, there was a striking difference between the United States — the highest at 1,994 hours — and western Germany — the lowest at 1,527 hours. However, no inferences about the overall direction of working hours should be drawn as the manufacturing sector has been a declining sector in these countries.

One can conclude that working time arrangements in industrialized countries have been characterized by increasing complexity, and that the duration of working time is becoming increasingly disaggregated according to the needs of enterprises and sectors and the preferences expressed by workers. The segmentation of the labour market into sectors or occupations, which are characterized by differences in the length of working hours, may allow more individual choice about the relative trade-offs between increased income or more free time in the future. This issue of whether short or long hours are freely chosen, however, will be a sensitive one, as such diversity could aggravate existing income inequality.

Conclusions

The main themes presented above can be summarized as follows:

(1) Mandatory worksharing policies adapted at the national level by law are probably not capable of creating substantial employment, although voluntary worksharing undertaken at the enterprise level may be useful as a temporary, defensive measure to preserve employment in periods of economic difficulty.

(2) Sustained employment generation is most likely to come from economic growth, i.e. increases in productivity and output. Working time policies which permit or encourage flexibility should, therefore, be pursued to enhance competitiveness and growth.

(3) Flexibility in working time should not be equated with the dismantling of social protection, as regulation is still necessary to protect safety, health and the well-being of workers, and certain forms of flexibility will require adaptation of existing regulations. The cost of measures to ensure social protection will not diminish the benefits of flexibility, but rather serve to reinforce them.

(4) Significant increases in labour participation rates by women have been a major factor in significantly altering basic ideas about working time. These changes have called into question even the concept of a standard work-week, and have materially affected the

---

[52] ibid.; M. Beaston: "Progress towards a flexible labour market", in *Employment Gazette*, February 1995. pp. 55-66.

[53] Statistics of the Institut der Deutschen Wirtschaft (IW — Institute of the Germany Economy), cited in Bundesvereinigung der Deutschen Arbeitgeber Verbände (BDA — Confederation of German Employers' Associations): *Arbeitgeber*, Vol. 10, No. 47, 1995, p. 709.

organization and length of working time, in many cases to allow working parents to reconcile their work and family responsibilities. Providing balance between work and other aspects of life is not only a humane issue, but it is also a strategic one.

(5) Reductions in working time in the future are both likely and desirable for the general well-being of workers as productivity and output increases. Working time reductions, however, are likely to be uneven, as there may be an increasing segmentation of the labour force between persons who choose to work relatively long hours to maximize income and those who work shorter hours to have more time for non-work interests. The goal should be to ensure that such choice is voluntary and that there are minimum standards for all workers. Strong involvement of the social partners is paramount.

Part II:
Working time trends in law and practice

Working time trends in law and practice

Introduction

This Part of the *Digest* focuses on the regulation of working time, be it through legislation, collective agreements or practice. It starts with a brief summary of some of the major trends in the extent of working time in the different regions of the world. This is followed by 16 country studies which describe in some detail current and developing trends in working time legislation and practice in the countries concerned. All studies are presented in a similar pattern, each starting with an overview, including statistics, which is followed by separate sections on normal hours of work, overtime and absolute maximum hours, rest periods, shop-opening hours, paid annual leave, public holidays and other types of leave, and, in some cases, shift and night work. Special references to certain occupations and special categories of workers are often made.

The brief summary of trends is based on the information contained in the country studies, but also on other sources. A great deal of information was assembled for this Part of the *Digest* and some 26 draft country studies were originally prepared. Due to a lack of time and space, it was not possible to include them all in this issue. Nevertheless, the review of all of this information made it possible to compare the situation and developments in the different regions and provide some general observations.

The statistics used to compare the trends in average weekly hours of work from 1984 to 1994 are based on the ILO *Year Book of Labour Statistics*[1] (1994 and 1995 issues) and the data mentioned in the country studies, unless otherwise indicated. Two different ways of calculating average weekly hours of work are used: hours actually worked and hours paid for. The first refers to hours worked during normal periods of work, including average overtime; the second comprises, in addition to hours actually worked, hours paid for but not worked, such as paid annual leave, paid public holidays, paid sick leave and other paid leave. Average weekly hours tend to be slightly higher when statistics are based on hours paid for. Normal hours of work are the legal or collectively agreed hours without overtime.

Overview of working time trends by region

Trends in Western Europe

The past decade has witnessed successful efforts in a number of Western European countries, either generally or within certain sectors, to reduce normal hours of work to the 35- to 37.5-hour range. The 37.5-hour week is the legal norm in Norway and the 37-hour week is the general norm through collective agreements in Denmark. In the United Kingdom and Germany, a 35- to 37.5-hour week has been more or less achieved in a number of sectors, although the majority of settlements have been in the 36- to 37.5-hour range. A number of unions have announced their intention to press for a generalized 35-hour week, although there

---

[1] ILO: *Year Book of Labour Statistics*, Vol. 53, 1994; ibid.: *Year Book of Labour Statistics*, Vol. 54, 1995.

appears, for the moment, to be little concrete action towards such a goal outside very specific occupations or sectors.

From 1984 to 1994, average weekly hours actually worked or paid for in non-agricultural activities remained stable (as in France, the Netherlands, Norway, Sweden and the United Kingdom), or decreased slightly [as in Belgium, Germany (former Federal Republic), Portugal, Spain and Switzerland]. In 1993, weekly hours ranged from 32.6 hours in Belgium to 40.1 hours in the Netherlands. In the manufacturing sector, the average weekly hours showed a very slight reduction in all countries, but decreased by as much as three hours per week in Germany. (See Tables 1 and 2 below.)

In many European countries, recent trends have been marked by efforts towards a greater degree of flexibility concerning a range of working time issues. For example, some countries, such as France and Norway, have introduced laws which allow, either directly or by agreement of the social partners, to extend the reference period for overtime beyond a week so that hours may be averaged over a longer period of time. This allows enterprises to respond to seasonal shifts in demand during both peak and slack periods. No overtime premiums have to be paid, as long as the absolute maximum hours of work during any given week are respected and the average of hours during the reference period are the legally mandated normal hours. Also, there has been a tendency towards more flexibility in terms of allowing additional shifts, including evening, night and weekend shifts, most notably in France and Germany. Finally, there has been a certain liberalization of shop-opening hours, with a new Sunday trading law in the United Kingdom and a revision of the law in France, which allows slightly more possibilities for extended shop hours and Sunday openings.

It was found that paid annual leave and paid leave for public holidays have remained remarkably stable and have not been a determining factor in changes in working time duration. Rather, the number of hours worked per week has been the crucial factor in changes in the duration of working time.

Trends in Central Europe

Since the transition from a planned economy to a market-oriented economy, many countries in this region have adopted new labour laws which specify labour standards on working time, enhance the role of collective bargaining and, in some cases, allow considerable flexibility in the arrangement of work schedules, normally subject to negotiations between the social partners. In Poland, for example, normal weekly hours of work are legally 42 in industry; but in agriculture, commerce and offices, they can be averaged over the period of a month. In practice, normal weekly hours of work have been brought down to 40 hours or less through collective agreements. Restrictions on overtime have become similar to legal rules in other European countries. In manufacturing, hours actually worked have decreased from 152 hours per month in 1984 to 137 hours per month in 1991.

In Hungary, the new labour code adopted in 1992 permits considerable variations from the standard 44-hour week according to sector and subject to collective agreements, provided that limits do not exceed 12 hours a day and correspond to eight hours a day on average over a period of up to a maximum of six months. In agriculture and manufacturing, annual hours limits are also set. In certain occupational categories, legislation assigns the responsibility of determining working time entirely to the social partners. In practice, approximately 90 to 92 per cent of all employees now work between 36 and 43 hours a week. In manufacturing, actual hours of work decreased very slightly from 147.1 hours per month in 1984 to 145.7 hours per month in 1994, with a low of 136.4 hours per month in 1992. However, figures are not strictly comparable due to changes during this period in the statistical methods used.

Actual hours of work in the manufacturing sector in the Czech Republic have also decreased over the last decade. In state industry, average actual hours were 43 per week in 1984 and 40 per week in 1991 in the former Czechoslovakia. Since 1990, the statistics based on enterprises with 25 or more employees show a slight increase from 39.7 hours per week to 40.2 hours per week in 1994.

Trends in North America

In Canada, the average weekly hours of work have been declining. However, considering only full-time workers, average weekly hours remained virtually unchanged from 1975 to 1994 at just over 42 hours per week. In fact, a polarization of hours of work has been observed, with an increase from 17 to 22 per cent of all employed males working more than 50 hours a week and a similar increase in part-time employment from 14 to 23 per cent, the majority of which is female.

At the same time, Canadian trade unions have been negotiating for shorter working hours. Under collective agreements, the percentage of workers with normal hours of work of less than 40 hours per week has increased from 48 per cent in 1986 to 53 per cent in 1994. An even more notable reduction of working time has been achieved since the mid-1960s in annual hours of work, essentially through increased paid annual leave and the addition of paid statutory public holidays.

In the United States, hours of work have been remarkably stable over the period 1984 to 1993. For the civilian labour force working in the manufacturing sector, weekly hours of work paid for have increased slightly from 40.7 in 1984 to 42 in 1994. For production and construction workers and non-supervisory employees in the private sector, average weekly hours paid for have decreased slightly from 35.2 hours in 1984 to 34.7 hours in 1994 (these figures include both full-time and part-time employment). Paid annual leave in the United States is relatively modest in comparison to Western Europe, and the highest level of annual working hours in manufacturing is to be found in the United States (see Table 3 below). One interesting aspect of the working time discussion has been the virtual absence of debate concerning reducing working hours as a means to combat unemployment. Workers and their representatives appeared to be more willing to reduce wages and benefits as the price for preserving their jobs rather than trying to negotiate for reductions in working hours.

Trends in Oceania

In Australia, the principle of a 38-hour work-week was established at the federal level in 1983. In some industries, this had already come into practice earlier, as the 40-hour work-week became generally applicable in 1947. Through collective bargaining, normal hours of work at present typically range from 35 to 37 hours per week. Enterprise-level negotiations, which are encouraged by federal legislation, have resulted in agreements aiming to make working hours more flexible and allow up to 12 hours of work a day under certain conditions. The actual weekly hours of work have remained stable since 1984, around 33 hours per week, but increased in industries due to an increase in overtime hours. The rise in part-time work from 17.1 per cent in 1982 to 24.4 per cent in 1992 has probably reduced average working hours in the different services, but comparable statistics are not available for all sectors.

New Zealand has a relatively deregulated framework for the determination of working time. Whereas legislation mandates a working week of not more than 40 hours, there is ample scope for collective or individual negotiations to diverge and even agree on longer working weeks. Parallel to the changes allowing for more flexibility in working time arrangements, which were introduced by legislation adopted in 1987 and 1991, shop-opening hours were also deregulated and shops may now open 24 hours a day on any day of the week. A trend towards a four-day work-week is also evident, particularly in the retail, restaurant and hotel sectors. Average hours of work paid for have remained stable over the last decade at around 39 hours per week. However, as in other countries, weekly hours actually increased or remained stable in most sectors, except services, where they decreased slightly. Average overtime hours are relatively high in manufacturing and construction (around 3.5 hours per week), but only 30 minutes per week on average in services.

Trends in Asia

The Japanese Government has announced its intention to try to achieve a reduction in actual annual hours of work to 1,800 hours by the year 1996. To this end, the law was changed in 1993 so that normal hours of work would be reduced from 44 to the current standard of 40 hours per week, but there are numerous exceptions based on the size and type of company. At the same time, the five-day working week was actively promoted and about 65 per cent of enterprises now work five days a week. The amount of legally mandated overtime pay was also increased. Moreover, the new law has rules which allow working hours that are unevenly distributed to be averaged over a longer period of time, typically over either a three-month or one-year period.

The trend towards shorter working hours can also be observed in practice. The average hours actually worked in all non-agricultural activities decreased from 40.7 in 1984 to 36.6 hours per week in 1994. In the manufacturing sector, weekly hours are slightly higher, but also decreased considerably from 41.7 hours in 1984 to 37.7 hours in 1994. Nevertheless, actual annual working hours remain among the highest in the industrialized world, principally because Japanese workers actually take much less vacation than their counterparts in other industrialized countries even when they are entitled to it. (See Table 3 below.)

In some countries or areas in Asia, which are sometimes referred to as emerging market economies, weekly hours of work have declined but remain substantially higher than those prevalent in industrialized countries. For example, in the Republic of Korea, working hours in non-agricultural activities decreased from 52.4 hours in 1984 to 47.5 hours in 1993. Hours in manufacturing decreased from 54.3 in 1984 to 48.9 hours per week in 1993. This can be attributed in part to the legal reduction of normal hours from 48 to 44 hours per week in 1989. In a number of cases, normal hours of work have been further reduced to 42 a week through collective agreements, and some firms have adopted a system of alternating five- and six-day work-weeks. However, average weekly overtime, which has also decreased since 1980, remains high at around six hours per week. As in Japan, workers take only a fraction of their paid annual leave entitlement, but data on annual hours of work are not available.

In Hong Kong, average actual hours of work decreased slightly in non-agricultural sectors from 47.6 hours in 1984 to 45.8 hours per week in 1994, and remained unchanged in manufacturing, being 44.8 hours per week in 1984 and 44.6 hours in 1994.

In some emerging market economies, weekly hours of work actually increased. For example, in Singapore, the average for all non-agricultural activities increased slightly between 1984 and 1994 from 45.6 to 47 per week, and in manufacturing, hours of work increased from 47.8 to 49.3 for the same period.

Nonetheless, efforts to legally mandate shorter normal hours of work or to arrange work so that employees can have a two-day weekend regularly or every other week are continuing. In China, for example, legal hours of work were reduced from 48 hours per week to 44 in 1994, and then in 1995 to 40 hours per week. Although it is still too soon to evaluate the most recent legal change, at least some firms have already adopted the alternating five-day/six-day work-week.

The situation in some developing countries also poses novel issues which are not always present in industrialized countries. For example, in the Philippines, office workers were recommended to adopt Government guidelines to work a compressed work-week of five, rather than six days, as an energy conservation measure.

Trends in Africa

Many developing countries have reduced their normal hours of work, which often only affect formal sector employees, but average actual hours of work remain higher than in most industrialized countries. There are not many African countries with statistics on weekly hours of work. In Egypt, in manufacturing establishments with ten or more persons employed, average weekly hours paid for declined from 56 hours in 1985 to 52 hours in 1992.

In South Africa, where the normal weekly hours established in legislation are 46 for most sectors, hours actually worked in manufacturing decreased from 46.5 in 1984 to 44.7 in 1992. Many industrial agreements fix normal hours at 40 a week. In the trade, restaurants and hotels sectors, weekly hours actually worked were somewhat lower at 35.6 in 1984 and 34.6 in 1992. Data as to the percentage of persons working part time in these sectors are not available.

Trends in Latin America

In the emerging market economies of Latin America, trends are mixed, similar to those observed in Asia. In Argentina (Greater Buenos Aires), for example, average working hours per week declined slowly from 47.3 in 1974 to 43.7 in 1992, due in part to an increase in part-time work, which grew from 10 to 15.8 per cent during the same period. In more recent years, it appears that average weekly hours are again increasing, but comparable statistics are not available.

In Brazil, the new constitution adopted in 1988 established normal hours of work at 44 hours per week, down from 48 hours set by the 1934 Constitution. As a result, actual weekly hours averaged over the year went down, but the percentage of those working overtime increased. In the Greater São Paulo region, for example, the percentage of those working overtime increased from 20.3 per cent in 1987 to 39.8 per cent in 1994. This tendency is due to low salaries and the high administrative cost of hiring new workers. However, the reduction of working time and overtime is being discussed as a means of maintaining the level of employment, particularly in trade union circles.

In Mexico, actual hours of work in manufacturing increased from 43.4 hours per week in 1984 to 44.8 hours in 1994, with a high of 46.4 hours in 1985 and 1986. A similar trend can be observed in Chile, where weekly hours actually worked increased slightly from 43.6 in 1984 to 44.6 in 1994, and had been at a peak of 45.3 in 1991.

Comparison of trends

Weekly hours

Table 1 below summarizes the working time trends from 1984 to 1994 for the countries or areas referred to in this overview. For some of them (Argentina, Brazil, Denmark, Hungary, Mexico and South Africa), there are no overall national data on weekly hours actually worked or paid for, but in some cases, there are data on weekly hours in manufacturing (see Table 2). Before comparing the countries in Table 1, it should be pointed out that the length of average weekly hours is not comparable between countries, because the population base or sample differ considerably from one country to another. Whereas, in principle, they concern all sectors of non-agricultural activities, in some countries certain economic sectors are excluded; in others, some agricultural activities are included. In some cases, data refer only to the private sector. Sometimes the information is limited to a few sectors and the average is obtained on this limited basis.

However, in general, the data should be consistent within each country and provide an indication of working time trends in the countries concerned. Comparing the trends, it can be observed that, in most countries, average weekly hours of work, including overtime, have remained stable or have changed very little over the last ten years. Only in countries where the average hours were relatively long is there a marked decrease. This is particularly the case in Japan and the Republic of Korea.

Average weekly hours worked in manufacturing (Table 2) present a much more varied picture. Whereas in the majority of countries or areas the trend is towards a decrease or stability in hours actually worked or paid for, in some countries the average has in fact gone up. This is the case in Australia, Mexico, New Zealand, Singapore and the United States.

Table 1. Hours actually worked per week in non-agricultural activities

Country or area	1984	1985	1986	1987	1988	1989	1990	1991	1992	1993	1994
Australia	33.8	33.0	32.7	33.1	33.4	33.1	33.3	33.2	33.0	33.0	33.2
Belgium	33.7	33.3	33.2	33.2	33.6	33.9	33.7	33.0	32.6	32.6	---
Canada*	32.0	32.0	31.8	31.9	32.1	31.7	31.3	30.8	30.5	30.6	---
France	39.0	38.9	38.9	39.0	39.0	39.0	39.0	39.0	39.0	39.0	38.9
Germany*	40.9	40.7	40.5	40.2	40.2	40.1	39.7	39.3	39.0	38.0	38.3
Japan	40.7	40.6	40.4	40.6	40.6	40.2	39.5	38.8	37.9	36.8	---
Korea, Rep.	52.4	51.9	52.5	51.9	51.1	49.2	48.2	47.9	47.5	47.5	---
Netherlands*	40.4	40.3	40.3	40.2	40.1	40.1	40.1	40.2	40.1	40.1	---
New Zea.*	39.4	39.6	38.9	38.8	38.6	38.8	38.7	38.5	38.7	38.9	39.2
Norway	35.0	35.5	35.8	35.2	35.8	35.7	35.3	35.0	34.9	34.9	35.0
Spain	37.6	37.2	37.4	36.1	36.5	36.8	36.7	36.6	36.1	---	---
Sweden	---	---	36.2	36.3	36.5	36.7	36.9	36.8	36.7	35.4	35.8
UK	---	43.6	43.6	43.7	44.1	44.3	44.2	43.5	43.6	43.5	---
USA*	35.2	34.9	34.8	34.8	34.7	34.6	34.5	34.3	34.4	34.5	34.7

(* = hours paid for)

Table 2. Hours actually worked per week in manufacturing

Country or area	1984	1985	1986	1987	1988	1989	1990	1991	1992	1993	1994
Australia	36.2	36.9	37.1	37.3	37.9	37.7	38.1	37.6	38.0	38.1	38.7
Belgium	33.7	33.1	33.0	33.0	33.4	33.6	33.4	32.7	32.3	32.4	---
Canada*	38.4	38.6	38.4	38.7	38.9	38.7	38.2	37.8	38.3	38.6	---
Denmark	33.0	32.1	32.8	32.1	31.8	31.8	31.5	31.5	31.5	31.5	---
France	38.7	38.6	38.6	38.7	38.7	38.7	38.7	38.7	38.7	38.6	38.6
Germany*	41.0	40.7	40.4	40.1	40.0	39.9	39.5	39.2	38.9	37.6	38.0
Hong Kong	44.8	44.8	45.2	44.5	45.9	44.8	44.0	45.2	43.0	44.9	44.6
Japan	41.7	41.5	41.1	41.3	41.8	41.4	40.8	40.0	38.8	37.7	---
Korea, Rep.	54.3	53.8	54.7	54.0	52.6	50.7	49.8	49.3	48.7	48.9	---
Mexico	43.4	46.4	46.4	44.2	44.9	45.1	45.4	45.6	45.5	45.0	44.8
Netherlands*	40.3	40.3	40.1	39.9	39.8	39.8	39.9	39.9	39.8	39.8	---
New Zea.*	40.4	40.7	39.6	40.2	39.9	40.5	40.7	40.4	41.1	41.6	42.0
Norway	37.7	38.2	38.4	37.2	37.7	37.7	37.0	36.8	36.8	36.8	36.9
Singapore*	47.8	46.5	47.7	48.4	47.4	48.6	48.5	48.7	48.7	49.2	49.3
South Africa	46.5	45.9	46.4	46.2	47.2	47.5	45.4	44.9	44.7	---	---
Spain	36.5	36.3	36.7	35.4	35.8	36.8	36.7	36.6	36.3	---	---
Sweden	38.1	38.3	38.3	38.4	38.5	38.5	38.5	38.4	38.5	37.3	37.8
UK	43.5	43.7	43.7	43.8	44.3	44.5	44.3	42.9	43.2	43.1	---
USA*	40.7	40.5	40.7	41.0	41.1	41.0	40.8	40.7	41.0	41.4	42.0

(* = hours paid for)

Annual working time

The most appropriate way of comparing working time around the world would be to take into account the different elements that make up working time over the span of a year. This becomes more and more necessary as the number of averaging schemes, shift patterns and flexible working time arrangements increase. No internationally recognized method of calculating annual hours of work has yet been devised. However, some models are currently being used.

Eurostat has developed a model to estimate actual annual working time for all employees (taking the mean of full- and part-time workers) in European countries.[2] Comparing working time from 1983 to 1993 for 12 countries, it found that, in general, annual hours had fallen from an average of 1,702.5 hours in 1983 to 1,668.8 (down 33.7 hours). In 1993, the longest hours were worked in Portugal — 1,822.6 a year — followed by Greece with 1,810.3 a year, and the shortest in the Netherlands, with 1,451.7 a year. Considering only full-time workers, annual hours increased slightly in the United Kingdom and France, while they declined in Germany and Italy. The duration of actual annual hours for full-time employees is lowest in Italy and Belgium— 1709.7 hours and 1711.2 hours respectively — and highest in the United Kingdom, Ireland and Portugal, with 1952.7, 1859.1, and 1857.1 hours respectively.[3]

Another model is the one used by the Institute of the German Economy (IW)[4] to analyse actual annual hours of work in manufacturing. In Table 3, one sees a similar pattern as in Table 2 of both increasing and decreasing trends. During the period 1980 to 1994, actual annual hours increased in Canada, Italy and the United States, and decreased in France, Germany, Japan, Sweden and the United Kingdom. There appears to be a striking difference, in manufacturing at least, between the United States — the highest at 1,994 — and western Germany —, the lowest at 1,527 hours.

[2] Eurostat: "Le temps de travail dans l'Union européenne: Estimation de la durée effective annuelle (1983-1993)", in *Statistiques en bref: Populations et conditions sociales*, No. 4, 1995, p. 3.

[3] ibid., p. 5.

[4] Statistics of the Institut der Deutschen Wirtschaft (IW — Institute of the German Economy), cited in Bundes-vereinigung der Deutschen Arbeitgeber Verbände (BDA — Confederation of German Employers' Associations): *Arbeitgeber*, Vol. 10, No. 47, 1995, p. 709.

Table 3. Actual annual hours of work in 1980 and 1994 in manufacturing

Country	1994	Difference since 1980
United States	1994	+118
Japan	1964	-194
Canada	1898	+46
United Kingdom	1826	-18
Italy	1803	+61
Norway	1667	-2
Sweden	1620	-188
Netherlands	1615	-80
France	1607	-106
Denmark	1581	-68
Belgium	1581	-32
Western Germany	1527	-175

In developing countries, the annual hours are likely to be much higher. In Argentina, for example, actual annual hours (average normal hours plus overtime) in industry amounted to 2,198 in 1992.

From the statistical tables presented here, it appears that, in general, trends in working time are rather stable with only minor reductions over the last ten years, except in Japan and the Republic of Korea. Any increases in certain sectors were often counterbalanced by a decrease of working hours in the service sector, due to increases in part-time working. In manufacturing, where there has traditionally been little part-time work, trends are more mixed. In most industrialized countries, however, manufacturing has been a declining sector relative to total employment, and trends in this sector may not be significant for total working time trends. Furthermore, the increase in actual working time in manufacturing is strongly linked to increases in overtime work.

From the country studies it is apparent that, in practice, the organization of working time differs greatly from basic legal standards, due to the important role that collective negotiation plays in this area. It is also evident that working time is becoming more flexible, with an increase in averaging schemes and more possibilities to vary daily and weekly working hours. This is a development which meets the needs of employers to remain competitive in the global economy, but can also enhance the freedom of choice of individual workers.

Argentina

Overview and trends

Overview

With changes over time in federal and provincial jurisdictions, the evolution of statutes regulating working time in Argentina has been complex and, at times, contradictory. The primary source of regulation on working time is the National Constitution,[1] which provides that legislation guarantee workers a "limited working day" and "paid breaks and holidays". In the development of relevant laws, emphasis was placed on both the duration of working time and the provision of rest periods.

In 1905, the first law regulating working time was enacted with Act No. 4661 prohibiting work on Sundays.[2] In 1929, Act No. 11,544 established a working day of eight hours and a working week of 48 hours.[3] Act No. 11,640 of 1932 introduced the so-called "English Saturday", with Saturday work limited to morning hours only in the city of Buenos Aires and the national territories, but not in the provinces.[4]

During the 1930s, some provinces also enacted their own regulations on weekly rest and shop-opening hours, establishing a 44-hour working week. However, other provinces maintained the 48-hour working week. Act No. 11,544 of 1929 on statutory hours of work and Decree No. 16,115 of 1933, issuing regulations implementing this Act, have together provided the basic national statutory framework on hours of work for many decades.[5]

The situation arose whereby some parts of the country had a statutory working week of 44 hours and, in other regions, 48 hours per week was the legal norm. To correct this, Act No. 11,544 on statutory hours of work was amended,[6] stating that the Act only stipulated the maximum number of working hours and so did not impede the introduction of a shorter working week. In 1969, however, this amendment was repealed and the new Act superseded all provincial laws dealing with working time matters.[7] This meant that those provinces with

---

[1] F.C. Roth: "Argentina", in A.P. Blaustein and G.H. Flanz (eds.): *Constitutions of the countries of the world* (Dobbs Ferry, Oceana Publications, 1995). Section 14 bis.

[2] Act No. 4661 respecting Sunday rest, dated 31 August 1905 (*Leyes Nacionales*, Vol. 13, No. 2, 1903-1905, p. 516).

[3] Act No. 11,544 respecting the eight-hour day, dated 12 September 1929 (*Boletín Oficial*, No. 10,614, 17 September 1929, p. 501) [LS 1929-Arg.1A].

[4] M. Ackerman and A.O. Goldin: "Argentina", in R. Blainpain (ed.): *International Enclyclopaedia for Labour Law and Industrial Relations* (Deventer, Kluwer, 1990), p. 93.

[5] Act No. 11,544, op. cit.; Decree No. 16,115/33 to regulate Act No. 11,544, dated 16 January 1933 (*Boletín Oficial*, 28 January 1933), as amended up to Decree No. 2882, dated 15 November 1979 (*Boletín Oficial*, No. 24,297, 21 November 1979, p. 5).

[6] Decree-Act No. 10,375, dated 12 June 1956 (*Anales de Legislación Argentina*, Vol. XVI-A, 1956, p. 499).

[7] Act No. 18,204 to institute a uniform system of weekly rest to be observed throughout the Republic, dated 12 May 1969 (*Boletín Oficial*, No. 21,683, 15 May 1969, p. 1) [LS 1969-Arg.1].

44-hour working weeks had to introduce a 48-hour working week in line with the federal capital and other provinces. However, this only applied to new employment contracts, and thus, in the same province or even in the same enterprise, employees could work different hours for the same wage. Therefore, in 1974, Act No. 20,744 respecting contracts of employment was enacted, allowing the provinces to fix working hours as long as they were not less than 44 hours per week.[8] Subsequently, various provinces proceeded to fix weekly maximum working time at 44 hours. However, the above-mentioned Act was amended in 1976 by Decree No. 390,[9] establishing that working time be uniform throughout the entire nation (i.e. a 48-hour working week) and regulated by Act No. 11,544 of 1929 on statutory hours of work. Supreme Court jurisprudence has since upheld this provision, by denying validity to provincial laws fixing a maximum limit lower than 48 hours per week.

Presently, the main legal sources regulating working time remain Act No. 11,544 of 1929 on statutory hours of work and Act No. 20,744 of 1974 on contracts of employment. The latter provides that a shorter working week can be fixed through collective bargaining.

The National Employment Act of 1991 added new complementary statutory provisions, allowing — through collective bargaining — more flexibility in the organization of working time, particularly as concerns reduced hours of work and the calculation of average working time over a one-year period.[10]

Trends

The length of average normal working hours per week in the greater Buenos Aires region slowly, but steadily, declined from 47.3 hours per week in 1974 to 43.7 hours per week in 1992. However, in recent years, there appears to be a trend of increasing weekly hours of work. The decline in the 1970s and 1980s represents an average annual reduction rate of -0.4 per cent and is shown in Table 1.

Another trend that can be observed during the same period is the increasing participation of part-time workers in the labour market. Part-time workers represented 10 per cent of the total working population in 1974. This figure increased to 15.8 per cent in 1992. This increment is shown in Table 2.

---

[8] Act No. 20,744 to approve the rules governing contracts of employment, dated 11 September 1974 (*Boletín Oficial*, No. 23,005, 27 September 1974, p. 2), as amended up to Act No. 24,013, dated 5 December 1991 (*Boletín Oficial*, No. 27,286, 17 December 1991, pp. 4-10) [LS 1974-Arg.2; 1976-Arg.1; DDS 1991-ARG1].

[9] Decree No. 390 to approve the code governing contracts of employment, dated 13 May 1976 (*Boletín Oficial*, No. 23,410, 21 May 1976, p. 2), as amended up to Act No. 24,465, dated 23 March 1995 (*Boletín Oficial*, No. 28,112, 28 March 1995, pp. 1-2) [LS 1976-Arg.2; DDS 1995-ARG1].

[10] National Employment Act, Act No. 24,013, dated 5 December 1991 (*Boletín Oficial*, No. 27,286, 17 December 1991, pp. 4-10) [LLD 1991-ARG1].

Table 1. Average working hours per week (Greater Buenos Aires)[11]

Category	1974	1980	1990	1992
All employed workers	47.3	45.0	44.5	43.7
Part-time workers ①	18.9	19.4	19.0	18.5
Full-time workers: Self-employed ②	54.5	51.7	52.6	52.1
Wage-earners A ③	41.5	40.4	40.8	40.3
Wage-earners B ④	66.4	62.3	59.9	61.1

① Workers working up to 30 hours per week, irrespective of the type of activity.
② Self-employed, whatever the length of their working week, and domestic employees working more than 30 hours per week.
③ Workers not working overtime (normal hours of work).
④ Workers working overtime (actual hours of work).

Table 2. Percentage distribution of working population according to number of hours worked per week (Greater Buenos Aires)[12]

Category	1974	1980	1990	1992
All employed workers	100.0	100.0	100.0	100.0
Part-time workers	10.0	11.8	13.6	15.8
Full-time workers Self-employed	25.4	27.9	24.8	26.7
Wage-earners A	45.7	42.4	41.8	39.7
Wage-earners B	18.9	17.9	19.8	17.8

One explanation for the reduction of the average weekly working hours is this steady growth of part-time workers in the Argentine labour market, which does not necessarily express a preference of workers for part-time work. According to statistical data, 36 per cent of part-

[11] A. Monza: *Reducción de la jornada de trabajo y creación de empleo: Algunas reflexiones sobre el caso argentino*, unpublished report prepared for the ILO (Buenos Aires, 1994).

[12] ibid.

time workers were involuntarily working part time in 1974, and by 1992, this figure rose to 42 per cent.[13]

The average weekly hours of work of the two main groups of wage-earners A (working normal hours of work) and B (working overtime) are shown in Table 3 according to economic sectors. The trend reflects a decline in the working week between 1974 and 1992, but the differences in hours of work between economic sectors remained much the same. There was, however, more variation between branches of activity for workers working overtime in addition to the decline in normal hours of work.

Table 3. Average weekly hours of work for wage-earners by economic sector (Greater Buenos Aires)[14]

Economic sector	1974	1980	1990	1992
Total				
Wage-earners A	41.5	40.4	40.8	40.3
Wage-earners B	66.4	62.3	59.9	61.1
Industry				
Wage-earners A	42.8	41.1	42.3	41.4
Wage-earners B	64.4	61.7	59.1	60.8
Construction				
Wage-earners A	42.5	41.3	42.2	41.1
Wage-earners B	69.4	61.7	59.1	60.8
Finance, insurance and business services				
Wage-earners A	39.4	39.7	40.4	40.0
Wage-earners B	73.5	64.5	60.3	61.9

[13] ibid.

[14] ibid.

Economic sector	1974	1980	1990	1992
Public administration				
Wage-earners A	36.9	37.9	38.2	36.9
Wage-earners B	73.4	66.2	65.5	62.4
Education and health				
Wage-earners A	38.5	38.1	37.9	37.5
Wage-earners B	72.7	69.2	58.5	59.0
Commerce and personal services				
Wage-earners A	42.6	41.1	42.1	41.4
Wage-earners B	61.3	59.7	59.7	61.3

Table 4 illustrates the hours of work per week by major types of economic activity in Greater Buenos Aires in 1993.

Table 4. Normal hours of work per week by major division of economic activity in 1993 (Greater Buenos Aires)[15]

Major division	1993
Mining and quarrying	45.5
Manufacturing	44.0
Electricity, gas and water	40.9
Construction	41.1
Trades, restaurants and hotels	48.6
Transport, storage and communication	51.5
Financing, insurance, real estate and business services	33.5
Community, social and personal services	33.5
Total (all non-agricultural sectors)	41.8

[15] Information provided to the ILO by the Instituto Nacional de Estadística y Censos, 1994.

The potential impact of the reduction of the working week on employment in Argentina is influenced by the complexity of the labour market. Demographic pressures, the increasing proportion of women in paid employment and technological innovations are factors which are changing the structure of urban labour markets as part of the structural adjustment process.[16] Given global trends in this respect, together with the patterns observed in the tables above, it is possible that the working week could be shortened in the future. The reduction of working time could be an element in the development of national policies to regulate the labour market and promote employment.[17] In this context, the question could be raised as to what extent would statutory reform be useful in reducing working time, as, for different reasons, around 60 per cent of the working population in Argentina is excluded from the scope of existing legal provisions.[18]

A general labour agreement[19] signed by the Government and the main employers' and workers' organizations in 1994 addresses a series of issues in relation to creating employment, increasing competitiveness of the national economy and improving social equity. Two sections include working time issues. With regard to measures for promoting employment, the agreement covers the regulation of apprenticeship and part-time contracts, for which there are specific working time regulations. This agreement reflects the consensus reached between the Government and the employers' and workers' organizations on introducing more flexible clauses on working time, annual holidays and suspension of employment in collective agreements, as long as they are agreed by the parties and within the limits established in the legislation.

In the 1990s, the Government eased legislative requirements for enterprises undergoing economic difficulties, as well as for small and medium-sized enterprises. In 1992, Decree No. 2072/92 allowed enterprises facing a crisis situation to modify many operational arrangements, including working time. The enterprise must submit proposed changes to the Ministry of Labour for approval.[20] In 1995, Act No. 24,467 introduced special statutory measures for small and medium-sized enterprises, which in Argentina generate around 40 per cent of the national income and provide employment to approximately 60 per cent of the total workforce.[21]

The Act defines a small enterprise as an undertaking with less than 40 workers and with limited annual sales turnover. The ceiling for the sales figure is established according to the

---

[16] Monza, op. cit.

[17] ibid.

[18] According to Monza, the following occupational groups are excluded: rural workers (around 11 per cent of the total workforce), urban self-employed (28 per cent), part-time urban wage-earners (13 per cent), full-time domestic employees (5 per cent), and a portion of full-time urban clandestine wage-earners (about 5 per cent).

[19] Agreement for employment, productivity and social equity. *RELASUR*, No. 4, 1994, pp. 195-216. (The agreement was signed on 25 July 1994 by the Government and the main employers' and workers' organizations.)

[20] "Plan para empresas en crisis: Su regulación", in *Boletín Oficial*, No. 28,028, 1994, pp. 1-2.

[21] Act No. 24,467 respecting small and medium-sized enterprises, dated 23 March 1995 (*Boletín Oficial*, No. 28,112, 28 March 1995, pp. 2-6) [DDS 1995-ARG2].

type of sectoral activity.[22] With a view to promoting employment, small and medium-sized enterprises are permitted to use a variety of contractual arrangements under less restrictive administrative procedures, in particular, fixed-term contracts, contracts for launching a new activity, contracts providing initial employment for youth and on-the-job training contracts (as established in the National Employment Act, 1991, Sections 43-65).[23]

As regards paid annual leave, the Act provides for collective agreements in small enterprises to modify the legislative provisions on procedures, requirements, periods of advance notification and preferred annual leave periods.[24] The only provision that cannot be modified concerns the right of workers to be granted annual leave during summertime at least once every three years, as provided in the 1976 Decree respecting contracts of employment.[25]

The Act also provides that workers attending a vocational training course of interest to the enterprise may request the employer to adapt their daily working hours to ensure their participation.[26]

Collective bargaining

Since 1991, an increasing number of collective agreements have been negotiated as a result of new statutory norms linking wage increases to productivity improvements. From official records, it can be observed that 33 per cent of agreements include working time as an issue and labour cost reduction as an objective.[27]

In this respect, there are several examples of collective agreements where the length of some types of leave and justified absences have been reduced; the length of the actual working day has increased; compensatory supplements for overtime hours and holidays have been reduced; premiums have been introduced for regular attendance or punctual arrival at work; working schedules have been reorganized; and rules for the distribution of annual leave have been agreed.[28]

According to the Ministry of Labour and Social Security, these trends are positive, but the dynamics of the negotiations are far from reflecting a process of "reduction or redistribution of working time" which, in some market economy countries, is transforming the approach to working time and the relations between workers and employers. In Argentina, there is a close link between the length of the working day and fluctuations in economic activity, and

---

[22] ibid., Section 83.

[23] ibid., Section 89.

[24] ibid., Section 90.

[25] Decree No. 390, op. cit., Section 154.

[26] Act No. 24,467, op. cit., Section 96.

[27] Ministry of Labour and Social Security, Technical Advisory Committee on Productivity and Remuneration, Document No. 2, August 1993, cited in *RELASUR*, op. cit., p. 151.

[28] Ministerio de Trabajo y Seguridad Social: *El sistema argentino de relaciones laborales: Informe RELASUR*, Colección Informes OIT No. 40 (Madrid, 1994), p. 151.

the reduction of working hours — with or without a reduction in wages — is a means of adjusting or regulating employment. A reduction in hours of work may be a sign of better working conditions in other countries, but in Argentina, it is more likely to be a reflection of problems in economic cycles.[29]

While the legal annual working hours — 2,450 hours per year — are comparatively high compared to annual hours of work in industrialized countries, the normal working hours in industry are similar to those in industrialized countries. Differences are more marked when comparing the much higher number of overtime hours worked in Argentina with those in industrialized countries. The following table illustrates the trend in overtime hours in Argentina between 1990 and 1992.[30]

Table 5. Average annual hours in industry[31]

Year	Normal annual working hours	Overtime hours per year
1990	1,885	164
1991	1,927	188
1992	1,957	241

In 1993, the percentage of workers working overtime hours averaged 6 per cent of the total number of persons in paid employment. The total number of overtime hours was 1.9 per cent of the total number of hours worked.[32] In May 1995, the Ministry of Labour and Social Security reported that the number of overtime hours has recently declined due to an increase in normal working hours.[33]

Today, in Argentina, there is considerable debate on the reduction of weekly working hours, the limitation of overtime hours and the introduction of other working time measures. In recent years, there appears to be an increase in working time, reaching an average of 46 hours per week in 1995.[34] From the employers' point of view, reducing the working day still just

[29] ibid.

[30] ibid.

[31] Ministerio de Trabajo y Seguridad Social, *El sistema argentino de relaciones laborales*, op. cit., p. 152.

[32] Instituto Nacional de Estadística y Censos, op. cit.

[33] Information provided to the ILO by the Ministry of Labour and Social Security, 1995.

[34] "Un poquito a cada uno", in *CASH*, Suplemento Económico de *Página/12*, No. 267, 11 June 1995, p. 3 (statement of Dr. E. Kritz, consultant to the Minister of the Economy).

does not make sense, as productivity levels are far below those in other industrialized countries and wage rates are high compared to those in neighbouring countries.[35]

The issue of working time is linked to the problem of job distribution and the maintenance of living and productivity standards. While the promotion of multi-skilling and job mobility within enterprises is important, the main problem in Argentina is the precarization of jobs and the tendency for workers to be expulsed from the labour market.[36] Legislative reform could contribute to a better distribution of existing jobs. For instance, if the statutory weekly hours of work were reduced from 48 to 44 hours, this could have a positive impact on employment. Another measure that could be undertaken would be to fix a lower limit for overtime hours by repealing the relevant law (Decree No. 2882/79), which increased an earlier limit on overtime hours from 200 to 300 hours annually.[37]

Normal hours of work

Law

The legal definition of "working hours" is the time during which a worker is at the employer's disposal, in so far as he or she is not able to engage in any other activity on his or her own account.[38] The normal duration of work must not exceed eight hours daily or 48 hours weekly for persons in a dependent employment relationship, except for employment in agriculture, stock-raising and domestic work or in undertakings in which only members of the family of the head, owner, occupier, manager, director or principal person in charge are employed.[39]

Young persons

Young persons between the ages of 14 and 18 years may not be employed on any type of work for more than six hours a day or 36 hours a week. The working hours of young persons over 16 years of age may, with the prior authorization of the administrative authority, be extended to eight a day or 48 a week.[40] Apprentices cannot work more than six hours a day or more than 36 hours a week.[41]

---

[35] ibid. (statement of Dr. D. Funes de Rioja, Director of the Social Politics Department, Unión Industrial Argentina).

[36] ibid. (statement of Dr. Julio Godio, senior specialist on workers' activities, ILO Multidisciplinary Team in Santiago, Chile).

[37] ibid. (statement of Dr. H. Recalde, Professor of Labour Legislation, University of Buenos Aires).

[38] Decree No. 390/76, op. cit., Section 197.

[39] Act No. 11,544, op. cit., Section 1.

[40] Decree No. 390/76, op. cit., Section 190.

[41] Act No. 24,465 to amend the Act respecting contracts of employment and regulations and to establish special means to promote employment and apprenticeship contracts, dated 23 March 1995 (*Boletín Oficial*, No. 28,112, 28 March 1995, pp. 1-2) [DDS 1995-ARG1], Section 4.

Agricultural workers

In 1980, a specific legal regime for agricultural workers was established by Act No. 22,248/80.[42] However, there is no direct reference to the maximum duration of daily working time: "hours of work shall conform to the practice and customs of each region and to the nature of the business". Nevertheless, limits are set indirectly due to the required break and rest periods.

Practice

According to a collective agreement of General Motors in Argentina (GMA), the average working time is set at 2,128 hours per year.[43] Reduced working hours on some weekdays can be offset by longer hours of work on other days. Statutory provisions on the maximum length of the working day and daily breaks are respected. For the calculation of annual hours of work, paid and unpaid leave periods are considered days worked.

Another agreement, reached between an enterprise (Sevel Argentina SA) and the Unión Obrera Metalúrgica (UOM) in September 1995, reduces the working day for a six-month period. This temporary arrangement was introduced to save jobs. In practical terms, the length of normal shifts was reduced to four six-hour shifts or four seven-and-a-half-hour shifts, depending on the type of work. Accompanying this reduced working day schedule are reductions in remuneration and benefits, such as canteen services, meal breaks, compensation for overtime hours, payment of the thirteenth month salary, remuneration on national holidays, annual leave, and other types of leave and justified absences.[44]

Overtime and absolute maximum hours

Law

Workers are not obliged to work overtime, except in cases of *force majeure* due to potential or actual danger, accidents, or where exceptional requirements of the national economy or the enterprise make overtime necessary. In no case may overtime hours exceed three hours per day, 48 hours per month or 320 hours per year.[45]

---

[42] Act No. 22,248 to approve nation-wide rules governing agricultural work, dated 3 July 1980 (*Boletín Oficial*, No. 24,461, 18 July 1980), as amended up to Act No. 24,013, dated 5 December 1991 (*Boletín Oficial*, No. 27,286, 17 December 1991, p. 4) [LS 1980-Arg.1; LLD 1991-ARG1].

[43] Collective agreement between General Motors of Argentina SA and the Sindicato de Mecanicos y Afines del Transporte Automotor (SMATA). The collective agreement is valid from 1 November 1993 to 31 October 1998.

[44] Agreement signed on 26 September 1995 in the Centro Operativo El Palomar of Sevel Argentina SA in Villa Bosch, province of Buenos Aires. The agreement included some clauses obliging the enterprise to rehire all workers who were dismissed so far, to maintain existing staff in their jobs, and to ban all new dismissals with the exception of those based on disciplinary reasons.

[45] Decree No. 16,115, op. cit.

Exclusions and exceptions

Excluded from maximum hour limits are family enterprises; shiftworkers, provided that the average of hours worked over a period of at least three weeks does not exceed the maximum limits; researchers; stock-exchange brokers who are remunerated exclusively by commission; workers who render their services outside the establishment and therefore are not directly supervised by the employer; night watchpersons who may work a 12-hour day; harbour and maritime workers; bus drivers; musicians; football players; health-service workers; journalists and radio-telegraphists.

Jobs requiring preparatory or complementary tasks can also be excluded from the normal maximum limits. These are subject to a special regulation by the executive power, and include both ongoing, daily activities (such as machine maintenance) and periodical activities (such as making an inventory).

Temporary exceptions to the legal maximum limits on hours of work may be approved to allow enterprises to deal with extraordinary demands of work.[46] Authorizations are issued for a limited period. The number of supplementary working hours may not exceed three hours a day, 48 hours a month or 320 hours a year for each worker. In all cases, the hours worked in excess must be remunerated as overtime hours.[47]

Work classified by law or by the labour administrative authority as dangerous, arduous or unhealthy may not be performed by women and minors less than 18 years of age. Male workers older than 18 years of age may only undertake such work for six hours a day or 36 hours weekly. This may be extended to seven hours on any day, but the weekly limit of 36 hours must be respected. If the working day combines day and night work, working hours under unhealthy conditions should not exceed three hours per day.[48]

In the case of ordinary working days, employers must pay overtime premiums, whether undertaken with or without permission from the competent administrative authority. The rate is equal to an additional 50 per cent of the normal wage. On Saturdays after 13:00, on Sundays and on public holidays, overtime is paid at twice the normal wage.[49]

Domestic employees

The legal employment status of domestic employees was established by Decree No. 326/56.[50] However, domestic workers employed for less than a month, or for less than four hours a day, or for less than four days a week in the service of a given employer are excluded.[51] The

---

[46] Act No. 11,544, op. cit., Section 4(b).

[47] Decree No. 2889/79, op. cit.

[48] Decree No. 390/76, Sections 176, 191 and 200.

[49] ibid., Section 201.

[50] Decree No. 326/56 concerning domestic employees, dated 14 January 1956 (*Boletín Oficial*, 20 January 1956).

[51] ibid., Section 1.

statutory provisions only apply to live-in domestic workers and no limits on their maximum working time are stipulated.

Practice

The law provides that collective agreements may provide for reductions in daily working hours, as well as establish methods for calculating the upper limits for reference periods longer than a week, as long as the legal limits are respected when hours of work are averaged. The two parties may freely agree upon limits on and compensation for overtime hours worked beyond the normal hours fixed. Individual contracts may also establish daily hours of work shorter than the legal normal hours of work.

A sample of 72 collective agreements, representing 53.3 per cent of the sectors concerned, found scarce reference to the length of daily working time or to current relevant legislation. Only 9.7 per cent of collective agreements had established daily working hours and weekly periods of between 40 to 44 hours.[52]

A General Motors Argentina collective agreement provides that overtime hours be paid in the same month in which they have been worked, if there are no hours owed by the workers. Tasks performed during overtime hours are paid according to statutory provisions. Each overtime hour is paid the effective monthly remuneration divided by 193.6.

Collective agreement 60/89 of the Sindicato Gráfico Argentino (workers in newspapers and in the printing industry) limits overtime hours to six hours per week.[53]

Rest

Law

Rest breaks

There are no applicable statutory provisions on rest breaks. Pauses and periods of inactivity due to the productive process are part of normal daily working time. Breaks due to the worker's unilateral decision are not counted as working time.[54]

Young workers. Workers under 18 years of age, who work both in the morning and in the afternoon, benefit from a two-hour break, unless a continuous working day reducing or eliminating the break is authorized. Enterprises are prohibited from requesting young workers to undertake their work at home.[55]

---

[52] Information provided to the ILO by the Unión Industrial Argentina, 1995.

[53] ibid.

[54] Decree No. 390/76, op. cit., Section 197.

[55] ibid., Sections 174-175.

Agricultural workers. Breaks of between two and four-and-a-half hours must be granted for meals and rest, the length of the break is to be decided by the National Committee for Agricultural Work, according to the season of the year and the geographical location of the establishment.[56]

Daily breaks

There must be at least a 12-hour break between the end of one working day and the beginning of the next.[57]

Agricultural workers. An uninterrupted break of not less than ten hours must be granted between the end of one working day and the beginning of the following day.However, the length of this pause could be reduced according to production needs. In this case, compensation equivalent to the reduction should be granted within the following fortnight.[58]

Domestic employees. A nightly rest period of at least nine consecutive hours and a three-hour daily rest period between morning and afternoon duties is required.[59]

Weekly rest

No worker may be employed between 13:00 on Saturday and Sunday midnight.In exceptional cases, as prescribed by law, a compensatory rest period of the same length must be granted for hours worked during the weekly rest period.[60]

Agricultural workers. Working on Sunday is prohibited, unless the activity cannot be postponed due to production or maintenance needs. A compensation day should be granted to the worker during the fortnight following any Sunday on which work is performed. The prohibition to work on Sunday does not apply to regular activities that must be undertaken on that day due to their nature or because they are carried out on the basis of rotating shifts. In this case, workers should be granted a day of compensatory rest during the following week. Financial compensation complementary to the compulsory rest time is also required.[61]

Domestic employees. A weekly rest time of 24 consecutive hours or, if that is not possible, two half-days a week beginning at 15:00.[62]

[56] Act No. 22,248/80, op. cit.

[57] Decree No. 390/76, op. cit.

[58] Act No. 22,248/80, op. cit., Sections 14-15.

[59] Decree No. 326/56, op. cit., Section 4.

[60] Decree No. 390/76, op. cit., Section 204.

[61] Act No. 22,248/80, op. cit., Sections 16-18.

[62] Decree No. 326/56, op. cit., Section 4.

Practice

Depending on the nature of the business's activity, meal breaks are between 15 to 30 minutes.[63] Collective agreements frequently specify breaks of between ten to 60 minutes for snacks or lunch.[64]

A General Motors Argentina collective agreement provides for a daily rest period of 12 hours between two consecutive working days.

Shop-opening hours

Law

Shop-opening hours are not regulated. In the case of financial institutions, opening hours are regulated by Act No. 21,526.[65]

Practice

Shops are open from 8:00 to 20:00 with a break at noon. On Saturdays, shops are open in the morning. Shopping centres are open Monday to Sunday from 10:00 to 22:00 with a compensatory rest day for employees. Banks are open to the public Monday to Friday from 10:00 to 15:00. Insurance companies are open Monday to Friday from 12:00 to 19:00. Public offices are open Monday to Friday from 10:00 to 18:00.[66]

Public holidays

Law

In Argentina, there are two categories of feast days: the so-called "obligatory holidays" and "non-working days". There are ten national obligatory feast days: 1 January, Good Friday, 1 May, 25 May, 10 June, 20 June, 9 July, 17 August, 12 October and 25 December.[67]

The statutory provisions governing rest on Sundays apply to national public holidays. On any such day, a worker is entitled to receive the remuneration corresponding to a normal working day, even if it falls on a Sunday. A worker who performs services on any such day is entitled to receive twice his or her normal remuneration for a working day.[68]

[63] Ministry of Labour and Social Security, op. cit.

[64] Unión Industrial Argentina, op. cit.

[65] Act No. 21,526 respecting financial institutions, dated 14 February 1977 (*Boletín Oficial*, No. 23,602, 21 February 1977, p. 3).

[66] Information provided to the ILO by the Confederación General del Trabajo, 1995.

[67] Act No. 21,329 on public holidays, dated 9 June 1976 (*Boletín Oficial*, No. 23,425, 14 June 1976, p. 2).

[68] Decree No. 390/76, op. cit., Section 166.

Workers paid on a daily basis have the right to be paid for public holidays, as long as they have worked for the same employer for a period of 48 hours or six days within the ten days prior to the holiday, or worked the previous day (to the holiday) and continue to work during any of the five following working days.[69] The limit on working hours on public holidays is the same as for normal working days.[70] Some of these holidays may be moved to Monday, especially when they fall on another weekday.[71]

There also are two non-working days, namely the day before Good Friday and 8 December.[72] The 24th of December is also a non-working day for banks and public administrations. This second category of feast days is optional in the private sector. Insurance companies and schools are also closed on these days, in accordance with specific sectoral regulations. Given the "optional" nature of the non-working days, the worker's remuneration is the same as for a normal day.[73]

Practice

Almost all collective agreements have established their "industry day". It is current practice, however, to work on this day, but with double pay.[74]

The collective agreement of General Motors Argentina strictly follows the statutory provisions concerning national holidays and non-working days and remuneration on these days.

Paid annual leave

Law

The minimum period of paid annual leave for workers is 14 days for up to five years of employment; 21 days for between five and ten years of employment; 28 days for between ten and 20 years of employment; and 35 days for more than 20 years of employment.[75] In all cases, days are consecutive days, but this provision may be modified by collective agreement.

For workers to have the right to a full annual leave period every year, they must have rendered services during a minimum period of half of the working days of the year to which the leave corresponds.[76] The paid annual leave period should start on a Monday, or on the following

---

[69] ibid., Section 168.

[70] Ministry of Labour and Social Security, op. cit.

[71] *El sistema argentino de relaciones laborales*, op. cit., p. 150.

[72] Act No. 21,329, op. cit., Section 1.

[73] Decree No. 390/76, op. cit., Section 167.

[74] Unión Industrial Argentina, op. cit.

[75] Decree No. 390/76, op. cit., Section 150.

[76] ibid., Section 151.

day if the Monday is a holiday. Where a worker has not completed the minimum period of service, he or she is entitled to an annual rest period calculated on the basis of one day of rest for every 20 days of actual work.

Employers should grant annual leave between 1 October and 30 April of the following year (i.e. during the summer period). The employer must inform workers in writing of their annual leave at least 45 days in advance. However, the same provision allows collective agreements to establish other holiday periods when the special nature of the work so requires. When leave is not granted simultaneously to all workers, the employer must organize the leave period to ensure that all workers are granted leave in summer at least once every three years.[77]

Paid annual leave has to be remunerated prior to the leave period. Different mechanisms have been designed to calculate the amount according to the salary system.[78] For example, for monthly remunerated jobs, the amount to be paid for each day of leave is calculated at one-twenty-fifth of the monthly salary.

Compensation in cash for the omission of granting annual leave is prohibited. The only exception to compensation in cash occurs in the case of termination of the employment contract. In such case, workers receive compensation proportional to the fraction of the year worked.[79]

Young workers

Workers younger than 18 years are entitled to a minimum period of 15 consecutive days of paid annual leave. Conditions for annual leave are the same as for other workers.[80]

Agricultural workers

The following consecutive, remunerated annual leave periods must be granted to agricultural workers: ten days for less than five years of work; 15 days for between five and ten years of work; 20 days for between ten and 15 years of work; 30 days for more than 15 years of work.

For these periods to be granted, workers should be at work during no less that half of the annual effective working days. Compensation days are also provided in case workers have not accomplished the minimum working days. For annual leave periods of 20 days or more, the employer — with the worker's agreement — may divide them into two periods. In all cases, remuneration should be paid in advance.[81]

Omission to grant annual leave cannot be compensated by money. The only exception to this provision occurs when the labour contract is terminated and annual leave has not been taken.

---

[77] ibid., Section 154.

[78] ibid., Section 155.

[79] ibid., Sections 156 and 162.

[80] ibid., Sections 150-164 and 194.

[81] Act No. 22,248/80, op. cit., Sections 20-22.

There is an established procedure for calculating the financial compensation to be granted to agricultural workers.[82]

Domestic employees

The length (consecutive working days) of paid annual leave for domestic workers varies according to seniority on the job: ten days for one to five years; 15 days for five to ten years; 20 days for more than ten years.

Domestic workers are entitled to be granted one hour a week to attend religious services.[83]

Practice

The Ministry of Labour and Social Security reports that the length of paid annual leave has remained stable since 1980.

The collective agreement of General Motors Argentina follows the legislation concerning paid annual leave, its distribution and length. Some special leaves (i.e. death of spouse, child or a relative) can be added to annual leave if occurring during the annual leave period.

Other types of leave

Law

National legislation provides for "special leave" periods to cover the personal needs of workers.

Ten days are granted for marriage; three days for the death of a spouse, a partner, a child or a parent; two days for the birth of a child; two days for school and university exams, with a maximum of ten days per calendar year; and one day for the death of a brother or sister. These days are remunerated as special leave days, and are calculated according to the salary system.[84]

Leave is also granted for making a blood donation (during the donation day); taking up an official appointment to which the worker has been elected (for the period of appointment plus 30 days); to fulfill a judicial or civic obligation (as needed); and for voluntary fire-fighting (in case of emergency).[85]

Agricultural workers have the right to the same special leave periods.[86]

---

[82] ibid., Sections 23 and 25.

[83] Decree No. 326/56, op. cit., Section 4.

[84] Decree No. 390/76, op. cit., Sections 155 and 158-159.

[85] Unión Industrial Argentina, op. cit.

[86] Act No. 22,248/80, op. cit., Section 24.

Practice

In collective agreements, other special leave may be granted, such as on the "industry day", or for the sickness or death of a relative, or for menstruation.[87]

In addition to the statutory special leave provisions, the General Motors Argentina collective agreement provides up to five days per calendar year for the serious illness of a family member, on condition that the worker is the only available person to care for the sick relative; one day, up to three times per calendar year, for blood donation, on condition that the donation is for the worker's own family or for another employee of GMA or the spouse of the employee. The attendance of the worker for appointments with the Ministries of Labour, Public Health or Justice, police or other official services is paid for the length of the appointment. Other unpaid special leave that may be granted includes leave for a worker who has been granted a fellowship to undertake research or a vocational training course in another locality or for personal reasons, which is only granted exceptionally for well-justified reasons. For unpaid special leave to be granted, the members of each working team should be in agreement, to ensure that group work is not jeopardized.

Shift and night work

Law

Persons employed on shift work are permitted to work more than eight hours in any one day or more than 48 hours weekly, on condition that the average number of hours worked over a period of not less than three weeks does not exceed eight hours per day or 48 hours per week.[88]

The period of night work for adult male workers is defined as between 21:00 and 06:00 of the following day. Working hours during the night may not exceed seven hours. However, this limit does not apply to work performed in alternating shifts.[89] Women and minors are prohibited from night work during the period from 20:00 to 06:00 of the following day. Woman and boys over 16 years old may, however, work up to 22:00 where manufacturing establishments operate a continuous three-shift system.[90]

When a work schedule combines day and night working hours, each hour worked during the night period (e.g. between 21:00 and 06:00) should be reduced by eight minutes. If work is performed during these eight-minute-per-hour periods, it should be compensated at the same rate as overtime hours.

---

[87] Unión Industrial Argentina, op. cit.

[88] Act No. 11,544, op. cit., Section 3(b).

[89] Decree No. 390/76, op. cit., Section 200; Act No. 11,544, op. cit., Section 2.

[90] Decree No. 390/76, op. cit., Sections 173 and 190.

Practice

The collective agreement of General Motors Argentina provides for the consideration of requests to change working time schedules for workers attending vocational training or university courses. Workers may change their shifts as long as workers performing equivalent work on different shifts agree to rotate, and that this agreement is communicated to the enterprise.

Australia

Overview and trends

Overview

Australia is a federal state with jurisdiction for labour relations, and more particularly working time issues, shared between the federal and state levels of government.[1] Federal jurisdiction is based on the federal constitution which states that the central government may adopt laws with respect to "conciliation and arbitration for the prevention and settlement of industrial disputes extending beyond the limits of any one State",[2] leaving to the states the power to legislate in most other instances. The federal labour relations system regulates approximately one-half of the workforce, while all the states combined regulate the other half. Conditions of employment, including working time issues, have traditionally been determined by compulsory conciliation and arbitration decisions called "awards", made by industrial relations commissions which function as independent industrial tribunals at both the federal and state level. While traditionally the industrial relations commissions of the states tended to follow the principles adapted by their federal counterpart, this appears to be changing as there have been legislative changes, at both the federal level and in some states, to decrease significantly the influence of the award system, which tended to facilitate highly centralized determination of working conditions in most workplaces, and encourage decentralized bargaining at the enterprise level directly between the employer and the employees, either individually or collectively. In May 1990, shortly before the reforms were introduced, approximately 80 per cent of all Australian workers had their terms and conditions of employment governed by either federal or state awards.[3]

The reform process to encourage decentralized enterprise level agreements began at the federal level in 1988 with the amendment of the Industrial Relations Act, which was supposed to permit employers and trade unions to agree on terms and conditions of employment and to have that agreement certified by the federal industrial relations commission (the "federal commission"),[4] even if certain parts of it did not conform to the federal commission's general principles. However, because the federal commission took a restrictive view of the amended law and refused to certify a number of agreements which it claimed were contrary to the public interest because they did not conform to the commission's principles, the Industrial Relations Act was again amended in 1992 and 1994 to encourage enterprise-level agreements and to reduce the federal commission's power to refuse to certify an agreement. After these

---

[1] The Northern Territory and the Australian Capital Territory are not legally states, but they have been granted self-rule powers which give them powers equivalent to states for purposes of analysis and they are, by consequence, treated as if they were states for describing the situation concerning working time issues in Australia.

[2] Section 51(35) of the Constitution of Australia, cited in M.J. Pittard: "Australia", in W. Kaplan, J. Sack and M. Gunderson (eds.): *Labour arbitration yearbook* (Toronto, Lancaster House, 1993), p. 347.

[3] Australian Bureau of Statistics: *1992 Labour statistics Australia* (Canberra, 1993), p. 131.

[4] The federal industrial relations commission is formally named the Australian Industrial Relations Commission.

amendments, the law allowed the conclusion of agreements on certain conditions of employment which were inconsistent with the federal commission's generally applicable standards. The amended law did not, however, abolish the award system completely, but recast it to function as "a safety net".[5] Awards were to set "fair and enforceable minimum wages and conditions of employment that are maintained at a relevant level" and to act "as a safety net ... underpinning direct bargaining".[6] In addition, however, the new legislation includes certain minimum standards to govern employment relations. The federal commission will not arbitrate in enterprise bargaining cases, but only conciliate, leaving the primary responsibility for reaching an agreement on the parties concerned.

There has been broad political support to facilitate enterprise-level bargaining and to move away from the centralized award system. Enterprise-level bargaining has been encouraged so that the social partners can negotiate agreements tailor-made to suit their workplace, and the primary responsibility for the successful outcome of negotiations rests with the parties concerned. These reforms were introduced with the goal of implementing cooperatively and constructively changes that were needed to improve productivity and to compete internationally, while ensuring that workers are adequately protected.[7]

There have also been changes in legislation in a number of states to facilitate decentralized bargaining at the enterprise level. These changes have been the most far reaching in Victoria, where the compulsory system of conciliation and arbitration was abolished as of 1 March 1993 and all previous awards lapsed as of that day. New awards require the consent of all employers and employees involved. Individual as well as collective employment agreements can be directly negotiated without the approval of any third party, although the parties can agree that a previous award will continue to apply to their particular workplace. The new legislation also establishes certain minimum standards concerning conditions of work including, with respect to working time issues, minimum paid annual leave. In the states of New South Wales, Tasmania and Western Australia, enterprise bargaining has also been introduced which allows agreements to be entered into with individual employees. While it is possible for trade unions to be parties to such enterprise agreements in these states, it is not required as it is in South Australia and Queensland. Compulsory arbitration exists in all states except Victoria, but it is to be phased out in Western Australia.[8]

---

[5] Industrial Relations Act 1988, Act No. 86, dated 8 November 1988 (*Acts of the Parliament*, 1988), as amended up to Act No. 158, dated 15 December 1994 (*Acts of the Parliament*, 1994).

[6] ibid., Section 88.

[7] R. Hamilton: "Employment matters in 1993", in *Journal of Industrial Relations*, Vol. 36, No. 1, March 1994, pp. 117-134; information provided to the ILO jointly by the Government of Australia and the Australian Chamber of Commerce and Industry, May 1995.

[8] "Australia. Industrial relations Accord: One more step to workplace bargaining?", in *International Labour Review*, Vol. 132, No. 2, 1993, pp. 143-149. See also C. Fox and J. Teicher: "Victoria's Employee Relations Act: The way to the future?", in *Australian Bulletin of Labour*, Vol. 20, No. 3, September 1994, pp. 194-210.

Trends

A five-day, 40-hour week was the standard work-week already in 1947, and remained the generally applicable standard working week largely until the early 1980s,[9] although labour unions fought successfully for a 35-hour week in the 1970s in some industries, such as the coal mining, oil and stevedoring industries. In the early 1980s, unions pressed for a more generalized 35-hour week but were unsuccessful. In December 1981, the Metal Industry Award reduced normal weekly hours from 40 to 38. After this, the trend was to seek a 38-hour week in most industries, and, in September 1983, the federal commission — in a major decision — established the general principle of a 38-hour work-week, which is still applicable.[10] More generally, however, some studies seem to indicate that, although standard working hours have changed very little over the past several decades, annual working hours have decreased if entitlements to annual leave, sick leave and other types of leave are taken into account.[11]

The legal changes to the federal law to facilitate agreements at the enterprise level appear to have had only a limited impact in the private sector. As of 1993, the overwhelming majority of enterprise-level agreements were in the manufacturing sector and were confined to unionized companies, frequently the larger ones.[12] It would appear, however, that changes are more likely to take place concerning the arrangement of working hours and whether premium pay should be due for certain work performed during time traditionally considered as non-social hours or during what has been historically considered overtime periods, i.e. evening and night work, weekend work, public holidays, and supplementary hours after one's regularly scheduled hours. Recent developments include more shift work to make better use of capital equipment and reduce cost and disruption associated with the shutting down and restarting of equipment; the introduction of staggered starting and finishing times as well as meal breaks to achieve a greater spread of normal working hours; compressed work-weeks which may, for example, consist of longer shifts over shorter periods of time, such as 12-hour shifts over a three-day period; use of a reference period longer than one week so that average working hours per week are calculated over two or more weeks, with supplementary hours worked during peak periods balanced by having additional days off subsequently or shorter hours of work during subsequent working weeks; and the elimination of overtime and other premium rates for work during unsocial hours or for shift work, and the incorporation of these supplementary payments into one all-inclusive, higher annual salary.[13]

[9] Confederation of Australian Industry: *Flexibility of working time in Australia* (Melbourne, 1989), Appendix 2, p. 20.

[10] Government of Australia and Australian Chamber of Commerce and Industry, op. cit.

[11] P. Dawkins and M. Baker: "Australia", in G. Bosch, P. Dawkins and F. Michon (eds.): *Times are changing: Working time in 14 industrialised countries* (Geneva, International Institute for Labour Studies, 1994), pp. 48-55.

[12] Hamilton, "Employment matters in 1993", op. cit.

[13] Government of Australia and Australian Chamber of Commerce and Industry, op. cit.

There has also been a trend towards increased part-time work.[14] In 1982, some 17.1 per cent of the workforce worked part time, of which 3.8 per cent were men and 13.3 per cent were women. In 1992, however, 24.4 per cent of the workforce was employed part time, of which 6.1 per cent were men and 18.3 per cent were women.[15]

Normal hours of work

Law

Although there is no generally applicable federal law on normal hours of work, the federal commission, through award determinations, has established 38 hours per week as the broad norm. At the state level, state commissions have tended to follow the standard established by the federal commission. Some states also have statutory limits. In New South Wales, although the state commission of New South Wales has established a 38-hour week as a broadly applicable standard, it has legislation which provides that weekly hours of work should not exceed 40, but can be averaged over 52 weeks.[16] In Queensland, the law provides that, in the absence of an award or an agreement, six days in any period of seven consecutive days are the applicable limits, with 40 hours in any period of six consecutive days and eight hours in any day.[17]

Practice

Awards at the federal and state level have usually established normal hours of work per week to be 38, with a daily maximum of eight hours. A growing number of awards allow daily hours of up to 12 hours under certain restricted conditions. In some industries, shorter hours of work, typically in the range of 35 to 37 hours per week, have been achieved.[18] Available statistics on the average weekly hours of work in Australia indicate only a very slight decrease in average hours of work since 1984, which is at present just over 38 hours for all non-agricultural activities. Table 1 gives the average hours of work for full-time adult employees, including overtime. If part-time workers are included, the average is considerably lower at

---

[14] See, inter alia, P. Robertson: "Some explanations for the growth of part-time unemployment in Australia", in *Australian Bulletin of Labour*, Vol. 15, No. 5, December 1989, pp. 384-389; K. Norris: "Recent trends in labour mobility and in job durations", in *Australian Bulletin of Labour*, Vol. 19, No. 1, March 1993, pp. 49-55; and J. Mangan and J. Steinke: "Working-time reductions: A survey of the Australian experience", in *Industrial Relations Journal*, Vol. 19, No. 4, Winter 1988, pp. 322-327. For an analysis of the potential economic consequences of part-time work, see B.H. Casey and S.W. Creigh: "Part-time job creation: An option for Australia?", in *Journal of Industrial Relations*, Vol. 28, No. 4, December 1986, pp. 534-544.

[15] *1992 Labour statistics Australia*, op. cit., p. 40.

[16] New South Wales Industrial Relations Act 1991, Act No. 34, dated 11 November 1991 (*The Statutes of New South Wales*, 1991), as amended up to Act No. 40, dated 2 June 1994 (*The Statutes of New South Wales*, 1994), Section 23.

[17] Queensland Industrial Relations Act 1990, Act No. 28, dated 15 June 1990 (*Queensland Government Gazette*, 1990), as amended up to Act No. 14, dated 11 April 1995 (*Queensland Government Gazette*, 1995), Section 221(2)..

[18] Government of Australia and Australian Chamber of Commerce and Industry, op. cit.

33.2 hours per week. It should be observed that statistics on actual hours worked were not available for the different services which are the sectors most likely to be affected by part-time work. This explains why the average weekly hours decreased slightly since 1984, despite the fact that actual working hours slightly increased in the sectors mentioned in Table 2.

Table 1. Hours of work paid for per week by major divisions of economic activity[19]

Major division	1984	1985	1986	1987	1988	1989	1990	1991	1992	1993	1994
Mining and quarrying	41.8	42.1	42.0	42.3	43.3	44.2	43.9	42.4	43.5	43.2	42.8
Manufacturing	40.9	41.3	41.4	41.5	41.7	41.8	41.3	40.4	40.7	41.1	40.2
Electricity, gas and water	39.5	39.5	38.9	39.3	39.1	39.2	39.2	38.7	39.0	39.1	38.5
Construction	40.4	41.1	41.2	40.9	42.0	40.2	41.6	42.3	40.9	41.2	40.2
Trades, restaurants and hotels	40.4	40.2	40.1	40.1	40.2	39.9	39.9	39.4	39.5	39.6	37.7
Transport, storage and communication	40.6	43.1	40.7	40.6	40.8	41.2	40.5	40.4	40.4	41.3	40.7
Financing, insurance, real estate and business services	38.6	38.7	38.7	38.8	38.7	38.9	39.1	38.6	38.6	39.0	37.1
Community, social and personal services	37.8	38.0	37.8	37.8	37.8	39.8	38.2	38.1	38.1	38.3	37.0
Total (all non-agricultural activities)	39.6	40.1	39.7	39.8	39.9	38.8	39.8	39.5	39.4	39.7	38.4

Table 2. Actual hours of work per week in major divisions of economic activity

Major division	1984	1985	1986	1987	1988	1989	1990	1991	1992	1993	1994
Mining and quarrying	36.7	37.3	37.1	37.7	39.7	40.1	41.3	41.4	40.8	42.7	43.6
Manufacturing	36.2	36.9	37.1	37.3	37.9	37.7	38.1	37.6	38.0	38.1	38.7
Construction	36.8	37.7	38.0	38.3	38.9	38.5	38.8	38.6	38.8	39.1	39.9
Transport, storage and communication	35.1	36.1	35.7	36.0	36.6	36.5	37.1	36.3	37.6	37.8	36.7
Total (all non-agricultural activities)	33.8	33.0	32.7	33.1	33.4	33.1	33.3	33.2	33.0	33.0	33.2

[19] Bureau of Statistics, International Labour Office [covers full-time adult non-managerial employees only]. N.B. Comparable statistics for other countries normally include part-time workers.

Special categories of workers

Normal hours of work of federal public servants are 36¾ hours per week; or seven hours and 21 minutes per day. Hours of work are normally scheduled Monday through Friday.[20] Hours of work can be averaged over a period of ten working days, but the maximum flexitime credit or debit allowed is ten hours.[21] The 38-hour work-week is also the standard in the nursing profession, but there are varying practices regarding shift arrangements. Attempts to introduce 12-hour shifts have met with resistance and it is common to have a maximum limit of ten hours per shift.[22]

Overtime and absolute maximum hours

Law

There are no generally applicable laws at the federal or state levels concerning limits to overtime, compensation for overtime or absolute maximum hours of work.

Practice

Awards or agreements may provide for limits to overtime, although there is no generally applicable standard.[23] The conditions under which overtime may be worked vary from industry to industry. While overtime in a number of cases is voluntary, many awards state that employers may require employees to work "reasonable overtime". However, what constitutes "reasonable overtime" will depend on the circumstances of the case. Prior authorization and notification must be given where and when such action would be seen as reasonable under the circumstances. A requirement to work overtime can also be implied in a contract of employment.[24]

Compensation for overtime is generally either a premium payment or compensatory time off. In some cases, compensatory time is also granted at a premium rate. Compensation for overtime is frequently at a premium rate of 50 per cent for the first three hours and doubletime thereafter. However, there is a trend towards payment of doubletime after two hours, particularly in some state jurisdictions. Sometimes awards may also provide for a minimum payment regardless of overtime actually worked. A requirement of at least two hours' pay when an employee is required to be present at work for overtime is contained in some

---

[20] Information provided to the ILO by the Community and Public Sector Union, June 1995. Public service is governed by the General Conditions of Service, Professional Officers Association, Australian Government Employment Award 1990.

[21] ibid., Australian Government Employment (Flexible Working Hours) Award 1988.

[22] M. Vidovich, Australian Nursing Federation: *The nursing industry in Australia*, working paper presented to the Asian Tripartite Workshop on Working Time Arrangements, Bangkok, 18-22 July 1994.

[23] Government of Australia and Australian Chamber of Commerce and Industry, op. cit.

[24] ibid.

awards.[25] Recent statistics indicate that the total amount of overtime hours worked as well as the percentage of persons working overtime has been decreasing.[26]

Special categories of workers

In the nursing industry, overtime rates apply for hours worked in excess of scheduled shifts. Special compensation is payable to workers who are required to be available by telephone or paging device for duty. Premium rates are applicable for evening, night and weekend shifts. Flexitime has been applied on an experimental basis in some cases. Nurses "bank" time worked in excess of their scheduled hours on busy days and "spend" it later when it is convenient to them and the department.[27]

In the public service, staff may be required to work overtime and premium payment is due, subject to prior authorization and the fulfilment of certain conditions. Certain staff, including those in managerial positions, are not entitled to overtime compensation. Overtime is compensated during weekdays, as well as on Saturdays, at time-and-a-half for the first three hours and doubletime thereafter. Doubletime is paid for all work performed on Sundays.[28]

Rest

Law

The only legislation at the federal or state level is a law in Queensland which provides that, where practicable, employees shall have a ten-minute rest break during each four-hour period of work on any day. This rest time is calculated as part of working time.[29]

Practice

Awards and agreements generally provide for a meal break of between 30 minutes and one hour during an employee's hours of work. Usually, an employee will not be required to work for more than five hours without a meal break. Awards also provide that if employees continue to work without taking a meal break, they are entitled to overtime until a meal break is given. Meal breaks are often paid if the break is during overtime or shift work. Provision may also be made for a work pause or tea break during normal working hours. A work pause is usually ten to 20 minutes in the morning or afternoon or both, although work pause provisions are not as common as meal break provisions. Most awards and agreements provide

---

[25] ibid.

[26] Australian Bureau of Statistics: *Job vacancies and overtime, Australia, February 1995* (Canberra, March 1995). For a longer term perspective, see M. Wooden: "Overemployment, unemployment and the work sharing debate", in *Australian Bulletin of Labour*, Vol. 19, No. 4, December 1993, pp. 314-321.

[27] Vidovich, *The nursing industry in Australia*, op. cit.

[28] Community and Public Sector Union, op. cit.

[29] Queensland Industrial Relations Act 1990, op. cit., Section 221(7).

that meal breaks are unpaid and work pauses are paid.[30] In the public service, at least 30 minutes must be taken between 12:00 and 14:00 and up to two hours may be taken, depending on work requirements. Lunch breaks are unpaid.[31]

With respect to daily rest, awards and agreements usually provide for a minimum period of rest between the end of overtime work and the commencement of a new shift. The minimum period of rest traditionally was eight hours, but it is now commonly ten hours. If the minimum break is not observed, all work performed is paid at overtime rates until the prescribed rest period is provided.[32] In the public service, employees are entitled to have at least eight consecutive hours off between the termination of duty on one day and the commencement of duty the following day, as well as reasonable travelling time to cover going to and from their place of work.[33] Nurses are generally entitled to a minimum of nine-and-a-half hours of rest between shifts.[34]

Normal weekly hours vary, but there is commonly a rest break on Saturday and Sunday. Some industries provide more flexible arrangements, for example, nine days of work scheduled over a two-week period, or work scheduled on Saturday with a day off during the regular Monday to Friday week.[35]

Shop-opening hours

Law

Shop-opening hours are regulated by state law. The terms of regulations vary from state to state, but generally these hours range from 08:00 to 16:00 or 09:00 to 17:30 or 18:00 on weekdays, with provision made for late-night shopping on one or two nights of the week. Most shops are open for at least part of Saturday. Some industries are excluded from the general restriction on Sunday trading. Retail establishments are generally closed on public holidays.[36]

Public holidays

Law

There are ten federal public holidays in Australia. Depending on the jurisdiction, up to three additional holidays are also declared in a given state. In Queensland, it is provided that work

---

[30] Government of Australia and Australian Chamber of Commerce and Industry, op. cit.

[31] Community and Public Sector Union, op. cit.

[32] Government of Australia and Australian Chamber of Commerce and Industry, op. cit.

[33] Australian Government Employment Award 1990, op. cit.

[34] Vidovich, *The nursing industry in Australia*, op. cit.

[35] Government of Australia and Australian Chamber of Commerce and Industry, op. cit.

[36] ibid.

on public holidays is paid at the rate two-and-a-half times the regular rate for a minimum of four hours of work.[37] In the Northern Territory, doubletime pay is obligatory for work required on public holidays for employees who earn less than A$ 401 per week.[38]

Practice

Employees covered by federal awards normally have an entitlement to at least 11 paid public holidays, and those covered by state awards are entitled to between ten and 11 paid public holidays. Federal public service employees are granted up to 13 paid public holidays, depending on the number of state public holidays in the locality where they work. Awards and agreements usually provide for doubletime pay for work on public holidays, although time-and-a-half pay is also practised. Federal public servants may be required to work on public holidays if it is in the interest of the service concerned, and they are to be paid at two-and-a-half times their regular rate of pay.[39]

Paid annual leave

Law

There is no federal statute on entitlement to paid annual leave, although the award system has fixed the minimum national standard for most workers at four weeks' paid annual leave after a year of service with the employer. Legislation in the Australian Capital Territory, New South Wales, the Northern Territory, South Australia, Victoria and Western Australia all grant an entitlement to four weeks of paid annual leave.[40] Shiftworkers in the Australian Capital Territory and the Northern Territory are entitled to supplementary paid annual leave according to certain conditions (see below under **Shift and night work**). Most states provide for a premium payment of 17.5 per cent of the salary (referred to as annual leave loading).

---

[37] Queensland Industrial Relations Act 1990, op. cit., Section 222(3).

[38] Northern Territories Public Holidays Act 1981, Act No. 71, dated 11 December 1981 (*Northern Territory Gazette*, 1981), as amended up to Act No. 28, dated 30 June 1993 (*Northern Territory Gazette*, 1993).

[39] Government of Australia and Australian Chamber of Commerce and Industry, op. cit.

[40] Australian Capital Territory Annual Holidays Act 1973, Act No. 46, dated 29 November 1973 (*ACT Gazette*, 1973), as amended up to Act No. 106, dated 15 January 1992 (*ACT Gazette*, 1992), Section 5. New South Wales Annual Holidays Act 1944, Act No. 31, dated 8 December 1944 (*The Statutes of New South Wales*, 1944), as amended up to Act No. 112, dated 8 December 1992 (*The Statutes of New South Wales*, 1992). Northern Territory Annual Leave Act 1981, Act No. 70, dated 18 September 1981 (*Northern Territory Gazette*, 1981), as amended up to Act No. 28, dated 30 June 1993 (*Northern Territory Gazette*, 1993), Section 6. South Australia Industrial and Employee Relations Act No. 52, dated 16 June 1994 (*South Australian Government Gazette*, 1994), Section 71 and Schedule 4 (minimum standard, but may be deviated from by industrial agreement). Victoria Employee Relations Act 1992, Act No. 83, dated 24 November 1992 (*Government Gazette*, 1992), as amended up to Act No. 114, dated 7 December 1993 (*Government Gazette*, 1993), Schedule 1(1). Western Australia Workplace Agreements Act 1993, Act No. 13, dated 23 November 1993 (*Government Gazette of Western Australia*, 1993), as amended up to Act No. 1, dated 9 May 1995 (*Government Gazette of Western Australia*, 1995), Section 17; Minimum Conditions of Employment Act 1993, Act No. 14, dated 23 November 1993 (*Government Gazette of Western Australia*, 1993), Division 3.

However, this is now prohibited in Victoria as of 1992.[41] In the Australian Capital Territory, annual leave pay is equal to regular pay.[42] If a public holiday falls during the period of leave, the duration of paid annual leave is increased accordingly.

Practice

The generally accepted minimum national standard for annual leave is four weeks after each year of service with an employer, whether determined by award or enterprise agreement. Pro-rata paid annual leave is usually available for a period less than the required 12 months of continuous service. In the federal public service, paid annual leave is also four weeks. In addition, federal public service employees, who are engaged in seven-day shift work or who work in a remote locality, are entitled to an extra week of paid annual leave. Provisions for public service employees at the state level may be greater than the generally accepted national minimum standard of four weeks. For example, the minimum paid annual leave for Northern Territory public servants is six weeks.

In the private sector, awards or enterprise agreements may provide five weeks of paid annual leave for workers in remote locations, regular Sunday workers or continuous shiftworkers (see below under **Shift and night work**). Many awards prescribe that paid annual leave can be taken in two separate periods. One period of leave, however, must be of at least three weeks' duration. Under federal awards, employees and employers may also agree to allow up to one week's paid annual leave to be taken in single days.[43] According to the Government, enterprise bargaining should allow the social partners to negotiate more flexible arrangements concerning paid annual leave provisions.

Other types of leave

Law

Long-service leave

Long-service leave is paid leave granted to employees who have had a substantial number of years of service with the same employer, and can typically last two or more months, although in some jurisdictions the length of the leave period is calculated in weeks. At the federal level, long-service leave is determined by federal awards and agreements. In the federal public service, long-service leave entitlement is three months after ten years of service.[44] In the states, long-service leave is prescribed by state legislation. The standard private sector entitlement for long service leave is 13 weeks (three months) after 15 years of

---

[41] Victoria Annual Leave Payments Act 1992, Act No. 60, dated 17 November 1992 (*Government Gazette*, 1992), as amended up to Act No. 64, dated 17 August 1993 (*Government Gazette*, 1993).

[42] Australian Capital Territory Annual Holidays Act 1973, op. cit., Section 5.

[43] Government of Australia and Australian Chamber of Commerce and Industry, op. cit.

[44] ibid.

service, unless state legislation imposes different minimum requirements. Below is a summary of state legislative provisions on long service leave.

Australian Capital Territory. Two months after ten years of service, with a proportional amount of long-service leave accruing at the same rate after every five years of service, i.e. one month for every five subsequent years.[45]

New South Wales. Two months' leave after ten years of service, and one month for every five years thereafter.[46]

Northern Territory. Three months after ten years of service, with an equal entitlement after a subsequent ten years of service.[47]

Queensland. Thirteen weeks' leave (three months) after 15 years of service, with prorated entitlement to long-service leave if employment has lasted more than ten and less than 15 years and employment is terminated.[48]

South Australia. Thirteen weeks' leave (three months) after ten years of service, and 1.3 weeks for every subsequent year.[49]

Tasmania. Thirteen weeks' leave (three months) after 15 years of service, and 8⅔ weeks for every following ten-year period; if employment lasts seven, but not 15 years of service, there is an entitlement to prorated long-service leave.[50]

Victoria. Thirteen weeks' leave (three months) after 15 years of service, and 4⅓ weeks' (one month) for every five years thereafter.[51]

[45] Australian Capital Territory Long Service Leave Act 1976, dated 16 June 1976 (*ACT Gazette*, 1976), as amended up to Act No. 1, dated 1 March 1993 (*ACT Gazette*, 1993). Sections 3-4.

[46] New South Wales Long Service Leave Act 1955, Act No. 38, dated 5 November 1955 (*The Statutes of New South Wales*, 1955), as amended up to Act No. 112, dated 8 December 1992 (*The Statutes of New South Wales*, 1992). Section 4(1).

[47] Northern Territory Long Service Leave Act 1988, Act No. 72, dated 18 September 1988 (*Northern Territory Gazette*, 1988), as amended up to Act No. 59, dated 14 December 1990 (*Northern Territory Gazette*, 1990). Section 8.

[48] Queensland Industrial Relations Act 1990, op. cit. Division 3.

[49] South Australia Long Service Leave Act 1987, Act No. 73, dated 5 November 1987 (*South Australian Government Gazette*, 1987), as amended up to Act No. 93, dated 17 December 1992 (*South Australian Government Gazette*, 1992). Section 5.

[50] Tasmania Long Service Leave Act 1976, dated 15 December 1976 (*Tasmania Gazette*, 1976), as amended up to Act No. 68, dated 25 November 1994 (*Tasmania Gazette*, 1994). Section 7. Slightly different rules apply to miners and state employees.

[51] Victoria Employee Relations Act 1992, op. cit. Section 56.

Bereavement leave

Western Australia provides an entitlement of two days of paid leave in the event of the death of a spouse (or *de facto* spouse), child or step-child, or parent or step-parent.[52] Awards in most jurisdictions also frequently grant two days' paid leave for the death of a close relative.[53]

Practice

Other types of leave which may be provided in various awards or agreements or by custom include leave for jury duty, trade union training leave, study leave, special leave and special family leave.[54]

Leave for jury duty

Although employees who are called for jury service are paid a daily allowance from the court, under some awards the employer is required to pay the difference between the amount paid by the court and the employee's regular rate of pay.

Trade union training leave

Although this is not a standard form of leave, it is found in some awards and agreements. The provisions most commonly provide that the employee may be absent for up to two weeks on trade union training leave, but only one week is to be paid for by the employer.

Study leave

This leave is available to an employee to attend courses or undertake studies which may be helpful in the person's work. This type of leave may be paid or unpaid.

Special leave

Special leave may be available: when moving residences or moving to a different state for job purposes, to give blood, to fulfil religious obligations, or to attend a seminar or conference. Special leave may be paid or unpaid, depending on the purpose of the leave.

Special family leave

This form of leave is to support family members when they are ill, usually for between three to five days, and it may be either paid or unpaid, depending on the agreement. Many

---

[52] Western Australia Minimum Conditions of Employment Act 1993, op. cit. Section 27.

[53] Government of Australia and the Australian Chamber of Commerce and Industry, op. cit.

[54] ibid.

agreements also provide that employees can use their paid sick leave credits for this purpose as well.

Federal public service

A novel trend in the public service is to allow workers to take four weeks' unpaid leave a year (without affecting their annual leave entitlements) and to have their salary for 48 weeks averaged over 52 weeks. This provision is still only available in a few sectors of the public service, but is becoming more popular.[55] In the federal public service, there are other forms of leave for varying periods (in addition to those listed above), some of which are paid and some of which are unpaid. These types of leave include: staff organization leave; leave to engage in employment in the interest of the federal public service; campaign leave; leave for full-time defence service or for specified defence service or defence service training; leave for work in the interests of defence or public safety; arbitration leave and leave to prepare evidence in arbitration proceedings; leave to accompany a spouse on a posting; leave to be a witness; leave for local government purposes; leave to participate in emergency services; leave for attendance at international sporting events; special recreational leave; leave to engage in private sector employment; and leave without pay (up to 12 months which can be extended).

Shift and night work

Law

The Northern Territory provides that, in addition to the regular four weeks of paid annual leave, shiftworkers who work regularly on weekends and public holidays are entitled to an extra week of annual leave. Shiftworkers on continuous shifts, who have been employed for a period of 12 months, are entitled to a further half-day per month during which continuous shifts have been worked.[56] In the Australian Capital Territory, shiftworkers are entitled to five weeks' paid annual leave instead of four. Other jurisdictions have not legislated on this subject.

Practice

Shiftworkers and night workers benefit from similar, although not identical, provisions in terms of premium pay and other benefits. For example, premium pay for shiftworkers employed outside normal hours ranges from 15 to 30 per cent, while night workers normally receive a 30 per cent premium payment.[57]

---

[55] Additional information provided to the ILO by the Government of Australia, June 1995.

[56] Northern Territory Annual Leave Act 1981, op. cit. Section 6(2)-(3).

[57] Government of Australia and Australian Chamber of Commerce and Industry, op. cit.

Shiftworkers normally receive a rest period of two consecutive days after the completion of normal weekly hours.[58] Some awards and agreements prescribe a minimum period of rest between the end of an overtime shift and the commencement of a new shift.

Seven-day shiftworkers in the federal public service are entitled to an extra week of paid annual leave in addition to the normal four weeks per year.[59] Nurses who perform rotating shift work are also entitled to an extra week of paid annual leave.[60]

[58] ibid.

[59] Community and Public Sector Union, op. cit.

[60] Vidovich, *The nursing industry in Australia*, op. cit.

Brazil

Overview and trends

Overview

In Brazil, the number of working hours is determined both by law and by practice. The Federal Constitution,[1] the *Consolidação das Leis do Trabalho* (Consolidation of labour laws, hereinafter referred to as CLT),[2] and several laws and other statutory instruments provide for the regulation of working hours in general, as well as for specific occupational groups or categories of workers. Collective agreements, which may be applied exclusively or in combination with legal instruments, also establish working time rules for certain categories of workers.

The Federal Constitution establishes the rights and duties of workers, which are developed in more detail in the CLT.[3] The CLT was promulgated by Legislative Decree No. 5452 on 1 May 1943. Until then, labour laws were numerous and somewhat inaccessible as they were scattered and not incorporated in a sole legal instrument. The CLT unified, modified and arranged all the labour laws into an organized and structured labour code. Labour regulations adopted after 1943 are considered additions to the CLT.

The CLT provides for rules on all subjects related to labour and to workers in general. For some categories of workers, there are special provisions, such as on working time, rest breaks, annual leave and safety at work. These special provisions apply to radio operators, bank employees, port workers, chemists, typists, maritime crew, journalists, teachers, vendors, watchpersons, managers, underground miners, cold storage workers, telephone operators, drivers, cinema employees and railway workers.

For some occupations, there are specific legal regulations: Act No. 5811/37 (elevator operators); Act No. 3999/61 (physicians); Acts Nos. 4950A/66, 5194/66 and 6691/78 (engineers); Decree No. 1323/62 [air service (ground) personnel]; Act No. 3857/60 (musicians); and Act No. 7183/84 (aircraft personnel).

Trends

From 1934 to 1988, Brazilian Constitutions established a limit of 48 working hours per week and eight daily working hours. During the discussions of the Constitutional Assembly, which drafted the current Constitution promulgated in 1988, workers' unions campaigned strongly

---

[1] Constitution of the Federal Republic of Brazil, dated 5 October 1988 (*Diário Oficial*, No. 191-A, 5 October 1988, pp. 1-32).

[2] Legislative Decree No. 5452 to approve the consolidation of labour laws, dated 1 May 1943 (*Diário Oficial*, Vol. 82, No. 184, 9 August 1943, p. 11,937), as amended up to Act No. 9022, dated 5 April 1995 (*Diário Oficial*, No. 67, 6 April 1995, p. 1) [LS 1943-Braz.1; 1945-Braz.2; 1949-Bra.2; 1951-Bra.1; 1952-Bra.1; 1955-Bra.1; 1957-Bra.1; 1967-Bra.2; 1970-Bra.1A-G; 1977-Bra.1; 1977-Bra.3; 1985-Bra.1].

[3] Constitution, op. cit., Sections 7-10.

for a 40-hour work-week, which was supported by a significant number of politicians. The new Constitution maintained the eight-hour normal working day but reduced the weekly limit to 44 hours. The daily limit is not generally reflected in collective agreements, which tend to arrange working hour schedules from Monday to Friday, so as to avoid working on Saturdays. Thus agreements, while usually maintaining the 44-hour weekly limit, commonly adjust the number of daily working hours to allow for two consecutive days of weekly rest.

A Bill of Law, presented to the Congress in 1994, proposed a reduction in working hours for the workforce as a whole, by bringing weekly hours down to 40, although maintaining an eight-hour day.[4] At the same time, there is a trend in recent years for a greater proportion of workers to perform overtime. In 1987, 20.3 per cent of workers employed in Greater São Paulo in industry, commerce and services worked overtime. This figure increased to 39.8 per cent in 1994.[5]

Constitutional provisions aimed at reducing overtime have, however, been limited. The economic situation in Brazil in the recent past, with high inflation rates and severe declines in purchasing power, has encouraged workers to compensate for the devaluation of their salaries through overtime. For employers, overtime is a cheaper solution than hiring additional workers, particularly for those activities which require an increase in the labour force during certain periods of the year or during times of accelerated economic growth.

Another trend affecting working hours in Brazil during the last decade is the growth of outsourcing, whereby large companies resort to two types of schemes: contracting of a "satellite" company (unrelated company) to supply the same services as an eliminated production line; and abolition of a certain number of positions and the hiring of the services of other companies to provide personnel to perform the same activities. In both cases, salaries are often lower and working hours are usually different from those of the contracting company.[6]

The debate on the flexibility of working time is part of a broader discussion on the modernization and simplification of labour legislation and reduction of social costs in Brazil. In this respect, technological innovation, productivity and competitivity will no doubt be significantly influenced by the Government's policies concerning economic globalization within the context of the MERCOSOL agreement (Argentina, Brazil, Paraguay and Uruguay).

Working time is constantly associated with the issue of employment in the sense that reducing working hours and/or overtime work could have an effect on the maintenance of the level of employment. This is the opinion of unions which are in favour of a prohibition on overtime work, based on the argument that overtime work constitutes an obstacle to the creation of new jobs. In reality, the rise in the number of new jobs which was expected with the eight-hour

---

[4] Bill of Law No. 0453/94, presented on 16 June 1994 by the *Camara dos Deputados* (House of Representatives).

[5] Information provided to the ILO by the Departamento Intersindical de Estatística e Estudos Sócios-Económicos (DIEESE — Joint Trade Union Department of Statistics and Socio-economic Studies), July 1995.

[6] Information provided to the ILO by the Central Única dos Trabalhadores (CUT — Sole Workers Central), July 1995.

daily limit imposed by the new Constitution did not happen, being replaced by a rise in the number of overtime hours. This tendency is due to low salaries and to the high administrative costs of hiring new workers.[7]

Normal hours of work

Law

According to the Constitution, the working day of urban and rural workers may not exceed eight hours and the working week is limited to 44 hours. The Constitution provides that arrangements may be made by a collective labour agreement or convention for compensation of hours and a reduction in the workday. It also provides for a six-hour workday for work performed in uninterrupted shifts, unless otherwise agreed through collective bargaining.[8]

For miners working underground, the CLT establishes six hours daily and 36 hours weekly. These limits may be increased to eight hours daily and 48 hours weekly, or decreased to less than six hours daily and 36 hours weekly under collective agreement or by written agreement between an employer and an employee.

Monthly or annual limits are not referred to in the legislation. Several other statutory or legal instruments regulate the hours of work per day, month or week in accordance with the requirements of certain occupations. For example, elevator operators,[9] bank employees,[10] telephone operators[11] and engineers[12] work six hours per day and 30 hours per week. Public servants work eight hours a day, but have a 40-hour week; musicians may work five hours per day.[13] Aircraft personnel may work from 11 to 20 hours a day, depending on the flight.[14]

Young workers

Hours of work for young workers between 12 and 14 years of age are the same as for other workers. Young persons between 12 and 14 years old must, however, be employed only on light work which is not harmful to their health or normal development. They must also be

---

[7] CUT, op. cit.

[8] Constitution, op. cit., Section 7(xiii)-(xiv).

[9] ibid., Section 7.

[10] CLT, op. cit., Section 224.

[11] ibid., Section 227.

[12] Act No. 4950-A/66 on remuneration of qualified professionals in engineering, chemistry, architecture, agronomy and veterinary science, dated 22 April 1966 (*Diário Oficial*, 29 April 1966); Act No. 5194/66 to regulate the profession of engineer, architect and agronomist, and for other purposes, dated 26 December 1966 (*Diário Oficial*, No. 244, 27 December 1966, p. 14,892), as amended up to Act No. 6619/78, dated 16 December 1978 (*Diário Oficial*, 19 December 1978).

[13] Information provided to the ILO by the Ministry of Labour, May 1995.

[14] Act No. 7183/84 to regulate the aircraft personnel profession and for other purposes, dated 5 April 1984 (*Diário Oficial*, No. 68, 6 April 1984, pp. 4969-4979).

guaranteed the right to attend school to obtain at least a primary education. Young workers under 18 years of age may not be employed at night or on dangerous or unhealthy work or work prejudicial to their morals.[15]

Practice

In general, legal limits are observed. In some cases, collective bargaining has established a different distribution of the working time during the day and/or the week. For example, a collective agreement signed in Joinville (SC) between employers and workers of the textile clothing sector, effective 1 June 1994 to 31 May 1995, contains some of the standard rules on daily working hours, followed in many other collective agreements. It states the following options:

(a) one week of 40 working hours (five days of eight hours), followed by one week of 48 hours (six days of eight hours);

(b) week of 44 working hours: eight daily hours from Monday to Friday and four working hours on Saturday;

(c) week of 44 working hours from Monday to Friday, Saturday off and compensation of hours during weekdays;

(d) week of 44 working hours: Monday to Friday from 22:00 to 05:00 and Sunday from 22:30 to 05:00;

(e) week of 44 working hours: Monday to Thursday from 22:00 to 05:00; Fridays, one week from 22:00 to 08:00; every other Saturday from 21:00 to 05:00.[16]

Table 1 shows the average actual weekly working hours in different sectors of the economy in the metropolitan area of São Paulo.[17]

---

[15] CLT, op. cit., Sections 402-405 and 411.

[16] Information contained in the data base Sistema de Acompanhamento de Negociações Coletivas (SANC), July 1995, document no. 940139.

[17] Figures are not available for Brazil as a whole. However, the State of São Paulo is responsible for 40 per cent of Brazil's GDP, concentrates its largest and most diverse industries, and is the basis of the Brazilian trade union movement. P. Montagner and S.M. Chagas Brandão: "Recessão e racionalização produtiva: Implicações para o mercado de trabalho", in São Paulo em Perspectiva, Vol. 8, No. 1, January-March 1994, p. 156.

Table 1. Average actual weekly hours of work in Greater São Paulo[18]

Year	Industry		Commerce		Services	
	Hours worked	% working overtime	Hours worked	% working overtime	Hours worked	% working overtime
1985	46	22.4	50	41.8	43	23.8
1986	46	22.8	49	43.8	43	23.6
1987	46	20.3	49	41.8	44	24.2
1988	45	21.3	49	43.4	43	25.6
1989	47	42.1	47	57.7	42	36.7
1990	43	34.8	46	49.0	42	32.4
1991	43	35.3	47	53.6	42	33.6
1992	42	36.7	46	53.0	41	34.5
1993	43	38.7	47	55.3	41	32.7
1994	43	39.8	47	54.4	41	33.3
Jan. 1995	44	47.0	48	58.7	44	40.9
Feb. 1995	45	50.9	49	64.8	43	40.0
Mar. 1995	41	38.7	44	50.6	38	30.4
Apr. 1995	42	35.5	46	54.0	41	33.3

Table 1 indicates that the average actual weekly working hours until 1988, when the legal limit was 48 hours, was 46 hours and 22 minutes. Since 1988, when the legal limit was lowered to 44, the average actual working hours have been around 44, but the percentage of those working overtime increased.

Agreements for some occupations establish a shorter number of working hours than those indicated in the Constitution. This is the case, for instance, of bus drivers in the city of São Paulo (seven hours a day and 40 hours a week) and workers in photographic arts (six hours daily and 36 hours weekly).[19] Other collective agreements provide for longer working days,

[18] DIEESE, op. cit. Since November 1988, legal normal working hours were reduced from 48 to 44 hours per week.

[19] CUT, op. cit.

for example, for nurses and watchpersons who have working days of 12 hours, followed by a 36-hour break.[20]

In rural areas, the schedule of the working day may be determined by seasonal factors due to the nature of the rural work itself and/or to the practices of each region. However, the constitutional limits must be observed.

Enterprises in some industrial sectors are expressing an interest in the averaging of work hours on an annual basis. For example, in the metallurgy sector of São Paulo, enterprises are initiating negotiations on flexibility clauses on annual hours schemes to better match production with demand.[21] In the State of Minas Gerais, unions in the metallurgy, steel and steelworks sectors agreed to a collective agreement on annual working hours, within legal parameters, in order to facilitate the flexibility of the scheduling of working hours.[22]

Overtime and absolute maximum hours

Law

The CLT establishes a maximum limit for overtime of two hours per day by an agreement in writing between the employer and the employee or by a collective contract of employment.[23]

Hours of work may be prolonged beyond the statutory limits or the limits fixed by agreement in the event of urgent necessity, in order to meet cases of *force majeure* or to carry out or complete work which cannot be postponed or which failure to carry out might entail manifest loss. Notice of such overtime must be given to the competent authority within ten days. In cases of overtime for reasons other than *force majeure*, hours of work may not exceed 12 a day unless another limit is expressly fixed by law.[24]

In the event of interruption of work due to an accidental cause or *force majeure* rendering work impossible, the hours of work may be prolonged, but not more than by two hours, on the number of days needed to make up lost time. They may not exceed ten hours per day and may not be prolonged on more than 45 days in a year. Prior authorization must be obtained from the competent authority.[25]

Overtime may be compensated in two different ways: by a wage premium or by time off. The Constitution and the CLT establish that, for overtime work, a minimum of 50 per cent of the

---

[20] Ministry of Labour, op. cit.

[21] Sistema de Acompanhamento de Negociações Coletivas, op. cit., document no. 940138.

[22] DIEESE, op. cit.

[23] CLT, op. cit., Section 59.

[24] ibid., Section 61(1).

[25] ibid., Section 61(2).

hourly wage be paid in addition to the normal pay. For overtime during public holidays, the premium is 100 per cent of the hourly wage.[26]

For overtime work due to reasons of *force majeure*, the remuneration must be at least equivalent to that for normal hours of work. For urgent work that cannot be postponed, there is a 25 per cent premium.[27]

In accordance with a collective agreement or contract, overtime hours can be compensated by working reduced hours on other workdays, as long as normal weekly hours are not exceeded.[28]

Exemptions to the provisions on overtime work include canvassers; travelling salespersons and persons working outside an undertaking who are not subject to a fixed timetable; managers; and employees in stevedoring services and in dockers' services in ports.

For women workers, a 15-minute break is granted before starting overtime hours.[29]

Practice

The legal limit of a maximum of two hours of overtime per day is respected. Compensation for overtime, in practice, is based mainly on wage premiums, which can be considerably higher than the legal requirements as a result of collective bargaining.[30] For example, a 75 per cent premium is payable for the first two hours of overtime in the building and furniture making sector in São Paulo and in the plastics production sector in Santa Catarina. The footwear industry in Pernambuco pays a 100 per cent overtime premium for the first two hours.

For overtime after two hours on Mondays to Fridays, wage premiums range from 70 to 100 per cent. For overtime work on holidays, some sectors pay premiums of more than the legal 100 per cent; for example, the vegetable oils and paints sector in Rio de Janeiro pays a 130 per cent premium and in the food, coffee and salt industry in Paraíba, a 200 per cent wage premium is payable.

Besides wage premiums, overtime may also be compensated by time off. For instance, an agreement in the cement industry in the State of Pará states that one hour of overtime from Monday through Saturday is to be compensated by one-and-a-half hours of time off, and for one hour of overtime on Sundays, two hours off are given.[31] The most common provision,

[26] Constitution, op. cit., Section 7(xvi); CLT, op. cit., Section 59(1).

[27] CLT, op. cit., Section 61(2).

[28] ibid., Section 59(2).

[29] ibid., Section 384.

[30] Ministry of Labour, op. cit.; information provided to the ILO by the Confederação Nacional da Industria (CNI — National Confederation of Industry), July 1995.

[31] Sistema de Acompanhamento de Negociações Coletivas, op. cit.

however, is that overtime hours are compensated by reducing hours of work on other working days, as stated in the law.

A combination of days off plus a wage premium is typically used for overtime on public holidays and/or rest days.

A Bill of Law modifying the legal wage premium is under consideration by the Federal Chamber of Deputies.[32] It would establish that, under collective agreement, the maximum limit for overtime work would be two hours; the wage premium for the first hour would be 50 per cent (100 per cent for hazardous activities), and for the second hour, 100 per cent (200 per cent for hazardous activities); and that time off could replace the wage premium. In the absence of a collective agreement and in case of *force majeure*, the union or labour authority would have to be notified of the extension of working hours and the wage premium would be 70 per cent (120 per cent for hazardous activities) for the first hour and 120 per cent (220 per cent for hazardous activities) for the second hour.

Rest

Law

Rest breaks

Workers who have a working day of six or more hours are entitled to one unpaid break after four hours of work. The length of the break is a minimum of one hour and, except as otherwise provided by an agreement in writing or a collective contract, may be no more than two hours. The break may be shortened to less than one hour with the authorization of the Ministry of Labour, if requirements for the establishment of canteens are respected and employees do not have to work overtime.[33]

Workers who have a working day of between four and six hours have one unpaid break of 15 minutes after four hours of work.[34]

There are some cases in which the law requires the rest break to be paid. Employees performing typewriting, bookkeeping or accounting work have a paid ten-minute break for every 90 minutes worked.[35] Workers in cold storage chambers must rest 20 minutes after every one hour and 40 minutes worked.[36] Underground mining workers have a 15-minute break every three hours worked.[37]

---

[32] Bill of Law No. PL 01005/88, presented on 11 October 1988 by the *Camara dos Deputados* (House of Representatives).

[33] CLT, op. cit., Section 71.

[34] ibid., Section 71(1).

[35] ibid., Section 72.

[36] ibid., Section 253.

[37] ibid., Section 298.

Daily rest

Daily rest must be for a minimum of 11 hours between two consecutive workdays.[38]

Weekly rest

The Constitution provides for paid weekly rest, preferably on Sundays. The duration of weekly rest, according to the CLT, is of 24 consecutive hours, coinciding totally or partially with Sunday.[39]

In cases of work which cannot be delayed and of *force majeure*, work may be carried out during the weekly rest period with previous authorization of the labour authorities. Such authorization is permanent in the case of work which, on account of its nature or for reasons of public interest, must be carried out on Sundays. In other cases, temporary permits may be issued for a specified period, which may not exceed 60 days on each occasion.[40]

Some activities are allowed to be carried out seven days a week for public convenience or due to the nature of a company's activities. Some examples are water, gas and electricity production; flower cultivation; bread baking; livestock production; steel and petroleum production; meat, fish, poultry and egg marketing; services provided by pharmacies, gas stations, hotels, hospitals, sport centres and car rental agencies; port, navigation and airline services.[41] The daily limit for all these cases is eight hours.

Compensatory measures provided for activities carried out seven days a week are usually a day off on another day of the week or a wage premium of 100 per cent.[42]

Practice

Rest breaks and daily rest are usually in accordance with the law. In most sectors of the economy, mainly in the urban areas, the working week is normally five days, Monday to Friday. Consequently, the weekly rest break generally coincides with Saturday and Sunday.

Shop-opening hours

Law

Shop-opening hours are determined by municipal administrations. Such hours may vary depending on the region and the nature of activities of the establishment. In general,

---

[38] ibid., Section 66.

[39] Constitution, op. cit., Section 7(xv); CLT, op. cit., Section 67.

[40] Decree No. 27,048/49 regulating paid weekly rest and public and religious holidays, dated 12 August 1949 (*Diário Oficial*, 16 August 1949), Section 8.

[41] CLT, op. cit., Section 67; Decree No. 27,048/49, op. cit., Section 7.

[42] Decree No. 27,048/49, op. cit., Section 6.

commerce and services start at 09:00 and close between 18:00 and 22:00. Most shops are closed on Sundays.[43]

Bank opening hours are subject to regulation by the Central Bank.[44] They are open to the public from Monday through Friday from 10:00 to 16:00 in some cities, and from 09:00 to 15:00 in others. They are closed on Saturdays and Sundays.

Public holidays

Law

Act No. 605/49 provides that civic holidays are determined by federal law and that religious holidays must be established by municipal law, according to local traditions, within the limit of four per year, including Good Friday.[45] In 1980, 12 October was declared a national holiday.

National level

Act No. 662/49 establishes the following national holidays: 1 January: World Peace Day; 1 May: Workers' Day; 7 September: National Day; 15 November: Republic Day; and 25 December: Christmas. Act No. 1266/50 establishes that 21 April (Tiradentes Day) and days of general elections are national holidays.

Municipal level

Paid public holidays in the city of São Paulo, as determined by Act No. 7008/67, are the following: 25 January: Foundation Day; Good Friday; Corpus Christi; 2 November: All Saints Day. In the city of Rio de Janeiro, Decree No. E1914/67 determines the following holidays: 20 January: Foundation Day; Good Friday; Corpus Christi; 2 November: All Saints Day.

Practice

Carnival is not a legal holiday. Shrove Tuesday is not worked in most places, but the length of the Carnival holiday can vary from one to four days.

In cases where work on public holidays is allowed, limits to such work and compensation are regulated by the same criteria as those applied to weekly rest.

---

[43] Ministry of Labour, op. cit.

[44] Act No. 4178 abolishing work on Saturdays in financial establishments, dated 11 December 1962 (*Diário Oficial*, 24 December 1962).

[45] Act No. 605 on paid weekly rest and public and religious holidays, dated 5 January 1949 (*Diário Oficial*, 14 January 1949).

Paid annual leave

Law

The CLT states that all employees have the right to paid annual leave. The minimum period of service required to qualify for basic annual leave is 12 months from the beginning of the contract. The length of such leave is proportional to the number of absences from work of the employee, as follows: 30 calendar days if not absent for more than five times; 24 calendar days if absent between six and 14 times; 18 calendar days if absent between 15 and 23 times; 12 calendar days if absent between 24 and 32 times. Absence from work does not include special leave for family events and civic obligations (see below under **Other types of leave**); leave for maternity or miscarriage; employment accident or incapacity for work for which sickness benefits are payable; absences authorized by the enterprise; suspension of work due to charges against the employee, which were later dismissed; and absences on days on which the employee was not required to work.[46]

There are no provisions for additional paid annual leave to be granted on the basis of length of service, age or specific working conditions.

The Constitution establishes a wage premium of one-third of the normal salary for the annual leave period.[47] Collective agreements for most occupations usually provide that the beginning of annual leave must not coincide with weekends or holidays. Since the economic recession of 1990, industry has been promoting mandatory collective leave as a way to adapt production to demand.[48]

Annual leave must be taken in only one period. Under exceptional circumstances, it could be taken in two periods, one of which should be no less than ten calendar days. Employees under 18 and over 50 must take holidays in only one period.[49]

Where more than one member of a family works at the same enterprise, they are entitled to take annual leave at the same time, as long as this is not detrimental to the work.[50]

Workers under 18 are entitled to take annual leave during school holidays.[51]

Collective annual leave may be granted to all employees at the same time in an enterprise or in particular departments of an enterprise. The leave may be taken in two annual instalments, as long as neither is less than ten calendar days. The Ministry of Labour must be given at least 15 days' notice of the dates on which such leave is to begin and end.[52]

---

[46] CLT, op. cit., Sections 130-131.

[47] Constitution, op. cit., Section 7(xvii).

[48] DIEESE, op. cit.

[49] CLT, op. cit., Section 134.

[50] ibid., Section 136(1).

[51] ibid., Section 136(2).

[52] ibid., Section 139.

An employee is entitled to be paid cash compensation in lieu of actually taking annual leave for one-third of the number of days of leave. In this case, two-thirds are actual leave and one-third is financial compensation, provided that a minimum of 20 days are actually taken.[53]

Other types of leave

Law

The CLT provides for paid leave as follows: two days for the death of a spouse, ascendant, descendant, brother or sister, or dependent; three days for marriage; five days for the birth of a child; one day every 12 months for blood donation; two days to register as an elector; as long as necessary to comply with requirements of military service.[54]

Shift and night work

Law

The Constitution determines that the working day for shift work is six hours, unless otherwise agreed in collective agreements. A 15-minute break must be scheduled for every four hours worked.[55]

The Constitution guarantees higher salaries for night work than for day work.

The CLT provides that one hour of night work is equivalent to 52 minutes 30 seconds, and must be paid at a rate higher than for day work. This is not applicable to cases where work is organized in weekly or fortnightly shifts. Night work activities are those performed between 22:00 and 05:00 for urban workers and 21:00 and 04:00 or 05:00 for rural workers. For rural night work, an average premium of 25 per cent is payable.[56]

Practice[57]

Collective agreements provide for a variety of working time arrangements. Workers in water sanitation in Bahia State receive a wage premium of 30 per cent of the normal salary for dangerous work, 32.5 per cent for work during rest periods and 26 per cent for night work.

Employees in the graphics industry in Amazonas State may work on a Sunday, but must have one Sunday off per month.

---

[53] ibid., Section 143.

[54] ibid., Section 473; Constitution, op. cit. [provisions in reference to Section 7(xix) providing for an unspecified period of paternity leave].

[55] Constitution, op. cit., Section 7(xiv).

[56] Ministry of Labour, op. cit.

[57] Sistema de Acompanhamento de Negociações Coletivas, op. cit.

Working time arrangements for miners in Minas Gerais State include six eight-hour days and four days off for continuous rotating shifts; or six eight-hour days and two days off, followed twice by schedules of five eight-hour days and two days off for semi-continuous shift work (6x2, 5x2, 5x2). The average weekly hours are 36 as required by law. A wage premium of 50 per cent of the basic salary is paid. Pauses of 30 minutes are included in daily working time.

A collective agreement for dairy workers in the Minas Gerais State provides for shift work of up to eight hours per day and 44 hours per week.

Mining, marble and stone quarrying workers in Espirito Santo State can work 12-hour shifts, followed by 36 hours off, with wage premiums for night periods.

Timber extraction workers in São Paulo State have agreed to a reduction of the meal break to 30 minutes, with a wage premium of 7.5 per cent of the basic salary.

The wage premium for night work is 30 per cent for candle and soap industry workers in Pernambuco State, for textile workers; workers in the glass, crystal and optical industry; workers in the ceramics, building and brick, and furniture industries in the State of São Paulo; and for workers in the food, bread and dairy industry of the State of Santa Catarina. For typographers in the states of São Paulo and Pernambuco, and for workers in the footwear and glove industry in Pernambuco State, the premium for night work is 35 per cent. A 40 per cent wage premium for night work is payable for coffee industry workers in São Paulo State. In Pernambuco State, workers in the plastic materials industry receive a 50 per cent wage premium for night work. In the State of São Paulo, a 50 per cent premium for night work is paid to employees working with dental and medical equipment, in tinsmith workshops, and in car repairs.

Canada[1]

Overview and trends

Overview

Canada is a federal state in which the federal Parliament and provincial legislatures share authority to enact labour laws under the Constitution Act, Sections 91 and 92. Most labour regulation takes place at the provincial and territorial level, and in some provinces and territories this regulatory authority is delegated to the local level.

Federal jurisdiction covers subjects of a national, international or interprovincial nature. In addition, the federal Parliament has the power to regulate undertakings within a province which are in the general interest of Canada or in the interest of two or more provinces. Most regulation of labour matters at the federal level, including working time issues, can be found in the Canada Labour Code.[2] This regulatory framework applies to approximately 10 per cent of the workforce.

Provincial authority to regulate labour matters, including working time, is derived from the power of the provinces to enact property and civil rights legislation. Given that the right to enter into contract is a civil right, and that labour laws place certain restrictions on contracts between employers and workers, they are characterized as property and civil rights legislation. Provinces also have the right to legislate with respect to local undertakings. Although the federal Parliament has the exclusive authority to pass laws dealing with the two territories of Canada, the Yukon and Northwest Territories, it has enacted legislation to grant the territorial governments the right to legislate on property and civil rights issues and questions of a local and private character. Thus the territorial governments have virtually the same powers as the provinces to legislate on labour standards.[3]

Trends

Between 1986 and 1994, working hours have been reduced, although the reductions have been very gradual. For example, based on a review of collective agreements covering establishments with more than 500 workers, it was found that 48 per cent of full-time workers in 1986 had a work-week of less than 40 hours, and that this percentage had increased to 53 per cent

---

[1] The main texts used to prepare this country study are CCH Canadian Limited: *1995 Canadian master labour guide*, 9th edition (North York, Ontario, 1995); CCH Canadian Limited: *Canadian Labour Law Reports* (North York, Ontario, 1995) (which contains both summaries and the texts of most relevant laws); and Human Resources Development Canada: *Employment standards legislation in Canada: 1995-1996 edition* (Ottawa, 1995).

[2] Canada Labour Code (*Revised Statutes of Canada*, Ch. L-2, 1985), as amended up to 15 December 1994 (*Revised Statutes of Canada*, Ch. 41, 1994).

[3] Human Resources Development Canada: *Employment standards legislation in Canada: 1995-1996 edition* (Ottawa, 1995), p. 1. See also D. Bellemare and L.P. Simon: "Canada: The case of Quebec", in G. Bosch et al. (eds.): *Times are changing: Working time in 14 industrialized countries* (Geneva, International Institute for Labour Studies, 1993), p. 106.

in 1994. Since the mid-1960s, however, reductions in working time have been more evident in annual hours of work, essentially because of increases in both the length of paid annual leave and the number of paid statutory public holidays, rather than significant declines in weekly hours of work. Unions have been prime movers in obtaining reductions in working hours.[4] In 1993, approximately 29.5 per cent of the labour force belonged to a union and 37.6 per cent of all non-agricultural jobs were held by unionized workers.[5]

An official advisory report has concluded that, in the last several years, there has been a certain polarization in the duration of working time for different categories of workers. Although the average working week had declined to approximately 37 hours per week in 1994, this figure is misleading because it counts both part-time and full-time workers. In fact, the principal reason for the decline in average weekly hours was the increase in part-time employment, from approximately 14 per cent in 1975 to 23 per cent in 1994. Weekly hours for full-time workers remained virtually unchanged between 1975 and 1994 at just over 42 hours per week.[6]

The advisory report also noted two interesting developments. The first was that hours of work by some full-time workers had actually increased as of 1994. And the second was that most new job creation in Canada has been in part-time employment, while most job loss has been in full-time work. The report stated that, as of July 1994, approximately 22 per cent of all employed males were working more than 50 hours a week, up from 17 per cent in 1976. Of those working long hours, approximately 69 per cent were men. By contrast, approximately two-thirds of those working part time were women. The report found that this difference in hours of work between certain categories of men and women could also have the effect of polarizing income and opportunities.[7]

The report concluded that there were several factors which led employers to prefer having some full-time employees work longer hours rather than hiring new workers. The first factor deterring the engagement of new workers was the fixed costs associated with new personnel, such as recruitment, training and benefit costs. With respect to benefit costs, the report noted that they can add up to approximately one-third of payroll costs in some enterprises. Paid annual leave was found to be the largest benefit cost, followed by employer-sponsored pension and related benefits, such as health and disability insurance. The last category of fixed costs was legislated payroll taxes for unemployment insurance, provincial heath care, workers' compensation and the statutory pension contributions. It was noted that most of these fixed costs did not increase if an employee worked longer hours. The second factor influencing the trend towards longer hours by full-time workers was a desire by enterprises to use capital equipment more efficiently. In some cases, this was influenced by changes in

---

[4] Human Resources Development Canada: *Report of the Advisory Group on working time and the distribution of work* (Ottawa, December 1994), p. 14.

[5] Bureau of Labour Information, Human Resources Development Canada: *Union membership in Canada, 1993: A directory of labour organizations in Canada* (Ottawa, 1994), p. 1.

[6] Human Resources Development Canada, *Report of the Advisory Group on working time ...*, op. cit., pp. 14-15.

[7] ibid., pp. 14-15 and 18-20.

technology itself. The third factor contributing towards longer hours of work by full-time workers was that supplementary hours worked by many salaried workers were not compensated by the employer and hence a type of "free good".[8]

Normal hours of work

Law

Normal hours of work are fixed on a daily or on a weekly basis, or both. Thus, they are eight hours a day and 40 hours a week at the federal level and in British Columbia, Manitoba, the Northwestern Territories, Saskatchewan and the Yukon Territory. In Alberta, they are eight hours and 44 hours. The latter weekly figure is also in force in New Brunswick, Ontario and Quebec. Whereas the standard is 40 hours per week in Newfoundland, it reaches 48 in Prince Edward Island. These limits indicate the hours beyond which overtime is normally paid. There are numerous exclusions and exceptions in most jurisdictions.

Exclusions and exceptions to legal standards for normal hours of work

Federal

Exclusions. Managers, superintendents and members of the architectural, dental, engineering, legal and medical professions.

Exceptions. Where there is an established practice requiring or permitting an employee to work in excess of standard hours (1) for the purpose of changing shifts, (2) pursuant to the exercise of seniority rights contained in a collective agreement, or (3) as a result of exchanging shifts with another employee, then there is an exception to the limit on standard hours. Furthermore, an employer may establish or modify a work schedule that exceeds the normal limits of eight hours per day and 40 hours per week if the average hours of work for a period of two or more weeks do not exceed 40 hours per week and if at least 70 per cent of the employees affected approve the arrangement or if it has been agreed to in a collective agreement.

Alberta

Exclusions. Managerial, confidential and supervisory employees, farm labourers, domestic employees, public employees, municipal policemen, certain salespersons, chartered accountants, lawyers and extras in a film.

Exceptions. Ten hours a day or 191 hours per month: field catering, geophysical exploration, land surveying, logging and lumbering, employees of a municipal district employed in road construction, maintenance or snow removal, oil well servicing. Ten hours a day or 60 hours per week: ambulance drivers, taxicab drivers. Nine hours a day or 54 hours per week:

[8] ibid., pp. 16-17.

employees in irrigation activities other than office employees. Nine hours a day or 48 hours per week: cultivation and preparation of trees, shrubs and plants. Ten hours a day or 44 hours per week: highway and railway construction and brush clearing.

British Columbia

Exclusions. There are numerous categories of employees excluded under the Employment Standards Act Regulation. Examples of employees excluded include, but are not limited to, agricultural and horticultural workers, police officers, student nurses, school bus drivers, commercial fishermen, professionals and managers.

Manitoba

Exclusions. Professional employees, farm labourers, domestic workers employed for less than 24 hours a week in a private home, employees in fishing activities, voluntary employees for specific organizations, independent contractors, persons employed in a private home as a sitter or companion for a child or an aged, infirm or ill member of the household, students in training, persons employed under a rehabilitation or therapeutic project, certain provincial government employees, construction workers, commissioned travelling salespersons, workers employed in a business where only members of the employer's family are employed.

Exceptions. Upon authorization by the Board, exceptions may be granted for a variation of working hours to accommodate the rotation of shifts with the hours worked averaged over a number of weeks. Other daily, weekly, or monthly hours may be permitted, provided that the alternative limits are found to be fair and reasonable where the hours set by legislation are determined by the Board as not feasible for certain industries.

Newfoundland

Exclusions. Professionals and students in professional training. Also excluded from receiving overtime in excess of normal hours are live-in housekeepers or babysitters working under an arrangement permitting these workers to take time off with pay in lieu of overtime after 40 hours work in a week; agricultural workers other than those employed in the production of fruit and vegetables in greenhouses and nursery operations; and persons employed in the raising of livestock.

Northwest Territories

Exclusions. Managerial employees.

Nova Scotia

Exclusions. There are numerous categories of employees excluded by regulation or law. Examples of such employees include, but are not limited to, supervisory and managerial employees or those employed in a confidential capacity, certain farm labourers, domestic employees, certain apprentices, specified professions or students of such professions, automobile, real estate and insurance salespersons, employees on fishing vessels and teachers. Also excluded are ambulance drivers or attendants, persons employed in a building where they reside as janitors, watchpersons or superintendents, and service station employees if the station where they work is required to remain open more than 48 hours in a week.

Exceptions. An employee in the transport industry who is required to be away from his or her home base overnight has standard hours of 96 hours during any two consecutive weeks, after which he or she is eligible for overtime payment. Hours of work in the construction industries are contained in a schedule approved by the Labour Minister. If, by collective agreement or custom, the hours of work on one or more days of the week are less than the normal hours of work fixed by the administrative authorities, the hours of work may be exceeded on the remaining days of the week, according to an agreement between an employer and the workers or their representatives.

Ontario

Exclusions. There are numerous categories of employees excluded by regulation or law. Examples of employees excluded include, but are not limited to, supervisory and managerial employees, domestic employees, construction workers, resident janitors or caretakers, full-time firefighters, fishing or hunting guides, persons engaged in landscape gardening, mushroom growing, horticulture and certain other agricultural activities, certain categories of professionals, teachers, funeral directors and embalmers, and homeworkers.

Exceptions. Sixty hours per week: highway transport employees; 55 hours per week: workers engaged in road building; 50 hours per week: local cartage employees; 50 hours per week: hotel, motel, tourist resort, restaurant and tavern employees who work 24 weeks or less in a calendar year and who are provided with room and board; 50 hours per week: fresh fruit and vegetable process workers; 50 hours per week: sewer and water main construction workers.

Prince Edward Island

Exclusions. Salespersons whose income is primarily derived from commissions on sales, farm labourers who are not engaged in a commercial undertaking, persons employed for the sole purpose of protecting and caring for children in private homes, employees of non-profit organizations who are required to reside at a facility operated by their employer, and employees covered by a collective agreement.

Exceptions. The Board may exempt specific employers or industries from the normal hours of work as established in the Employment Standards Act, and may substitute other standards for which overtime rates will apply for hours worked in excess of these alternative standards. In granting an exception, the Board considers (1) the seasonal nature of the work; (2) the effect of the extended hours on the health and safety of the workers; (3) work requirements that include the need to have the workers on the premises, although they may not be actually working; and (4) the duration of the proposed work schedule.

Quebec

Exclusions. The consort of the employer and their ascendants and descendants; students employed in social or community non-profit organizations; executive officers of undertakings; employees who work outside establishments whose working hours cannot be controlled; employees assigned to harvesting, canning, packaging and freezing fruit and vegetables during the harvesting period; employees of a fishing, fish processing or fish canning industry; farm workers; employees whose main duty is the care, in a dwelling, of a child or of a disabled, handicapped or aged person, if that work does not serve to procure a profit for the employer; construction workers; certain contract workers; and students who work during the school year in establishments selected by an educational institution pursuant to a job induction programme approved by the Ministry of Education.

Exceptions. Sixty hours per week: watchpersons other than those employed by commercial surveillance services; 55 hours per week: employees working in a remote area or on the James Bay territory; 53 hours per week: domestic employees living in the employer's home; 47 hours per week: employees working in a forestry operation or sawmill; 40 hours per week: employees in the retail food trade in specified regions.

With the permission of the Employment Standards Commission, an employer may arrange working hours such that higher than normal hours of work are performed in one week and are compensated with fewer hours in another week, as long as the average weekly hours over a defined period are equivalent to the normal hours of work. This approval is not needed if there is a collective agreement approving this practice or it is allowed by administrative decree.

Saskatchewan

Exclusions. Managerial employees; persons engaged primarily in farming, ranching or market gardening; certain professional employees and students learning their profession; firefighters; road construction and maintenance workers; commercial travellers who travel regularly between two or more localities; certain logging industry employees; designated workers in certain northern locations; driver-salespersons outside cities who sell dairy, bakery or carbonated beverages; field employees of the public service; automobile salespersons; and operators of residential service facilities required to be on the premises overnight.

Exceptions. Eighty hours averaged over two weeks: employees of city newspapers; hours averaged over one year: oil truck drivers; workers covered by industrial standards schedules for particular industries.

With the permission of the administrative authorities and by collective agreement or, if no union exists, by agreement of a majority of the concerned workers, working hours can be arranged to be ten hours a day, 40 hours per week without the obligation to pay any overtime.

Yukon Territory

Exclusions. Employees who are members of the employer's family; workers employed in mineral exploration; travelling salespersons; supervisory and managerial employees; members of certain professions; guides or outfitters; watchpersons or caretakers; farmer workers; sitters, domestic employees and persons receiving a supplement to benefits under section 38.1 of the Unemployment Insurance Act, 1971.

Exceptions. If it is agreed in a collective agreement or, if there is no union, by agreement of a majority of workers, then normal hours of work may be arranged to be ten hours a day over a period of four days a week (40 hours per week), or 12 hours per day over a period of three days a week (36 hours per week) without the payment of any overtime. Moreover, if the administrative authorities determine that the nature of the work is such that it is reasonable to have an irregular distribution of hours of work, then they may order that working hours be averaged over two or more weeks. Similarly, if the workers are not represented by a union and the employer reaches an agreement with the majority of the workers to distribute irregularly hours of work, then the administrative authorities may order that the hours of work be averaged over a period of two or more weeks.

Practice

Table 1 provides an overview of trends in average weekly hours paid for from 1984 to 1993 for the different economic sectors. It can be observed that, in general, weekly hours have remained remarkably stable over this period.

Table 1. Hours of work per week by major divisions of economic activity[9]

Major division	1984	1985	1986	1987	1988	1989	1990	1991	1992	1993
Mining and quarrying	41.0	39.6	39.9	39.8	40.9	39.6	40.1	39.4	39.5	39.6
Manufacturing	38.4	38.6	38.4	38.7	38.9	38.7	38.2	37.8	38.3	38.6
Electricity, gas and water	40.3	40.5	40.6	41.0	41.3	40.8	41.2	41.2	40.7	40.7
Construction	37.3	37.7	37.6	38.2	38.5	38.1	38.1	37.2	36.7	36.6
Trades, restaurants and hotels	27.5	27.5	27.3	27.2	27.1	26.8	26.9	26.4	26.0	26.2
Transport, storage and communication	37.6	37.5	37.3	36.9	38.6	38.0	37.0	36.8	36.5	36.2
Financing, insurance, real estate and business services	27.1	27.4	27.1	27.1	27.5	27.9	28.0	27.5	27.7	27.7

[9] Bureau of Statistics, International Labour Office [hours paid for].

Major division	1984	1985	1986	1987	1988	1989	1990	1991	1992	1993
Community, social and personal services	28.3	28.3	28.3	28.2	28.4	27.9	27.8	27.8	27.7	27.7
Total (all non-agricultural activities)*	32.0	32.0	31.8	31.9	32.1	31.7	31.3	30.8	30.5	30.6

*   Includes forestry and logging.

Figure 1 shows the distribution of normal weekly hours of work in major collective agreements in 1986 and 1994. Although gradual decreases in weekly working hours have also occurred since the 1960s, the principal reductions in working time have taken place on an annual basis in the form of increases in the average length of annual paid leave and because of the increase in the number of statutory public holidays.

Figure 1. Normal weekly hours of work in major collective agreements, 1986 and 1994[10]
(Note: Excludes the construction industry.)

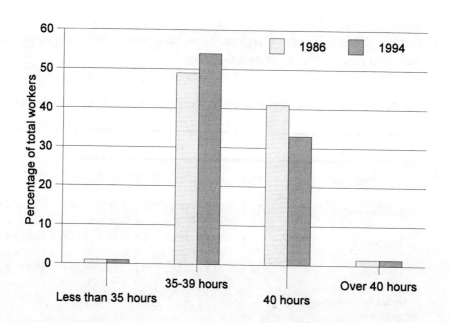

[10] Human Resources Development Canada, *Report of the Advisory Group on working time ...*, op. cit., p. 14.

Overtime and absolute maximum hours

Law

Limits to hours of work

The federal jurisdiction, a number of provinces and one territory have legal limits on the maximum hours of work. In a number of cases, there are exceptions for emergencies. Exceptions are also sometimes allowed for shift work, where the limit for maximum hours of work is determined in reference to the average hours worked over the shift cycle which may be established over a period of more than one week. Five provinces and one territory, however, have no limitations on maximum hours of work. In some cases, there may be a legal limit established, beyond which a worker can refuse overtime, which is lower than the maximum hours of work. The exclusions to the maximum hours of work limitations are largely the same as those to the normal hours of work beyond which overtime must be paid (see above under **Normal hours of work**).

Table 2. Maximum limits on hours to work

Federal	48 hours per week. The administrative authorities may issue a permit to allow work in excess of 48 hours per week in exceptional circumstances. In certain cases, daily and weekly hours can be averaged over two or more weeks, so that the total hours of work do not exceed 48 hours or the maximum working hours as permitted in a particular industrial establishment. This is normally found in situations where there are irregular working hours due to the nature of the work.
Alberta	12 hours per day, upon permission by the administrative authorities. Exceptions may be granted for emergencies.
British Columbia	None in general. Workers, however, may not work for more than eight hours in or about a coke oven, smelter, concentrator or mineral separation plant in any 24-hour period, except when necessary for changes in shifts.
Manitoba	None (right to refuse overtime after 40 hours per week).
New Brunswick	None
Newfoundland	None
Northwest Territories	Ten hours per day; 60 hours per week

Nova Scotia	The limit of 48 hours per week may be exceeded for accidents or urgent work.
Ontario	Eight hours per day; 12 hours per day upon permission of the administrative authorities; 48 hours per week (right to refuse overtime after 48 hours per week), with exceptions in emergencies. Weekly hours can be extended by 12 hours to 60 hours per week upon permission of the administrative authorities for work by engineers, firefighters, full-time maintenance workers, receivers, shippers, delivery truck drivers and their assistants, watchpersons and others engaged in similar occupations. For other workers, an extension of maximum working hours cannot exceed 100 additional hours per year over the legal maximum of 48. An extension of working hours may be permitted because of the special character of the work performed, or because of the perishable nature of the raw material to be processed. A permit may be issued for hours in excess of the legal limit of 48, but does not require a worker to work the additional time without his or her consent. An employee's maximum hours of daily work are subject to any schedule in force under the Industrial Standards Act.
Prince Edward Island	None
Quebec	None
Saskatchewan	48 hours per week (employees have the right to refuse overtime after 44 hours per week). For employees of hotels, restaurants, educational institutions, hospitals and nursing homes, working hours shall be limited to 12 hours in any one day. Industrial standards schedules establish hours of work for the industries which are covered by those schedules.
Yukon Territory	None generally applicable. Persons who work in mines are not to work in excess of normal hours.

Overtime

Overtime is payable for work in excess of the normal daily, weekly or other period of normal hours. Throughout the jurisdictions, the rate of overtime pay is 1.5 times the regular rate after the normal daily or weekly hours, as set out above. In British Columbia, the compensation of hours worked after 11 hours a day or 48 hours a week is higher (two times the regular rate).

In principle, workers have the right to refuse overtime work, at least beyond certain weekly limits established by law, unless there is some type of emergency situation. As indicated above, some categories of workers are excluded from the standards applicable to normal hours of work and are, in principle, also excluded from overtime pay. In other cases, exceptions have been allowed so that specific limits to normal hours of work can be established that are different from those that are generally applicable, or which permit the averaging of hours of work over a period of two or more weeks to determine if normal hours of work on a weekly basis have been exceeded. In some cases, this averaging is allowed to facilitate the scheduling of shift work (see above under **Normal hours of work**).

Compensatory rest

In some jurisdictions, compensatory rest can be given in lieu of paying overtime, subject to certain conditions being satisfied. Below are indicated the jurisdictions which regulate this matter.

Alberta. The employer and a majority of workers may, through their union representatives, negotiate a collective agreement or, where there is no union, make another type of agreement, to provide that compensatory time can be given in lieu of overtime pay, provided that (1) time off is taken during a period when the worker could have otherwise been working; (2) when time off is not actually provided or taken the worker is paid overtime; (3) time off is to be taken within three months from the end of the pay period in which it was earned, although the agreement may provide for a longer period of time or the administrative authorities may authorize a longer period of time; (4) and any modification or termination of the agreement requires at least one month's written notice to the other party. Time off in lieu of overtime pay is considered as hours of work and paid as wages. All workers affected by the time off agreement are to be provided with a copy of the agreement.

Newfoundland. An employer can have an agreement with a live-in housekeeper or babysitter, such that this person has time off in lieu of pay for overtime for hours worked in excess of 40 hours a week.

Quebec. At the request of the worker or pursuant to a collective agreement, the employer may provide paid time off, equivalent to the time worked plus 50 per cent, in lieu of paying overtime wages. In such a case, the paid time off must be taken within 12 months of the performance of the overtime hours at a time mutually agreed upon between the worker and the employer.

Practice

Hourly paid overtime averaged 2.2 hours per week in manufacturing in 1993. High levels of overtime were regularly worked in the transportation equipment sector (auto, auto parts, aerospace: 3.3 hours per week); refining (3 hours per week); primary metals and machinery industries (2.9 hours per week); and the paper industry (2.8 hours per week). Other sectors of economic activity where overtime has been reported to be prevalent include mining, utilities, communications, transportation and construction. Many of these are male-dominated, with above average base rates and arrangements for overtime. In the overall workforce, men are more likely to work paid overtime (approximately 10 per cent) than women (approximately 6 per cent). One survey has indicated that women engage in more unpaid overtime than men.[11]

Rest

Law

In some jurisdictions, there are specific provisions concerning rest breaks, as well as daily and weekly rest. Minimum rest breaks for meals provided for by law are, in principle, unpaid and are not counted as hours of work.

Rest breaks

Alberta. An employer must allow an unpaid or paid rest break of at least 30 minutes during a shift in excess of five consecutive hours, unless (1) an accident occurs, there is urgent work of a necessary character, or there are other unforeseeable circumstances; (2) the administrative authorities issue a permit exempting an employer from the rest-break requirement; (3) different rest breaks are agreed to according to a collective agreement; or (4) under particular circumstances it would not be reasonable for the worker to take a break.

British Columbia. Workers are not allowed to work longer than five hours without a meal break of at least 30 minutes.

Manitoba. No worker is permitted to work longer than five hours without a meal break, which must be of a minimum duration of one hour, unless another arrangement is approved by the administrative authorities or is negotiated as part of a collective agreement.

New Brunswick. Workers are not permitted to work more than five hours without a 30-minute rest break for a meal.

Newfoundland. Workers must have a one-hour rest period after each five hours of work. There are exceptions to this provision for workers who are crew members of ferry boats, for workers who are subject to a collective agreement, or for workers who work alone or in circumstances where it would be impractical for them to take a rest break. A collective agreement or employment contract may provide for rest breaks which differ in duration and timing.

Ontario. Workers are not permitted to work more than five hours without a minimum rest period of 30 minutes for a meal. However, a shorter break can be authorized by the administrative authorities, provided that the worker has a rest period after five hours of work.

Prince Edward Island. Workers are to be given a rest period of at least 30 minutes for a meal after five hours of work.

---

[11] Human Resources Development Canada, *Report of the Advisory Group on working time ...*, op. cit., pp. 18-20.

Quebec. Minimum meal breaks are 30 minutes unless otherwise provided for by administrative decree or collective agreement. A worker is considered to be at work during a coffee break.

Northwest Territories. Workers are not permitted to work more than five hours without a minimum rest period of 30 minutes for a meal.

Yukon Territory. A worker is entitled to a meal break of at least 30 minutes. The break is to be given after five hours of work to employees who work ten hours or less on a given day, and after six hours to those who work ten hours or more.

Daily rest

British Columbia. There must be a minimum eight consecutive hours of rest after a worker has worked a shift, except in emergencies.

Newfoundland. Workers must take eight consecutive hours off in each 24-hour period of employment, except in an emergency situation.

Yukon Territory. A worker must be given a rest period of at least eight hours between each shift worked, except in an emergency. Upon request of the employer, the administrative authorities can determine that the minimum eight-hour rest period would pose an unreasonable burden on the employer and this minimum rest period can be reduced to six hours.

Weekly rest

Federal legislation, as well as that of Manitoba, New Brunswick, Newfoundland, Nova Scotia, Ontario, the Northwestern Territories, Prince Edward Island, Quebec and Saskatchewan, provides for a weekly rest of one day, or 24 consecutive hours, and — except for Quebec and Saskatchewan — state that the rest is to be taken preferably on Sunday. In Ontario, the duration of the weekly rest is increased to 36 consecutive hours per week for retail employees, and in Saskatchewan, where the weekly rest applies to persons usually employed for 20 hours or more per week, it is of 48 hours for persons employed in establishments with more than ten workers. In Alberta, the weekly rest can be postponed: workers are entitled to one day per week, or two, three or four consecutive days in each two-week, three-week or four-week period. The weekly rest is longer in British Columbia (32 consecutive hours per week) and the Yukon Territory (two full working days, if possible one being a Sunday).

Exclusions to legal standards for weekly rest

Federal. Persons in managerial functions, and members of the architectural, dental, engineering, legal and medical professions.

Alberta. Employees of a farm or ranch whose employment relates directly to certain defined agricultural activities. Similarly, public service employees, municipal police officers and others specified by legislation who are exempt from the law establishing weekly rest and other employment standards.

British Columbia. Bus operators; truck drivers and helpers; motorcycle operators; persons employed in the operation of dining, lodging or recreational facilities servicing industrial employees in rural areas; ambulance drivers and attendants; and other categories of workers specified by regulation. Similarly, members of specified professions, students on a work experience or occupational training programme, sitters (for a child or an elderly or ill person) and persons receiving income assistance under a specified government programme are exempt from the law establishing weekly rest and other employment standards. Upon application by the employer, the administrative authorities may approve a different weekly rest arrangement where it is shown that those legislated are unsuitable.

Manitoba. Watchpersons, janitors and firefighters who live in the building in which they are employed, unless the nature of the work is such that it cannot reasonably be performed within an average of ten hours of actual work per day; persons in supervisory, managerial or confidential positions; workers who are involved in repairing or replacing equipment or machinery that is broken or who perform work of a similar emergency character in the plant where they are employed; persons employed for a period not exceeding three hours during their rest period when the sole purpose of the employment is to feed and attend horses where such work is part of their usual duties; persons engaged in public emergency work; and workers employed in a plant that has obtained an exemption from the administrative authorities.

New Brunswick. Agricultural operations employing three or fewer employees for a substantial part of the year; employees whose work involves dealing with emergency situations; part-time workers who are usually not employed for more than three hours per day; or employees who are designated as being outside the scope of the employment standards law.

Newfoundland. Persons in managerial or supervisory positions; persons engaged in emergency work; workers in designated undertakings; workers or employers that have applied for and received an exemption; workers subject to collective agreements pursuant to specified labour relations legislation; workers who are employed in remote areas of the province and who inform the employer that they do not desire that the provisions on rest apply to them; and those who work alone or where it would otherwise be impractical to take the specified rest.

Northwest Territories. Domestic employees in private homes; trappers and persons engaged in commercial fisheries; members and students of designated professions; managerial or supervisory personnel.

Nova Scotia. In cases of accident or other unforeseeable circumstances beyond human control.

Ontario. For the provision which mandates that 24 hours of consecutive rest per week is applicable to workers who are employed in hotels, restaurants or cafés in towns having a population of 10,000 or more, certain categories of workers (such as watchpersons, janitors, superintendents, forepersons, or persons who are not employed for more than five hours a day) are exempted. For the provision which mandates 36 hours of consecutive rest per week for retail employees, this obligation does not apply to workers who are employed by retail establishments whose primary purpose is to sell prepared meals; rent accommodation; to be open to the public for education, recreation or amusement purposes; or to those involved in selling goods and services which are related to the above. For certain industries, schedules to the appropriate legislation specify the days and rest periods to be taken by workers.

Prince Edward Island. Farm labourers, persons whose primary income is derived from commissions on sales, or those governed by collective agreements.

Quebec. The provisions of the law do not apply to workers employed by small farms; workers who are employed to care for children, the aged, or the disabled in a non-profit establishment; construction workers; or students employed in a job induction programme.

Saskatchewan. Managerial employees; workers engaged primarily in farming, ranching or market gardening; and teachers subject to specified legislation. The administrative authorities may grant an employer an exemption from the rest requirements when it would create a hardship for the employer or the employees for a specified period not exceeding one year.

Yukon Territory: Under specified circumstances, an employer may require an employee to work up to 28 days without a day of rest and, in addition, seven more continuous days if it is necessary to finish a project undertaken in the first 28 days. An employee who works such a long continuous period is entitled to have at least one day of rest for each seven days of work and to take those days of rest in a continuous period. Also exempt from the rest provisions are members of an employer's family; travelling salespersons; managerial and supervisory employees; members of certain professions; persons working as guides or outfitters to assist others in recreational wilderness activity; farm workers; persons who search for minerals; watchpersons or caretakers; domestic employees or sitters who are employed to provide services, such as cooking, cleaning, and looking after children or the disabled, although employees of business or day-care facilities providing such a service are not excluded.

Shop-opening hours

Law

The issue of shop-opening hours is largely dominated by the question of whether retail establishments can operate on Sundays. There has been a trend in favour of authorizing retail establishments to be open on Sundays in a number of jurisdictions in Canada for practical reasons, such as cross-border shopping, economic recession and the increased participation of women in the workforce, and also because of a recent decision of Canada's highest federal court. The Supreme Court of Canada has declared federal legislation entitled the "Lord's Day Act" unconstitutional as an infringement of the constitutional guarantee of freedom of religion. The federal Lord's Day Act prohibited the sale or purchase of goods and land, and from engaging in any work, business or labour activity for gain on Sunday, and appeared to have had as its purpose the protection of Sunday as the universal day of worship.

The federal Lord's Day Act was a criminal statute, but provided that the provinces could legislate in this area and allow commercial activity at their discretion. In some cases, provincial legislation further devolved the discretion to regulate this question to the municipal level. There remain some provincial Lord's Day Act statutes in force. However, these statutes typically do not prohibit activity on Sunday, but state affirmatively that certain types of activity may take place. In some cases, such provincial Lord's Day Acts were adopted to take advantage of a provision of the federal Lord's Day Act which provided that provinces had the authority to derogate from the prohibition against Sunday work contained in the federal law. Most current provincial legislation, however, is essentially secular in character, and often states that there should be at least one day of rest per week and, if possible, on Sunday (see above). Restrictions on shops opening on Sunday have subsequently been upheld in a number of judicial challenges at the provincial level as a justifiable measure to ensure that most people have a common day of rest and that families can be together. These court decisions have tended to recognize a potential for inconvenience or imposition on persons who worship on a day other than Sunday, but have indicated that the burden is insignificant or trivial and that there are valid secular reasons for having one common day of rest per week. Typically, however, for the owner of a chain of stores, all such stores must close on a day other than Sunday and all must be open on Sunday. In some jurisdictions, persons who have a day of worship other than Sunday can operate their stores on Sunday if they close at least once a week on another day. In some jurisdictions, liberalization of Sunday opening of retail establishments has been progressive to maintain public support, and eventual acceptance of, Sunday shopping. Below is a summary of the situation as it applies to the different jurisdictions in Canada.

Alberta

No Sunday closing or retail business holiday legislation, although municipalities have the power to regulate store hours.

British Columbia

The provisions of the Holiday Shopping Regulations Act, which regulated the opening of retail establishments on Sunday, was struck down by the British Columbia Court of Appeal. In practice, Sunday shopping is widespread.

Manitoba

The Retail Business Holiday Closing Act enumerates a certain number of holidays on given days of the year and also states that Sunday is a holiday. According to the law, no retail establishment shall be open for business on a holiday. Exceptions, however, are numerous and include (1) goods and services in connection with prepared meals or living accommodation; (2) establishments selling liquor; (3) establishments where the number of persons working, including the owner, is not more than four; (4) pharmacies that sell designated goods; (5) gas stations; (6) stores selling nursery stock, flowers, or fresh fruit and vegetables; (7) laundromats and other coin-operated services; (8) rentals of motor vehicles or boats; (9) tourist, recreational, educational or amusement facilities; and (10) retail establishments regulated by a particular legal regime established by the provincial legislature.

Retail businesses open for 24 hours every day can also be open on Sunday, provided that no more than six persons, including the owner, are employed on any holiday and no more than two are employed at any one time. For emergency work or special events, the administrative authorities may also issue permits.

An exemption can also be granted to retail businesses which close on Saturday. If closed on the immediately preceding Saturday, the business may be open on Sunday. If the owner has a retail business with more than one establishment, then all the establishments must be closed on the preceding Saturday and all must be open on Sunday.

New Brunswick

According to the Days of Rest Act, the weekly day of rest is designated as Sunday in the interest of having a uniform day of rest as far as practicable. Activities which are exempt include (1) sporting, recreational, entertainment or amusement activities; (2) transportation services; (3) commercial fishing and marine farming; (4) farming and food processing; (5) garden supply stores; (6) preparation of meals for sale; (7) hotels and similar accommodation; (8) convenience stores not employing more than three persons; (9) drug stores; (10) gas stations; (11) activities in connection with religious worship; (12) activities in connection with the supply of utilities and heat; (13) activities in connection with the morning edition of a newspaper; (14) ambulance services; (15) police and firefighters; (16) retail businesses located in a provincial or national park; (17) mining, smelting and oil refining; sugar bush and sugar refining operations; (18) telecommunications activities; and (19) laundromats.

By regulation, other activities that are exempt include (1) premises licensed under the Liquor Control Act; (2) beer manufacturers; (3) alcohol distillers or wine producers; (4) the viewing or displaying of real estate which may be sold on a day other than the day of weekly rest; (5) activity necessary to the preparation of a daily or weekly newspaper; (6) pulp and paper industry activities; (7) shipping and navigation industries; (8) ship building and repair activities; (9) antique or craft stores; (10) flea markets; (11) licensed retail liquor stores where there are usually no more than three persons, including the owner, to run the establishment.

The administrative authorities may also grant exemptions, upon application, for (1) retail businesses engaged in designated activities; (2) businesses or industries which function continuously; (3) for persons who wish to work or operate a business on that day because the person cannot work another day because of his or her religious beliefs or conscience; or (5) the retail business is in a tourist area. Exemptions of a temporary character to all retail businesses in a region may also be granted during a festival or other special event.

Newfoundland

The Shops Closing Act lists Sunday as a holiday and it applies to retail and wholesale trade and business activity. If a municipality takes action to regulate shop opening, the provincial authorities may exempt that municipality from the operation of the Act. There are numerous exceptions to the Act, and typical exceptions include drug stores, gas stations, convenience stores and retail businesses in tourist areas.

Northwest Territories

There is no legislation restricting work on Sunday.

Nova Scotia

There are two laws restricting Sunday openings. The first is the Lord's Day (Nova Scotia) Act, which defines the period of closing as from 12 noon on Saturday to 12 noon on Sunday. The council of a municipality may issue a permit authorizing the operation of certain establishments and the periods of opening for the following types of stores: grocery stores; confectionery stores; stores catering to tourists which sell handicrafts, novelties and souvenirs; fruit stands; flea markets or rummage sales; laundromats; and billiard halls and pool rooms. Subject to law, it is also lawful to operate any time during this period a gas station, a drug store and a restaurant. After 14:00 on Sunday, it is permitted to charge admission and employ persons in connection with public games or contests, performances or public meetings.

The second law restricting Sunday opening is the Retail Business Uniform Closing Day Act, which includes Sunday as a day for uniform closing. The Act prohibits retail activity generally on Sunday, but there are exemptions for the following activities or stores: (1) drug stores; (2) the sale of agricultural products by the producer, the sale of maple sugar products, or the sale of Christmas trees; (3) gas stations; (4) restaurants and accommodation facilities, as well as camping, food, beverage, recreation or tourist information facilities; (5) private clubs; (6) public games, contests or performances; (6) the renting of motor vehicles or small boats for personal use; (7) transportation services; (8) telecommunications and broadcasting; (9) newspaper publishing; and (10) the provision of goods and services on an emergency basis.

Ontario

The One Day's Rest in Seven Act provides that the weekly day of rest should be on Sunday, whenever possible. Under the Retail Business Holidays Act, in principle retail businesses are to be closed on a holiday, which includes statutory holidays and also Easter Sunday. There are exceptions for certain stores or activities involving the sale of certain products, including the following: (1) small stores selling only food, tobacco, antiques or handicrafts; (2) pharmacies; (3) gas stations; (4) nursery stock, flowers and associated accessories, fresh fruit and vegetables; (5) newspapers, periodicals and books; (6) art galleries; (7) liquor stores duly licensed; (8) goods and services for sale in duly licensed tourist stores; (9) educational, recreational or amusement activities; and (10) goods and services sold in connection with the provision of prepared meals, living accommodation, laundromats and other coin-operated services, vehicle or boat rental, and vehicle or boat servicing and repair.

In addition, the council of a municipality may adopt bylaws to permit retail establishments to be open on holidays in order to develop and service tourism. Exemptions may also be given in a municipality for up to five holidays a year during a period in which there is a fair, festival or other special event.

Any retail business which always closes on a day of the week other than Sunday may be open on Sunday.

The Employment Standard's Act provides that employees of retail businesses may refuse to work on Sundays or holidays. Even if the employee has agreed to work on a Sunday or holiday, he or she can later refuse the work if 48 hours notice is given to the employer. The employer cannot take, or threaten to take, any retaliatory action against an employee who refuses to work on Sundays or holidays. The right to refuse work on Sunday, however, does not apply to retail businesses which are engaged primarily in the selling of prepared meals, the renting of living accommodation, being open to the public for educational, recreational or amusement purposes, or selling goods and services ancillary to the above activities.

Prince Edward Island

The Retail Business Holidays Act prohibits the carrying out of retail business on holidays, which is defined to include Sunday, except the last Sunday in November and the Sundays preceding Christmas Day. The prohibition does not apply to (1) gas stations; (2) convenience stores; (3) automatic laundries; (4) restaurants and other eating establishments; (5) services involving accommodation, camping, recreational services and facilities, and tourist information; (6) tourism services offered by tourism operators; (7) drug stores; (8) taxis and other transport services; (9) telecommunication and broadcasting services; (10) video stores; (11) bakeries; (12) flower shops; (13) yard sales and flea markets; (14) mobile canteens; (15) roadside fruit and vegetable stands; (16) open houses for the showing of real estate; and (17) craft fairs. Additional exemptions may be granted by regulation.

A person, who for reasons of religious belief or conscience closes his or her business one day of the week other than Sunday, may operate the retail business on Sunday.

The Lord's Day (P.E.I.) Act provides that the administrative authorities may fix the period of time on Sunday during which a person may provide a game, contest, sport, motion picture, theatrical performance, concert, recital, lecture or exhibition of an educational, artistic or cultural nature. There are numerous exceptions to the Act which permit retail business activity on Sunday, many of which are similar to the exceptions in the Retail Business Holidays Act.

Quebec

The Sunday Observance Act was repealed in 1986. The Hours and Days of Admission to Commercial Establishment Act sets out the days and times when retail businesses may be open to the public. Easter Sunday and other holidays which fall on Sunday are fixed as retail business holidays. Opening hours for establishments are fixed between the hours of 08:00 and 21:00 Monday through Friday, and 08:00 and 17:00 on Saturday and Sunday. On 24 and 31 December, hours are between 08:00 and 17:00, and on 26 December, hours are between 13:00 and 17:00 where it falls on a Saturday or a Sunday, and 13:00 and 21:00 where it falls on another day of the week.

There are numerous exceptions to the limitations on opening hours on the days when it is permitted to be open according to the Act. These include establishments which sell the following items: (1) meals, foodstuffs or alcoholic beverages for consumption, either on or off the premises; (2) pharmaceutical, hygienic or sanitary products; (3) tobacco and related items; and (4) fuel and motor oil.

Establishments which may operate outside of the days and hours fixed in the Act include those located in an air terminal or a hospital, at a place where sports activities take place, and at a cultural centre. Other commercial establishments which may operate outside the days and hours fixed in the Act include those selling works of art, handicrafts or antiques; flowers or inedible horticultural products; foodstuffs or other products which are accessories to services undertaken in connection with a leasing contract for goods or services.

Saskatchewan

Under the Lord's Day (Saskatchewan) Act, municipalities may adopt bylaws to permit specified public games or sports for which attendance is charged, which are to be held between the hours of 13:30 and 18:00 on Sundays. Cinemas, musical performances, amusement rides and rodeos may be held after 13:30 on Sundays. A public authority may operate transportation and eating facilities, charge for attendance for sports and games, and operate golf courses, swimming pools, zoos, curling rinks and employ workers for the carrying out of such activities.

The Industrial Standards Act contains schedules for specific industries and zones, and these schedules frequently state that work may be done on certain days on the week, excluding Sundays.

Yukon Territory

Pursuant to a provincial Lord's Day Act, municipal councils may pass bylaws, after an affirmative majority vote of the electors, to permit specified sports, movies and performances, and business connected to such activities, after 13:30 on Sundays.

Public holidays

Law

The number of statutory paid public holidays varies among jurisdictions. Six jurisdictions — the federal jurisdiction, Alberta, British Columbia, Saskatchewan, the Northwest Territories and the Yukon Territory — provide nine paid public holidays. Ontario and Quebec provide eight public holidays; Manitoba, seven; New Brunswick, six; and Newfoundland, Nova Scotia and Prince Edward Island, five.

At the federal level, the following public holidays are given: New Year's Day, Good Friday, Victoria Day, Memorial Day, Canada Day, the first Monday in August, Labour Day, Thanksgiving Day, Remembrance Day, Christmas Day and Boxing Day. Although public holidays vary at the provincial level, with some provinces having particular public holidays of their own, public holidays which are common to all jurisdictions include New Year's Day, Good Friday, Labour Day and Christmas Day. Canada Day is also a public holiday in every jurisdiction, except Newfoundland. Other public holidays that are common in many jurisdictions include Victoria Day, Thanksgiving Day and Remembrance Day.

Most jurisdictions have requirements which employees must satisfy before the public holiday is paid. Fairly representative are requirements in New Brunswick which state that an employee has no right to pay for a public holiday not worked if he or she (1) has worked for an employer less than 90 days (although most jurisdictions require only 30 days) in the previous 12-month period; (2) has failed to work the regular scheduled day of work without cause before or after the public holiday; (3) has failed to report for and perform the work without cause after having agreed to work on the public holiday; or (4) is employed under an arrangement where the employee can elect to work when asked. Conditions may vary from province to province. Only Saskatchewan, however, grants public holidays with pay unconditionally.

In most jurisdictions, it is usually possible for an employer to agree with the employee or union representative to substitute time off on a public holiday for time off on another day, which cannot be normally later than the employee's next paid vacation leave. The statutes also frequently provide that, when a public holiday falls on a non-working day, such as a Saturday or Sunday but also a day of the week if that is normally a non-working day, the employee shall benefit from a paid day off on the working day immediately preceding or just after the public holiday.

The pay for a public holiday not worked is usually the employee's regular pay, except for Newfoundland, where it is two times the regular rate of pay. In certain industries, such as construction, however, it is a lump-sum payment at the end of the year of 3.5 or 4 per cent of gross annual earnings. The pay for a public holiday worked is usually the regular pay plus one-and-a-half times regular pay, although there are some variations (see below). As stated previously, some jurisdictions also offer the possibility of giving the employee another day off with regular pay rather than paying a premium for work performed on the public holiday.

Legislation in several jurisdictions — the federal jurisdiction and British Columbia, Manitoba, Newfoundland, Nova Scotia, Ontario and the Yukon Territory — contains special provisions for work performed in continuous operations. Similar provisions are also frequently applicable in a number of jurisdictions concerning, *inter alia*, seasonal industries, hotels and other living accommodation, tourist resorts, restaurants, amusement facilities, hospitals and gas stations. These more flexible provisions typically provide that, for work performed on a public holiday, the worker is to receive the regular pay plus (1) one-and-a-half times regular pay; (2) another day off with regular pay; or (3) regular pay for the next non-working day.

There is no qualifying length of service requirement for entitlement to public holidays and premium pay for holiday work in the Yukon Territory. In Manitoba and Nova Scotia, wages must have been earned for at least 15 of the 30 calendar days preceding the holiday. A length of service of 30 days is required in the other provinces, except for Prince Edward Island and Quebec (60 days), and New Brunswick (90 days) and Ontario (three months).

Paid annual leave

Paid annual leave is a right of every employee in Canada in all jurisdictions, unless the worker is excluded from the application of employment standards legislation. In all jurisdictions except Saskatchewan, employees are entitled to two weeks' paid annual leave after each completed year of employment. In Saskatchewan, employees are awarded three weeks of paid annual leave after one year and four weeks after ten years. In other jurisdictions, increased annual leave is also provided for legally after a certain number of years of service.

The employer determines when an employee can take paid annual leave, within limits laid down by law. The leave must be granted to the employee within a certain number of months after the date on which the worker becomes entitled to it. The period can vary from four months in New Brunswick, to ten months in the federal jurisdiction, British Columbia, Manitoba, Newfoundland, Nova Scotia, the Northwest Territories, Ontario, Prince Edward Island and the Yukon Territory, to 12 months in Alberta, Quebec and Saskatchewan.

Most jurisdictions indicate whether the paid annual leave can be given in one or more unbroken periods, although legislation from the federal jurisdiction, Manitoba, the Northwest Territories and the Yukon Territory do not. The laws of the other jurisdictions, however, usually provide that paid annual leave can be broken into periods of one week at the employer's request, but that periods shorter than one week cannot be imposed by the employer unless the employee consents. Nine jurisdictions require that notice be given to the employee as to when leave is to begin, with the notice period ranging from one to four weeks. Generally, the laws require that leave be paid at least one day before it begins. If a public holiday occurs during the leave period, the leave is extended by one day or the employee shall be granted another working day off with pay at a mutually agreed time. Finally, in the event of termination of the employment relationship, any portion of unused paid annual leave must be paid to the employee.

With the exception of Saskatchewan (three weeks with pay of 3/52 of annual earnings; four weeks after ten years with 4/52 of annual earnings), the basic paid annual leave period is of two weeks, with 4 per cent of annual earnings. Both the length of the leave and the level of pay are increased for long service in Alberta, British Columbia, Manitoba, the Northwestern Territories and Quebec (three weeks after five years; 6 per cent of annual earnings), while — under the federal legislation — the leave increases after six years (6 per cent of annual earnings).

Other types of leave

Law

Several types of leave or justified absence are recognized by one or more jurisdictions in Canada. These include bereavement leave, leave for jury duty or in connection with court proceedings, leave for voting, and leave to be married or to attend a family member's marriage.

Bereavement leave

Bereavement leave for the death of a family member is provided for by legislation in the federal jurisdiction (three days, paid); New Brunswick (for defined immediate family members: three days, unpaid; for more extended defined family members: one day, unpaid); Newfoundland (one day, paid, plus two additional days, unpaid); Nova Scotia (for defined immediate family members: three days, unpaid; for more extended defined family members: one day, unpaid); Prince Edward Island (three days, unpaid); Quebec (for defined immediate family members: one day, paid, plus three additional days, unpaid; for more extended defined family members: one day, unpaid); Saskatchewan (five days without pay); and the Yukon Territory (three days without pay). In some jurisdictions, relatively short minimum employment service is required before an employee is eligible (e.g. three months in the federal jurisdiction, Saskatchewan; one month, New Brunswick).

Leave for jury duty or in connection with court proceedings

Leave for jury duty is provided for by law in Alberta, Manitoba, Newfoundland, Nova Scotia, Ontario, Prince Edward Island, Quebec and Saskatchewan. Typically, these provisions do not require that the leave granted is paid, but do contain sanctions against an employer who takes adverse employment action against an employee who responds to a summons for jury service. In Nova Scotia, the law also states that the employer is to give the employee an unpaid leave of absence when required by summons or subpoena to appear as a witness in a judicial proceeding.

Leave for voting

The federal jurisdiction and all the provinces and territories provide for paid time off for voting. Three consecutive hours are allowed in all jurisdictions, except Prince Edward Island (one hour if the person's employment does not permit one hour of his or her own time); the federal jurisdiction and British Columbia (four hours); and Quebec (four hours in addition to the meal break). In a number of jurisdictions, workers engaged in certain transportation sectors are excluded. Alberta, New Brunswick, Ontario, Quebec and the Yukon Territory also have provisions to allow employees paid time off to vote in municipal elections.

Leave to be married or to attend a family member's marriage

This type of leave is provided for in Quebec. Workers are given one day of paid leave for their own wedding, and one day without pay for the wedding of their children or those of their consort, and of their father, mother, brother or sister.

Practice

Educational or training leave

Collective agreements in some cases provide for educational or training leave, which may be paid or unpaid. This leave may be for the purpose of teaching the person new skills, updating existing knowledge or skills, or for retraining.

Shift and night work

Law

Provisions of federal law applicable to shift work are found essentially as exceptions to the normal hours of work provisions or to the maximum hours of work provisions summarized above. Typically, these provisions allow for work beyond normal hours of work if necessary for the changing of shifts, or place limitations on maximum hours of work for certain types of shift work. These provisions frequently also allow the averaging of hours over periods of time of two or more weeks to arrive at a calculation of average weekly hours when determining compliance with normal hours of work provisions and eligibility for overtime or compensatory rest. Exceptions allowing for averaging over two or more weeks are frequently intended to facilitate an easier rotation of shifts. There are also certain exceptions applicable to persons who perform shift work on public holidays, which give alternatives to the payment of premium wages for work on such days (see relevant headings above).

There are no special legislative provisions applicable to night work.

Denmark

Overview and trends

Overview

Weekly working hours have been established at 37 across virtually all sectors of the economy since 1990, giving Denmark the shortest generalized weekly hours of work among European countries. An interesting feature of the evolution towards the 37-hour work-week is that it has resulted almost exclusively through collective bargaining at the central and sectoral level.[1] Exceptionally, the Government intervened in the spring of 1985, as the workers' and employers' organizations were unable to agree on terms of collective agreements that were up for renewal. By an Act of Parliament, terms were imposed for a reduction of the working week for civil servants to 39 hours as of December 1986. Although this reduction applied formally only to civil servants, it had the effect of producing a general reduction of the weekly hours to 39.[2]

A feature of the Danish labour market is that there is a concerted effort among the social partners in different sectors to have relatively uniform settlements concerning working time issues. While certain sectoral variations exist, there is a strong tendency to have the normal working week the same throughout the economy.[3] A multitude of both employer and worker organizations negotiate individual collective agreements. In 1991, there were some 600 collective agreements in force. The collective bargaining process is coordinated by two central organizations: the Landsorganisationen i Danmark (LO — Danish Confederation of Trade Unions) and the Dansk Arbejdsgiverforening (Danish Employers' Confederation).[4] The uniformity achieved in terms of working hours extends also to non-organized employment, where the 37-hour week is also generally considered the norm.[5]

Other working time issues are similarly deregulated and established by collective bargaining, most notably rules concerning overtime and premium pay on public holidays. Legislation does have some role and supplies standards, for example, for minimum periods of rest, paid annual leave and shop-opening hours. Since the adoption of the Council Directive concerning certain aspects of the organization of working time[6] and the Council Directive on the protection of

---

[1] From a working week of 48 hours in 1920, the hours of work decreased by only one hour until 1958. The ensuing reduction of the working week by ten hours was achieved over a period of 32 years. See "Danemark: Evolution des salaires et de la durée du travail", in *UIMM Social International*, No. 523, December 1993, p. 11.

[2] "Denmark: The reduction and restructuring of working hours", in *European Industrial Relations Review*, No. 231, April 1993, p. 25.

[3] ibid.

[4] Ministry of Labour, the Danish Employers' Confederation and the Danish Confederation of Trade Unions: *Labour relations in Denmark: The self-regulatory system* (Copenhagen, 1991), pp. 1-8.

[5] "Denmark: The reduction and restructuring of working hours", op. cit.

[6] Council Directive 93/104/EC concerning certain aspects of the organization of working time, dated 23 November 1993 (*Official Journal*, Vol. 36, No. L307, 13 December 1993, pp. 18-24).

young people at work,[7] working time issues are, however, no longer solely within the Danish regulatory domain. These Directives allow member States of the European Union either to change their legal regulation or to ensure that, in practice, the conditions in these Directives are respected. It would seem likely that many of the provisions will be implemented through the traditional collective bargaining process, keeping with the social partners' preference to negotiate certain working time issues without government intervention. Such a conclusion is strengthened by the inclusion of a "European Union clause" in the recent industry agreement.[8] This clause requires that the Directive concerning certain aspects of the organization of working time be implemented in written employment contracts.

Trends

The Danish working week has been reduced in stages. In 1974, it was brought down to 40 hours; subsequently small additional reductions were introduced; and, in September 1990, 37-hour working week was introduced. Since then, however, the downward trend seems to have been halted and, instead of further reductions, there seems to bea move towards a more flexible distribution of working hours.

According to statistics for the period 1983-1992, Denmark experienced significant reductions in working time. The hours usually worked, i.e. the normal hours of work plus average overtime, declined from 40.5 hours per week in 1983 to 38.8 per week in 1992. Hours actually worked per week, i.e. excluding annual leave, sick leave, and leave or absence for other reasons, decreased from 40.6 in 1983 to 37.5 in 1992, while the number of persons who worked more than their usual hours almost doubled, growing from 5.5 to 9.9 per cent. Part-time work continued to be of particular importance: the percentage of the workforce which works part time was among the highest in Europe. In the period 1983-1992, part-time work in agriculture increased from 8.80 to 19.94 per cent of total employment, was relatively stable in industry rising very slightly from 10.77 to 10.98 per cent in 1992, and actually decreased in services from 30.33 to 27.20 per cent.[9]

Most collective agreements were renegotiated in the spring of 1995 for a period of two years, except in industry, where the March 1995 agreement will remain in force for three years.[10] One of the marked trends in these negotiations was the absence of a discussion of further reductions in the working week. The trend seems to be to stabilize working time at current levels and to have greater flexibility in the distribution of working hours over time, largely due to employer demands. In major sectors, such as industry, transport, office and clerical work, normal hours of work may be flexibly distributed up to 45 hours per week and averaged

---

[7] Council Directive 94/33/EC on the protection of young people at work, dated 22 June 1994 (*Official Journal*, Vol. 37, No. L216, 20 August 1994, pp. 12-19).

[8] "Danemark: Convention collective de trois ans dans l'industrie", in *UIMM Social International*, No. 538, April 1995, p. 11.

[9] Eurostat: "Working time in the European Union: The average working week from 1983 to 1992", in *Statistics in focus: Population and social conditions*, No. 1, 1995, p. 3.

[10] "Danemark: Convention collective de trois ans dans l'industrie", op. cit., p. 10.

over a period of 26 weeks. The averaging period in industry had previously been six weeks. In the construction sector, the period for averaging in 1995 was 22 weeks, while in trade and commerce it was 16 weeks.[11] However, a remaining issue is the notice period required by employers for averaging hours. The present rules on averaging weekly hours give little scope for employers to change working hours in response to immediate changes in workload. This possibility has existed in shops for many years.[12]

Among the many factors which influenced the reduction of working hours in the 1980s, the wish to curb rising unemployment seems to have been important.[13] However, statistical information assembled by the Danish Employers' Confederation seems to suggest that the reduction was not effective as a means of increasing employment, but that the main effect was to cause an increase in the amount of overtime worked.[14]

In 1993, a series of measures aimed at combating unemployment were enacted by the Social Democrat-led coalition. One of the principal measures was an expanded system of leave opportunities, which included extending existing parental leave up to 52 weeks, and the introduction of educational and sabbatical leave for up to 52 weeks. Participants in such schemes originally received 80 per cent of maximum unemployment benefits, although in the case of sabbatical leave, the benefit was subsequently lowered to 70 per cent.[15] In the case of educational leave, however, the person receives 100 per cent of the maximum unemployment benefit. The two central organizations took opposing views on the reform. The Danish Employers' Confederation was strongly opposed, as they feared it would increase expenditure for employers, while the Danish Confederation of Trade Unions maintained that the new programmes would create up to 100,000 jobs.[16] These measures were introduced on a trial basis for one year as of 1 January 1994. They were found to be partially successful,[17] and by the end of 1994, it was decided to maintain the extended parental leave as well as the educational leave on a permanent basis, while the temporary trial period for sabbatical leave was extended for three years. Sabbatical leaves granted under this law may not extend beyond 1 March 1999.[18]

Another way to combat unemployment has gained some attention in Denmark. A group of garbage collectors in the town of Aarhus devised a scheme according to which three of them teamed up and worked cycles of three weeks on and one week off, which allowed them to draw 80 per cent of maximum unemployment benefits on the week off. Under such a scheme, these three garbage collectors could offer employment for three weeks to a fourth member

[11] Information provided to the ILO by the Danish Employers' Confederation, April 1995.

[12] "Denmark: The reduction and restructuring of working hours", op. cit., p. 27.

[13] Danish Employers' Confederation, op. cit.

[14] ibid.

[15] Act No. 435 respecting paid leave, dated 30 June 1993 (*Lovtidende A*, Vol. 87, No. 435, 1 July 1993, pp. 2354-2357), as amended up to Act No. 7, dated 9 January 1995 (*Lovtidende A*, No. 3, 17 January 1995, p. 45).

[16] "Labour market reform", in *European Industrial Relations Review*, No. 244, May 1994, p. 17.

[17] "Denmark: End to bargaining in site", in *European Industrial Relations Review*, No. 255, April 1995, p. 6.

[18] Act No. 435 respecting leave, op. cit.

of the group on equal terms, i.e. work for three weeks and unemployment benefits for one week. The Danish authorities in the municipality decided to accept this scheme, commonly referred to as the "garbage collectors' proposal", even though it did not fully conform to the requirements of the law for payment of unemployment benefits, and was outside the three types of extended leave recently adopted. Some prominent economists and the Danish Employers' Confederation opposed the scheme, arguing that the worksharing scheme would reduce labour market flexibility when the expected economic upturn arrived, while the Danish Confederation of Trade Unions took the position that the model would threaten the unemployment insurance scheme. Although the Government found the "garbage collectors' proposal" interesting as a concept, it was decided to not allow the programme to continue in 1995 as it did not conform to the legal requirements for paying unemployment benefits. Interestingly, however, the Danish Confederation of Trade Unions and most of its member unions did not, as of August 1994, support the idea of redistributing work as a strategy to fight unemployment, but found that unemployment could be reduced by more economic growth, intensification of training and education measures, and the acceptance of a certain social responsibility to employ potentially marginalized groups of workers.[19] According to a survey in Denmark, worksharing is positively viewed by the public, and 71 per cent of the respondents indicated that they would be willing to share their work with others, and two-thirds of these people said that they would do so without full financial compensation.[20]

Normal hours of work

Law

There is no generally applicable legislation with respect to normal weekly hours of work.

Young workers

According to the Act respecting the working environment, working time for young persons under 18 years of age shall not exceed the number of daily hours for adult workers in the occupation established by collective agreement, with, in any event, a daily maximum of ten hours.[21] Young workers attending vocational education establishments shall have working time arranged to allow them to attend classes. The Minister of Labour may lay down rules prescribing the extent to which young persons under 18 years of age may be employed in excess of the normal hours of work for any occupation.

[19] "LO changes unemployment strategy", in *European Industrial Relations Review*, No. 247, August 1994.

[20] "Denmark: Worksharing idea spreads", in *European Industrial Relations Review*, No. 241, February 1994, p. 5.

[21] Act No. 681 respecting the working environment, dated 23 December 1975 (*Lovtidende A*, No. 65, 1975, p. 1951), as amended up to Notification No. 139, dated 23 March 1987 (*Lovtidende A*, No. 18, 25 March 1987, p. 452) [LS 1975-Den.1], as implemented by, inter alia, Notification No. 372 respecting rest periods and rest days, dated 15 August 1980 (*Lovtidende A*, No. 43, 1980, p. 1134).

Practice

The common norm throughout the labour market is a 37-hour work-week. Both daily and weekly hours of work are generally established by collective agreement. Many collective agreements allow for a fair amount of flexibility in when work is performed, usually with minimum and maximum hours of work per day. Minimum hours of work are usually five or six hours per day, and maximum hours of work are frequently ten. Hours of work per week are normally scheduled Monday through Friday, although Saturday work is not usually forbidden in collective agreements. The apex employers' and workers' organizations coordinate bargaining between their members when agreements are renewed, with the result that working time issues are often very similar in different collective agreements.[22]

Overtime and absolute maximum hours

Law

There is no generally applicable legislation on overtime or absolute maximum hours of work per week or per day. Daily hours of work are indirectly regulated by the Act respecting the working environment, which contains certain minimum daily rest requirements (see below under **Rest**).[23]

Practice

In collective agreements, situations which justify overtime include rush orders, replacement of sick workers, late arrival of ships and unforseen events in general. Many collective agreements only state that the employees are entitled to premium payment when working overtime. Prior notification, usually the day before or the same day at noon, is often required, failing which additional compensation should be paid. A typical schedule for overtime payment is the normal rate of pay plus a 50 per cent premium for the first three hours, and a 100 per cent premium for subsequent hours. In some agreements, overtime remuneration is expressed in fixed amounts, but follows the same principle of increasing the premium after a certain number of overtime hours.[24]

Although there is no legislation on overtime, court decisions have interpreted overtime provisions in collective agreements. An overtime provision in a collective agreement has been interpreted as an obligation for a worker to perform overtime if asked by the employer. If the agreement contains limits on overtime, an employer may not exceed these limits without the consent of the trade union which is party to the agreement. However, even if the agreement

[22] P. Jacobsen: *Legal and contractual limitations to working-time: Denmark*, Working Paper No. WP/94/37/EN (Dublin, European Foundation for the Improvement of Living and Working Conditions, 1994), p. 4.

[23] Act No. 681 respecting the working environment, op. cit., Section 50(2).

[24] Danish Employers' Confederation, op. cit.

does not contain any overtime limits, it has been found in certain cases that an employer has breached the collective agreement if overtime is used systematically.[25]

Most collective agreements include rules on daily and weekly maximum hours and overtime payment. Depending on the collective agreement, the restriction on the use of overtime is frequently in the form of requiring compensatory time for each hour of overtime in excess of a certain limit. Examples of such limits are industry, eight hours each four-week period; construction, five hours per week; hotels and restaurants, 24 hours each four-week period.

Compensatory time off may also incorporate a premium. For example, in the Danish public service, compensatory time is normally given with the same premium as that for overtime, i.e. 50 per cent, and employees can choose whether they prefer to receive their regular rate of pay plus a 50 per cent premium of compensatory time, i.e. 1.5 hours for each hour of overtime.[26]

According to the Danish Employers' Confederation, average overtime hours per week were 1.7 for skilled workers, 2.1 for unskilled male workers and 0.7 for unskilled female workers.[27] Since 1980, there has been a trend towards an increased use of overtime. A study covering the period 1986 to 1990 examined the development of the hours worked in relation to normal hours of work as then established by collective agreements.[28] It concluded that men worked more than normal hours more frequently than women, and that working more than the norm was concentrated among medium, and especially higher, paid employees. Unskilled workers appeared to work above normal hours in a not insignificant number of cases. The proportion of employees working above established normal hours seemed to have increased since the reduction of working time which occurred in 1987.[29]

---

[25] Jacobsen, op. cit., p. 19.

[26] Information provided to the ILO by the Danish Public Service, July 1995.

[27] Danish Employers' Confederation, op. cit.

[28] "Denmark: The reduction and restructuring of working hours", op. cit., p. 27.

[29] Eurostat: *Labour force survey: Results 1992* (Luxembourg, 1994), pp. 154-155 (Table 1) and pp. 158-159 (Table 2).

**Table 1. Full-time employees, average hours usually worked per week
by sector of economic activity, 1992[30]**

Sector	All	Males	Females
Agriculture	42.2	42.9	38.9
Industry	38.3	38.6	37.4
Energy & water	37.2	37.2	---
Mineral extraction, chemicals	39.3	39.1	39.8
Metal manufacture, engineering	38.2	38.4	37.3
Other manufacturing industries	38.2	38.8	37.3
Building and civil engineering	38.3	38.4	37.1
Services	38.9	40.1	37.7
Distributive trades, hotels	39.7	41.0	37.5
Transport and communication	39.8	40.5	37.6
Banking, finance & insurance	39.6	41.0	37.7
Public administration	38.3	38.6	37.8
Other services	38.2	39.1	37.8

Rest

Law

The daily rest required by law is 11 consecutive hours in a 24-hour period, although this can be reduced to eight hours for shiftworkers and agricultural workers up to 30 days per year. The law states that it is preferable that weekly rest take place on a Sunday and on the same day by all employees of the enterprise. A weekly rest of 24 hours immediately after a daily rest period is also required by law. This amounts to 35 hours (11 plus 24) for regular workers, and 32 hours (eight plus 24) for shift- and agricultural workers.

In the case of work in ports and warehouses consisting of loading, unloading and connected operations mainly carried out by casual workers on a shift basis, the rest period may be reduced to nine hours.

Where a natural catastrophe, accident, mechanical breakdown or any similar unforeseen event disrupts the normal running of an enterprise, an exception may be made to these provisions.

[30] ibid.

Exceptions may also be permitted by the Labour Inspectorate where (1) the nature of the work is such that its performance cannot be postponed, or (2) special types of work render such exceptions necessary. In such cases, an exception in respect of a particular rest period may be made without prior permission where such permission cannot be obtained in time. Notice of the exception must, however, be given in writing to the Labour Inspectorate at the earliest opportunity.

The Minister of Labour may set rules for the daily rest period in occupations, fields or types of work where circumstances make it necessary to do so, including rules as to the reduction of the length of the daily rest period to eight hours and the hours at which the rest period is to be taken. Accordingly, the rules on daily and weekly rest do not apply to persons in managerial and supervisory functions. Daily rest may be limited to eight hours for a maximum of 14 days per calendar year during periods of taking inventories and annual bookkeeping. This also applies for shops and department stores during the 14 days preceding Christmas.[31]

There is no generally applicable regulation for meal or rest breaks.[32]

Young workers

The daily rest of young persons under the age of 18 must be not less than 12 hours in every 24 hours. This rest period should normally be placed between 08:00 and 18:00. Exceptions may be authorized by the Labour Inspectorate.

Practice

Most collective agreements contain regulations on daily breaks. Such periods are not considered as part of the daily working time and are not paid. Usually, there will be a lunch break of 30 minutes. If the break is interrupted or if the employee is required to be at the disposal of the employer, the employee will receive compensation, commonly in the form of having such time counted as normal hours of work or by having such time being paid for as overtime. There are some agreements, especially in the white-collar sector, where breaks are included in the daily working time and paid as such. In a number of establishments, work pauses for tea or coffee are paid for as working time.[33]

Shop-opening hours

Law

Shops are required to be closed from Saturday at 17:00 until Monday at 06:00, as well as on public holidays, Constitution Day and Christmas Day. As of 1995, weekly shop-opening

---

[31] Notification No. 372 respecting rest periods and rest days, op. cit.

[32] Act No. 681 respecting the working environment, op. cit.

[33] Jacobsen, op. cit., p. 20; Industrial Relations Services: *Working time in Europe: The duration and flexibility of working time in 17 European countries* (London, 1991), EIRR Report No. 5, p. 61.

hours were deregulated. On Easter Saturday, the Saturday preceding Whitsunday and the last Saturday before Christmas, opening hours extend to 20:00. Shops may not be open on Constitution Day or Christmas Day. By special permission, other opening hours may be granted for tourism purposes. There are exceptions to these rules for pharmacies. The sale of certain specified products, such as gasoline and flowers, may be conducted on Sundays as well. The law prohibits the sale of alcoholic beverages containing 2.8 per cent or more of alcohol on weekdays from 20:00 until 06:00, on Saturdays from 17:00 until Mondays to 06:00, as well as on public holidays, Constitution Day and Christmas Day. Shopkeepers must ensure that customers do not have physical access to such alcoholic beverages outside regular opening hours.[34]

The present law was put into effect as of 1 July 1995 in an effort to deregulate partially shop-opening hours. It repealed a previous law, which entered into force on 1 October 1994.[35] Criticism was voiced concerning the exception to shop-opening hours which allows certain goods to be on sale outside the specified hours, and the obligation of shopkeepers to ensure that customers do not have physical access to goods which are not to be sold outside the regulated hours. The present law provides for a revision in the year 2000.

Public holidays

Law

There is no generally applicable legislation which specifies conditions for work on public holidays or whether time off should be granted on such days.

Practice

Although rarely expressly stated in collective agreements, it is a widespread practice to consider the religious days of the Danish church as work-free days. There are nine religious holidays: New Year's Day, Easter Thursday, Good Friday, Easter Monday, the Day of Prayer (12 May), Ascension Day, Whit Monday, Christmas Eve and Christmas Day. There is a varying practice with respect to Labour Day (1 May). It is relatively frequent that collective agreements specify that Labour Day is a public holiday, although this is normally not the case for shops and service establishments. It is current practice, however, to provide that the afternoon of Constitution Day (5 June) is not worked.[36] Thus, globally, the number of public holidays varies between 9.5 and 10.5 days. If it is necessary for the proper functioning of the enterprise, employees can be required to work on public holidays. The rules concerning premium pay for work on public holidays are the same as those concerning work on Sundays.[37]

---

[34] Act No. 371 respecting shop-opening hours, dated 14 June 1995 (*Lovtidende A*, No. 84, 1995, p. 1678).

[35] Act No. 169 respecting shop-opening hours, dated 16 March 1994 (*Lovtidende A*, No. 36, 1994, p. 749).

[36] Jacobsen, op. cit., p. 24; Ministry of Labour, op. cit.

[37] Jacobsen, op. cit., p. 25.

Paid annual leave

Law

The right to annual leave is regulated in the Act respecting vacations, which provides for five weeks of vacation.[38] Annual leave is calculated according to a six-day work-week, even though most employees work only five days a week. Only Sundays and public holidays are not counted. Annual leave is granted at the rate of two-and-a-half days for every month of employment in a calendar year for a total of 30 days per year. Where a person has been employed for less than one year, the leave entitlement is to be calculated in proportion to the duration of employment. The right to annual leave is separate from the right to annual leave pay under the law. All employees, even new employees, have the right to five weeks of annual leave per year. However, to be entitled to annual leave pay, the employee must have worked during the preceding qualifying year. Employees who have worked partially in the preceding qualifying year, but who have not qualified for a full 30 days of annual leave pay, may supplement their paid leave days with unpaid days so the total leave will be 30 days. Three weeks (18 days) should be taken in the period from 2 May to 30 September, unless an individual or collective agreement so provides.

The Act applies to all employees in the private and public sectors, with the exception of civil servants, employees covered by the Act on agricultural and domestic servants, who are covered by separate laws which have virtually identical provisions.[39] Employees employed by the month are entitled to their usual remuneration during the vacation, plus a supplement of 1 per cent of their wages in the reference year. For other employees, vacation compensation amounting to 12.5 per cent of earnings in the reference year is due. An employee must, in principle, take annual leave in order to receive his or her annual leave pay, subject to some minor exceptions. A new worker who has no entitlement to annual leave pay, because he or she is a new entrant to the workforce or has had an interruption of employment, is not required to take annual leave without pay during the qualifying year, although, as stated above, the person does have this option.[40]

If the employment relationship is terminated, annual leave pay due is paid. However, when a worker changes employers, paid annual leave is carried over to the new employment relationship and can be taken during the qualifying year when the employee has not yet earned his or her allowance to annual leave pay with the new employer. This is possible because sums due as annual leave pay are paid into a special leave fund by each employer and are carried over to the new employment relationship when there is a job change.

---

[38] Act No. 273 respecting annual leave, dated 4 June 1970 (*Lovtidende A*, No. 17, 1970, p. 695), as amended up to Act No. 102, dated 3 March 1993 (*Lovtidende A*, No. 25, 1993, p. 413) [LS 1970-Den.2; 1971-Den.2A; 1978-Den.1].

[39] Jacobsen, op. cit., p. 25.

[40] ibid., pp. 25-26.

Practice

Workers' entitlement to paid annual leave does not seem to be improved under collective agreements, except for annual leave for senior white-collar workers, whose leave period may be increased.[41] To the extent that the issue is regulated in collective agreements, it is in connection with the annual leave pay.[42]

Manufacturers typically close down for three weeks in July. They have resisted efforts to stay open and distribute vacations more evenly, although there is a tendency to have three-week closures start in the second week of July rather than the first week. Contrary to the expectations of some observers, it appears that most employees also prefer to take their vacation during the traditional shut-down period.[43]

Other types of leave

Law

As of 1 January 1994, the rules concerning the right to extended parental leave, educational leave and sabbatical leave were substantially amended with the aim of increasing employment (see above under **Overview and trends**).[44] Parental and maternity leave are not covered here, as they have been extensively illustrated in another ILO publication.[45]

Educational leave

This leave is available to persons over 25 who are covered by the state unemployment insurance programme and who have been employed for at least three of the last five years. This leave may last between one week and one year (two years in the case of unemployed people), but can only be used once in a period of five years. The leave can, however, be divided into shorter periods. The person receives no remuneration from the employer, but receives 100 per cent of the maximum unemployment benefit. The agreement of the employer is required, and there is no legal obligation to re-employ the worker. Employers are not obliged to replace the person on leave with a substitute, but where they do recruit an unemployed person, they receive a state subsidy of 43 kroner per hour if the employment takes place under a vocational training scheme.

---

[41] Industrial Relations Services, *Working time in Europe ...*, op. cit., p. 25.

[42] Jacobsen, op. cit., p. 27.

[43] "Summer closures stay", in *Industrial Relations Europe*, Vol. 21, No. 248, August 1993, p. 4.

[44] Act No. 435 respecting leave, op. cit.

[45] *Conditions of Work Digest* on "Maternity and work", Vol. 13, 1994.

Sabbatical leave

Like educational leave, sabbatical leave is available to people over 25 who are covered by the state unemployment insurance programme and who have been employed for at least three of the last five years. This leave may last for a minimum of 13 and maximum of 52 weeks. Those participating receive no remuneration from the employer, but receive an allowance corresponding to 70 per cent of the maximum unemployment benefit. Under the previous rules, the allowance was 80 per cent of the maximum unemployment benefit. The agreement of the employer is required, and there is no legal obligation of re-employment, but employers are obliged to replace the person on leave with an unemployed person.

Time off to seek new employment

The Act on white-collar workers provides that an employee, who has given or received notice of termination of employment, is entitled to have the necessary time off work in order to seek new employment.[46]

Practice

The legislation on extended parental, educational and sabbatical leave proved more popular than was expected. While the estimate was that some 20,000 persons would apply for leave during 1994, 31,000 applications had been accepted by mid-March 1994.[47] By the end of June 1994, some 63,000 people were on leave. The average length of leave — 39 weeks — was also longer than foreseen.[48] While the effect on unemployment was less encouraging than expected and the profile of those taking leave — predominantly female and low-paid — fuelled discussion about the position of women in the labour market, a desired shift from child-care to educational leave seems to have contributed to the decision to maintain the educational leave programme while maintaining the right to sabbatical leave only for a temporary period.[49]

Other types of justified absences are customarily recognized in practice by some establishments. Many collective agreements contain provisions which entitle employees to leave for union training. Although such leave is frequently not paid, in some collective agreements it is. Similarly, it is customary for an employer to grant unpaid leave if the employee has received a political mandate. However, this situation is normally not covered by collective agreement and it is granted at the discretion of the employer, who may terminate the employment relationship if such duties unduly interfere with the performance of the individual's work.

[46] Jacobsen, op. cit., p. 32.

[47] "Denmark: Labour market reform", op. cit., p. 17.

[48] "Denmark: Leave still popular", in *European Industrial Relations Review*, No. 247, August 1994.

[49] "Denmark: Changes in use of leave", in *European Industrial Relations Review*, No. 255, April 1995, p. 6.

It is also customary in many establishments to give time off to employees for several personal reasons, such as the birth of a child, the death of a close relative, the birthday of the employee and of certain close relatives (a 50th birthday or another round number of years). Usually, however, such time off is unpaid.[50]

Shift and night work

Law

There is no legislation on shift work. With respect to night work, the Act on the working environment places no generally applicable limits on night work except the mandated rest period of 11 hours during a 24-hour period. However, night work is regulated for young persons, and employees between the ages of 15 to 18 years are not permitted to work from 20:00 to 06:00. Exceptions to this rule may be authorized by the Labour Inspectorate. In the evenings, young persons may be allowed to work until 15 minutes after closing time in shops which are permitted to stay open longer, provided they have a rest period of at least one hour after normal closing hours. Work during such extended hours should not in any event be beyond 22:00 and should not occur more than four times a year. In bakeries and agriculture, young persons may start work at 04:00. In hotels and restaurants, 16- to 18-year olds may be allowed to work until 24:00.

Practice

Until 1965, shift work was regulated principally by sectoral agreement. At that time, however, the two apex workers' and employers' organizations agreed on a central agreement on shift work which, subject to renegotiation every two years, was in force until February 1995. The renewal of the central agreement in February 1993 contained provisions allowing for more flexibility in the arrangement of working time and, for example, allowed for an averaging period up to one year. It is also not unknown for the employees themselves to be given the opportunity to arrange their working hours within the framework of the weekly working time.[51] In February 1995, with the expiration of the two-year central agreement on shift work, it was decided to reintroduce a sectoral approach. In the latest three-year industry agreement, there are provisions on shift work.[52] The steelworkers' agreement (in force as of August 1994) also has provisions and specifies that weekly working hours are 37 hours for normal day work, 36 hours for two-shift service, and 35.66 hours for three-shift work.[53]

---

[50] Jacobsen, op. cit., pp. 32-34.

[51] "Danemark: Renouvellement de l'accord sur le travail posté", in *UIMM Social International*, No. 521, October 1993, p. 15.

[52] "Danemark: Convention collective de trois ans dans l'industrie", op. cit.

[53] "Danemark: Salaires et conditions d'emploi des ouvriers dans la sidérurgie", in *UIMM Social International*, No. 537, March 1995, p. 10.

France

Overview and trends

Overview

Working time is extensively regulated by law in France. This body of legal regulation is compiled and consolidated in the French Labour Code (*Code du Travail*). The legal regulation of working time also uses administrative decrees to allow flexibility for certain industries or occupational groups.

Road and maritime transportation, public hospitals (although not private ones), underground mines and certain nationalized enterprises, such as the railways, and electric and gas facilities, are subject to specialized regulatory regimes and are not covered by the Labour Code. Agricultural workers are covered by the Rural Labour Code (*Code rural du Travail*).[1]

The rate of unionization is relatively low. Approximately 65 per cent of establishments, many of them small and medium-sized firms, are estimated to be without union representation. Often, working time arrangements are concluded with the works council or the staff representatives or by referendum. In other cases, the employer makes formal or informal agreements with individual workers.[2] Collective agreements of either an inter-industry or industry character are signed by a national federation of employers and one or several national union federations. Frequently, they establish guidelines for industry agreements in certain sectors. Most collective agreements are concluded at the enterprise level, although industry-wide agreements at the sectoral level have also been concluded.[3] While, in the past, collective agreements could only increase the protection or benefits accorded by law to workers, there have been a series of changes in the law since 1982 which have allowed collective agreements to provide for derogations to the law in specific instances, resulting in less protection or benefits than statutorily mandated. However, unions which were not party to the agreement have the right to oppose such derogations, provided that they, individually or jointly, received 50 per cent of the votes in the preceding election of workers' representatives.[4]

Trends

In 1982, the Government introduced a statutory 39-hour work-week and extended statutory paid annual leave from four to five weeks. These policies were designed to save or create jobs by reducing working time in a period of economic recession, although the impact of the measures on the unemployment figures proved difficult to ascertain.

---

[1] J. Rojot: *Legal and contractual limitations to working-time: France*, Working Paper No. WP/94/38/EN (Dublin, European Foundation for the Improvement of Living and Working Conditions, 1994), p. 10.

[2] ibid., pp. 49-50.

[3] ibid., pp. 46-47.

[4] ibid., p. 4. See, e.g., Act No. 82-957 respecting collective bargaining and the settlement of collective labour disputes, dated 13 November 1982 (*Journal Officiel*, No. 265, 14 November 1982, p. 3414).

Legal texts adopted in 1982, 1986, 1987 and 1993 have all allowed new forms of flexibility in the arrangement of working time. According to one source, only a limited number of enterprises, typically large ones, have taken advantage of the new possibilities offered by changes in the law.[5] These changes allow employers to schedule working hours to cope with periods of peak demand without having to pay overtime if the excess hours worked can be averaged by scheduling less than normal hours of work during slack periods. A number of changes in the law have also allowed companies to use expensive capital equipment more intensively by allowing the extention of operating time. For example, changes in the law have allowed compressed work-weeks involving significant weekend work, and some companies, particularly in industry, have taken advantage of these provisions by introducing weekend shifts. In some cases, these changes in the law have increased the length of working hours of establishments or allowed more exceptions to the general prohibition of Sunday work — the traditional day of rest in France — with the consequence of increasing the engagement of part-time and other atypical workers in some sectors. Despite objections from trade unions to part-time work, it has become an integral part of French employment.[6] Overall part-time employment, however, only grew modestly between 1983 to 1992, with the percentage of employees working part time increasing from 12.03 to 16.25 in services, 3.62 to 4.23 in industry, and actually declining slightly from 16.49 to 15.96 in agriculture.[7]

The Government has encouraged the reduction of working time, through collective agreements, as a means of sharing work among those currently employed and those who are unemployed. For example, an Act adopted in 1993 provided financial incentives in the form of reduced social security contributions where, as a result of a negotiated working time reduction of at least 15 per cent, employment in the firm increased by 10 per cent within six months. The 1993 Act contained financial incentives for the hiring of part-time workers, and for progressive early retirement of workers without significant loss of benefits.[8] Similarly, the Government has taken measures to reduce working time in the public sector with the goal of maintaining or increasing employment.[9]

During the 1990s, a significant number of private enterprises have adopted programmes to reduce working time with the aim to stop the growth of, or reduce, the number of persons dismissed for economic reasons. In a number of cases, the workers concerned have either experienced a decrease in salary or have agreed to moderate wage claims for a certain time.

---

[5] Rojot, op. cit., p. 49.

[6] ibid., p. 35.

[7] Eurostat: "Working time in the European Union: The average working week from 1983 to 1992", in *Statistics in focus: Population and social conditions* (Luxembourg), No. 1, 1995, p. 9.

[8] Act No. 93-1313 respecting labour, employment and vocational training, dated 20 December 1993 (*Journal Officiel*, 21 December 1993).

[9] "Worksharing and redundancies", in *European Industrial Relations Review*, No. 239, December 1993, p. 16; "Company employment agreements break new ground", in *European Industrial Relations Review*, No. 240, January 1994, p. 13.

In some cases, these salary decreases were degressive to minimize the impact on lower-paid workers.[10]

Like other member countries of the European Union, France has to conform to the Directive on working time of 23 November 1993 and the Directive on the protection of young people at work of 22 June 1994, both of which have working time provisions.[11]

Normal hours of work

Law

Normal hours of work are legally 39 hours per week and cannot exceed ten hours per day. The law is subject to exceptions, which are fixed by an administrative decree.[Article L.212-1].[12] However, averaging schemes permitted by law allow normal hours to extend beyond 39 hours per week without the payment of overtime if they are balanced out by shorter hours in other weeks, subject to specifically applicable rules (see below under **Overtime and absolute maximum hours**). In certain occupations, the spreadover of a normal working day (i.e. the repartition over the day of normal hours of work) is regulated by decree. For example, in retail selling of items other than food, the length of the working day cannot exceed ten hours for a full day's work and five hours for a half-day's work. In retail selling of food, the maximum length of the working day cannot exceed 12 hours for a full day's work, and six hours for a half-day's work. In road transport, the maximum length of the working day cannot be more than 12 hours a day for a driver.[13]

The Act establishing the 39-hour week is applicable to industrial and commercial establishments and their dependent organizations, be they private or public, non-religious or religious, even if they are establishments which have a vocation for teaching or non-profit activities. Also covered are public and ministerial offices, the liberal professions, corporations, professional associations and associations of any nature. Workers who are employed in family establishments under the authority of the father, mother or responsible person, are also covered, as are artisanal establishments and cooperatives, as well as their dependent organizations [Articles L.200-1 and 212-1].

Occupations which are expressly excluded from the Act establishing the 39-hour week include the following: caretakers, managers and workers employed by the owners of privately owned buildings, travelling salespersons and commercial travellers, domestic servants, mothers'

[10] G. Aznar, Agence régionale pour l'aménagement du temps: *Répertoire 1994 des "innovations temps de travail"* (Paris, CATRAL, 1994), p. 30.

[11] Council Directive 93/104/EC concerning certain aspects of the organization of working time, dated 23 November 1993 (*Official Journal*, Vol. 36, No. L307, 13 December 1993, pp. 18-24); Council Directive 94/33/EC on the protection of young people at work, dated 22 June 1994 (*Official Journal*, Vol. 37, No. L216, 20 August 1994, pp. 12-19).

[12] Labour Code, Act No. 73-4, dated 2 January 1973 (*Journal Officiel*, 1973), as amended up to 1994 [Dalloz: *Code du Travail* (Paris, 1994)]. All citations to legal provisions in this text are to the Labour Code.

[13] Ministère du Travail, de l'Emploi et de la Formation professionnelle: "Guide partenaires: Le temps de travail", in *Magazine Partenaires*, No. 14, Supplement, May 1995, p. 6.

helpers, managers of an establishment who have the power to decide conditions of work including working-time questions, officers of corporations, employers, and self-employed persons.[14]

Regulatory exceptions to the Act are made for certain branches or industries because of the nature of the work; the fact that the workers have civil servant status; or the fact that other public employees hold special positions. Although the Rural Labour Code has brought many agricultural workers within the ambit of the 39-hour week, there are still a number of agricultural occupations which are exempt from its application. There are also permanent derogations fixed by administrative decree for certain occupational categories, often because there is a need for preparing or finishing certain tasks outside of the normal hours of work for an establishment, or because work must be performed the same day for technical or other exceptional reasons. These permanent exceptions vary according to the occupation and are fixed in terms of daily, and not weekly, limits, usually anywhere from 30 minutes to two hours. These excess hours cannot be carried over to another day.[15]

Another exception to the legal limit of 39 hours per week concerns workers who are employed in occupations with substantial slack time because there are no clients or because of an interruption of the production process or some other valid reason, but who stay at the disposal of the employer. The recurring nature of such slack hours in industries such as hairdressing, water transport and certain engineering occupations led to the adoption of the notion of equivalent hours, which applies in certain occupations determined by decree. Under this concept, a working week of 42 to 43 hours is considered as equivalent to 39 hours of actual work because, although the worker is technically at the disposal of the employer, he or she is actually doing little or no actual work for part of the time. Although the practice of equivalent hours is still legally recognized, there has been a trend away from it: either workers are paid for all hours that they are at the disposal of the employer or they are paid at a slightly higher rate.[16]

Practice

In practice, normal hours of work vary between 35 to 39 hours per week.[17]

Changes in the law, which give financial incentives for a 15 per cent reduction of working time, are designed to encourage employers to reduce working hours to at least 34 hours per week. In a number of cases, establishments have reduced individual working hours to this extent.[18]

---

[14] Rojot, op. cit., p. 10, citing Ordinance No. 82-41, dated 16 January 1982.

[15] ibid., pp. 10 and 12.

[16] ibid., p. 11.

[17] Incomes Data Services (IDS): "Hours and holidays 1995", *IDS Study*, No. 590, November 1995, p. 12.

[18] See Aznar, op. cit.

Normally, work is organized around a five-day work-week, with Saturday and Sunday being rest days. However, the 39-hour week can be spread over six days with one day of rest, or five-and-a-half days with a day-and-a-half of rest. More rarely, the working week is spread over four or four-and-a-half days.[19]

Overtime and absolute maximum hours

Law

Overtime is limited to 130 hours per year. For certain occupations, exceptions are provided for by administrative decrees (for equivalent hours) or through collective agreements, which are allowed to decrease or increase this amount, beyond which the authorization of the Labour Inspector is necessary [Article L.212-6].[20]

Overtime payment and compensatory time

Overtime is normally paid after 39 hours per week, unless there is an averaging scheme, in which case overtime is payable after 44 hours per week. For hours worked in excess of the weekly limits fixed by law, by decree (for equivalent hours) or by collective agreement, overtime is paid at the normal rate of pay plus a premium of 25 per cent for the first eight hours of overtime and of 50 per cent for any additional hours.

In addition, workers are entitled to compensatory rest after 42 weekly hours of work. A distinction is made between enterprises which employ more than ten workers and those which employ ten or less.

In enterprises which employ more than ten employees, the worker has the right to obligatory compensatory rest equal to 50 per cent of the overtime worked. If more than 130 hours of overtime are worked in one calendar year, the obligatory compensatory rest is equal to the amount of overtime worked beyond this limit [Article L.212-5-1].

In enterprises which employ ten employees at most, no compensatory rest is obligatory until a worker has reached 130 hours of overtime during a calendar year. Only then are workers entitled to obligatory compensatory rest equal to 50 per cent of the overtime worked beyond the annual limit of 130 hours.

For overtime work of an urgent character, i.e. for rescue work or to prevent or deal with the consequences of an accident (see Article L.221-12), obligatory compensatory rest is due at the rate of 20 per cent for overtime work performed after 42 hours per week.

Compensatory rest must normally be taken for an entire day, each day off being equivalent to eight hours of compensatory rest. In certain sectors, to be determined by an administrative decree, it can be taken by the half-day [Article L.212-5-1]. Special rules are applicable to seasonal work [Article L.212-5-2] and shift work [Article L.212-5]. The rest day must

---

[19] Ministère du Travail, de l'Emploi et de la Formation professionnelle, op. cit., p. 26.

[20] ibid., p. 10.

normally be taken within two months of the corresponding overtime work, and outside the period 1 July to 31 August. It cannot be added to paid annual leave.[21]

A collective agreement, concluded at the level of the industry, enterprise or plant, may permit the replacement of part or all of any premium pay due for overtime hours by the granting of paid compensatory rest. In those enterprises which are not subject to a collective agreement, the granting of paid compensatory rest in lieu of premium overtime pay is subject to the absence of opposition by the works council or, if none exists, the staff representatives. The hours of overtime so compensated are not counted against the annual limit of 130 hours per worker which the employer can use without prior authorization [Article L.212-5]. This provision encourages the granting of compensatory rest rather than overtime pay. In addition, several measures have been introduced to increase flexibility in the use of hours worked and, in certain cases, reduce the number of hours for which an overtime premium is to be paid.

The impact of flexible options on overtime pay

Statutory flexibility options allow the averaging of time worked over several weeks. They apply if there is a collective agreement at the level of the industry, the enterprise or the plant.

In one flexibility scheme, referred to as "type 1 variation", weekly hours can be changed over the course of a year and go up to the weekly maximum of 48 hours in a given week, provided that the average weekly hours worked over the year do not exceed 39. Hours worked above 39 hours in any week, however, give rise to overtime and compensatory rest according to law, but are not counted against the annual maximum of 130 hours [Article L.212-8].

Another flexibility scheme is referred to as "type 2 variation". The average weekly hours, computed over one year or a shorter period, must amount to 39 hours, and the normal maximum weekly hours must not exceed 44, subject to exceptions as provided for by law [Article L.212-8]. Workers must be granted a reduction in effective working time, financial compensation or training time, or measures for employment maintenance or creation must be introduced. Under this scheme, hours worked over 39 and up to 44 per week, which are balanced by reduced working time in other weeks, are not counted in the 130-hour overtime annual maximum, are not paid at the overtime rate and do not give rise to compensatory rest. Hours worked in excess of 44 hours per week are considered as overtime.

With the 1993 Act, another possibility for averaging working hours over part or all of the year was adopted. It allows the employer to spread work unevenly over the period in question, as long as the statutory limits of ten hours per day, 48 hours per week, and 46 hours per week over any given period of 12 weeks are respected, in which case no overtime is due. The key condition to this arrangement is that it must result in a collective reduction of working time, which is to be, on average, below the statutory limit of 39 hours per week. This arrangement must be the result of a collective agreement, which can be concluded at the level of the industry, the enterprise or the plant [Article L.212-2-1].

[21] ibid., pp. 10-11.

Other flexibility options permit a worker with responsibility for children to ask that his or her working time be spread unevenly through part or all of a year by modification of the individual's contract of employment. It is not necessary that working time be reduced or that a collective agreement be negotiated. The legal maximum hours must be respected and the arrangement must conform to the relevant administrative decree [Article L.212-2-1].

In many branches of activity, the law also allows an employer to grant individual workers exceptions from the hours of work applied collectively to all workers if the works council, or the staff representatives if there is no such council, are not opposed, and the Labour Inspector or another responsible government official is informed in advance. If there are no staff representatives in an enterprise, individualized work schedules are authorized by the Labour Inspector after it is established that the workers concerned are in agreement. Under such a flexible agreement, a worker can work excess hours in one week and compensate by having reduced hours in another week. If the average weekly hours worked during the reference period do not exceed the legal limits, overtime is not payable [Article L.212-4-1]. An administrative decree limits the hours transferred per week to three hours and the maximum accumulated transfers to ten hours, although the decree also provides that enterprise-level collective agreements can derogate from these limits.[22]

Absolute maximum hours

Daily. The limit of ten hours per day can be extended to 12 hours per day with administrative authorization for exceptional cases involving work which has a special deadline because of the nature of the task; contractual obligations of the enterprise; seasonal work; work involving increased activity during certain days of the week; or industry- or enterprise-level collective agreements [Article L.212-1].[23]

Weekly. Absolute maximum hours are 48 hours per week. In exceptional circumstances, certain enterprises can be authorized to exceed the maximum limit of 48 hours per week without, however, exceeding 60 hours a week. Such authorization is given, for a limited period of time, by the Labour Inspector, who must be informed of the views of the works council or, if none exists, the staff representatives [Article L.212-7].

Annually. No generally applicable statutory provision. Absolute annual maximum hours result from the combined application of the annual limit on overtime and of obligatory compensatory rest and, where applicable, of annualized schemes (see above).

Young workers

Workers under 18 years old cannot work more than eight hours a day or 39 hours per week. However, the Labour Inspector can grant an exception to this rule, allowing for up to five additional hours of work per week if the occupational health physician is in agreement. The

---

[22] Rojot, op. cit., p. 44.

[23] ibid., p. 6. See also "Council finally adopts working time Directive", in *IDS European Report*, No. 385, January 1994, pp. 20-22.

daily or weekly hours of younger workers cannot, however, be more than the corresponding hours of adult workers in the establishment. The establishment must also allow a younger worker or apprentice the necessary time to attend training courses [Article L.212-13].

Practice

The situation in enterprises can be very much influenced by the terms of collective agreements. For example, the limit on overtime (130 hours per worker per year), which, as noted above, influences the amount of compensatory time off for hours worked in excess of that limit, is 94 hours per year in the metalworking industry.[24]

Table 1 shows that hours actually worked between 1984 and 1994 remained very stable, both in non-agricultural activities and in manufacturing.

Table 1. Hours actually worked per week by employees[25]

	1984	1985	1986	1987	1988	1989	1990	1991	1992	1993	1994
Non-agricultural activities*	39.0	38.9	38.9	39.0	39.0	39.0	39.0	39.0	39.0	39.0	38.9
Manufacturing	38.7	38.6	38.6	38.7	38.7	38.7	38.7	38.7	38.7	38.6	38.6

* Excluding water, communication, public administration and private domestic services.

Statistics available for 1992 (see Table 2) show that the average weekly hours usually worked by full-time employees were higher in agriculture than in industry for males and females considered together, although female workers in the manufacturing industries (other than metalworking) worked slightly longer than agricultural female workers. Hours worked in the service sector were lower than hours in agriculture and industry for males and females considered together, although males worked slightly longer hours, mainly due to their comparatively high hours in transport and communication and in banking and finance.

---

[24] Union des Industries métallurgiques et minières (UIMM): "Chapitre III: Horaire supérieur à l'horaire hebdomadaire", in *Legislation sociale, Vol. 3* (Paris, 1994), p. 2.

[25] Bureau of Statistics, International Labour Office.

Table 2. Full-time employees, average hours usually worked per week by sector of economic activity, 1992[26]

Sector	All	Males	Females
Agriculture	40.9	41.4	39.2
Industry	40.0	40.2	39.4
Energy & water	39.3	39.5	38.8
Mineral extraction, chemicals	39.9	40.0	39.6
Metal manufacture, engineering	39.9	40.1	39.1
Other manufacturing industries	40.1	41.7	39.5
Building and civil engineering	40.2	40.2	39.6
Services	39.5	40.6	38.3
Distributive trades, hotels	41.5	42.5	40.0
Transport and communication	40.2	40.6	39.0
Banking, finance & insurance	40.9	41.9	39.8
Public administration	39.8	40.6	38.8
Other services	37.0	37.4	36.7

Rest

Law

Rest breaks

There are no generally applicable provisions, except for young workers under 18 years, who cannot work more than four-and-a-half hours without a rest break [Article L.212.14].

Daily rest

There are no generally applicable provisions. To comply with the Directive on working time, measures will have to be taken to ensure that workers enjoy a minimum daily rest of 11 consecutive hours.

[26] Eurostat: *Labour force survey: Results 1992* (Luxembourg, 1994), pp. 154-155 (Table 1) and pp. 158-159 (Table 2).

Weekly rest

A full day's rest (24 hours) is required, although derogations are provided for by law in exceptional situations [Articles L.221-2; 221-4]. The day of weekly rest is fixed by law on Sunday, although there are provisions for numerous exceptions, which are applicable either on the basis of the type of work involved or may be negotiated by collective agreement.

Exceptions to weekly rest requirements

Some exceptions to the weekly rest requirements are applicable to establishments which provide goods or services that are essential to a modern economy and which need to function seven days a week. In other cases, work on Sunday may be allowed because of the technical nature of an industry; because of the economic importance of making intensive use of expensive equipment; because the goods involved are perishable; or because losses would occur if the processing of the goods was interrupted. Work on Sunday may also be allowed for convenience to the public for shopping or to engage in recreational activities, or because the work is in a locality characterized by important tourist activity. In such cases, the day of rest is normally given by rotation on another day, or compensatory time is given at a later more convenient time. In exceptional situations, however, weekly rest can be temporarily suspended.

Establishments that are statutorily authorized to give the day of weekly rest by rotation on a day other than Sunday include those which are engaged in the following types of activities: the production of food for immediate consumption; hotels, restaurants and cafés; shops selling tobacco; flower shops; hospitals, clinics, asylums, psychiatric facilities, retirement homes, health facilities, drug stores and pharmacies; public baths; newspapers and other news enterprises; enterprises in the entertainment industry (e.g. theatres, concert halls, cinemas); transport and chair-rental enterprises; lighting, water distribution and power companies; land transport (except the railways, for which a special regulation applies), air transport and other categories of transport enterprises; telecommunication enterprises; and show rooms and other permanent expositions where the aim of the activity is to sell to the public [Article L.221-9].

Weekly rest may also be given by rotation on a day other than Sunday in industries where the raw material is susceptible of rapid alternation and in industries in which any interruption of the work would result in the loss or depreciation of the goods which are being produced. Although normally a collective agreement is called for in such instances, in industries where there is no collective agreement, the authorities may fix the terms of the derogation by administrative decision [Article L.221-10].

In industries which operate on a continuous basis, either because there are reasons to maintain a furnace in constant operation or because there are other reasons why operations should be continuous, then the specialists involved are given their day of weekly rest according to an administrative regulation. The number of rest days should be at least equal to the number of weeks of work during the period in question; such rest days should include as many Sundays as possible [Article L.221-11].

In addition, weekly rest may be given by rotation in touristic localities which receive an exceptional number of visitors, or where there is a cultural activity of a permanent character, as well as in localities where thermal bathes exist. Establishments which can benefit from these exceptions include retail sales stores which sell goods or services that are related to tourist activity; are of a sportive, recreational, cultural nature; or are otherwise of a character to facilitate vacation activities [Article L.221-8-1].

Another exception which allows weekly rest to be given on a day other than Sunday is in industrial enterprises which function with two groups of workers, one group of which has as its function to replace other workers during the day or days of traditional weekly rest. This derogation has to be the subject of a collective agreement in the enterprise [Article L.221-6]. In addition, where it would be prejudicial to the public or otherwise compromise the normal functioning of the enterprise to have weekly rest granted simultaneously to all of the workers on Sunday, weekly rest may be given by rotation [Article L.221-6].

When security guards or concierges of commercial or industrial establishments cannot be given a day of weekly rest, they must be subsequently given a day of compensatory rest [Article L.221-15].

In retail establishments where weekly rest is normally given on Sunday, this day of rest can be cancelled on five Sundays during the course of a year by an administrative order of the mayor after he or she has received the views of the organizations of workers and employers concerned. The workers deprived of their day of weekly rest must be granted compensatory rest and a bonus payment equal to 30 per cent of their normal pay [Article L.221-19].

When establishments have continuous operations for only part of the year, the days of weekly rest can be deferred, although the worker concerned should benefit from at least two days of weekly rest per month. Seasonal workers can also have their weekly rest deferred according to administrative regulation [Article L.221-21].

Work is authorized to take place on the day of weekly rest for the work of loading and unloading in ports and other places of handling goods in accordance with administrative decrees [Article L.221-20]. For those industries which are determined by administrative regulation and which deal with perishable items or otherwise have to respond to an extraordinary increase in workload, the day of weekly rest can be suspended no more than twice a month and no more than six times during the year. Hours worked on the day of weekly rest are considered overtime and are to be counted towards the total number of overtime hours allowed for by law [Article L.221-22].

Weekly rest may be temporarily suspended, subject to conditions specified in law on an exceptional basis for certain types of work or certain occupations. These include emergency work to organize rescue operations, to prevent imminent accidents, or to repair damage to material, installations or the building as a result of an accident. This suspension of weekly rest is applicable not only to the enterprise in question, but to any other enterprise which undertakes urgent repair work on behalf of the damaged enterprise. In either case, the workers who have their weekly rest suspended are to be given a day of compensatory rest for the suspension of the customary weekly rest day [Article L.221-12].

Weekly rest may be suspended a half-day in industrial and commercial establishments for those persons who are responsible for the maintenance of machinery, cleaning of the establishment, care of horses, and generally for all maintenance work which must be done on the day of traditional rest and which is indispensable to avoid a delay in restarting operations during the normal hours of work. When workers have worked two half-days on the traditional day of rest, they are to be given an entire day of compensatory rest [Article L.221-13].

In establishments of the State as well as in those establishments which work on behalf of the State, as well as in the interest of national defence, weekly rest can be temporarily suspended [Article L.221-25].

The suspension of weekly rest is not applicable to young workers under 18 years of age [Article L.221-14].

Practice

The main trend concerning rest has been to have a shorter pause for the mid-day meal break of between 30 to 45 minutes so that the total working day, i.e. the spreadover, is shorter while normal hours remain constant. Certain collective agreements also allow for work pauses during production, which are paid as working time.[27]

Shop-opening hours

Law

Shops may be open up to 13 hours per day, six days a week. In principle, retail establishments are closed on Sunday, although small food shops may be open until 13:00. Other exceptions can be granted by the administrative authorities.[28]

Practice

After considerable debate, in 1992 the Government decided not to abolish the prohibition of work on Sunday, although it adopted legal provisions which allowed for a number of additional exceptions to the law. In 1995, there was a debate whether shop-opening hours should be extended further and, especially, whether more Sunday work should be authorized, particularly for retail establishments, which are currently limited to working five times per year on Sunday, subject to permission from the administrative authorities (assuming they do not fall under another exception to Sunday work) [Article L.221-19].[29]

---

[27] Ministère du Travail, de l'Emploi et de la Formation professionnelle, op. cit., p. 14.

[28] J.-Y. Boulin: "Esclave du dimanche", in *Futuribles*, April 1992, pp. 54-62, citing the Act of 1906.

[29] See generally "La bataille du dimanche", in *Futuribles*, April 1992, pp. 35-68.

Public holidays

Law

There are 11 public holidays, but only 1 May, Labour Day, is a paid public holiday legally [Article L.222-5]. There is no legal obligation to grant time off or pay workers for other public holidays if they do not work. However, workers under the age of 18 are not allowed to work on any public holidays [Article L.222-2], subject to certain exceptions [Article L.222-3].

The 11 public holidays are 1 January, New Year's Day; Easter Monday; 1 May, Labour Day; 8 May, Victory Day 1945; Ascension; Whit Monday; 14 July, National Day; 15 August, Assumption Day; 1 November, All Saints Day; 11 November, Armistice Day 1918; 25 December, Christmas Day [Article L.222-1] (actual dates for certain holidays, such as Easter and other religious holidays, are subject to change). An employee who works on a public holiday has no legal right to be paid higher wages.

Practice

By custom or collective agreement, many employers observe public holidays and do not require their employees to work. Many collective agreements provide for payment of observed holidays for workers with a minimum length of service. If work is performed on a public holiday, collective agreements also usually provide for premium pay.[30]

Paid annual leave

Law

By law, there are a minimum of five weeks of paid annual leave.

A worker must have effectively worked a month before having the right to paid annual leave. Such leave is accumulated at a rate of 2.5 working days per month to attain 30 working days per year [Article L.223-2]. Young workers and apprentices who are under 21 have the right, if they request it, to have an additional 30 days of leave without pay [Article L.223-3]. In addition, women workers or apprentices aged 21 or younger are allowed two supplementary days of paid annual leave for each dependent child [Article L.223-5].

The law gives a broad definition of what is considered to be effective work, and covers absence from work because of sickness, accident, military service, taking of compensatory rest or maternity leave [Article L.223-4].

The periods for using paid annual leave are normally fixed by collective agreement and must include the period from 1 May to 31 October [Article L.223-7]. Exceptions, however, may be applicable to agricultural workers covered by the Rural Labour Code [Article L.223-7-1]. If there is no collective agreement, the employer should fix the periods of vacation to be taken with the staff representatives and the works council. The scheduling of vacation should take

---

[30] Rojot, op. cit., p. 26.

into account the worker's seniority as well as his or her family situation, including the vacation alternatives of the worker's spouse if he or she works. Workers in the same enterprise who are married have the right to take their vacations together [Article L.223-7].

When paid annual leave does not exceed 12 days, it must be taken as one uninterrupted period.

During the period from 1 May to 31 October, the worker is entitled to take at least 12 days (two weeks) and no more than 24 days (four weeks) of paid annual leave. Exceptions can be agreed with a worker who has a valid reason, e.g. returning to his or her country of origin if the person is a foreigner, for desiring to take vacation in a area geographically remote from France. The leave period of 12 to 24 days can be taken at different times, although there must be at least one uninterrupted period of 12 days (two weeks). If the number of days of paid annual leave taken outside the period from 1 May to 31 October is more than six, then the worker is attributed two supplementary days of paid annual leave. If the number of days of paid annual leave taken outside this period is three to five, the worker has an extra day of supplementary paid annual leave. When paid annual leave is granted at the same time as the temporary closing of the enterprise, the splitting of paid annual leave during the period from 1 May to 31 October is possible with the consent of the works council or, in none exists, of the staff representatives, with the agreement of the workers concerned [Article L.223-8].

Compensation for paid annual leave normally amounts to one-tenth of total remuneration, which includes extra payments, during the reference period. However, the law also stipulates that the worker can be paid no less than what he or she would have earned if the person had not taken paid leave and continued to work [Article L.223-11].

Paid annual leave must be taken and cannot be compensated for by an additional cash payment, although, if a worker's contract is terminated before the worker has been able to take all of his or her leave, cash payment for accumulated paid annual leave is authorized [Article L.223-14]. Similarly, cash payment in lieu of taking paid annual leave is permitted for special categories of workers where the nature of the work is of such an irregular character that taking leave would be impractical.[31]

Practice

In practice, paid annual leave varies between five and six weeks. Paid annual leave may be increased over the statutory minimum of five weeks because of seniority, age, or because additional leave has been negotiated.[32]

---

[31] D. Perrod-Marron: "Congés non pris, congés non dus", in *Droit du Travail*, Vol. 43, Nos. 8-9, August-September 1992, p. 4.

[32] IDS, "Hours and holidays 1995", op. cit., p. 12; Ministère du Travail, de l'Emploi et de la Formation professionnelle, op. cit., p. 18.

Other types of leave

Law

French law authorizes sabbatical leave as well as leave or justified absence to cover a range of needs, including vocational, trade union or leadership training; family events; the performance of public functions; teaching assignments; and starting or taking over a business. The law also requires that the employer should, to the extent feasible, permit any worker to arrange his or her work schedule so that participation in regularly supervised sports activity is possible. This provision, however, is more in the nature of requiring a certain degree of flexibility in the scheduling of an employee's work than a type of leave [Article L.221-4-8].[33]

Educational or vocational training leave

Several types of leave have been established to facilitate education or vocational training for workers. The means of putting such leave into practice is, in some cases, subject to negotiation between employers and workers in the industry concerned. Mandatory contributions by the employer towards such educational and vocational training expenses are required for some types of leave.

Leave for vocational training for young persons under 25

A young worker who has not had any vocational training has the right to paid leave for this purpose, if it is needed during the first two years of employment up to the age of 25. The period of training can be for up to 200 hours.

Leave for workers' and union training

Workers who would like to participate in educational and training programmes have the right to do so for up to 12 days per year, if they request unpaid leave. These programmes are to be given by a training centre run by a union or otherwise certified by the Ministry of Labour. The employer can deny such leave if it would be prejudicial to the functioning of the enterprise or if it would exceed the limit fixed by the Ministry of Labour on the number of workers who can be on such leave at the same time. In addition, there is leave that is granted for economic training of workers who are members of the works council of an establishment. The maximum length of the leave is five days, and these days can be counted in the 12 days accorded for workers' and union training. There is also leave for training purposes granted to workers' representatives who participate on the committee of heath, safety and working conditions. The length of this leave is related to the size of the enterprise. For enterprises with less than 300 workers, the leave is three days; for those with 300 or more workers, five days. These days can be counted in the 12 days available for workers' and union training.

---

[33] See Rojot, op. cit., pp. 29-34. See also J.-G. Lamand: "Congés et absences du salarié", in *Semaine Sociale Lamy*, No. 684, 21 February 1994.

Leave for young persons under 25 to be trained as youth leaders or coordinators

This leave must be for a programme organized by a centre certified by the Ministry of Culture. It is unpaid and can be for up to six days per year.

Leave for family reasons

Paid leave is permitted for the following events: marriage, four days; birth or adoption of a child, three days; death of a spouse or a child, two days; marriage of a child, one day; death of the father or mother, one day.

Leave to perform public functions

There are three main categories of leave: leave for political activities; leave for judicial activities: and leave for activities of a social or civic character.

Political activities. If an employee is elected to the National Assembly or the Senate, the two chambers of the national Parliament, his or her contract of employment is suspended. Employees of an establishment have the right to an unpaid leave of absence of up to 20 days to be candidates in elections to Parliament. For locally elected officials, e.g. to a municipal council, general council (at the departmental level) or regional council, employees of an establishment are allowed an unpaid leave of absence to exercise their duties, subject to a limit specified by law, which in 1994 amounted to 1,014 hours a year. The authorities are responsible for any payment of these elected officials for the exercise of their public functions. When locally elected officials are on unpaid leave of absence, their absence is considered as time effectively worked for the calculation of paid annual leave, for rights linked to seniority and social benefits.

Judicial activities. Employees have the right of paid leave to participate in the functioning of the Labour Court. The employer can eventually be reimbursed by the State for the costs associated with the absence of a worker. There is also a right of paid leave for training to participate in the functioning of the Labour Court up to six weeks. The employer can charge the expenses associated with this absence to the money contributed by the employer for the continuing education of employees. There is also an unpaid leave for an employee who works in an establishment of at least 11 employees, and who has been designated by a recognized union or professional organization, to act in a representative capacity before the Labour Court. The period of absence cannot exceed ten hours per month.

Employees also have the right to an unpaid leave of absence to participate as assessors in social security tribunals, in mixed commissions of conciliation for the resolution of problems anticipated by the Labour Code, and to participate as a member of a jury in a criminal case.

Activities of a social or civic character. Employees are given unpaid leave to participate in the meetings of the board of directors of a social security organization; in the functions of organizations that deal with immigrants; in family associations; in organizations dealing with the problems of employment and training; and in a jury of examination. There is also a unpaid leave of absence for participating in the activities of humanitarian organizations which assist victims of natural disasters for a maximum 20 days. Leave can be granted to be a representative of an association or mutual benefit organization, up to a maximum of nine days a year.

Leave for teaching or research purposes

Workers with a minimum of one year's service may be permitted to take an unpaid leave of absence for up to one year to teach or undertake research in a public or private educational institution which is certified by the State, or to teach in a programme of continuing education authorized by the State. This leave can also be taken on a part-time basis, determined on the basis of either four hours per week or 18 hours per month.

Leave to start or take over a business

A worker who has worked 36 months in an enterprise and wants to start or take over a business can normally benefit from a leave of absence for one year. This leave is renewable once for a maximum leave of two years. The worker has to request his or her reinstatement three months in advance, and is entitled to either his or her previous position or an equivalent one.

Sabbatical leave

A worker who has been employed with an enterprise for at least three years and whose history of total employment, i.e. time with present and previous employers combined, amounts to at least six years is eligible. The worker can request sabbatical leave for a period of six to 11 months, and can use the time for any purpose.

Shift and night work

Law

The regulation of shift work focuses on workers who are organized to work on distinct shifts which follow one another. The workers on each team normally work and rest at the same time. Shift work by successive teams may be continuous shift work (24 hours a day, seven days a week); semi-continuous shift work (24 hours a day, with a weekly work stoppage); or discontinuous shift work (work stoppage during the night and at the end of the week).

Workers who are employed permanently in continuous shift work may not work more than 35 hours per week on average. It was anticipated that this provision would lead to a system of five shifts, where three shifts would work and two shifts would rest, with each employee working 33 hours and 36 minutes per week.[34]

There is also a provision which prohibits the employing of workers on successive shifts. There is, however, an exception for reasons connected with the imperative functioning of the

---

[34] Rojot, op. cit., p. 34; Ministère du Travail, de l'Emploi et de la Formation professionnelle, op. cit., p. 25.

enterprise. However, when work by the same employee on the second shift exceeds two hours, then the reasons for this have to be communicated by the employer to the Labour Inspector within 48 hours [Article R.212-13].

There are also provisions for employees who are engaged to work extended shifts during periods of traditional rest for other workers. Such arrangements should normally be permitted when there is an enterprise- or plant-level collective agreement or, in the absence of such an agreement, when the Labour Inspector has given authorization after consultation with the works council or, if none exists, with the staff representatives. When these teams are to work no longer than 48 hours consecutively, for example during a weekend, then work up to 12 hours each day is authorized. The authorization of the Labour Inspector is necessary to work 12-hour shifts, even if there is a collective agreement, because it is an exception to the ten-hour day limit fixed by the law [Articles L.221-5-1; R.221-14 to 221-17]. If, however, these teams are to work for a total consecutive period which exceeds 48 hours, then work only up to ten hours per day is allowed [Article R.221-17]. Workers who work these special shifts on the weekend are entitled to an increase of 50 per cent over what they would normally receive in compensation. However, this 50 per cent premium is not legally obligatory if these relief teams are scheduled to work during the week [Article L.221-5-1]. The effect of these provisions is that a worker who works two 12-hour shifts on the weekend receives 150 per cent of normal pay or pay equivalent to 36 hours of work during the week. If a worker works three ten-hour shifts, with two of them being on the weekend, he or she will receive 150 per cent for the two weekend shifts and regular pay for the day during the week, or pay equivalent to 40 hours of work during the week.

Where operating time per day is longer than the working time of one shift, but where production or business activity is not necessarily continuous or carried out by successive teams, a type of shift work known as relay work may be used to ensure coverage during all operating hours. Relay work may also be used in work situations where the total length of time between the beginning of the working day and its conclusion is long, but actual working hours are broken up in distinct periods between which there is no work for relatively significant periods. Such shift work in some industries may be subject to an administrative decree, or otherwise addressed in collective agreements at the industry, enterprise or plant level.[35] Otherwise such shift work is not regulated in detail, other than through the principal provisions applying to normal hours of work, maximum hours of work, overtime and compensatory rest.

In principle, night work — which is defined to be work between 22:00 and 06:00 — is forbidden for workers under the age of 18. However, in special situations, exceptions can be granted by the Labour Inspector for commercial establishments and entertainment productions. With respect to the bakery, restaurant and hotel business, an administrative decree fixes the conditions under which exceptions can be granted. If necessary to prevent imminent accidents or to undertake repairs necessary as a result of an accident, exceptions can be obtained to the general prohibition against night work. The minimum rest period for younger workers who perform night work is 12 consecutive hours [Articles L.213-7 to 213-10].

[35] Rojot, op. cit., p. 42.

Practice

Through collective agreement, meal breaks are sometimes paid as working time for shift work by successive teams of workers.[36]

---

[36] Ministère du Travail, de l'Emploi et de la Formation professionnelle, op. cit., p. 14.

Hungary

Overview and trends

As far as the determination of working time is concerned, the history of Hungarian labour law is divided into several periods. Act No. 2/1967[1] determined the duration of working time and, up to 1979, it fell under statutory provisions and was outside the competence of collective agreements.

In 1984, significant changes in the legal scope of collective agreement were made.[2] The regulation of issues related to the performance of work, rest times and remuneration were allowed to fall within the competence of collective agreements. Moreover, the determination of the work schedule and variations in flexible working hours arrangements were also subject to the agreement of the contracting parties. The autonomy of the contracting parties, however, still did not extend to the determination of the duration of the working time, which was specified by statutory provisions.

The next stage in the evolution of working time legislation came in 1989.[3] Although the duration of working time was still defined by statutory provision, the general working time framework of a given employer was fixed, within limits established by statute, by collective agreement.

From 1962 to 1992, working time was specified on a weekly basis. Act No. 2/1967 originally established normal hours of work at 44 to 48 hours a week.[4] The Government was authorized to fix a shorter or, exceptionally, a longer work-week exceeding 48 hours as well. In accordance with this statutory flexibility, weekly hours of work were fixed at 44 hours in industry and in the building industry, and 48 hours in all other branches of the economy. A shorter work-week — 40 to 44 hours — was fixed by statute for industrial and construction employers operating continuously or in three or more shifts a day. An even shorter work-week of 36 to 42 hours could be specified for positions hazardous to health by ministerial decree, with the agreement of the Ministers of Labour and Health.

It should be noted in connection with the weekly specification of working time that, until the 1979 amendment of the Labour Code, employees had been entitled to a single rest day only and that daily working time was eight hours.

Weekly working time was established generally at 44 hours in 1979. The weekly working time of industrial and construction employers operating continuously or which used three or

---

[1] Labour Code, Act No. 2 of 1967 (*Magyar Közlöny*, No. 67, 8 October 1967, p. 503), as amended up to Decree No. 8, dated 23 April 1990 (*Maygar Közlöny*, No. 35, 23 April 1990, p. 751) [LS 1967-Hun.2; 1971-Hun.2; 1979-Hun.1].

[2] See Decree No. 24 to modify the Labour Code, dated 31 October 1984 (*Magyar Közlöny*, No. 46, 31 October 1984, p. 784).

[3] See Act No. 5 to modify the Labour Code, dated 25 March 1989 (*Magyar Közlöny*, No. 19, 25 March 1989, p. 383).

[4] Labour Code 1967, op. cit., Section 37(2).

more shifts was fixed at 44 hours by ministerial decree in the same year. The autonomy of the contracting parties was extended to allow a collective agreement to prescribe a biweekly second day of rest in addition to the traditional one day a week of rest. As for the duration of working time in specialized sectors, the Minister was entitled to fix a framework for weekly hours of work exceeding 44 hours in agricultural production and manufacturing.

In 1989, the legal duration of the working time decreased once more. Pursuant to the law as amended, a collective agreement could specify a 40- to 42-hour week for any given employer. Working time was allowed to remain longer in agricultural production and manufacturing, but it was not to exceed 2,500 hours annually, including overtime, in these sectors. The management of agricultural cooperatives (as employers) could, in agreement with their employees, raise the annual hours limit to 3,000 hours.

The length of working time is to be distinguished from its scheduling. The relevant legislation allowed working time to be fixed on a monthly or annual basis. In general, monthly and annual work schedules used to be characteristic of seasonal jobs and, in particular, agricultural ones.

The actual duration of working time was influenced to a significant extent by overtime performed, in accordance with the relevant legislation, under collective agreements. As for limits on overtime, until 1992 only indirect restrictions applied, the most important one stipulating at least eight hours of rest for the employee between two workdays. Other statutory restrictions on overtime applied to female workers, minors, mothers with small children, and positions especially hazardous to health or particularly dangerous.

Act No. 2/1967 originally fixed basic paid annual leave at 12 days, with supplementary leave proportional to the period spent in employment: one additional day after every two years, not exceeding 12 days.[5] Moreover, supplementary leave was granted to various categories of workers, such as mothers with more than one child, pregnant and child-bearing women, minors, and those employed in certain positions. The employee was entitled to his or her average salary for the leave period in all circumstances. Moreover, it was within the employer's competence to give extraordinary and unpaid leave, and instances of compulsory unpaid leave were also defined under the law.

As for the cumulation of the various supplementary leaves, the general rule was, with some exceptions, that they could not be added up. The one more favourable for the employee had to be chosen.

In summary, it could be said that, in the period from 1967 to 1992, the determination of working time was governed by legal regulation above all. Collective agreements played a secondary role, owing to the restrictions placed on the contractual autonomy of the parties. The duration of legal working time, specified on a weekly basis, underwent a gradual decrease during this period.

In the period under scrutiny, the job creation and job preservation implications of working time had not been considered seriously, and the relevance of working time in relation to issues

---

[5] ibid., Section 42.

concerning competitivity and wages were only highlighted by the new Labour Code, which was established by Act No. 22/1992.[6]

Normal hours of work

Law

Section 117 of Act No. 22/1992 fixes the legal working time at eight hours a day. The parties concerned may fix a shorter or, in positions that are partially or fully of a standby character, a longer working time not exceeding 12 hours. If the work in question is especially hazardous to health or particularly dangerous, law or collective agreement may specify a period of time, up to six hours, within the working day that may be devoted to the hazardous or dangerous activity, and they may also prescribe other restrictions. The statutory provision fixing a framework for annual hours of work at 2,500 to 3,000 hours is still valid in the agricultural and manufacturing sectors.

In certain occupational categories, legislation assigns the elaboration of working time solely to the competence of collective agreements. Thus, the working hours and off-duty time of employees serving on ships and in engine rooms of waterborne power-machines, or of those who work as navigators, flight attendants, technicians and operators or drivers of aircraft service equipment in civil aviation, or as officials of regular national and international passenger traffic by road may be regulated by collective agreements. These agreements may have provisions which differ from standards prescribed by law.[7]

Working time may be specified by taking the daily working time as a point of departure for a reference period of a week or longer up to one year. It is essential that, even if working time is defined on an annual basis, the daily hours of work are not to exceed 12 hours and, with the exception of seasonal work, shall correspond to the daily working time of eight hours on average over a period of two months, or over a maximum period of four months for collective agreements providing otherwise, or over a maximum period of six months for collective agreements including several employers and providing otherwise.[8]

The provisions of the Labour Code qualify as generally applicable standards. The law on working time applies to both the public and the private sector, to male and female workers alike in all sectors, with the exception of agricultural production and manufacturing.

According to Act No. 23/1992 on the legal status of public servants, actual working time shall correspond to the legal standard, although averaging over an eight-week period is allowed.[9]

---

[6] Labour Code, Act No. 22, dated 30 March 1992 (*Magyar Közlöny*, No. 45, 4 May 1992, pp. 1613-1642) [LLD 1993-HUN1].

[7] ibid., Section 117(4).

[8] ibid., Section 118(3).

[9] See Act No. 23/1992 respecting the legal status of public servants, dated 5 May 1992 (*Magyar Közlöny*, No. 46, 5 May 1992, pp. 1645-1662), Section 39.

Act No. 33/1992 on the legal status of civil servants sets their weekly working time at 40 hours.[10]

Practice

According to official statistics, nearly 50 per cent of men work 36 to 40 hours per week, and roughly 30 per cent work 41 to 43 hours per week. The corresponding figures for female workers are 60 and 23 per cent, respectively. Approximately 90 to 92 per cent of all employees work between 36 and 43 hours a week.[11]

The registration of collective agreements is not compulsory under Hungarian law. Consequently, no official data are available as to how collective agreements determine the arrangement of working time. It is quite certain, however, that, in accordance with the Hungarian tradition, one-employer collective agreements prevail, and the new regulation described above (explicit reference to multi-employer collective agreements) reflects a legislative intent to stimulate the conclusion of more collective agreements whose effect extends to a whole sector or sub-sector.

According to industry sources, the normal hours of work in the metalworking industry are 40 hours per week.[12]

Overtime and absolute maximum hours

Law

If working time is not divided into different workdays in advance, then work carried out over and above the legal daily normal hours qualifies as overtime.[13]

Overtime is subject to special conditions. Thus, overtime on four consecutive days shall not exceed a total of eight hours. No legal departure shall be made from this provision. The upper limit for overtime shall be 144 hours annually or, in the event of a provision in the collective agreement that departs from this, a maximum of 200 hours, or exceptionally 300 hours if it involves collective agreements which cover several employers. Overtime shall be compensated. The employee shall be normally entitled, in addition to his or her regular pay, to a 50 per cent wage premium. If, under the agreement of the parties, the employee is entitled to time off instead of receiving a wage premium, this shall not be less than the length of the overtime

---

[10] Act No. 33/1992 respecting the legal status of civil servants, dated 2 June 1992 (*Magyar Közlöny*, No. 56, 2 June 1992, pp. 1953-1964), Section 39(1).

[11] Hungarian National Office of Statistics.

[12] Union des Industries métallurgiques et minières (UIMM): "Durée du travail et congés payés en Europe de l'est", in *UIMM Social International*, No. 537, March 1995, p. 27.

[13] Labour Code 1992, op. cit., Section 127(3).

worked. The time off shall be allocated by the end of the month subsequent to the performance of the overtime work.[14]

An employee obliged to do overtime work on his or her weekly rest day shall be entitled to regular pay plus a 50 per cent wage premium and another rest day, or doubletime pay and no rest day.

In the event of standby duty, a premium corresponding to 25 per cent of regular pay is due to be paid the employee.[15]

No minor (defined to be an employee under 18 years of age) shall be assigned overtime work or standby duty, and no legal departure shall be made therefrom (not even if overtime is assigned in the interest of preventing or averting accidents, natural disasters or serious damage).

The most essential restriction on working time is that the daily working time shall not exceed 12 hours, except for positions that are partially or fully of a standby character.

In the event of work that is especially hazardous to health or particularly dangerous, such activity cannot exceed six hours in a working day. No exceptions are allowed.[16]

Practice

No official data are available as to the use of overtime since, as previously mentioned, collective agreements are not subject to compulsory registration in Hungary.

According to industry sources, maximum overtime hours in the metalworking industry are 144 annually.[17]

Rest periods

Law

A rest break shall be granted during the working day if daily working time exceeds six hours. If continuous operation or production in three or more shifts makes it impossible to interrupt working time or, in positions of a standby character or in positions in which lunch breaks can be ensured within working hours, the break shall be provided during working hours. Under such conditions, the employee shall be entitled to a rest break after every three consecutive hours of continuous work. As opposed to previous legislation, the duration of the break is not defined under the law. In practice, it usually lasts 30 to 60 minutes.

---

[14] ibid., Section 147.

[15] ibid., Section 149.

[16] ibid., Section 120(3).

[17] UIMM, op. cit., p. 27.

Daily rest shall consist of 11 hours of rest between the completion of a day's work and the commencement of the next day's work. The collective contract or the agreement of the parties involved may depart from that but, in the case of such a derogation, eight hours of rest time may be ensured.[18]

Employees are entitled to two days of rest per week and one of these shall fall on Sunday. If the work schedule makes it impossible to observe this rule, the employee shall be entitled to an uninterrupted rest period of at least 42 hours a week. This shall include a Sunday or, if the particular job is of a nature that it is performed on Sunday, another full calendar day. Rest periods may, with the exception of a position that is hazardous to health, be allocated together, biweekly or, in cases defined under the collective agreement, even monthly, provided that one rest day is allocated on Sunday.

Practice

The allocation of rest basically corresponds to the relevant legislation. Collective agreements usually depart from the standards established by law only with respect to the specification of weekly rest days. Thus, employers working under a continuous or constant work schedule often allocate rest periods together on a monthly basis.

Shop-opening hours

Law

Shop-opening hours are regulated under Act No. 1/1978 on internal trade. Article 19 of the Act only specifies a general framework, stating that shop-opening hours can be established so as to meet supply requirements, the shopping habits, the living and labour conditions of the population, and that they should take into account the living and working conditions of commercial workers as well.[19]

Local governments are entitled to regulate the opening hours of shops operating under their territorial competence by governmental decree within this legal framework.

Otherwise, no central regulation exists with respect to shop-opening hours.

Practice

With respect to shop-opening hours in practice, it is increasingly frequent for some establishments, such as food store chains, to operate under multi-shift or continuous schedules. There are an ever increasing number of 24-hour shops in Hungary.

Most shops, however, are open from 10:00 to 18:00, 10:00 to 13:00 on Saturday, while some food stores are open from 07:00 to 18:00 on both weekdays and Saturdays. Other institutions

---

[18] Labour Code 1992, op. cit., Section 123(1)-(2).

[19] Act No. 1 of 1978 on internal trade (*Magyar Közlöny*, 1978).

that provide services to the public, such as banks, are usually open from Monday to Friday from 09:00 to 17:00.

Public holidays

Law

Under Section 125 of the Labour Code, employees shall not be obliged to perform work on public holidays — 1 January, 15 March, Easter Monday, 1 May, Whitsun Monday, 20 August, 23 October, and 25 and 26 December.

On public holidays, an employee shall be given work regularly only by an employer who operates continuously and, by definition, also operates on these days.

The Minister of Labour regulates, on an annual basis, changes in the work schedule which are made according to the dates on which public holidays fall, with the proviso that no Sunday shall be declared a workday.

Employees obliged to work on a public holiday shall be entitled, in addition to their wages for the day, to their normal pay.

Practice

The Hungarian practice does not deviate from legislation in this respect.

Paid annual leave

Law

After 1 July 1992, the previous, at least formally uniform, labour legislation was replaced by three qualitatively different acts: Act No. 22/1992 (the Labour Code), Act No. 23/1992 on the legal status of civil servants, and Act No. 33/1992 on the legal status of public servants. This fact is mentioned because the acts in question regulate paid leave in different ways.

Under the Labour Code, the employee shall be entitled to paid annual leave comprising basic and supplementary leave after every calendar year spent in employment. Basic paid annual leave is 20 workdays and increases in proportion to the employee's age. The total paid leave of an employee turning 45, for example, is 30 days.[20]

Minor employees shall be entitled to five days of supplementary leave annually, up to and including the year when they turn 18.[21]

The allocation of leave shall be determined by the employer after discussion with the employee. Except in the first three months of employment, the employer shall allocate one-

[20] ibid., Sections 130-131.

[21] ibid., Section 132(1).

quarter of the basic leave at a time, as requested by the employee. The employee shall announce his or her request at least 15 days prior to the commencement of the leave. Leave shall be allocated in more than two instalments only at the employee's request.[22]

In order to avoid any abuse, leave shall be allocated in the year in which it is due. In the event of an extraordinarily justified economic interest, the employer shall allocate leave no later than 31 January of the subsequent year. If the leave cannot be granted in the year in which it is due owing to the employee's illness or another valid reason that prevents the employee from taking leave, it shall be allocated within 30 days after the elimination of the obstacle in question.[23] As an authoritative rule, leave cannot be redeemed by money.

Under the Act on the legal status of civil servants, civil servants shall be entitled to basic paid annual leave of 25 workdays. Supplementary leave shall be allocated according to the rank of the civil servant: ten and nine days for public servants with higher and secondary educational qualifications, respectively. Moreover, senior civil servants shall be entitled to additional supplementary leave. The only departure from this regulation is that, for manual workers employed by organizations that come under the jurisdiction of the Civil Servants' Act, the Labour Code applies.[24]

Under the Act on the legal status of public servants, public servants in the lower and medium public servant categories shall be entitled to basic paid annual leave of 20 workdays, and those in the higher categories, to basic leave of 21 workdays. A public servant shall be entitled to supplementary leave equalling the number of his or her given payment category (payment categories are calculated on the basis of time spent in public service employment and change after every third year).[25]

An employee, public servant or civil servant shall be entitled to his or her average salary during time spent on leave.

Practice

In practice, the duration of leave of most workers does not differ from that specified under the applicable legislation. There is a certain deviation with respect to the allocation of leave, however. It is general practice, especially among larger employers, to draw up an annual leave plan from which deviations are allowed only in extraordinarily justified cases. Collective agreements tend to grant supplementary leave to mining workers and those employed in the electric energy sector.

---

[22] ibid., Sections 134-136.

[23] ibid., Section 134(3).

[24] Act No. 33/1992, op. cit., Section 41.

[25] ibid., Sections 55-56.

Other types of leave

Law

Pursuant to the Labour Code, workers shall be entitled to various other types of leave, some of them paid, some unpaid.

Employees who, by the parents' decision, play the greater role in the raising of their child (in practice, usually the female parent) or single parents shall be entitled to two, four and seven days of supplementary leave for one child, two children and more than two children under 16 years of age, respectively.[26]

The employee shall be entitled, under his or her study contract with the employer, to free time of a limited duration to pursue his or her studies. Most importantly, the employer shall ensure that the employee has four workdays of free time to study for exams for each subject studied, and ten workdays of free time for the completion of a thesis.[27]

Upon the employee's request, the employer shall grant unpaid leave for the purpose of looking after a child after the expiration of maternity leave, up to the time when the child reaches 3 years of age, or 10 years in the case of a chronically ill or seriously disabled child or, in the event of a child's illness, for the purpose of nursing the child at home for the duration of the illness.[28]

Upon the employee's request, the employer shall grant unpaid leave for protracted nursing or home care (foreseeably exceeding 30 days) of a close relative for the duration of the care period, up to a maximum of two years.[29]

Also upon the employee's request, the employer shall grant unpaid leave for a maximum of 12 months if the employee is building a house for himself or herself out of his or her private resources.[30]

The employee shall be exempted from the obligation to work for two workdays while fulfilling a public duty or upon the death of a close relative. Justified absence from work is also recognized for the duration of compulsory medical tests and for absence on account of donating blood (four hours at least if the donation takes place outside the workplace). Justified absence from work is also permitted if the employee is unable to report to the workplace because of circumstances beyond his or her control, or on the basis of regulations pertaining to employment, or if the employer has granted the employee permission not to report to work.[31] The employee shall be entitled to his or her average salary in the above cases of exemption from work, but not when the absence is due to circumstances beyond the

[26] Labour Code 1992, op. cit., Section 132(6).

[27] ibid., Sections 110-116.

[28] ibid., Section 138(4).

[29] ibid., Section 130(1).

[30] ibid., Section 140(1).

[31] ibid., Section 107.

employee's control. If the employee is exempted from work with the employer's permission, remuneration shall be due according to their agreement.

Practice

Collective agreements often specify special types of leave in other cases, in addition to those stipulated under the Labour Code. This is due to the fact that Act No. 22/1992 eliminated many types of supplementary leave that were specified under the former Labour Code and in corresponding executive orders. In practice, collective agreements limit the simultaneous allocation of special types of leave to a certain percentage of staff.

Shift and night work

Law

Certain aspects of shift and night work are regulated under the Labour Code. Workers employed on afternoon and night shifts are, for example, legally entitled to wage premiums. Work performed between 14:00 and 22:00 qualifies as afternoon work, and the shift supplement shall be 15 per cent of the basic wage. Work performed between 22:00 and 06:00 qualifies as night work, and the shift supplement is 30 per cent of the basic wage. An employee employed under a so-called non-stop working time schedule shall be entitled to an additional 5 per cent afternoon shift supplement and an additional 10 per cent night shift supplement.[32]

Practice

In practice, collective agreements often specify afternoon and night shift supplements exceeding those specified under the law.

---

[32] ibid., Section 146.

Japan

Overview and trends

Overview

Over the last decade, the Japanese Government has made significant efforts to lower the annual hours worked. In 1986, due to a six-day, 48-hour week, extensive recourse to overtime and the short period of annual leave entitlement (which was not fully utilized),[1] actual annual working time averaged 2,104 hours, which by far surpassed levels in all other industrialized countries. This figure included 172 overtime hours.[2] The goal set in 1987 was to reduce annual hours to 1,800 through the gradual introduction of a 40-hour week. The 40-hour week was to have been fully implemented by early 1990, but this could not be achieved. Pursuing the twin goals of economic growth and a reduction in working time proved to be a difficult challenge and exceptions were granted to maintain a 44-hour working week, particularly for small-scale enterprises. These exceptions are due to expire by the end of March 1997, but it may prove necessary to further extend them. In June 1995, the 40-hour regular work-week had been achieved at 95.1 per cent of enterprises with 301 or more employees; working time remained at 45.3 per cent at firms with 31 to 100 employees and at 37.3 per cent at firms with one to 30 employees (see Table 1 for the percentage of businesses with a 40-hour regular work-week by economic activity).[3]

In addition, the Government has promoted the introduction of a five-day working week to replace the six-day week. According to a survey in 1991, some 50 per cent of all employees enjoyed a five-day working week.[4] In late 1994, the Ministry of Labour reported that 98.2 per cent of financial institutions and insurance companies had introduced the five-day work-week.[5] As of 1994, the five-day week was required by law in the public service.[6]

Employees are often required to work overtime. There have been reports of overwork causing the death of workers (in Japanese, "karoshi").[7] There is no statutory limit on the number of overtime hours that can be performed, except for women working in industry. Efforts to reduce annual working hours have not included the introduction of statutory limits on over-

---

[1] The right to paid sick leave has only recently been included in collective agreements. However, annual leave days are often used instead.

[2] Union des Industries métallurgiques et minières (UIMM): "Durée du travail annuelle dans l'industrie", in *UIMM Social International*, No. 541, July 1995, p. 33.

[3] Japanese Trade Union Confederation: *The spring struggle for a better living 1996; RENGO white paper 1996: Challenge to change* (Tokyo, 1996), p. 60.

[4] Japan Institute of Labour: *Japanese working profile: Labor statistics 1993-94* (Tokyo, 1992).

[5] "Bank staffers lose bid to be paid for longer workday", in *Mainichi Daily News*, 23 December 1993.

[6] Act No. 33 concerning hours of work and leave, etc., of national public employees in the regular service, dated 15 June 1994 (*Kampoo*, No. 1420, 15 June 1994, pp. 2-5) [LLD 1994-JPN 1].

[7] "The Supreme Court's Hitachi decision on the duty to work overtime", in *Japan Labor Bulletin*, Vol. 31, No. 5, May 1992, p. 7.

time work, although the Ministry of Labour has issued administrative guidelines on maximum overtime hours.

Table 1. Percentage of businesses with a 40-hour regular work-week

Economic activity	301 or more employees	101-300 employees	30-100 employees	10-30 employees	1-9 employees
Manufacturing	96.7	63.7	34.9	25.9	27.1
Mining	50.0	47.4	26.1	6.4	5.3
Construction	97.8	36.8	15.6	15.6	7.9
Transportation	47.7	27.0	19.3	27.5	20.9
Cargo handling	65.2	53.2	35.6	30.0	36.4
Forestry	100.0	12.5	18.8	23.9	24.4
Commerce	95.8	71.0	47.6	32.5	28.5
Banking/advertisement	100.0	100.0	100.0	95.8	82.5
Movies and theatres	100.0	81.8	58.1	46.8	40.4
Communications	100.0	100.0	100.0	82.7	91.8
Education and research	100.0	72.6	55.5	49.6	54.7
Health	99.8	67.5	57.3	49.7	56.0
Entertainment and leisure	85.1	26.0	27.2	29.8	42.6
Cleaning/slaughtering	57.1	36.1	28.7	46.2	40.4
Other businesses	98.9	83.9	69.1	67.6	66.8

Statistics indicate that the number of annual hours of work has fallen considerably since measures to reduce working time were introduced (see Figure 1). However, caution must be exercised in interpreting this decline, which was influenced by several factors. Increasing or decreasing overtime is used to respond to fluctuations in demand.[8] The decline in the total actual working hours from 2,104 hours in 1986 to 1,894 hours in 1994 can be partly attributed to a reduction in the number of overtime hours worked.[9] Paid overtime declined by 17.4 per

---

[8] A recent study confirms that there is great reliance on working hour adjustments in response to cyclical changes in demand in Japan. M. Hashimoto: "Aspects of labor market adjustments in Japan", in *Journal of Labor Economics*, Vol. 11, No. 1, Part 1: Essays in honor of Jacob Mincer, January 1993, pp. 136-161.

[9] UIMM, op. cit.

cent in April 1994 compared with April 1993.[10] While the number of paid (reported) overtime hours have declined, unpaid overtime remains at high levels.[11] According to a survey in 1993, non-agricultural workers put in an average of 2,267 hours.[12] More recent statistics indicate that overtime hours are again on the rise. In the manufacturing sector, which reacts quickly to changes in the economy, the average monthly amount of overtime increased by 5.1 per cent in September 1994 to 12.5 hours, following a previous 3.6 per cent growth in August 1994.[13] The trend continued into the first quarter of 1995, reaffirming the preference of manufacturers to use overtime rather than create new jobs in response to increased production requirements in periods of economic recovery.[14]

Figure 1. Annual hours of work in industry, 1985-1994[15]

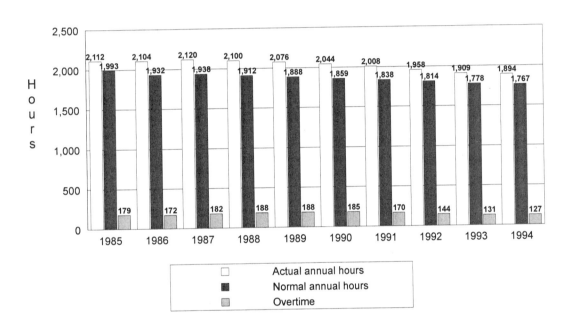

In 1987, the law was revised to allow for the averaging of working hours over a period of one month. With the revision of the Labour Standards Act in 1994, it became possible to average hours over a period of one week, a quarter or a year.

[10] R. Curtain: "Japan's response to the recession: Lessons for Australia?", in *Australian Bulletin of Labour*, Vol. 19, No. 3, September 1993, pp. 184-198.

[11] "The Supreme Court's Hitachi decision ...", op. cit.

[12] "The vanishing gift of overtime pay", in *Asahi Evening News*, 5 January 1995.

[13] "September overtime stays level", in *Mainichi Daily News*, 1 November 1994.

[14] K. Sado: "Labor and economic indices in the first quarter of 1995", in *Labour Issues Quarterly*, No. 28, Summer 1995, p. 20.

[15] UIMM, op. cit.

For example, a manufacturer of air conditioners with a workforce of 9,000 uses a seasonal work schedule. The workers put in a nine-hour day during the spring and summer periods and an eight-hour day during the autumn and winter periods. In order to keep the weekly hours of work within the statutory annual limit, the workers are offered a two-week holiday twice a year.[16]

A "free-time system" was introduced in 1990 in a company employing 500 research and development workers. Employees decide how many hours they work, and the company evaluates them according to their performance and not by the number of hours. They are required to work at least one hour per day, and are paid an allowance equivalent to 30 hours of overtime in addition to their basic salary, regardless of the actual number of hours worked. In addition, the company pays a performance-linked incentive bonus every six months. Another company devised a system of hiring employees to work nine months per year. They work for five days a week for nine months and then get three months off. Their salary amounts to between 84 and 92 per cent of that of regular employees.[17]

Normal hours of work

Law

Since 1977, the normal working time is eight hours a day and 40 hours a week. However, the weekly working time for large sectors of the labour market is 44 hours (see Table 2 below), due to the granting of exceptions to the law. These exceptions will expire on 31 March 1997.[18] Earlier exceptions allowing for a 46-hour week and even a 48-hour week expired on 1 April 1995.

[16] "Daikin to introduce variable working hours system for the year at production division", in *Japan Labor Bulletin*, Vol. 34, No. 2, February 1995, p. 3.

[17] "The vanishing gift of overtime pay", op. cit.

[18] Labour Standards Law, Act No. 49, dated 5 April 1947 (*Kampoo*, No. 303, 7 April 1947, p. 1), as amended up to Act No.79, dated 1 July 1993 (*Kampoo*, No. 107, 1 July 1993, pp. 2-6) [LS 1947-Jap.3; 1987-Jap.1], Chapter IV, Section 32.

Table 2. List of exceptions to the 40-hour work-week[19]

Type of industry	Number of employees				
	over 301	101-300	31-100	10-30	1-9
Manufacturing	40	44	44	44	46
Mining	44	44	44	44	46
Construction	40	44	44	44	46
Transportation	44	44	44	44	46
Cargo handling	44	44	44	44	46
Forestry	44	44	44	44	44
Commerce	40	44	44	44	46
Banking and advertising	40	40	40	40	40
Movies and theatres	40	40	44	44	46
Communications	40	40	40	40	40
Education and research	40	44	44	44	44
Insurance and health	40	44	44	44	46
Entertainment and leisure	40	44	44	44	46
Cleaning and slaughtering	44	44	44	44	46
Government offices	40	40	40	40	40
Other businesses	40	40	44	44	44

Young workers

Minors under 15 years of age may not be employed. Children under 15 and above 12 may be employed in light work, on condition that it is not injurious to their health and welfare, that working hours are outside of school hours, and that the permission of the Chief of the Labour Standards Office has been granted. Children under 12 years of age may be employed in motion picture production and dramatic performance companies only with the permission of the Chief of the Labour Standards Office.[20] The maximum working time for minors is 40

[19] Japanese Confederation of Labour, op. cit., p. 33..

[20] Labour Standards Law, op. cit., Section 56.

hours per week, including school hours, and the maximum daily hours of work are eight hours, including school hours. Minors are not allowed to work overtime or on holidays.[21]

Practice

Official statistics show a considerable decline in actual hours of work. In the industrial sector, annual working hours declined from 2,149 hours in 1987 to 1,961 hours in 1993. Comparative figures for the United States were 1,912 hours and 1,904 hours, and for Germany, 1,716 hours and 1,641 hours.[22] A Ministry of Labour survey conducted in 1994 indicated that scheduled weekly working hours in 1993 amounted to 39 hours and 51 minutes on average. This was reportedly the first time that scheduled working hours were less than 40 since the Ministry started compiling statistics.[23] However, both these surveys were based on businesses with more than 30 employees. As the exceptions to the 40-hour working week have been particularly frequent for small-scale enterprises, it may be assumed that the reduction of working time has not been as marked for these enterprises.

Overtime and absolute maximum hours

Law

According to the Labour Standards Law, overtime may be performed in the event of *force majeure* or "unavoidable temporary need".[24] Such a requirement, however, is subject to the approval of the Labour Standards Office. Overtime may also be provided for by way of a written agreement with the employees' trade union or a collective agreement, which must be submitted to the Labour Standards Office.[25] However, the Labour Standards Law does not restrict overtime hours of managers, supervisors and employees handling confidential matters, be they male or female.[26]

There is no statutory limit on overtime hours that may be worked by men. However, for employees engaged in dangerous work, the law provides for a maximum of two hours of overtime per day.[27] The Labour Standards Law, however, places a mandatory restriction on overtime by women. Female employees in manufacturing, mining, construction, transporta-

---

[21] ibid., Section 60.

[22] UIMM: "Durée annuelle du travail des ouvriers de l'industrie: Comparaison internationale au 1er novembre 1994", in *UIMM Social International*, No. 537, March 1995.

[23] "Working conditions and the labor market: Shorter hours progress", in *Japan Labor Bulletin*, Vol. 34, No. 1, January 1995, p. 1; "Japan's workweek slips below 40 hours", in *International Herald Tribune*, 13 October 1994. According to the latter source, the Government figures were based on a survey of 5,300 businesses with more than 30 employees.

[24] Labour Standards Law, op. cit., Section 33.

[25] ibid., Section 36.

[26] ibid., Section 41.

[27] ibid., Section 36.

tion and freight industries are limited to no more than six hours of overtime per week or 150 hours of overtime per year. They may not work on rest days. For women who work in accounting or financial positions in these industries, the limit is no more than 12 hours over a two-week period. Women working in other industries are limited to no more than 24 hours of overtime over a four-week period and 150 hours over the course of one year. They may only work once a month on their rest day.[28]

The minimum compensation for overtime work is a 25 per cent premium in addition to the ordinary wage rate.[29]

Practice

It is uncommon for employers to submit forms to the Labour Standards Office requesting approval for employees to work overtime. Most often, companies simply request employees to work overtime and pay them overtime wages. If work is required on a rest day, employees usually receive rest day wages (35 per cent premium) and are allowed to take the equivalent time off during another working day.[30]

[28] ibid.; Ordinance No. 3 promulgating standards applicable to women's work, dated 27 January 1986 (*Kampoo*, No. 17,685, 27 January 1986, p. 4), Section 3.

[29] Labour Standards Law, op. cit., Section 37.

[30] ibid., Section 33.

Table 3. Hours of work per week by major divisions of economic activity[31]

Major division	1984	1985	1986	1987	1988	1989	1990	1991	1992	1993	1994
Mining and quarrying ①	44.3	43.6	43.2	42.3	43.8	43.7	42.8	41.3	40.8	42.0	41.5
Manufacturing ①	41.7	41.5	41.1	41.3	41.8	41.4	40.8	40.0	38.8	37.7	37.6
Electricity, gas and water ②	43.6	43.6	43.5	44.0	43.9	43.5	42.3	42.9	41.8	40.7	---
Construction ①	43.6	43.5	43.8	44.0	43.9	43.2	42.6	41.6	40.7	40.1	39.6
Trades, restaurants and hotels ②③	49.4	49.6	49.5	49.3	49.1	48.6	47.6	46.7	45.6	44.9	---
Transport, storage and communication ①	41.7	42.6	42.6	43.3	43.8	43.5	42.9	41.6	40.8	40.5	40.1
Financing, insurance, real estate and business services ②④	46.9	47.4	47.1	47.5	47.2	44.8	43.7	43.0	42.3	41.8	---
Community, social and personal services ②	44.4	44.5	44.4	44.5	44.4	44.0	43.5	43.0	42.2	41.5	---
Total (all non-agricultural activities) ①⑤	40.7	40.6	40.4	40.6	40.6	40.2	39.5	38.8	37.9	36.8	36.6

① Establishment surveys of employees. ② Civilian labour force employed. ③ Excluding hotels.
④ Excluding business services. ⑤ Including business services and hotels.

Rest

Law

If daily working hours exceed six hours, employees are entitled to a 45-minutes break. A one-hour break must be given for work beyond eight hours. The break is not counted as working time. It may be divided and offered at any time of the day. Normally, the break should be given to all employees at the same time.[32] One day of weekly rest must be given (legally any day of the week). This does not apply to employers who grant four or more days of rest during a four-week period.[33] For work performed on rest days, workers are entitled to a 35 per cent

---

[31] Bureau of Statistics, International Labour Office [hours actually worked; employees].

[32] Labour Standards Law, op. cit., Section 34.

[33] ibid., Sections 32 and 35.

premium payment in addition to their normal hourly wage.[34] Public service employees are, subject to certain exceptions, legally entitled to Saturdays and Sundays off.[35]

Practice

Sunday is the traditional day of weekly rest. Sixty-five per cent of Japanese companies have a five-day working week.[36]

Shop-opening hours

Law

There are no generally applicable provisions. However, regulations in force require large retail stores to close at 20:00. Exceptionally, stores may remain open one hour longer for up to 60 days per year. Since May 1994, the number of days of obligatory closing was reduced from 44 to 24 days per year.[37] Regulations on opening times for banks provides that business hours be from 09:00 to 15:00.[38]

Practice

It is common for shops to remain open until 20:00, in particular in the metropolitan areas.[39]

Public holidays

Law

There are 14 national public holidays, as follows: 1 January (New Year's Day), 15 January (Adults Day), 11 February (Foundation Day), 20 or 21 March [Vernal (Spring) Equinox Day], 29 April (Green's Day), 3 May (Constitutional Memorial Day), 4 May (Golden Week Holiday), 5 May (Children's Day), 15 September (Aged People's Day), 22 or 23 September [Autumnal (Fall) Equinox Day], 10 October (Sports Day), 3 November (Culture Day), 23 November (Labor Day), 23 December (Emperor's Birthday). If one of these days falls on a Sunday, the following Monday is a holiday.

[34] ibid., Section 20.

[35] Act No. 33 of 1994, op. cit., Section 6.

[36] CCH Japan Limited: *Japan employers' handbook* (Tokyo, November 1994), para. 35-020, p. 40,501, citing statistics given by the Ministry of Labour.

[37] Information provided to the ILO by the Ministry of Labour, July 1995. "'Regular holiday' getting the ax at department stores", in *Mainichi Daily News*, 12 July 1994.

[38] Ministry of Labour, op. cit.

[39] "'Regular holiday' getting the ax at department stores", op. cit.

Public service employees are legally entitled to time off during the national (public) holidays,[40] as well as the days from 29 December to 3 January of the following year (Year End or New Year's holiday).[41]

Work on public holidays entitles an employee to premium pay of 35 per cent.[42]

Practice

It is not legally binding to give time off for public holidays in the private sector, but most companies give time off or rest day wages for work performed on public holidays.[43] Most companies also give additional leave during the "Golden Week" (early May), as well as several days at the end of the year.[44]

Paid annual leave

Law

Employees who have worked continuously for one year and have reported for work at least 80 per cent of the time are entitled to ten paid annual leave days. As length of service increases, the number of paid annual leave days increases by one day each year, up to a maximum of 20 days.[45]

Practice

The number of paid annual leave days increased by one day during the period 1988 to 1993. A slight increase in the rate of use of paid annual leave is also noticeable (from 50 per cent in 1988 to 56.1 per cent in 1993), although it remains relatively low.[46] The trend seems to be to encourage more use of paid annual leave days. In order to pursue the official governmental policy to reduce working hours, companies seem to prefer to offer extra paid annual leave days rather than cutting daily working hours.[47]

---

[40] *Japan employers' handbook*, op. cit., para. 35-020, pp. 40,501-40,502, citing to Act No. 178 concerning national holidays of 1948.

[41] Act No. 33 of 1994, op. cit., Section 14.

[42] Act No. 79 of 1993, op. cit.

[43] Wyatt: *1994/95 employment terms and conditions — Asia/Pacific* (Hong Kong, 1993), p. 119.

[44] *Japan employers' handbook*, op. cit., Section 35-020, p. 40,501; Ministry of Labour, op. cit.

[45] Labour Standards Law, op. cit., Section 36.

[46] Ministry of Labour, op. cit.

[47] "Days off are becoming more compulsory", in *Asahi Evening News*, 4 January 1995.

Other types of leave

Law

A law was passed on 5 June 1995, which entitles employees to family leave of three months. The law, which will enter into force in April 1999, is designed so that employees can care for their elderly parents or other family members (a spouse, a spouse's aged parents or children). Employers will not be allowed to refuse requests for the leave or dismiss employees for taking it.[48]

Practice

Most companies give their employees leave for certain occasions, such as for an employee's marriage, the birth of a child or the death of a close relative.

According to a Ministry of Labour survey (reported in August 1995), some 52 per cent of companies with 500 or more employees and 14 per cent of firms with less than 100 employees have introduced a family leave programme entitling employees to take leave to care for aged parents or other family members. Very few small-scale firms have adopted such a scheme.[49]

Shift and night work

Law

There are no generally applicable provisions for shift work. Women are generally prohibited from working between the hours of 22:00 and 05:00. There are, however, numerous exceptions, such as in health care and hotel and catering work.

Women may work until 22:30 in enterprises with shift systems.

[48] "New family leave bill becomes law", in *Japan Labor Bulletin*, Vol. 34, No. 8, August 1995, p. 4.

[49] ibid.

Korea, Republic of

Overview and trends

Overview

In the Republic of Korea, working time issues are determined by collective bargaining and by statute, although legislation appears to be the more important instrument in determining generally applicable standards. The most important labour law with respect to working time issues is the Labour Standards Law, which establishes, inter alia, minimum standards for normal hours of work, overtime, rest requirements, standards for work on public holidays, and paid annual leave.[1] In 1989, the weekly hours of work were reduced from 48 to 44 hours per week through amendment of the Labour Standards Law.[2] Weekly hours of work in some sectors are frequently higher than 44 hours per week because of overtime (see below under **Overtime and absolute maximum hours**).[3] Another interesting aspect of practice is that Korean workers normally take only a relatively small proportion of their legal entitlement to paid annual leave (see below under **Paid annual leave**).

Collective bargaining agreements take precedence over standards established by legislation only if such agreements increase benefits or protection afforded. As of December 1992, the rate of unionization of permanent workers was 19.8 per cent and the number of organized establishments has increased significantly since the late 1980s. Collective agreements tend to be reached at the enterprise level and, therefore, collective bargaining tends to be decentralized. In a number of cases, trade unions have succeeded in reducing normal weekly hours of work to 42, and in some sectors a five-day week has been introduced (see below under **Normal hours of work**).[4] It has been suggested by one observer that a 40-hour work-week will eventually be introduced in Korea through collective bargaining in the private sector.[5]

Trends

Although actual hours of work have decreased significantly during the period 1984 to 1993, having been reduced from 52.4 to 47.5 hours per week in all non-agricultural activities combined and from 54.3 to 48.9 hours per week in the manufacturing sector (see Table 2), these figures are still relatively high in comparison with hours in developed industrialized countries. According to one source, female workers and manual workers in the manufacturing sector have enjoyed greater reductions in weekly working hours than other employees, and the reduction has been more rapid in establishments employing more than 500 employees

---

[1] Labour Standards Law, Act No. 286, dated 10 May 1953 (*Labour Laws of Korea*, 1991), as amended up to Act No. 4220, dated 13 January 1990 (*Labour Laws of Korea*, 1992).

[2] ibid.

[3] Y.B. Park: *Labor in Korea* (Seoul, Korea Labor Institute, 1993), pp. 67-68.

[4] Wyatt: *1994/95 employment terms and conditions — Asia/Pacific* (Hong Kong, 1993), p. 159.

[5] ibid., pp. 150 and 159.

than in small and medium-sized enterprises.[6] There appear to be two reasons for reductions in hours of work. First, the amendment of the Labour Standards Law in 1989, which reduced normal weekly hours of work from 48 to 44, had a significant influence. Secondly, workers, especially in large enterprises, had indicated a preference for more leisure time and less overtime work.[7]

There appears to be a tendency for collective bargaining to play a more important role in fixing the working conditions of workers.[8] The Korean Government has also envisaged the amendment of labour legislation to reduce the direct intervention of the state in industrial relations and to allow for more flexibility with respect to working conditions. To do so, the Labour Law Research Committee, comprising representatives of workers, employers and public bodies, was set up to discuss amendments to labour legislation to introduce more flexibility for the arrangement of working hours.[9]

According to a member of the Federation of Korea Trade Unions (FKTU), the Korea Employers Federation (KEF) has favoured the introduction of flexible working hours, and the KEF has consequently argued for the revision of the Labour Standards Law.[10] The FKTU, however, has taken the position that priority should be given to the reduction, and not to the flexible arrangement, of working time. There appear to be three reasons for the position of the FKTU. First, Korean workers still have relatively long working hours and would like to have further reductions. Secondly, it is feared that a system allowing for the flexible scheduling of work could eliminate or reduce payment for overtime, which has traditionally been a significant component of workers' wages. And thirdly, Korean workers have already had an unsatisfactory experience with a flexible working hours system, which was adopted in December 1980 but subsequently repealed in November 1987. It appears that the flexible hours provisions were repealed because, in practice, they resulted in longer working hours and reduced rest periods.[11]

---

[6] Park, op. cit., pp. 65-68.

[7] M.S. Lim, Ministry of Labour: *Report on the rules and distribution of working hours in Korea*, working paper presented at the Asian Tripartite Workshop on Working Time Arrangements (Bangkok, 18-22 July 1994), p. 9.

[8] Park, op. cit., pp. 89-100.

[9] Lim, op. cit., pp. 13-14.

[10] K.O. Chung, Federation of Korean Trade Unions: *Working hour arrangements in Korea*, working paper presented at the Asian Tripartite Workshop on Working Time Arrangements (Bangkok, 18-22 July 1994), pp. 2-4.

[11] ibid., pp. 2-4.; see also Lim, op. cit., pp. 1-4.

Normal hours of work

Law

The Labour Standards Law provides that normal hours of work shall not exceed eight hours per day and 44 hours per week.[12] The hours of work specified in the law exclude rest periods. This legal provision covers all businesses and workplaces with five or more permanent workers. However, it may partially apply, according to Presidential Decree, to businesses and workplaces with four permanent workers or less. The law does not apply to businesses or workplaces which employ only relatives living in the same household or which have only domestic employees.[13] Other exceptions to the law apply to workers engaged in (1) cultivation of land, reclamation work, seeding and planting, picking, or other agricultural and forestry work; (2) livestock breeding, collection of marine products, regeneration of marine products, or cattle breeding, sericulture and fishery; (3) supervisory work, or intermittently assigned work approved by the Labour Relations Commission; and (4) other work as may be provided by Presidential Decrees.[14]

Workers in special or difficult working conditions

Workers engaged in underground work or other harmful or dangerous work — as specified by Presidential Decree — are not to work more than six hours per day and 34 hours per week.[15] Subject to approval by the Minister of Labour, these hours may be extended up to two hours per day or 12 hours per week.

Young workers

Young workers between the ages of 13 and 18 are not to work more than seven hours per day and 42 hours per week. Subject to agreement between the young person and the employer, hours of work may be extended one hour per day and six hours per week.[16] Such young workers are prohibited from engaging in any kind of work detrimental to morality or harmful to health, and may not work inside a pit.[17] Young workers are, in principle, forbidden to engage in night work or work on public holidays unless the person consents and approval has been obtained from the Minister of Labour[18] (see below under **Shift and night work**).

[12] Labour Standards Law, op. cit., Section 42(1).

[13] ibid., Section 10.

[14] ibid., Section 49.

[15] ibid., Section 43.

[16] ibid., Section 55.

[17] ibid., Sections 51 and 58.

[18] ibid., Section 56.

Practice

Normal working hours are usually Monday through Friday, with a half-day on Saturday. Some manufacturing firms have adopted a system of a biweekly alternating schedule, with five days of work scheduled in one week and six days of work of eight hours a day the following week. In a number of cases, trade unions have succeeded in reducing normal weekly hours of work to 42.[19] There are a limited number of enterprises which have introduced a five-day work-week. These enterprises are found mainly in the health sector, the electronics sector, and the wholesale and retail trade sector.[20] Normal weekly hours of work for public servants are 44 hours per week from March to October and 39 hours per week the rest of the year.[21] (See Tables 1, 2 and 3.)

Table 1. Hours of work per week by major divisions of economic activity[22]

Major division	1984	1985	1986	1987	1988	1989	1990	1991	1992	1993
Mining and quarrying	42.4	41.4	40.8	39.3	39.4	37.9	36.2	39.5	39.4	---
Manufacturing	54.3	53.8	54.7	54.0	52.6	50.7	49.8	49.3	48.7	48.9
Electricity, gas and water	49.4	50.0	50.4	50.0	50.9	48.2	47.8	48.6	49.1	---
Construction	49.1	49.0	48.6	48.1	47.9	46.6	45.8	45.6	46.0	---
Trades, restaurants and hotels	49.9	50.0	49.7	49.5	49.6	48.0	47.5	47.8	47.5	---
Transport, storage and communication	53.4	53.2	52.8	51.8	51.6	50.3	48.8	48.7	48.2	---
Financing, insurance, real estate and business services	45.9	45.8	45.2	45.3	45.9	44.5	43.6	44.2	44.3	---
Community, social and personal services	46.8	46.6	46.2	46.1	46.6	45.0	44.5	44.6	44.7	---
Total (all non-agricultural activities)	52.4	51.9	52.5	51.9	51.1	49.2	48.2	47.9	47.5	47.5

[19] Wyatt, op. cit., p. 159.

[20] Lim, op. cit., p. 13 [according to a survey conducted by the Ministry of Labour in July 1991 of 19,326 companies with 50 or more workers].

[21] ILO: *Report I: General report*, Joint Committee on the Public Service, Fifth Session, Geneva, 1994, document no. JCPS/5/1994, p. 26.

[22] Bureau of Statistics, International Labour Office [employees; hours actually worked].

Table 2. Frequency and distribution of the five-day work-week[23]

Year	Number of companies			Number of workers		
	Total	5-day week	%	Total	5-day week	%
1989	18,552	148	0.8	3,612,789	116,627	3.2
1991	19,326	217	1.1	3,657,672	126,121	3.4

Table 3. Hours of work per week in non-agricultural activities by sex and occupation[24]

Year	Sex		Occupation	
	Male	Female	Manual	Non-manual
1984	51.8	53.4	55.1	49.3
1985	51.5	52.8	54.6	49.0
1986	51.9	53.6	55.8	48.8
1987	51.5	52.6	54.9	48.5
1988	51.0	51.2	53.4	48.5
1989	49.2	49.2	51.5	46.9
1990	48.2	48.4	50.9	45.8
1991	48.7	47.4	50.8	45.8
1992	47.7	47.3	50.4	45.7
1993	47.7	47.1	---	---

[23] Lim, op. cit., p. 13.

[24] Park, op. cit., p. 66.

Overtime and absolute maximum hours

Law

Workers may work up to 12 hours of overtime per week, subject to agreement between the parties concerned.[25] With the approval of the Ministry of Labour and the agreement of the worker concerned, these limits may be extended when a special situation arises. In the case of an emergency when advance approval is impossible, working time may be extended, but an *ex post facto* approval must be obtained without delay.[26] When such extended hours are worked because there is an emergency situation, the Minister of Labour may order compensatory time off corresponding to the duration of such extended working hours if it is subsequently determined that the extension of working hours was inappropriate.[27] Special exceptions are applicable to hours of work and rest requirements, if the undertaking falls in one of the categories of activity considered as in the public interest (see below under **Rest**).

Overtime work is to be paid at the regular rate of pay plus a 50 per cent premium.[28]

Workers in special or difficult working conditions

Normal hours of work for underground or other harmful or dangerous work which are specified by Presidential Decree are limited to six hours per day and 34 hours per week, and may be extended up to two hours per day and 12 hours per week with the approval of the Minister of Labour.[29]

Women and young workers

Women workers may work overtime no more than two hours per day, six hours per week, or 150 hours per year.[30] Overtime work for young persons between 13 and 18 years of age may be no more than one hour a day and six hours per week.[31]

Practice

Substantial overtime work occurs in many sectors of economic activity in Korea, with the result that many Korean employees work relatively long weekly hours when compared to hours of work in developed industrialized countries (see Table 2). Average weekly overtime

---

[25] Labour Standards Law, op. cit., Section 42(1).

[26] ibid., Section 42(3).

[27] ibid., Section 42(4).

[28] ibid., Section 46.

[29] ibid., Section 43.

[30] ibid., Section 57.

[31] ibid., Section 55.

in all non-agricultural sectors of economic activity has decreased somewhat since 1980, but is still relatively high at six hours per week (see Table 4).

Table 4. Average weekly overtime[32]

Year	Hours of overtime per week
1980	7.2
1981	7.5
1982	7.4
1983	7.8
1984	7.8
1985	7.6
1986	7.9
1987	7.8
1988	7.2
1989	6.6
1990	6.5
1991	6.3
1992	6.0
1993	5.8
1994	5.8

Rest

Law

The law provides for a rest break of not less than 30 minutes for every four hours of work, and not less than one hour for every eight hours during the course of work.[33]

[32] Ministry of Labour: *The Labour*, No. 10, 1995, p. 72.

[33] Labour Standards Law, op. cit., Section 44.

Periods of rest may deviate from the established standards if the undertaking falls in one of the following categories of activity, which are considered as in the public interest: (1) transportation, sales and storage of goods, and finance and insurance; (2) movie production and entertainment, communication, educational research and investigation, and advertisement; (3) medical treatment, attendance, sanitation, hotel and restaurant services, burning and cleaning, and hairdressing; or (4) other business as specified by the Minister of Labour.[34] An employer may alter rest breaks when the enterprise falls under one of the categories mentioned as an exception in the legal provisions on hours of work (see above under **Normal hours of work**).

The law requires that workers be granted at least one or more days off each week.[35]

Public holidays

Law

There are 18 public holidays in Korea, although only one public holiday — Labour Day, 1 May — is required by law to be paid. The public holidays are: New Year's Day (two days), Lunar New Year (three days, depending on lunar calendar), Independence Day (1 March), Arbour Day (5 April), Labour Day (1 May), Children's Day (5 May), Buddha's Birthday (one day, depending on lunar calendar), Memorial Day (6 June), Constitution Day (17 July), National Liberation Day (15 August), Thanksgiving Days (three days, depending on lunar calendar), National Foundation Day (3 October), and Christmas (25 December).[36]

The law requires that a worker receive his or her regular rate of pay plus 50 per cent premium pay for work performed on a public holiday.[37]

Practice

These public holidays used to be applied to public employees only, but paid public holidays are granted in a number of collective agreements in many private sector companies, especially in large enterprises. However, it is still relatively common for workers in small and medium-sized enterprises to work on public holidays and receive premium pay.[38]

---

[34] ibid., Section 47-2.

[35] ibid., Section 45.

[36] Lim, op. cit.; Wyatt, op. cit., p. 159.

[37] Labour Standards Law, op. cit., Section 46.

[38] Park, op. cit., p. 69.

Paid annual leave

Law

In Korea, the notion of paid annual leave is somewhat complex because there are two types of leave which, taken together, form the equivalent of paid annual leave in other countries. The two kinds of leave provided include what is actually termed paid annual leave and monthly leave, which in essence is also a form of paid annual leave.

— *Paid annual leave.* Paid annual leave of ten days is granted to a worker who has one full year of service without absence, or eight days if the worker has been present for at least 90 per cent of the time during his or her year of service. In addition to the basic paid annual leave, an employer is required to grant one additional day of paid annual leave for each consecutive year of service until the employee is entitled to a total of 20 days altogether.[39]

— *Paid monthly leave.* The law also entitles an employee to one day of paid leave per month, which may be accumulated.[40]

— *Cumulative effect of legal provisions.* Taking paid annual leave and paid monthly leave together, workers are legally entitled to a minimum of 22 days of paid annual leave (broadly defined) per year and a maximum of 32 days after ten years of continuous service with the same employer.

Practice

A sample survey of 360 enterprises in 1989 showed that employees actually only use three days on average out of their combined paid annual and monthly leave entitlement. The reason for this phenomenon is that many employees are paid premium wages when they work on days on which they are entitled to paid leave, and such employees appear to prefer higher wages to free time. This is particularly the case in small enterprises. In most Korean establishments, three to six days of paid special summer leave are granted in addition. Most establishments provide this special leave without deducting it from the legally stipulated paid annual leave. According to the same survey, four days of paid special summer leave are taken on average.[41]

---

[39] Labour Standards Law, op. cit., Section 48.

[40] ibid., Section 47.

[41] Park, op. cit., pp. 68-69.

Other types of leave

Law

There are no other generally applicable provisions for other types of leave. For public servants, leave for family events varies from one to seven days, depending on the nature of the event.[42]

Practice

According to some collective agreements, employees are entitled to leave on the date of the anniversary of the founding of a company. They may also be entitled to leave for bereavement and special personal or family occasions.[43]

Shift and night work

Law

There are no generally applicable provisions on shift work. Night work, which is defined as work between 22:00 and 06:00, is required by law to be compensated with premium pay of 50 per cent over the worker's regular pay.[44] It is also forbidden to employ young workers and women workers to perform night work.[45]

---

[42] ILO, op. cit., p. 38.

[43] Lim, op. cit., p. 5.

[44] Labour Standards Law, op. cit., Section 46.

[45] ibid., Section 56.

Mexico

Overview and trends

Overview.

Mexico is the world's 13th largest economy and a major participant in world trade. The population is relatively young, with 58 per cent aged under 25 and less than 5 per cent aged 65 or over. Between 1979 and 1993, the service sector expanded, while the industrial sector declined, but employment in the *maquiladoras* (plants assembling duty-free imported equipment and materials for re-export) grew, accounting for about 10 per cent of employment in the manufacturing sector. The proportion of wage and salary workers declined from 62.9 per cent to 56.9 per cent. A relatively low open unemployment rate reflects the large number of persons in unstable, marginal and largely unregulated work in the informal sector or in contract work.

Article 123 of the Constitution[1] guarantees to all persons the right to work that is socially useful and that is carried out in conditions which respect their dignity. It calls for the adoption of laws to regulate conditions of work and sets out certain principles, such as equal pay for equal work, as well as fairly detailed standards regarding, *inter alia*, hours of work, night work and overtime compensation.

The current legislation, the Federal Labour Act,[2] came into force in 1970. It regulates working time along the provisions of Article 123 of the Constitution. It also requires employers to enter into collective agreements with the trade union to which their workers belong; such agreements are to include, among others, provisions regarding hours of work, rest and leave.[3] In the absence of a collective agreement, a written note of the conditions of work is to be drawn up in duplicate, for the records of the employer and the worker. This document must include, in particular, information on daily hours of work, rest days and paid annual leave.[4] Except for the safety and health standards, the provisions of the Act do not apply to family undertakings.[5]

The National Administrative Office of the Commission on Labor Cooperation, set up under the North American Free Trade Agreement (NAFTA), is to provide to the Commission

[1] Political Constitution of the United States of Mexico, dated 5 February 1917 (*Diario Oficial*, 1917), as amended up to Decree, dated 20 October 1993 (*Diario Oficial*, No. 18, 25 October 1993, p. 2).

[2] Federal Labour Act, dated 2 December 1969 (*Diario Oficial*, No. 26, 1 April 1970, p. 1; errata, ibid., No. 51, 30 April 1970, p. 2; errata: ibid., No. 29, 5 June 1970, p. 16), as amended up to 16 December 1987 (*Diario Oficial*, No. 14, 21 January 1988, p. 19) [LS 1969-Mex. 1; 1973-Mex.2; 1975-Mex.1; 1979-Mex.1].

[3] ibid., Sections 387 and 391.

[4] ibid., Sections 24-25.

[5] ibid., Section 352.

information on national labour law and its implementation. However, working time is not one of the areas where failure to observe national laws would result in trade sanctions.[6]

Trends

The Mexican economy has undergone significant changes over the past 15 years, including the privatization of many concerns, economic restructuring and technological innovation. The North American Free Trade Agreement (NAFTA) opens up a large export market, but heightens the need for productivity and enterprise efficiency. In this general context, many provisions of the Federal Labour Act appear outdated. Employers, in particular, regret the rigidity of the law, which, they feel, hampers the development of truly competitive enterprises. Since 1990, the need to revise the Act has been the subject of debate, although no agreement as to the scope of such a revision has been reached so far, and no actual proposed bill has reached Parliament.

Led by the Confederación Patronal de la República Mexicana (COPAMEX — Employers' Confederation of the Mexican Republic), employers favour a range of measures that would enable them to adapt the productive capacity of enterprises to the level and composition of demand. Flexibility is sought essentially on three fronts: (a) recruitment and dismissal, (b) remuneration and (c) working time.

Regarding the latter, the objective of employers is to achieve a more efficient use of the hours of work available and to minimize the need for costly overtime. Employers have thus called for the development of casual work, part-time work and temporary work, while being strongly opposed to daily or weekly limits on working time in the legislation. In order to respond to workload fluctuation, they would like to be able to reduce hours of work as, and when, necessary, with a corresponding reduction in pay. COPAMEX has proposed the introduction of measures, such as a reduction in the number of public holidays; the discontinuation of the "bridging" system, under which days falling between a public holiday and a normal rest day are not worked; a tighter control of absenteeism and tardiness; a limitation of justified absences; and the elimination of related contractual clauses.

A lack of consensus within the trade union movement has hampered the development of concrete proposals for change. There is, however, strong opposition to any measures that would enable employers to make unilateral decisions, especially as regards working schedules, as these may affect workers' health or their social and family life.[7]

---

[6] G.C. Hufbauer and J.J. Schott: *NAFTA: An assessment*, Revised edition (Washington, Institute for International Economics, 1993).

[7] G. Bensusán and C. García: *Opiniones sindicales sobre la reforma laboral*, Documentos de trabajo No. 46 (Mexico City, Fundación F. Ebert, 1993), pp. 26-27.

Normal hours of work

Law

In line with the corresponding provision in the Constitution, the law prescribes different normal daily hours of work according to when the work is performed. Day work, defined as work performed between 06:00 and 20:00, is not to exceed eight hours. Night work, defined as work performed between 20:00 and 06:00, is not to exceed seven hours. The third category envisaged in the law, "mixed hours of work", contains both day and night work. Such shifts are not to exceed seven-and-a-half hours. A shift including three-and-a-half hours or more of night work is considered as night work.[8] Within the above limits, hours of work are fixed by the worker and the employer.[9]

Read together with Section 69, which provides for at least one rest day with full pay every six days, these figures define normal weekly hours as 48 for day work, 42 for night work and 45 for "mixed hours".

Young workers

Article 123 of the Constitution provides for a minimum age of 14 years for access to employment. Special provisions for minors under 16 years of age include the prohibition of work after 22:00 in undertakings other than industrial establishments; maximum daily working hours (six hours, divided into two equal shifts, with an interval of at least one hour for rest); the prohibition of overtime and of work on Sundays or other compulsory rest days; and the provision of paid annual leave of no less than 18 working days. In addition, work should be assigned to minors below 16 in such a way that they have the necessary free time to complete their school curriculum and attend vocational training centres. Young workers under 18 years of age may not work at night in industry.[10]

Specific occupations

Part VI of the Federal Labour Act adapts certain rules to the nature of a number of specific occupations.

Special regulations regarding hours of work are especially frequent in occupations linked to the transport of goods and passengers, where hours of work are to be adapted to the needs of the service and may begin at any time (e.g. for crew members or railways).[11] The following are examples of such specific rules.

---

[8] Federal Labour Act, op. cit., Sections 60-61.

[9] ibid., Section 59.

[10] ibid., Sections 175-180.

[11] ibid., Sections 226 (crew members) and 252 (railways).

— **Seafarers**. Written contracts should stipulate daily hours of work and the annual leave period (which should be no less than 12 paid days); weekly rest should be respected even when the ship is at sea.[12]

— **Flight crews**. The total period of duty, to be stipulated according to the equipment used, should not exceed 180 hours a month. Actual flying time should not exceed 90 hours a month, nor, on a daily basis, the normal daily hours prescribed for day work, night work and "mixed hours of work" respectively. Any hour in excess is to be treated as overtime. Crew members are entitled to 30 calendar days of annual leave, increasing by one day for each year of service, up to a maximum of 60 calendar days.[13]

— **Dockers and other workers in zones of federal jurisdiction**. Workers who work on a rest day are entitled to a 16.6 per cent increase of the daily wage.[14]

Other specific rules exist in connection with the following:

— **Homeworkers**. Homeworkers are entitled to the payment of wages for one compulsory rest day in the course of each week under consideration and to paid annual leave.[15]

— **Domestic employees**. Meals and night rest periods are provided for, but their duration is not foreseen: they should be "sufficient".[16]

Practice

Many collective agreements contain provisions regarding normal hours of work. While some simply reproduce the legal requirements, others introduce reductions to normal daily and weekly hours, or changes in the arrangement of the statutory hours.

In manufacturing, the average of hours actually worked per week have remained relatively stable, increasing only slightly from 1984 to 1994. However, in several years the average was well above the present level (see Figure 1).

---

[12] ibid., Sections 195 and 198-199.

[13] ibid., Sections 223-225 and 233.

[14] ibid., Section 272.

[15] ibid., Sections 327-328.

[16] ibid., Section 333.

Figure 1. Hours actually worked per week in manufacturing, 1984-94[17]

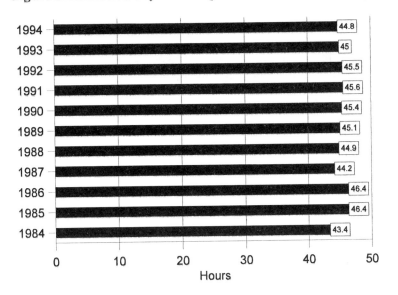

Changes have been observed in certain parts of the automobile industry and in the rubber industry, whereas other collective agreements in the automobile industry and in the sugar industry simply follow statutory provisions. For example, at the Ford Motor Company, which works a five-day week, normal weekly hours are 45, 40 and 42½ for the day, night and "mixed hours" shift. The same company had envisaged that the 45 weekly hours would be worked, on a rotating basis, over four 11½-hour days, with the remaining three days as days of rest. This experiment, however, was not carried out. Slightly lower hours are worked at Volkswagen de México (Volkswagen of Mexico), as follows: 44, 42 or 40, on the basis of a five-day week; normal shiftworkers and persons working regularly on the day shift have Saturdays off; the two weekly rest days are granted to other workers on the basis of needs for the use of productive capacity, and do not necessarily fall on a Saturday and Sunday. In the rubber industry, which is governed by an extended collective agreement, weekly hours were brought down to 40 for all workers.

There appear to be a few differences in approach between the manufacturing sector and the service sector. In the Banco de Comercio Exterior (External Trade Bank), weekly hours of work for day work are 35. In the Instituto Mexicano de Seguridad Social (Mexican Institute of Social Security), the normal working day for day-shift white-collar workers is 6½ hours, although they may be required to work eight hours.

A survey of 42 enterprises found that, after the devaluation of the Mexican peso in 1994, six enterprises started to practice a reduced working week — i.e. with Friday off —, while five others reduced the length of their working day by an average of two hours.[18] In an automobile

---

[17] Bureau of Statistics, International Labour Office.

[18] Survey carried out by the Asociación Mexicana de Ejecutivos en Relaciones Industriales (AMERI) on the "Plan laboral de emergencia"; preliminary results to the survey, cited in R. Wilde: *Tiempo de trabajo*, unpublished report prepared for the ILO, June 1995.

plant, a 50 per cent reduction in weekly hours was introduced, with a corresponding reduction in pay. The 24 weekly hours are worked over three days. In another, the normal 48 weekly hours are worked over four 12-hour days.

In several enterprises, efforts are made to avoid layoffs by using various possibilities. An example is to require workers to take their annual leave at times of low demand. In another factory, normal hours of work have been maintained, but, at times of low demand, workers are assigned to various tasks not directly related to production.

Overtime and absolute maximum hours

Law

The law allows overtime work in two sets of circumstances. In the event of a catastrophe or of imminent danger, in which the lives of the worker, of his fellow workers or of the employer are in danger, or if the very existence of the undertaking is imperilled, daily hours of work may be extended for the time strictly necessary to ward off the danger. The hours so worked will be paid at the same rate as normal hours of work.[19]

Normal hours of work may also be extended on account of exceptional circumstances, on condition that they are not allowed to exceed normal hours by more than three hours on no more than three days a week. The hours so worked will be paid at double rate.[20]

The law does not set other limits for overtime (e.g. over a certain number of weeks, over a month or over a year). In fact, the Act implies that time in excess of the nine hours of overtime referred to above may be worked, since it specifically provides for payment at the rate of three times the normal rate, without prejudice to sanctions (i.e. a fine) being imposed on the employer. However, the consent of workers is required, since they may not be forced to work more than nine hours of overtime in a given week.[21] The possibility of averaging hours over the week or any other period is not envisaged.

Thus, absolute maximum hours of work could amount to 54 a week throughout the year, and to more, with the worker's consent.

Since part-time work is not regulated in the Act, there are no provisions to regulate work performed by a part-time worker in excess of the contractual hours.

Practice

A survey carried out by an ILO-CIDA project found that 42 per cent of the enterprises interviewed were increasing the use of overtime; 37 per cent were reducing it; in another 16 per cent, there had been no changes; in 10 per cent of the enterprises, overtime increased in

[19] Federal Labour Act, op. cit., Sections 65 and 67.

[20] ibid., Sections 66-67.

[21] ibid., Section 68.

certain production areas only. According to a union representative in the food industry, workers consider overtime as necessary to complement their earnings.[22]

There is no intensive use of overtime in the *maquiladoras*. The majority of these enterprises do not practice them. In Tijuana, for example, workers average 1.6 hours of overtime per week. In the electronic sector, overtime averages 1.3 hours per worker per week.[23]

At IMASA (electricity company), when working four or more hours of overtime, workers are allowed a 30-minute break, which is paid at the overtime rate.[24]

Rest

Law

Rest breaks

Workers are entitled to a rest period of at least 30 minutes during the course of their continuous daily hours of work.[25] If workers are unable to leave the workplace for meals during the rest period, such periods are deemed to be hours actually worked, and are included in the daily hours of work.[26]

Daily rest periods

The legislation does not provide for daily rest periods. As a consequence, normal weekly hours may be worked over a reduced number of days (as shown by the few examples above). In view of the regulation of overtime (see above), this may also mean that actual daily hours may be high.

Weekly rest

Workers are entitled to at least one day of rest with full pay every six days. Regulations to be issued under the Act are to prescribe that the rest day shall fall on Sunday. Workers who are obliged to work on a Sunday are entitled to at least an extra 25 per cent of the normal daily remuneration. Hours of work may be so scheduled as to enable the workers to have Saturday afternoon off or some similar arrangement. In occupations which require continuous work, the days on which the weekly rest day is taken are to be fixed by mutual agreement between

---

[22] A. García, A. Hernández and R. Wilde: *Innovación en la empresa y dinamicá de negociación: Caso México* (Mexico City, ILO, 1994).

[23] J. Carrillo (ed.): *Mercados de trabajo en la industria maquiladora de exportación: Síntesis del reporte de investigación* (Mexico City, Secretaría del Trabajo y Previsión Social and El Colegio de la Frontera Norte, 1991), pp. 54-55.

[24] IMASA: *Contrato colectivo de trabajo 1994-1996*, Clause 21, p. 11.

[25] Federal Labour Act, op. cit., Section 63.

[26] ibid., Section 64.

the employer and the workers. Workers are not obliged to work on a rest day; their agreement must be obtained if their work is needed.[27]

Practice

Rest breaks

At the Ford Motor Company, besides the legal 30-minute break for meals or relaxation, workers enjoy two breaks of ten minutes each, one in the morning and the other in the afternoon.[28]

At the Instituto Mexicano del Seguro Social (Mexican Institute of Social Security), rest breaks, which are counted as effective working time, are linked to the hours worked: for six-and-a-half hours of work, workers have a 15-minute break; for eight hours, a 30-minute break; for eight hours or more, a 60-minute break.[29]

Weekly rest

At the Instituto Mexicano del Seguro Social (Mexican Institute of Social Security), workers have the right to two consecutive weekly rest days, which should be fixed, and should normally fall on Saturday and Sunday. However, depending on the needs of the service, other days may be agreed between the parties, provided that workers have two paid rest days every five working days.[30] Workers assigned to work away from their place of residence are entitled to an extra day of weekly rest at their place of residence for every weekly rest day taken at the place of assignment.

Shop-opening hours

Law

There are no generally applicable laws regulating shop-opening hours.

Practice

Banks have extended their hours of service to the public, with consequences on the hours of bank employees. For example, since 1993, the Inverlat-Comermex Bank is open to the public from 09:00 to 15:00. The bank employees now work from 8:45 until 16:00 or 16:30. The

---

[27] ibid., Sections 59, 69-71 and 75.

[28] Ford Motor Company SA de CV: *Contrato colectivo de trabajo 1992-1994* (Chihuahua), Clause 29, p. 16.

[29] Information provided to the ILO by the Instituto Mexicano del Seguro Social, May 1995.

[30] ibid.

compensation for the increase in hours of work amounts to 10 per cent of the former remuneration. At Bancomer, some branches are open to the public from 8:30 to 17:00.[31]

Public holidays

Law

The following days are paid public holidays: 1 January, 5 February, 21 March, 1 May, 16 September, 20 November and 25 December. In addition, every six years, 1 December, when the new Federal Executive takes office, is also a paid public holiday.[32]

Compensation for work on these days is a double wage, in addition to the normal wage payable in respect of the public holiday.[33]

Practice

Additional paid public holidays under collective agreements often include Maundy Thursday and Good Friday; the day of the Labor Union; 10 May (Mothers' Day); 15 September (when the National Holiday begins); 1 and 2 November ; 12 December; and 24 and 31 December.

Paid annual leave

Law

Workers who have been in the service of an employer for more than one year are entitled to paid annual leave.[34] The basic entitlement is no less than six working days, which is increased by two working days (up to a maximum of 12 days) for each subsequent year of service. After the fourth year of work, the leave is increased by two days for every five years of service. For casual or seasonal workers, the entitlement is proportional to the number of days worked in a given year.[35]

Workers must be allowed to take at least six days of their annual leave in one uninterrupted period. Workers whose entitlement is longer may split their leave, or be requested to do so.[36]

---

[31] Wilde, op. cit.

[32] Federal Labour Act, op. cit., Section 74.

[33] ibid., Section 75.

[34] ibid., Section 76.

[35] ibid., Section 77.

[36] ibid., Section 78.

When the employment relationship is terminated before completion of one year of service, the worker is entitled to remuneration proportional to the length of service.[37] Otherwise, the payment of compensation in lieu of annual leave is prohitibed.

Workers are entitled to an annual leave bonus of no less than 25 per cent of their salary. Both the bonus and the salary are to be paid before the beginning of the leave.[38]

Practice

Several collective agreements improve upon the provisions of the law, both in terms of the number of days of leave and of the amount of the associated cash bonus. Table 1 gives an example of the benefits provided.[39] However, there are significant differences in terms of the number of years over which an increase in the number of days of holidays is foreseen (which varied in the collective agreements examined from nine to 25) and in terms of the extra number of days (from 15 to 45).

Table 1. Increase in paid annual leave and cash bonus according to seniority in an enterprise

Years of service	Days of paid leave	Remuneration (as a percentage of wages)
1	7	136
2	9	151
3	11	151
4	13	166
6 to 8	13	166
9	15	166
10	15	181

Other types of leave

Law

The law does not provide for other types of leave.

---

[37] ibid., Section 79.

[38] ibid., Section 80.

[39] TREMEC: *Contrato colectivo de trabajo: Productividad 1995-1997*, Clause 121, p. 92.

Practice

Special paid or unpaid leave is granted by collective agreements for health, social, educational and welfare reasons, for public or trade union duties, or for personal reasons. Whether such leave is paid or unpaid is sometimes left to the decision of management on the merits of the case. No provision was identified in connection with leave to care for children or relatives. It is assumed that leave for personal reasons is used in such cases.

Health, social, education or welfare reasons

The Compañía de Luz y Fuerza del Centro provides for a certain number of days of paid leave per year, as required, to study under fellowships, to sit examinations or to attend congresses and symposia.[40]

Public or trade union duties

The Instituto Mexicano del Seguro Social provides for unpaid leave, as required, for public duties. Paid leave, according to the function, is granted workers for trade union representation.

The Compañía de Luz y Fuerza del Centro grants leave for public duties as required, paid or unpaid (management decision).

Leave for personal reasons

The Compañía de Luz y Fuerza del Centro grants workers up to ten months per calendar year of leave for personal reasons, paid or unpaid (management decision).

The Instituto Mexicano del Seguro Social grants workers up to three days of paid leave.

The Ford Motor Company grants workers three paid working days for the birth of a child. Compassionate leave ranges from three to five paid working days for the death of a brother or sister, a child or spouse.

The Nissan Mexicana plant grants workers 10,000 pesos and a six-day paid leave on marriage.

---

[40] Compañía de Luz y Fuerza del Centro and Sindicato Mexicano de Electricistas: *Contrato colectivo de trabajo 1994-1996*, Clauses 39, 41-42 and 44, pp. 31-35.

New Zealand

Overview and trends

Overview

Pursuant to the Employment Contracts Act 1991, many working time issues are subject to negotiation between the employer and the worker, either individually or collectively.[1] Special requirements for absolute maximum hours and rest, however, are applicable by statute to sectors, such as transportation, mining and health care, where questions of safety are paramount.[2] Nevertheless, there are some statutory requirements of general applicability with respect to working time issues. For example, the Minimum Wage Act 1983 mandates that employees should not work more than 40 hours a week, five days a week, exclusive of overtime, although the parties can agree by contract to work more than 40 hours a week as long as the terms and conditions are not harsh or oppressive.[3] Moreover, an Order pursuant to the Act establishes the overtime rate for minimum wage employees.[4] The Holidays Act 1981 mandates that employees should receive 11 paid public holidays per year, and three weeks of paid annual leave after having worked a qualifying year with the same employer.[5]

Following the adoption of the Employment Contracts Act 1991, there was a significant decline in the number of employees covered by collective agreements. It has been estimated that 721,000 employees were covered in the 1989-90 bargaining round, but that as of February 1993, there were only 428,000 employees covered. Another survey indicated that those covered could have declined to around 370,000.[6]

As to actual working time developments, the length of the working week tends to have been maintained at 40 hours, although some agreements providing for a working week in excess of the 40 hours have been reported. The distribution of working time over the week seems

---

[1] Employment Contracts Act 1991, Act No. 22, dated 7 May 1991 (*Statutes of New Zealand*, 1991).

[2] Information provided to the ILO by the Industrial Relations Centre, Faculty of Commerce and Administration, Victoria University of Wellington, April 1995. See also Wyatt: *1994/95 employment terms and conditions — Asia/Pacific* (Hong Kong, 1993), p. 239.

[3] Minimum Wage Act 1983, Act No. 115, dated 16 December 1983 (*Statutes of New Zealand*, 1983), as amended up to Act No. 27, dated 7 May 1991 (*Statutes of New Zealand*, 1991).

[4] Minimum Wage Order 1995, Order No. 20, dated 13 February 1995 (*Official Gazette*, 16 February 1995).

[5] Holidays Act 1981, Act No. 15, dated 23 July 1981 (*Statutes of New Zealand*, 1981), as amended up to Act No. 26, dated 7 May 1991 (*Statutes of New Zealand*, 1991).

[6] R. Harbridge and A. Honeybone: "The Employment Contracts Act and collective bargaining patterns: A review of the 1993/94 year", in R. Harbridge, A. Honeybone and P. Kiely (eds.): *Employment contracts: Bargaining trends and employment law update: 1993/94* (Wellington, Industrial Relations Centre, Victoria University of Wellington, 1994), p. 2.

to be changing though, particularly in the retail, hotel and restaurant sectors, as well as in some industries.[7]

Trends

In the 1980s, New Zealand was characterized by a system of labour relations generally and working time regulation in particular that was considered as highly regulated. The heart of the previous system was the Labour Relations Act 1973. Awards negotiated under the Labour Relations Act 1973 for different industries or occupations generally specified a 40-hour week, with a Monday through Friday work-week, and normal hours of work to be scheduled between 08:00 and 18:00. The Labour Relations Act 1987 encouraged and, to some extent, achieved more flexibility in the arrangement of working time, although the essence of the 1973 regulatory structure was retained.[8]

The industrial relations system supported by these laws had encouraged multi-employer bargaining. Once a trade union had negotiated and registered an award, the "blanket coverage" provision in the award bound all employers in that industry or any employers who hired personnel who worked in occupations covered by the award. As a result, multi-employer bargaining accounted for 77 per cent of all employees covered by registered awards or agreements in 1989 and 1990. The criticism of the former regulatory framework included claims that it was too rigid and not adapted to the emergence of new industries, skills and production methods. Critics said that it was badly adapted to the service sector, which needed to have more flexibility in arranging work outside the core period of Monday through Friday. It was considered important to be able to adapt to jobs which increasingly required weekend and shift work, particularly for work in the service sector which accounted for the majority of employment growth in recent years.[9]

The adoption of the Employment Contracts Act 1991 significantly altered the entire regulatory framework. The Act discourages multi-employer bargaining because of a legal impediment to strike action in support of such negotiation, and because there is no legal provision for extending a settlement to other employers in the same industry or occupation. The new Act's features, plus the opposition of the New Zealand Employers' Federation to multi-employer settlements, led to the virtual collapse of multi-employer bargaining and a shift towards bargaining at the level of the individual enterprise. Under the Act, bargaining may take place either in the context of collective bargaining or individually. Although the Employment Contracts Act does not place any limits on working time, the 40-hour week has not, however, been completely abolished. The former provision in the Labour Relations Act of 1987 is now contained in the Minimum Wage Act, with the significant difference that the present provision does not contain any requirement that the five days of work should be scheduled so as to

---

[7] Information provided to the ILO by the Industrial Relations Centre, Victoria University of Wellington, April 1995.

[8] ibid.

[9] Harbridge and Honeybone, op. cit.; G. Anderson, P. Brosnan and P. Walsh: "Flexibility, casualization and externalization in the New Zealand workforce", in *Journal of Industrial Relations*, Vol. 36, No. 3, December 1994, p. 491.

avoid Saturday and Sunday work. The consequence of these changes is that contract settlements, be they collective or individual negotiations, are more divergent and the likelihood of having premium rates of pay apply to certain types of work has been reduced and, in some instances, abolished. These outcomes, however, are not uniform across all sectors.[10]

Another significant aspect of the adoption of the Employment Contracts Act 1991 has been the decision to keep no public record of collectively bargained agreements. Employment contracts are now treated as no different from other commercial contracts, i.e. they belong exclusively to the contractual parties and there is no requirement that they should become part of the public domain.[11] Confidentiality of settlement has become an important aspect of negotiations. While Government policy has determined that there will be no public record of collective agreements, it has decided that, for "analytical and research" purposes, employers entering into collective employment contracts that cover 20 or more employees should forward copies of those contracts to the Secretary of Labour.[12] As a consequence, publicly available information about the precise terms of settlement has become more difficult to obtain, although collective information about trends is available from the Government. Previously, a Commission had registered collective agreements and published them, thus making the outcomes of bargaining quite transparent.

Parallel to the changes allowing for more flexibility in working time arrangements introduced first by the Labour Relations Act 1987 and subsequently by the Employment Contracts Act 1991, shop-opening hours were also deregulated. Until 1980, the Shop Trading Hours Act 1977 had prohibited the opening of most shops on Saturdays and Sundays.[13] In 1980, Saturday shopping was introduced and virtually all restrictions were lifted with the repeal of the Shop Trading Hours Act in 1990. Shops may now be open 24 hours a day any day of the week, with the exception of certain public holidays. One of the reasons advanced for the deregulation of shop-opening hours was that restrictions on weekend shopping were considered to have a detrimental effect on New Zealand's economy.[14]

The Government has also decided to undertake a general review of the Holidays Act 1981, which has very specific requirements for paid public holidays. The perceived need to have more flexible working time arrangements is one of the principal reasons for this review. According to the Department of Labour, the "current law is based on the idea that employees always work Monday to Friday, half past eight to five. In reality people now have a whole

---

[10] Harbridge and Honeybone, op. cit.

[11] ibid., p. 1.

[12] S. Hammond and R. Harbridge: "The impact of the Employment Contracts Act on women at work", in *New Zealand Journal of Industrial Relations*, Vol. 18, No. 1, April 1993, p. 18.

[13] "Open all hours?", in *Labour and Employment Gazette*, Vol. 36, No. 1, March 1986, p. 17.

[14] A. Smith: *Working time arrangements: The New Zealand experience*, paper presented at the Asian Tripartite Workshop on Working Time Arrangements (Bangkok, 18-22 July 1994).

range of working hours and days. There is an urgent need to attend to the widening gap between current working arrangements and the Holidays Act".[15]

Although there is some interest in modifying the Holidays Act 1981 with regards to public holidays, the Government is proceeding cautiously because of the politically sensitive nature of the issue. The general approach has been that most working time issues should be a matter of negotiation between the parties concerned.[16]

The New Zealand Council of Trade Unions (NZCTU), on the other hand, has argued in favour of a comprehensive review of employment rights, including those concerning working time. Among other things, the NZCTU has argued for limits on the hours of work a worker can be obliged to work in any given day or week, and for consideration of a statutory entitlement to premium payment for hours worked in excess of this limit. It has also argued for modification of the Holidays Act 1981 to recognize the rights of workers with non-traditional working patterns.[17]

In contrast, employers' organizations are largely satisfied with the legislative changes of a deregulatory nature enacted in recent years. However, the modification of the Holidays Act 1981 with respect to public holidays has been considered to be a possible area for further reform. Employers' organizations have called for the removal of statutory requirements concerning public holidays, which should be left to negotiation between the parties to the employment relationship.

Normal hours of work

Law

According to the Minimum Wage Act 1983, normal hours of work shall be fixed at 40 per week, exclusive of overtime, and the employer shall endeavour that these hours are worked on not more than five days per week. However, the parties may agree contractually to work more than a maximum of 40 hours per week, as long as the terms and conditions of employment are not harsh or oppressive.

Practice

According to information contained in a government database of over 2,500 collective agreements covering approximately 340,000 employees, 73 per cent of these employees worked a 40-hour work-week, and 24 per cent worked a 37.5 or 38 hour work-week in 1985. Some extension of the work-week beyond 40 hours was also evident, particularly in the transport and construction sectors. Collectively agreed contracts, however, covered only a minority of the total workforce. According to official data contained in the Household Labour Force Survey (HLFS), which covers employees who are covered by collective agreements

---

[15] Department of Labour: *Review of the Holidays Act 1981* (Wellington, 1995).

[16] Industrial Relations Centre, Victoria University of Wellington, op. cit.

[17] ibid.

as well as those who are not, over 400,000 workers (28 per cent of the workforce) worked more than 40 hours per week. Although the Monday through Friday week still remains the most common schedule (51 per cent of employees covered by the database), a significant number of employees (34 per cent) can be required to work any day of the week. A trend towards a four-day work-week is also evident, particularly in the retail, restaurant and hotel sectors.[18]

Table 1. Hours of work per week by major divisions of economic activity[19]

Major division	1984	1985	1986	1987	1988	1989	1990	1991	1992	1993	1994
Mining and quarrying	40.5	41.7	40.7	42.9	42.4	43.7	42.8	42.9	45.2	45.2	45.5
Manufacturing	40.4	40.7	39.6	40.2	39.9	40.5	40.7	40.4	41.1	41.6	42.0
Electricity, gas and water	41.0	41.2	40.8	40.9	40.1	40.5	40.7	40.3	41.1	40.9	41.2
Construction	42.7	43.5	42.4	42.2	41.8	42.8	42.6	41.8	42.2	42.9	43.3
Trades, restaurants and hotels	38.0	38.0	37.2	36.8	36.7	36.8	36.9	37.0	37.3	37.6	37.7
Transport, storage and communication	42.3	42.8	42.1	41.9	42.1	42.4	41.7	41.4	41.2	41.4	42.0
Financing, insurance, real estate and business services	37.6	37.6	37.5	37.7	37.6	37.8	37.4	37.1	37.1	36.9	37.5
Community, social and personal services	37.7	38.0	38.0	37.5	37.5	37.6	37.3	37.2	37.3	37.3	37.5
Total (all non-agricultural activities) *	39.4	39.6	38.9	38.8	38.6	38.8	38.7	38.5	38.7	38.9	39.2

*   Including forestry and logging.

Overtime and absolute maximum hours

Law

The Minimum Wage Act 1983 states that the maximum hours of work per week shall be fixed at 40, exclusive of overtime, unless the parties otherwise agree contractually. An Order pursuant to the Act also establishes a monetary amount of overtime pay for those who are paid the minimum wage. Thus, overtime is payable after 40 hours of work per week, unless

[18] Industrial Relations Centre, Victoria University of Wellington, op. cit.

[19] Bureau of Statistics, International Labour Office [hours paid for employees; establishments with the equivalent of more than two full-time employees].

the parties agree to a different arrangement by contract. There are no requirements for justifying under what circumstances overtime can be worked. However, if the amount of overtime was considered excessive by an employee, a claim could be made under either the Employment Contracts Act 1991 (as an action to the employee's disadvantage under the Act's personal grievance provisions that the hours are harsh or oppressive) or the Health and Safety in Employment Act 1992 (through a complaint to a Health and Safety Inspector).[20] The only other statutory limits on overtime apply in sectors which are regulated for safety reasons, such as the transportation, mining and health sectors, where maximum daily hours and required rest periods place restrictions on total hours worked, including overtime.[21]

Practice

Individual and collective contracts usually indicate that reasonable overtime must be performed on request. Compensation for overtime is subject to agreement between the parties and practice varies according to when overtime is worked. For overtime in excess of a normal working day, the most prevalent rate is time-and-a-half for the first three hours, and doubletime thereafter. However, time-and-a-half throughout is also common, and there is a slight trend towards this type of provision. Overtime pay can be triggered by contractual limits on daily or weekly hours of work, or both. Premium pay for work on public holidays is common and typically is paid at doubletime rates (in addition to the day off statutorily required). Overtime for weekend work is most commonly time-and-a-half for the first three hours of Saturday work and doubletime thereafter, whereas doubletime is the most common provision for Sunday work. Despite the above, weekend premium rates apply to only 55 per cent of the those in the Government's database of collective agreements.[22] An emerging trend is an increase in variations of premium rates of pay. Seen by sector, premium rates remain common in all sectors except the retail, hotel and restaurant sectors, as well as in the community, public administration and service sectors.[23]

According to official data, the average amount of overtime worked per employee is just under two hours per week. There are significant differences across industries. Employees in manufacturing and construction sectors work on average 3.5 hours of overtime a week. Public administration, business and financial employees work on average less than one hour of overtime per week, and employees in the public and community services work on average less than 30 minutes of overtime per week. The average amount of overtime worked per employee is getting less. Although there are virtually no restrictions on how employers and

[20] Information provided to the ILO by the New Zealand Employers Federation, Inc., May 1995.

[21] Industrial Relations Centre, Victoria University of Wellington, op. cit.; Wyatt, op. cit., p. 239.

[22] Industrial Relations Centre, Victoria University of Wellington, op. cit. See also R. Harbridge and A. Honeybone: *Working time and the application of penal rates of pay: A gender and industry analysis in the 1993/94 year*, paper presented to the Sixth Labour, Employment and Work Conference (Wellington, 24-25 November 1994), p. 11.

[23] Harbridge and Honeybone, "The Employment Contracts Act and collective bargaining patterns", op. cit., p. 11.

employees organize hours of work, there is only limited evidence, essentially in the manufacturing sector, of averaging schemes in the form of annualized hours.[24]

Rest

Law

There are no generally applicable provisions on work pauses, breaks, daily or weekly rest. Certain sectors where safety is a major concern, such as the transportation, mining and health sectors, have maximum daily hours and required rest periods. Although there are no formal requirements for weekly rest, the Minimum Wage Act 1983 specifies that, unless otherwise agreed to contractually, normal hours of work are not to exceed 40 hours per week, and that the employer shall endeavour to fix daily hours so that these are spread over no more than five days. As the parties can agree contractually to more hours of work per week, as the law itself does not specify that the five days of work a week have to be consecutive (and, by implication, that rest has to be consecutive as well), and as there is no guidance on when or how much overtime can be worked, the Minimum Wage Act 1983 cannot be said to fix firm weekly rest requirements but only indirect indicative standards.

Practice

According to the New Zealand Employers' Federation, employees normally receive a paid work pause of ten minutes during each four-hour working period, and during every two hours worked after an eight-hour day, provided that overtime is to be worked for at least an hour. An employee also normally benefits from an unpaid meal break of 30 minutes to one hour after no more than four hours of work, unless there is an alternative arrangement agreed to between the employer and employee concerned.[25]

According to information in the Government's database covering over 2,500 collectively agreed contracts, daily rest can only be determined indirectly by analysis of the maximum span of hours between the start and end of work, as fixed by contract. These daily span provisions, found in 57 per cent of the contracts, do not prevent work from taking place outside the range fixed by mutual agreement, but only serve to indicate the limits beyond which premium pay should be made. In the majority of contracts which contain such span of hours provisions, the span is 12 hours or less, and only 3 per cent of the employees in the sample had a clock hour span of more than 14 hours.

With respect to weekly rest, information from the Government's database indicated that in 51 per cent of the contracts, the traditional Monday through Friday working week was recognized, which would ordinarily give a two-day period of weekly rest. There has, however, been the emergence of a seven-day working week, which means that weekly rest is determined in function of how the work is organized and scheduled for such employees.

[24] Industrial Relations Centre, Victoria University of Wellington, op. cit.

[25] New Zealand Employers' Federation Inc., op. cit.

Around one-third of all employees have such working arrangements. And around 10 per cent of workers work a four-day week. The five-day week, Monday through Friday, is still prevalent in the manufacturing, energy, government administration and financial sectors; the seven-day week is common in the public and social services (health) sectors; and the four-day week is frequent in the retail, restaurant and hotel sectors.[26]

Shop-opening hours

Law

Legislation restricting shop trading hours was repealed in 1990.[27]

Shops can now open for 24 hours a day on any day of the week. Minimal restrictions still apply to certain public holidays: shops cannot open on Christmas Day, Good Friday or Easter Sunday, and can only open after 13:00 on Anzac Day. These restrictions do not apply to enterprises, such as petrol stations, dairies, takeaways and similar establishments.[28]

Public holidays

Law

The Holidays Act 1981 provides for 11 paid public holidays per year, and its provisions are applicable to all employees, whether part time, full time or casual. According to the Act,[29] these days include Christmas Day, Boxing Day, New Year's Day, the second day of January (or some other day in its place), Good Friday, Easter Monday, Anzac Day, Labour Day, the birthday of the reigning sovereign, Waitangi/New Zealand Day, and the day of the anniversary of the province (or some other day in its place). The right to paid leave on Anzac Day and Waitangi/New Zealand Day[30] is regulated in separate legislation.[31] Employers must provide no less than these 11 days, and employees are obliged to take those days in addition to their paid annual leave.[32]

Subject to agreement between the parties, work may be required on all public holidays. There is no specific remuneration required by law for such work, but employees must be given a

---

[26] Industrial Relations Centre, Victoria University of Wellington, op. cit.

[27] Shop Trading Hours Repeal Act 1990, Act No. 57, dated 3 July 1990 (*Statutes of New Zealand*, 1990).

[28] Industrial Relations Centre, Victoria University of Wellington, op. cit.

[29] Section 7A, Holidays Act 1981, op. cit.

[30] Waitangi is the place where the founding document of New Zealand was signed in 1840 between the British Crown and the indigenous people of New Zealand, the Maori.

[31] Anzac Day Act 1966, Act No. 44, dated 14 October 1966 (*Statutes of New Zealand*, Vol. 2, 1966); Waitangi Day Act 1976, Act No. 33, dated 1 November 1976 (*Statutes of New Zealand*, 1976).

[32] P. Kiely: "Employment law update", in R. Harbridge, A. Honeybone and P. Kiely (eds.): *Employment contracts: Bargaining trends and employment law update: 1993/94* (Wellington, Industrial Relations Centre, Victoria University of Wellington, 1994), p. 41.

day off in lieu without regard to the rate of pay on the public holiday. There are exceptions in the case of two specific holidays, Waitangi/New Zealand Day and Anzac Day. On these days, pay for work at a rate above that for an ordinary day absolves the employer of the requirement to also give in addition a paid day off in lieu of work on the public holiday.

Paid annual leave

Law

The minimum period of paid annual leave established by the Holidays Act 1981 is three weeks. It applies to full-time employees and prorata to part-time employees. Casual employees are to receive 6 per cent of their wages for the year as annual leave pay. The qualifying period is one year with the same employer. However, if employment is terminated after less than one year, the employee is entitled to payment of annual leave pay on a prorata basis, calculated at 6 per cent of gross ordinary earnings. At least two uninterrupted weeks is to be allowed within six months of entitlement to paid annual leave and the balance within 12 months. Unless the relevant employment contract provides otherwise, the employer fixes the time for paid annual leave after consultation with the employee, taking into account work requirements and the availability to the employee of opportunities for rest and recreation. The employer and the employee may agree to paid leave being taken wholly or partly in advance. The entitlement to the basic three weeks of paid leave cannot be lost once it has been earned, and is accumulated until it is taken or employment has been terminated. Although the employee can thus not be given a supplementary payment in lieu of taking his or her paid annual leave while in employment for the basic statutory minimum, an employer can pay an employee to work during any period of leave entitlement that is in excess of the statutory minimum.[33]

Practice

Additional paid annual leave based on service is a common provision in contracts. In the transportation sector, it is common to grant four weeks of leave after one year of service. According to the Government's database of collective agreements, across all sectors approximately 11 per cent of employees are entitled to a fourth week of paid annual leave after five years of service. This entitlement is available to the majority of employees in the restaurant and hotel sector, and a large proportion of workers in the construction sector. It was also found that 39 per cent of all contracts provided for a fourth week of entitlement after six years of service, and 30 per cent after seven years. The tendency is for a reduction of the qualifying period.[34]

[33] Holidays Act 1981, op. cit. The amendments did not change the rules regarding paid annual leave. See also Wyatt, op. cit., p. 240.

[34] Industrial Relations Centre, Victoria University of Wellington, op. cit. See also Hammond and Harbridge, op. cit., p. 24; R. Harbridge: "Privacy, redundancy and trends in leave", in *The Employment Contract*, No. 12, March 1995, pp. 7-8.

Other types of leave

Law

Special leave

The Holidays Amendment Act 1991 provides for a minimum of five days' special leave per year to any worker with over six months of service with the same employer. Special leave may be taken when the employee, the employee's spouse, a dependent child or parent of an employee is sick, or in the event of bereavement. This special leave may not be accumulated. In practice, many employers tend to grant more special leave than required by law.[35]

Military service

Employees who volunteer for military service are protected by law, provided the employee gives 14 days' notice of a period of service. The employer is required to keep the person's job open, and his or her service is regarded as unbroken with respect to terms and conditions of employment without any loss of benefits. Such leave is not required to be paid by the employer, and the employee may, but is not required to do so, take leave for military service from his or her entitlement to annual leave.[36]

Practice[37]

Bereavement leave

In the Government's database of over 2,500 collective agreements, it was found that bereavement leave is commonly a separate entitlement from the legally mandated special leave which can be used for a variety of purposes. Bereavement leave is normally less than five days, and three days is most prevalent. For 37 per cent of the workers in the sample, bereavement leave was granted at the employer's discretion.

Long-service leave

According to information derived from the Government's database of collective agreements, approximately 80 per cent of workers have contract provisions that provide for a period of special leave based on length of service.

---

[35] Industrial Relations Centre, Victoria University of Wellington, op. cit.

[36] Volunteers Employment Protection Act 1973, Act No. 25, dated 2 October 1973 (*Statutes of New Zealand*, Vol. 1, 1973), as amended up to Act No. 59, dated 30 March 1987 (*Statutes of New Zealand*, 1987). See also Wyatt, op. cit., p. 240.

[37] Industrial Relations Centre, Victoria University of Wellington, op. cit. See also R. Harbridge: "Trends in collective bargaining: New employees, parental leave and other leave entitlements", in *The Employment Contract*, No. 8, March 1994, p. 6.

Jury service, military service, and education and training

The Government's database of collective agreements also found that over 90 per cent of workers were covered by contract provisions which provided for other types of leave, such as jury service, military service, and education and training.

Shift and night work

Law

There are no generally applicable provisions.

Practice

The arrangement of shift and night work is subject to negotiation between the parties. Premium payment is frequently granted for work during inconvenient or unsocial hours, i.e. in the evening, during the night, or for weekend work (see above under **Overtime and absolute maximum hours**). Night work and certain types of shift work may attract premium rate payments irrespective of the length of the daily period for which the worker is engaged. Shiftworkers usually receive more favourable annual leave provisions than average workers, and frequently are granted a fourth week of paid annual leave after a year of service.[38]

---

[38] Industrial Relations Centre, Victoria University of Wellington, op. cit.

Norway

Overview and trends

Overview

The Norwegian tradition relating to working time issues is characterized by a close inter-action between law and practice. Generally, collective agreements between the major social partners, the Landsorganisasjonen i Norge (LO — Norwegian Confederation of Trade Unions) and the Næringslivets Hovedorganisasjon (NHO — Confederation of Norwegian Business and Industry) have been ahead of legislation. The trade unions have been in a relatively strong position, and membership in the larger national federations accounts for 66.6 per cent of the total workforce.[1]

The current legislation — the Working Environment Act (WEA) — dates from 1977. During its elaboration a revision of the working time provisions was discussed. The social partners did not, however, reach agreement on many issues and, as a result, Chapter X of the WEA (Hours of work) is largely based on the rules in its predecessor, the Work Protection Act.[2] The new law, however, introduced a greater amount of flexibility regarding working time arrangements. The social partners were given more freedom to extend and vary the framework for working hours through collective agreement reached at the central level; the newly founded working environment committees (compulsory in all enterprises with more than 50 employees) were assigned greater authority to permit exceptions to the rules; and the Labour Inspectorate was given wider powers to grant exceptions to the rules.

Subsequent modification of the WEA in 1984 granted representative worker organizations the right to deviate by collective agreement at the central level from restrictions established by the law for overtime work, work on Sundays and public holidays, and night work.

Further changes regarding working time were introduced to the WEA, effective as of 1 February 1995. These amendments did not change the framework for the length of working hours, overtime and use of night work, but allowed the parties, to a greater degree than before, to reach agreement at the local level on some working time issues.

A certain amount of flexibility in the labour force is provided part-time workers, who have exceeded 20 per cent of total employment for a number of years. Approximately one out of two women employed is a part-time worker, and among the European countries, only the Netherlands has a larger share of part-time working.[3]

---

[1] P. Johnsen and K. Lange: "Norway", in C. Brewster, A. Hegewisch, T. Lockhart and L. Holden (eds.): *The European human resource management guide* (London, Academic Press, 1992), pp. 393-438.

[2] Information provided to the ILO by the Ministry of Labour, May 1995.

[3] Statistics Norway: *Social survey 1993* (Oslo, Kongsvinger, 1994), p. 65; Ministry of Labour, op. cit.

Trends

In 1986, Norway experienced the most serious industrial conflict since 1931. As a result, there was an agreement to reduce weekly working time from 40 to 37.5 hours per week as of 1987.[4]

In 1992, a major industrial conflict between the social partners was only barely avoided. In addition to wage increases, the LO demanded improvements in working conditions in the form of working time reductions for working parents. Although the rights of working parents were not changed in the agreement, the Government subsequently extended the right to state-financed leave for workers with children.

The working time rules and collective agreements in force as of 1995 have been criticized as too inflexible by employers, who have claimed that the rules have prevented the adequate utilization of capacity in periods of heavy work. The recent changes of the WEA appear as a response to these concerns. The stated purpose of the Commission appointed to examine the WEA was "to adapt the Act to current economic and technological realities .... [and] to find a balance between consideration of fundamental worker rights and necessary economic adjustments". Based upon a survey of the experiences of Norwegian enterprises with the existing working hours rules, the Commission found that the criticism of working hours provisions and, in particular, restrictions on overtime, night work, and work on Sundays and public holidays, was overstated. The inflexible appearance of the law was largely due to a lack of knowledge concerning the flexibility actually offered by the Act. Although there were no major amendments made to the WEA's framework provisions on the length of working hours, overtime and the use of night work, the Act was amended to allow the social partners at the local level to agree on more flexible provisions and, in particular, for the increased use of overtime under certain conditions.[5]

The continuing high unemployment levels have led to a debate on whether it would be possible to achieve a better distribution of employment by reducing overtime work. The Norwegian Government, however, has referred to surveys which indicate that reduction of overtime does not necessarily lead enterprises to take on new employees, but rather to reductions in overall production. The Minister of Labour has rejected worksharing as a viable alternative to contain unemployment.[6] Another issue, which seems to have gained some attention in Norway, is the possible introduction of a right to educational leave.

---

[4] Trades Union Congress: "Norway", in *Review of working time in Britain and the Western Europe* (London, 1988), p. 38.

[5] Ministry of Labour, op. cit.

[6] ibid.

Normal hours of work

Law

Normal hours of work are legally 40 hours per week and nine hours per day.[7]

The WEA is applicable to all enterprises where there are one or more employees. Certain categories of work and workers not covered by the law include managerial staff, salespersons, commercial travellers, teachers, work in lighthouses, field work and expeditions.[8] Special rules apply to mining and to work on drilling platforms in the North Sea, as well as to sea-farers, people working in aviation, household assistants and agricultural workers. There are also special rules for shift and night work. However, the main rules, as well as other provisions in the WEA regarding the duration and structure of hours of work, may be modified by collective agreement. Furthermore, an employer whose enterprise is covered by collective agreement may make its provisions relating to working hours applicable to all employees who perform work of the nature covered by agreement, subject to approval by the Ministry of Labour.

Young workers

According to the WEA, children under 15 year of age may not be employed for ordinary work.[9] They may only carry out simple jobs, such as light messenger work.[10] Many heavy and dangerous jobs may not be carried out by young people between the ages of 15 and 18. People aged 14 or more may be employed for work as part of their schooling or practical vocational training. The working hours for children and young people must be such that it is not difficult for them to do their school work. Overtime and night work are not permitted for children and young people under 18 years of age, and they are entitled to an off-duty period of at least 12 hours between two working periods. The off-duty period shall always include the period from 21:00 to 07:00 for employees under the age of 16, and the period from 23:00 and 06:00 for employees from 16 to 18. Exceptionally, employees aged 16 or more may be called to work between 23:00 and 06:00 in cases of strict necessity.[11]

---

[7] Section 46, Act No. 4 respecting workers' protection and the working environment, dated 4 February 1977 (*Norsk Lovtidend*, Part I, No. 4, 14 February 1977, p. 77), as amended up to Act No. 2, dated 6 January 1995 (*Norsk Lovtidend*, Part I, 1995) [LS 1977-Nor.1; LLD 1995-NOR 1].

[8] ibid., Section 41.

[9] ibid., Section 34.

[10] Regulations concerning work by students in public schools above 13 years of age, with reference to Article 35(a)-(c) of the WEA, dated 22 September 1977, in Direktoratet for arbeidstilsynet: *Arbeid av barn og ungdom* (Oslo, 1990), pp. 5-6.

[11] WEA, op. cit., Sections 34-40; Regulations concerning work by students in public schools above 13 years of age, op. cit.; Regulations concerning exceptions from the prohibition of night work for persons under 18 years of age, with reference to Section 37(4), as amended up to 1986, of the WEA, dated 24 August 1977, in Direktoratet for arbeidstilsynet, op. cit., pp. 7-8; Regulations respecting young people at work where particular measures of precaution are required, dated 23 June 1993, Ministry of Labour, op. cit.

Oil extraction

There are special rules on working time in the oil extraction industry. The ordinary working hours shall not exceed 12 hours per day and 36 hours per week, on average, over a maximum period of one year. Representative worker organizations may conclude collective agreements concerning a different arrangement of working hours, notwithstanding these restrictions. Subject to the consent of the Ministry, an employer who has negotiated such a collective agreement may make the provisions regarding working hours applicable to all employees.[12]

Practice

In practice, normal working hours are 37.5 hours per week and 7.5 hours per day.[13]

Working time arrangements are frequently negotiated by collective agreement, and the majority of such agreements provide for more favourable provisions than the law.[14]

[12] Royal Decree concerning regulations respecting worker protection and the working environment, etc., in connection with exploration for and exploitation of submarine petroleum resources, dated 1 June 1979 (*Norsk Lovtidend*, 1979), as amended up to Royal Decree, dated 13 September 1985 (*Norsk Lovtidend*, 1985), in Petroleum Directorate: *Regelverksamling for petroleumsvirksomheten* (Collection of laws and regulations relating to oil extraction) (Oslo, 1992), pp. 169-174.

[13] Ministry of Labour, op. cit.; information provided to the ILO by the Confederation of Norwegian Business and Industry, May 1995.

[14] D. Anxo and H. Locking: "Politiques et évolution du temps de travail en Norvège", in R. Hoffmann and J. Lapeyre (eds.): *Le temps de travail en Europe: Organisation et réduction* (Paris, Syros, 1995), p. 147.

Table 1. Hours of work per week by major divisions of economic activity[15]

Major division	1984	1985	1986	1987	1988	1989	1990	1991	1992	1993	1994
Mining and quarrying	42.2	44.8	44.0	42.4	43.1	42.4	42.8	42.4	42.2	43.5	43.8
Manufacturing	37.7	38.2	38.4	37.2	37.7	37.7	37.0	36.8	36.8	36.8	36.9
Electricity, gas and water	37.4	37.9	38.6	37.8	38.9	37.7	36.8	36.1	36.5	36.8	36.6
Construction	39.5	40.3	40.3	39.1	40.3	39.8	39.2	38.9	38.6	39.0	39.3
Trades, restaurants and hotels	33.1	33.6	34.0	33.2	34.3	34.2	33.8	33.6	33.6	33.4	33.1
Transport, storage and communication	38.4	39.3	39.4	38.7	39.0	38.8	39.0	38.8	38.3	38.3	38.5
Financing, insurance, real estate and business services	36.7	36.7	37.4	37.2	37.4	37.8	37.4	37.3	37.4	37.4	37.0
Community, social and personal services	32.1	32.5	32.9	32.7	33.1	33.2	32.9	32.7	32.7	32.7	32.9
Total (all non-agricultural activities)	35.0	35.5	35.8	35.2	35.8	35.7	35.3	35.0	34.9	34.9	35.0

Overtime and absolute maximum hours

Law

Overtime is defined as work for longer hours than the normal hours of work as prescribed in the WEA, or as agreed upon in a collective agreement. Overtime is legally required to be paid at the rate of regular pay plus 40 per cent. Overtime work must not be established as a regular system and cannot be performed except in the following cases: (a) when unforseen circumstances or the absence of employees risk causing disruptions of work; (b) when overtime is necessary to prevent damage; (c) when there is an unforseen volume of work; and (d) when a special workload has occurred because of lack of manpower with special competence, seasonal fluctuations or other valid reasons. Individual employees have the right to be exempted from overtime and additional work on grounds of health and other valid personal reasons.

The basic statutory limits to overtime work are ten hours per week, 25 hours during four consecutive weeks, or 200 hours in a calendar year. Overtime must not, however, together

---

[15] Bureau of Statistics, International Labour Office [hours actually worked; employees; labour force sample survey; including agriculture, hunting, forestry and fishing].

with normal hours of work, result in an employee working more than 14 hours in any 24-hour period.[16]

Overtime can be extended in four ways. First, it can be extended by agreement with local employee representatives. In enterprises bound by a collective agreement, the employer and the elected representatives of the employees may conclude a written agreement, applicable for a period of up to three months, stipulating overtime work for up to 15 hours per week, provided that the total overtime worked does not exceed 40 hours in the course of four consecutive weeks and the total overtime work must not exceed 300 hours in the course of one calendar year for each individual employee. Total hours of work must not exceed 16 hours in one single 24-hour period. Such an agreement may be extended to all employees at an enterprise who perform work of the type covered by the agreement, but can only be imposed on individual employees who have agreed to perform such extended overtime.

Second, overtime can be extended by permission of the Labour Inspectorate which, in special cases, may permit overtime for up to 20 hours per week and for more than 200 hours in the calendar year.

Third, overtime can be extended by a collective agreement with a trade union. In this case, there are no statutory limits prescribed, but the employees must have expressed their willingness to work overtime.

Fourth, overtime can be extended by dispensation of the Labour Inspectorate when the work is of such a special nature that it cannot be adapted to the provisions of the WEA. In this case, the consent of the individual employees is not required, but they shall be assured a satisfactory standard of safety and welfare.

In the case of people working reduced hours or part time, hours in excess of the number of hours agreed upon, but within the normal hours of work for full-time employees, shall be regarded as additional hours. There is no legal right to be paid a premium for additional time, but in practice it is typically compensated with a premium which is nevertheless inferior to the overtime rate of pay.

It is possible to average working hours over certain periods of time. Generally, and by written agreement, averaging is permitted so that, over a period not exceeding one year, the hours of work correspond to the legally provided hours. However, working hours may not exceed 48 in any one week, and daily hours may not exceed nine hours. The agreement shall stipulate which weeks of the year shall have longer or shorter hours of work, unless this is to be decided by the employee.[17] With agreement with the worker's elected representatives, weekly maximum hours can be extended to 54 and the daily maximum hours to ten when the nature of the work so requires; when the work is characterized by seasonal variations; or when time off cannot be used in a satisfactory manner due to the location of the work. Hours that are longer than those normally provided for, i.e. 40 hours per week and nine hours per day, may

[16] ibid., Section 50(1).

[17] ibid., Section 47(1).

not be used for consecutive periods longer than six weeks.[18] With the permission of the Labour Inspectorate, the averaging of hours of work may extend over one year, irrespective of the daily and weekly hours of work limits.[19]

Practice

According to statistics, there has been a steady increase in overtime during the last ten years. Expressed as a percentage of overall hours worked, paid overtime was 4 per cent in 1984 as compared to 6 per cent in 1994. Sharp increases in 1986 and 1987 were attributable to the general reduction in working hours from 40 to 37.5 hours per week that was introduced by collective agreement during that period, according to the Ministry of Labour. The Ministry has also indicated that a fair amount of overtime is generated by the large oil industry, which has particularly high levels of overtime. In the manufacturing sector, the rise of overtime levels from below-average levels in the 1980s to average levels by 1993 has also contributed to the growth of overtime work. Overtime pay is normally double regular pay.[20]

Rest

Law

Rest breaks

Employees are entitled to at least one rest break when hours of work exceed five-and-a-half hours per day, and rest breaks should total at least 30 minutes when hours of work are eight hours or longer. When employees are required to work overtime for more than two hours after completing ordinary hours of work, they shall first be allowed a break of at least 30 minutes. Breaks which occur after the end of normal hours of work shall be subject to remuneration as overtime, but shall not be included in the number of hours of permitted overtime. If the break occurs before the end of normal hours of work, it shall be regarded as part of normal hours of work.[21]

Daily rest periods

Employees are to have a continuous rest period of at least ten hours between two working periods. This period can be reduced to eight hours by agreement between the employer and the elected representatives of the workers, if necessary, in order to ensure that services are provided in a suitable manner. In cases when a risk of serious disturbance to operations

[18] ibid., Section 47(2).

[19] ibid., Section 47(3).

[20] Ministry of Labour, op. cit.

[21] WEA, op. cit., Section 51(1).

occurs, a work assignment of a short duration during the rest period may be agreed to. The Labour Inspectorate may also consent to a shortening of the rest period in special cases.[22]

Weekly rest

Ordinary hours of work shall be assigned so that each week has a continuous rest period of at least 36 hours and that one full 24-hour day (midnight to midnight) is included in it. At enterprises with a collective agreement, agreement may be reached that this rest period shall, on average, be 36 hours, but never shorter than 28 hours in a single week. The period over which averaging of weekly rest periods is permitted shall correspond to the averaging period for hours of work. No work is to be performed from 18:00 the day before a Sunday or public holiday until 22:00 of the evening preceding the next working day. There are special rules for religious holidays (e.g. Christmas, Easter and Whit Sunday) and exceptions for various types of work. An employee who has worked on a Sunday or public holiday shall normally be allowed the following Sunday or public holiday off. The Labour Inspectorate may permit exceptions. By agreement for a period of up to six months, hours of work can be so arranged that the employees will be off on average every other Sunday and public holiday, provided that during at least every third week, the weekly day of rest shall be a Sunday or public holiday. Work schedules may differ from these in the hotel and restaurant sector.[23]

Practice

In practice, daily rest is normally 16 hours and weekly rest 36 hours.[24]

Shop-opening hours

Law

According to the Act respecting shop-opening hours of 1985, the local authorities may restrict local shop-opening hours outside certain time spans, but they may not restrict shop-opening hours between 06:00 and 20:00 on Monday through Friday; between 08:00 and 18:00 on Saturdays and the day before public holidays; and between 06:00 and 15:00 on the day before Easter Saturday, Whit Saturday, Christmas Eve and New Year's Eve.[25] On Sundays and public holidays, shops may be authorized to be open between 14:00 to 19:00 (for example, in tourist areas), with the exception of Christmas Day, Easter Sunday, Whit Sunday and Good Friday, when shops shall be closed. The Act does not apply to sales in smaller outlets, such as kiosks and newsstands, outlets linked to transportation and touristic areas, restaurants, sales of certain items such as petrol, sales by auction, sales in art galleries, and the like. Prior to

---

[22] ibid., Section 51(2).

[23] ibid., Section 51.

[24] Confederation of Norwegian Business and Industry, op. cit.

[25] Act No. 20 respecting shop-opening hours, dated 26 April 1985 (*Norsk Lovtidend*, Part I, No. 8, 15 May 1985, p. 344).

the 1985 Act, shop-opening hours were tightly regulated, and shops were normally permitted to be open only between 08:00 to 16:00.[26]

Practice

The right to establish local standards regarding shop-opening hours had been used by some 315 of the 442 local authorities. As of 1992, 242 counties had chosen to limit shop-opening hours to the maximum extent possible according to the law, i.e. prescribing that shops should not open before 06:00, nor close later than 20:00. Approximately 100 counties authorize Sunday shopping one to three Sundays per year in the period preceding Christmas.[27]

Public holidays

Law

There are 12 public holidays and these are New Year's Day, Maundy Thursday, Good Friday, Easter Sunday, Easter Monday, Ascension Day, Whit Sunday, Whit Monday, Christmas Day and Boxing Day.[28] The 1st and 17th of May are special holidays that, by separate legislation, have the status of "festivals".[29] Employees are entitled to pay during these two days only after a qualifying period of 30 days of service. Employees required to work on these two days are entitled to the premium pay applicable to Sundays according to the collective agreements in force or, in the absence thereof, at least 50 per cent of the ordinary wage. The provisions regarding the 1st and 17th of May may be set aside by collective agreement.[30]

The WEA defines work on Sunday or a public holiday to extend from 18:00 the day before to 22:00 of the evening preceding the next working day. Certain types of work are generally permitted during Sundays and public holidays, such as work that should not be interrupted; work in relation to transport and communication; work in theatres, hotels and restaurants; and work in relation to medical care and nursing. Work at retail establishments is exempted and regulated separately.[31] For other types of work, up to eight Sundays or public holidays per calendar year may be permitted, subject to an agreement with the workers' elected representatives or, without such prescribed limitations, by the Labour Inspectorate. Such work includes seasonal work, unexpectedly heavy workloads, natural occurrences or when impor-

---

[26] Act No. 5 respecting the closing of shops, dated 25 July 1913 (*Norsk Lovtidend*, 1913), as amended up to Act No. 7, dated 1 July 1926 (*Norsk Lovtidend*, No. 2, 1926, p. 356). See also Institut syndical européen: "Norvège", in *La fléxibilité du temps de travail dans le secteur du commerce en Europe occidentale* (Brussels, 1992), pp. 55-56.

[27] Institut syndical européen, op. cit., p. 55.

[28] Act No. 1 respecting Sundays and public holidays, dated 4 June 1965 (*Norsk Lovtidend*, No. 21, 8 July 1965, pp. 992-995).

[29] Act No. 1 relating to 1 and 17 May as festivals, dated 26 April 1947 (*Norsk Lovtidend*, No. 15, 6 May 1947, pp. 251-253).

[30] ibid.

[31] Act No. 20 respecting shop-opening hours, op. cit.

tant community interests render work imperative. Work on Christmas Day, on the Saturdays preceding Easter Sunday and Whit Sunday, or on Maundy Thursday and Good Friday can only be required if there is an express provision to that effect in an agreement or if permission is granted by the Labour Inspectorate.[32] An employee who has worked on a Sunday or public holiday shall be allowed the following Sunday or public holiday off.[33] The law does not specify the compensation to be provided.

A special type of individual agreement to work on Sundays and public holidays is also provided for in the law. Such an agreement can be made for the purpose of allowing the employee corresponding time off on the days that are equivalent to Sundays and public holidays in accordance with the employee's religion.[34]

Practice

The practice is to provide for regular pay plus a 100 per cent premium for work on Sundays and public holidays.[35]

Paid annual leave

Law

Since 1981, employees have been entitled to four weeks and one day of paid annual leave.[36] Although it was intended to institute a full fifth week of holiday, difficult economic conditions led to a decision not to go ahead with this project. The Act does not apply to employees on ships or to fishermen whose leave entitlements are regulated by special legislation.[37] Collectively agreed annual leave provisions are only permitted if they are the same or more favourable to the employees than the requirements of the Act. All days count as workdays, except Sundays and statutory church and public holidays.[38]

---

[32] WEA, op. cit., Section 44.

[33] ibid., Section 51(3)(iv).

[34] ibid., Section 45.

[35] Confederation of Norwegian Business and Industry, op. cit.

[36] Act No. 21 respecting annual leave, dated 29 April 1988 (*Norsk Lovtidend*, Part I, No. 7, 11 May 1988, pp. 233-244), as amended up to Act No. 34, dated 15 June 1990 (*Norsk Lovtidend*, Part I, No. 9, 5 July 1990, pp. 498-502).

[37] Royal Decree to establish regulations respecting holidays for employees on ships, dated 22 December 1989 (*Norsk Lovtidend*, Part I, No. 24, 18 January 1990); Act No. 43 respecting holidays of fishermen, dated 16 June 1972 (*Norsk Lovtidend*, Part I, No. 20, 25 July 1972, p. 770), as amended up to Act No. 83, dated 17 December 1982 (*Norsk Lovtidend*, Part I, No. 28, 6 January 1983, pp. 699-700).

[38] The Act does not refer to Labour Day (1 May) and Constitution Day (17 May). They are work-free days, but labelled "festivals", and not public holidays. As a consequence, annual leave taken to include these days would not allow for a deduction from the days counted as public holidays. Cf. Act No. 1 of 4 June 1965, op. cit., and Act No. 1 of 26 April 1947, op. cit.

The reference period for paid annual leave is the calendar year and the qualifying year for vacation pay is the preceding calendar year. Employees may claim annual leave irrespective of annual leave pay earned. However, employees may refuse to take annual leave to the extent that they have not qualified for annual leave pay which would compensate them during their absence on annual leave. The main vacation period is from 1 June to 30 September. Employees may demand to have three weeks of their paid annual leave during that period. By way of collective agreement, other rules may also apply concerning the right to transfer unused paid annual leave to a following year. However, no more than 12 days may be transferred. The general holiday pay is 10.2 per cent of the wages paid in the qualifying year. This is equivalent to a person's regular salary, plus a small additional supplementary vacation payment. The holiday pay is payable on the last normal day before the holiday.

Persons above 60 are entitled to six extra vacation days and to vacation pay of 12.5 per cent of wages earned in the qualifying year.

Practice

Although the law allows for certain variations to the provisions of the Holidays Act, the length of annual leave as provided for by law seems to be generally applied.[39]

Other types of leave

Law

Health, social or welfare reasons

Since 1982, there is a statutory right for employees to have their normal hours of work reduced for health or social reasons or other reasons relating to their well-being. This right is subject to the condition that the reduction of working hours can be arranged without particular inconvenience to the employer. The reduction of hours may be taken as rest periods.[40]

Care of a sick or disabled child

Employees having children under the age of 12 in their care have the right to take time off if the child is sick and it is necessary to stay at home. The same applies if the person who otherwise has the daily responsibility for the child is sick. This right is limited to ten days per year. A single parent has the right to 20 days of leave annually. If the employee has more than one child, the limits are extended to 15 days of leave annually for two-parent families and to 30 days for single parents. There are more extensive rights to leave for parents with chronically ill and disabled children and when children are hospitalized.[41]

---

[39] Confederation of Norwegian Business and Industry, op. cit.

[40] WEA, op. cit., Section 44A.

[41] ibid., Section 33A.

Care for terminally ill relatives

There is also a statutory right to 20 days' leave of absence to care for relatives at a terminal stage of illness.[42]

Public duties

Employees have a right to a leave of absence to undertake public duties. The limit imposed is "to such extent as is required in order to comply with statutory requirements to attend to public duties".[43]

Practice

In practice, additional single days off with pay are commonly given for the following reasons: death or funeral of a relative, examination and treatment by doctor or dentist, the rest of the day when the employee has to leave work because of illness, family members with acute illness, partner giving birth or being hospitalized, moving from one residence to another, and giving blood.[44]

Shift and night work

Law

Ordinary working time is statutorily limited to 38 hours per week for discontinuous shift work; work in two shifts regularly operated on Sundays and public holidays; for work involving an obligation to work at least every third Sunday; and in case of work principally performed at night. Furthermore, ordinary working time is limited to 36 hours per week for employees on continuous shift work, for those performing work underground in mines (the time spent going down to and up from the mine shall be counted as working time), as well as for workers carrying out certain tunnelling work and the blasting of galleries underground.

Work between 21:00 and 06:00 is considered as night work. Night work is generally not permitted. The law provides for a list of 17 exceptions, which include most prominently transport, health services, restaurants and hotels. A provision which requires prior consultation with locally elected representatives for the scheduling of night work was introduced in 1995. Night work may also be permitted in other cases when it is necessary, i.e. when an especially heavy workload arises at regularly recurring periods of the year or when there is an unexpectedly heavy workload. Such permission can be in the form of an agreement with the employees' elected representatives for a total period of up to six months in the course of one year. Night work can also be authorized by the Labour Inspectorate.

---

[42] ibid., Section 33B.

[43] ibid., Section 33C.

[44] Confederation of Norwegian Business and Industry, op. cit.

Practice

According to statistics by the Norges Offisielle Statistikk (NOS) (Norwegian Official Statistics), continuous seven-day shiftworkers work 33.6 hours per week; three-shift workers, 33.5 hours per week; and two-shift workers, 36.5 hours per week. Non-shiftworkers work the standard 37.5-hour week.[45]

---

[45] Norges Offisielle Statistikk: *Lønnstelling for arbeidere i oljeutvinning, bergverksdrift og industri: 3. kvartal 1990* (Wage census for workers in oil extraction, mining and manufacturing: 3rd quarter 1990) (Oslo, 1990), NOS C6, pp. 8-12, 132.

South Africa

Overview and trends

Overview

Labour relations and collective bargaining in South Africa have been traditionally characterized by a relatively high degree of centralization, both before and after the transition to a multiracial democracy. Industrial council agreements between employer organizations and trade unions, other national agreements or company agreements, and official wage determinations made by the Government under the Wage Act have established the terms and conditions of employment in most enterprises.[1] The Basic Conditions of Employment Act provides a minimum standard of terms and conditions of employment, and includes provisions on working time issues.[2] The Basic Conditions of Employment Act was amended in 1992 to cover domestic employees and in 1993 to cover agricultural workers. Public sector employees, however, are not covered by the Basic Conditions of Employment Act, but by the Public Service Act.[3] Collective bargaining and labour relations are dealt with by a new Labour Relations Act, adopted in 1995.[4]

Trends

Parliamentary elections (to the National Assembly and Senate) were held in April 1994 and elected Members will hold office until 1999. In addition, a multi-racial Government of National Unity was formed following the April 1994 elections. The Government of National Unity has outlined an ambitious set of reforms of labour market regulation.[5]

The South African Reconstruction and Development Programme[6] is the centrepiece of the new Government's efforts to institute reforms in general, and Section 4.8, "Labour and worker rights", deals with policies to be pursued on labour relations. Section 4.8, however, only deals with broad principles of labour relations, and not with working time directly. Goals under

---

[1] Incomes Data Services (IDS): *Employment in South Africa 1995* (London, 1995), p. 40. See also Wage Act 1957, Act No. 5, dated 19 February 1957 (*Government Gazette*, 1957), as amended up to Act No. 97, dated 3 October 1986 (*Statutes of the Republic of South Africa*, Vol. 10, No. 29, 1995, pp. 641-683) [LS 1957-SA1].

[2] Basic Conditions of Employment Act 1983, Act No. 3, dated 16 February 1983 (*Government Gazette*, 1983), as amended up to Act No. 66, dated 29 November 1995 (*Government Gazette*, Vol. 366, No. 16,861, 13 December 1995, p. 1) [LS 1983-SA1; 1984-SA1].

[3] Public Service Act 1994, Act No. 103, dated 1 June 1994 (*Government Gazette*, Vol. 348, No. 15,791, 3 June 1994, p. 1; Public Service Regulations 1994, Regulation No. 1091, dated 10 June 1994 (*Government Gazette*, Vol. 348, No. 15,804, Regulation Gazette No. 5350, 10 June 1994, p. 1).

[4] Labour Relations Act, Act No. 66, dated 29 November 1995 (*Government Gazette*, Vol. 366, No. 16,861, 13 December 1995, p. 1).

[5] IDS, *Employment in South Africa*, op. cit., p. 7.

[6] White Paper on Reconstruction and Development, Notice No. 1954, dated 15 November 1994 (*Government Gazette*, Vol. 353, No. 16,085, 23 November 1994, p. 1).

Section 4.8 include equal rights for all workers; extended rights to organize and join trade unions; the right to strike and picket on social and economic issues; the right to information from companies and governments; the right to a decent wage and safe and healthy working conditions; changes in the collective bargaining system; enhanced jurisdiction for industrial councils to negotiate industrial policy, training and education, job placement and job creation; an obligation for employers to negotiate changes with respect to production matters and workplace organization; an obligation for the Government to upgrade skills; affirmative action to end discrimination on the grounds of race and sex; development of skills of South Africans rather than resort to outside technical personnel; a legal prohibition of sexual harassment; ratification of ILO conventions; and restructuring of labour market institutions.

In February 1995, a Ministerial task team, which included representatives of labour, management and academia, submitted a report which identified problems with existing law, and made both detailed and highly complex recommendations for changes in some aspects of the law. Although there were many proposals for change, including implementation of Section 4.8 of the South African Reconstruction and Development Programme, the principal reform suggested which could affect working time issues included a recommendation for a new Labour Relations Act[7] which would, inter alia, provide for the establishment of an independent Commission for Conciliation, Mediation and Arbitration (the "Commission") based on its counterparts in the United Kingdom and Australia.

The new Labour Relations Act, which came into effect on 13 December 1995, provides for the establishment of workplace forums in establishments of more than 100 employees, if requested by representative worker organizations, to work with the employer to enhance efficiency through worker participation. The matters to be discussed in such workplace forums include changes in organization of work. The new Labour Relations Act also includes a statutory right for a reasonable amount of time off for trade union activities.[8]

Normal hours of work

Law

The weekly legal limit for normal hours of work for most employees is 46 hours, excluding meal breaks. Specific exceptions are applicable to farm workers whose working time extends to 48 hours, excluding meal breaks, and security guards who may work for up to 60 hours a week, including meal breaks. The legal limits set out in the law, however, do not apply to certain occupational categories, such as "outside sales assistants, a traveller, a traveller's assistant, a demonstration-salesman, a property salesman, or an insurance agent, nor to employees in or in connection with a shop or an office with a specifically provided level of salary".[9] The limit for employees of the commercial distributive trade is 45 hours a week, except if they work for "small employers" with less than four employees, or for "new

---

[7] Draft negotiating document in the form of a Labour Relations Bill, Notice No. 97 (*Government Gazette*, Vol. 356, No. 16,259, 10 February 1995, p. 1).

[8] Labour Relations Act, op. cit., Sections 78-94 and Schedule 2.

[9] Basic Conditions of Employment Act, op. cit., Section 2(3).

employers", who have been in business for less than 12 months.[10] Public servants have a normal working week of 40 hours over five working days.[11]

With respect to daily limits, day workers and casual employees[12] who work a five-day week are limited to 9:15 hours of work per day. Day workers on a six-day week are limited to eight hours a day, or five eight-and-a-half- hour days and one shorter day that shall not exceed five hours. Security guards who work a six-day week are limited to a ten-hour day. If they work a five-day week, they can work 12 hours per day.[13]

Practice

In practice, many collective agreements provide for shorter working hours per week than the statutory limit. According to one source, the average working week is about 43 hours.[14] There is, however, significant variation in weekly hours among different industries. For example, the auto-assembly agreement provides for a 40-hour working week,[15] and an agreement in the building industry provides for a 42-hour week.[16] However, the metal industry agreement provides for a 44-hour week,[17] and the motor industry agreement provides for a 45-hour week.[18] A private survey showed the following distribution of hours agreed to in 13 Industrial Council agreements and in 39 companies (Table 1):[19]

[10] Wage Act 1957, op. cit.; Wage Determination 478: Commercial Distrubtive Trade, Certain Areas, Government Notice No. R1314, dated 25 August 1995 (*Government Gazette*, Vol. 362, No. 16,627, Regulation Gazette No. 5560, 25 August 1995, pp. 1-80).

[11] Public Service Act, op. cit.; Public Service Regulations, op. cit.

[12] "Day worker" is defined to be an employee who is not a shiftworker, and "casual worker" is defined to be an employee who is employed by the employer on not more than three days in any week, but does not include a "regular day worker", who is defined as a domestic worker employed on not more than three days in any week for the same employer for a period of not less than four consecutive weeks. Basic Conditions of Employment Act, op. cit., Section 1.

[13] ibid., Section 4.

[14] IDS, *Employment in South Africa*, op. cit., p. 99.

[15] ibid.

[16] For most employees, excluding watchmen and some motor vehicle drivers. For the latter, a working week of 48 hours is prescribed. Building Industry, North and West Boland: Main agreement, Regulation No. 805, dated 9 June 1995 (*Government Gazette*, Vol. 360, No. 16,452, Regulation Gazette No. 5513, 9 June 1995, p. 1).

[17] IDS, *Employment in South Africa*, op. cit., p. 99.

[18] Motor industry: Main agreement, Regulation No. 838, dated 23 June 1995 (*Government Gazette*, Vol. 360, No. 16,466, Regulation Gazette No. 5519, 23 June 1995, p. 1).

[19] Carried out by Andrew Levy & Associates, Rivonia, South Africa, and cited in IDS, *Employment in South Africa*, op. cit., p. 99.

Table 1. Distribution of hours agreed to in industrial agreements and companies

Hours agreed	Industrial agreements	Companies
46	1	2
45	2	8
44	3	4
43	---	3
42.5	1	---
42	---	3
41.5	---	1
40	6	14
38.75	---	1
37.5	---	3

Table 2 below illustrates the average number of working hours in some sectors for which official statistics are available.

Table 2. Actual hours of work per week by major divisions of economic activity[20]

Major division	1984	1985	1986	1987	1988	1989	1990	1991	1992	1993
Manufacturing	46.5	45.9	46.4	46.2	47.2	47.5	45.4	44.9	44.7	---
Construction	44.8	45.4	46.0	45.1	45.6	43.8	43.5	44.4	44.3	---
Trades, restaurants and hotels	35.6	36.0	36.1	35.7	35.8	36.1	36.3	36.0	35.9	34.6

[20] Bureau of Statistics, International Labour Office [hours actually worked; employees; excludes Transkei, Bophutswana, Venda, Ciskei; other geographical coverage of samples not specified].

Overtime and absolute maximum hours

Law[21]

Subject to an agreement between the employer and the employee, overtime may be worked for a maximum of three hours per day or ten hours per week. A labour inspector may, upon application by an employer and after consultation with the employee or employees affected, increase the maximum limit for overtime work by a written notice. Domestic workers may work overtime for up to 14 hours per week. These limitations do not apply in case of emergencies.[22]

The statutorily provided minimum rate of overtime pay is one-and-a-third times the worker's regular rate of pay. At least doubletime pay is to be paid for work on Sunday. Alternatively, compensation can be offered in the form of one-and-a-third times regular pay plus the granting of an extra day of paid leave. Exempt from these requirements are employees in shops which by law are entitled to be open on Sundays, provided that the employees get another day off during the week.

The law also allows for a type of averaging to avoid overtime for domestic and farm workers. Normal daily working time for domestic workers and farm workers may be extended, subject to a written agreement: by eight hours per week for an agreed period not exceeding four months, with respect to a farm worker, and by four hours per week for a period not exceeding 26 days, with respect to a domestic worker, during any 12-month period. A corresponding reduction of working time in an equivalent time period subsequent to the period of extended working hours is then due within the same 12-month period for both categories of worker. If for some reason the corresponding reduction in working time does not take place within the 12-month period, the employer is liable to the employee for payment of the extended hours worked as overtime. In any event, the daily working hours of a farm worker may not be extended to more than 14 hours, and those of a domestic worker to more than 12 hours. No overtime may be worked by the domestic worker on days of extended working time, and farm workers may only work two-and-a-half hours of overtime per day and no more than six hours of overtime a week when on an extended working time schedule.[23]

In the public sector, the employer has an express right to require overtime on "any day of the week or at any time during the day or night". Although employees have no right to claim overtime remuneration for extra hours, the Public Service Commission may decide to offer such remuneration.[24]

The law addresses the question of absolute daily and weekly maximum hours of work by specifying a maximum daily spreadover and by weekly limits on overtime. The maximum daily spreadover is defined to mean the period "from the time when such employee first

[21] Basic Conditions of Employment Act, op. cit., Section 3.

[22] ibid., Section 8.

[23] ibid., Section 6A; Agricultural Labour Act, Act No. 147, dated 1 October 1993 (*Government Gazette*, Vol. 340, No. 15,173, 13 October 1993, pp. 1-11).

[24] Public Service Regulations, op. cit., Section G 1.2.

commences work until he ceases work for that day", and is limited to 12 hours, subject to exceptions.[25] For example, domestic workers and farm workers may have a daily maximum spreadover of 14 hours. There are also exceptions and special rules applicable to security guards and shiftworkers.

Practice

In the motor industry, the maximum ordinary daily working time is eight hours, excluding meal breaks. The ordinary daily working time can, however, be extended by a maximum of 30 minutes on any given day for employees working a six-day week, and by one-and-a-quarter hours for five-day a week employees. For some categories of employees (mainly clerical employees), an additional limitation is that ordinary working time must not terminate later than 20:00 Monday to Friday, and not later than 13:00 on Saturday. Senior managers are usually excluded from overtime limits and do not have any expectation to be paid for overtime worked. For other employees, there is a general limit of ten hours of overtime work per week, to which can be added an additional ten hours, subject to permission being granted by the competent authorities. Overtime for more than 60 hours over a period of four consecutive months is not permitted. The minimum payment for overtime for most categories of employees is one-and-a-half times regular pay for work between 06:00 and 24:00, and double pay for work between 24:00 and 06:00.[26] In the motor industry, it is provided that non-shiftworkers, as opposed to shiftworkers, are not required to work on Sundays.

The national agreement in the engineering industry (NICISEMI) provides that overtime should be paid at the rate of time-and-a-third for the first six hours, and time-and-a-half thereafter until the normal starting time of the employee's next shift. Overtime worked on Saturdays in an establishment on a five-day working week is paid at one-and-a-third times for the first six hours, and then one-and-a-half thereafter. In some companies, all overtime after Saturday at noon is payable at time-and-a-half.[27] The national agreement sets a rate of double pay for work on Sunday, with a minimum payment of the hours of a normal shift. Urgent maintenance work on Sundays attracts double pay, with a minimum of four hours' pay. There is a minimum of eight hours' pay if morning work extends into the afternoon.[28]

---

[25] Basic Conditions of Employment Act, op. cit., Sections 1 and 3.

[26] Motor industry: Main agreement, op. cit.

[27] IDS, *Employment in South Africa*, op. cit., p. 90.

[28] ibid.

Rest

Law

Rest breaks

Work shall not continue for more than five hours continuously without a meal break, which shall not be less than one hour. An employer may conclude an agreement with an employee to shorten the meal interval to no less than 30 minutes, but such an agreement shall not have force unless the employer (other than the employer of a domestic worker) has given notice to the Labour Inspectorate. Time for a meal break in excess of one hour and 15 minutes shall be regarded as working time, except in the case of farm or domestic workers. The provisions of the law do not apply to some categories of workers such as, for example, security guards, continuous shiftworkers, certain occupations where the nature of work is independently performed, and work in emergency situations.[29]

In the public service, meal breaks are to be provided for, but are not counted as working time.[30]

Weekly rest

Work on Sundays in factories and shops, with the exception of employment in a "continuous activity", is not permitted without written permission from a labour inspector (see below under **Shop-opening hours**).[31]

Work connected with operating mines and works and of machinery used in connection therewith is prohibited on Sundays, Christmas Day and Good Friday, unless it is essential for the maintenance of the mines or special permission has been obtained from an inspector of mines.[32]

Practice

Rest breaks

In the motor industry, employees are entitled to a meal break of at least one hour after five hours of continuous service. Subject to a special agreement registered with competent authorities, five-day employees may agree with the employer to have only a 30 minute break. In addition, employees are entitled to two ten-minute work pauses, one in the morning and

[29] Basic Conditions of Employment Act, op. cit., Section 7.

[30] Public Service Regulations, op. cit., Section G 1.3.

[31] Basic Conditions of Employment Act, op. cit., Section 10.

[32] Mines and Works Act 1956, Act No. 27, dated 2 May 1956 (*Statutes of the Union of South Africa*, Part I, 1956, pp. 493-517), as amended up to Act No. 13, dated 18 March 1991 (*Government Gazette*, Vol. 310, No. 13,117, 3 April 1991, pp. 1-7). Section 9.

one in the afternoon, which are paid and counted as part of working time.[33] Other industrial agreements sometimes provide for two 15-minute work pauses, one in the morning and the other in the afternoon, in addition to the meal break.[34]

Shop-opening hours

Law

A general restriction on shops being open on Sundays is imposed by the Basic Conditions of Employment Act.[35] Exceptions may be granted by a labour inspector. A general exception is granted to employers who, by law, are entitled to carry on business in shops on Sundays. The Act does not contain any other restrictions on shop-opening hours.

Public holidays

Law

According to the Public Holidays Act, there are 12 paid public holidays: New Year's Day (1 January), Human Rights Day (21 March), Good Friday, Family Day (Monday after Easter Sunday), Freedom Day (27 April), Workers' Day (1 May), Youth Day (16 June), National Women's Day (9 August), Heritage Day (24 September), the Day of Reconciliation (16 December), Christmas Day (25 December), and the Day of Goodwill (26 December).[36] The names of all public holidays are not universally accepted. For example, the Day of Reconciliation, previously known as the Day of the Vow by Afrikaners, is sometimes referred to as Dingaan's Day in memory of the Zulu ruler, Dingaan, who was defeated by the Vootrekkers at the Battle of Blood River on this day in 1838. Similarly, Human Rights Day is also known as Sharpeville Day; Freedom Day is sometimes referred to as Election Day; Youth Day as Soweto Day; and Heritage Day as Cultural Day.[37]

The 1994 law on paid public holidays applies to all employees, including farm and domestic workers. If a public holiday falls on a Sunday, the following Monday is deemed to be the holiday. Any public holiday can be exchanged for any other day by agreement, provided that the employee still receives the same number of paid public holidays. This is in recognition of the fact that not all South Africans will, for example, wish to recognize Christmas as a public holiday.

Employees are entitled to time off with pay on public holidays. Employees who work on a public holiday, which falls on a day which otherwise would be ordinary working time, get

---

[33] Motor industry: Main agreement, op. cit.

[34] IDS, *Employment in South Africa*, op. cit., p. 103.

[35] Basic Conditions of Employment Act, op. cit., Section 10.

[36] Public Holidays Act 1994, Act No. 36, dated 23 November 1994 (*Government Gazette*, Vol. 354, No. 16,136, 7 December 1994, p. 3).

[37] IDS, *Employment in South Africa*, op. cit., pp. 101-102.

either doubletime off based on the actual hours worked, or a premium of one-and-a-third times regular pay plus an extra day of paid leave. Employees working on a public holiday, which falls on a day which otherwise is not ordinary working time, are entitled to a full weekday's pay plus premium of one-third of regular pay for actual hours worked, as well as an extra day of paid leave.[38]

Paid annual leave

Law

Most employees are entitled to 14 consecutive days of paid annual leave for a period of 12 months of continuous service. Specifically enumerated categories, such as "an outside sales assistant, a traveller, a traveller's assistant, a demonstration-salesman, a property salesman, an insurance agent, a guard or a security-guard", are entitled to 21 days of consecutive leave. Occasional leave granted with full pay is deducted from this entitlement. Regular day workers[39] are entitled to one day of leave for every 26 working days of employment. Public holidays which fall during annual leave time are not counted as days taken on paid annual leave.[40]

In the public service, paid annual leave varies mainly in function of the length of service.[41] Officers employed less than ten years are entitled to 30 days' leave, and those employed for more than ten years to 36 days. Officers and employees at teaching and educational institutions which close completely during periods of school holidays are entitled only to 12 days of paid annual leave. Special rules apply to nursing personnel employed at institutions which provide a 24-hour service. Registered nurses employed at such institutions for less than ten years are entitled to 46 days of paid annual leave, and those employed for more than ten years are granted 52 days. Nursing assistants are entitled to 40 and 46 days of paid annual leave respectively. Part-time nursing personnel are entitled to 30 days of leave.[42]

Practice

Collective or other agreements may add to the amount of paid annual leave. Larger employers usually grant closer to four weeks' paid annual leave on average. Leave periods over four weeks are uncommon for blue-collar workers.[43] In the motor industry, the paid annual leave

---

[38] Public Holidays Act, op. cit., Section 11.

[39] Defined as "domestic workers employed on not more than three days in any week by the same employer for a period of not less than four consecutive weeks". Basic Conditions of Employment Act, op. cit., Section 1.

[40] Basic Conditions of Employment Act, op. cit., Section 12.

[41] Special rules apply to employees employed before 1 July 1966.

[42] Due to a law change, special rules apply to nurses appointed leave before 1 January 1968. Such registered nurses and nursing assistants are entitled to 48 and 54 days of leave respectively. Public Service Regulations, op. cit., Section 4.2.1(e) and (g).

[43] IDS, *Employment in South Africa*, op. cit., p. 100.

entitlement is three weeks for those with less than ten years of continuous employment and four weeks for those with more. In addition to the regular annual leave pay which is the equivalent of regular pay, some employees, such as vehicle body assembly employees above certain grades, are entitled to additional annual leave pay.[44]

Other types of leave

Law

The Basic Conditions of Employment Act does not provide for any types of leave other than annual and sick leave. The new Labour Relations Act enacted in October 1995, however, provides for the first time for paid time off for union activities.[45]

Practice[46]

Basic literacy training

Basic literacy training is fairly common among large employers. These programmes are usually offered to unskilled and semi-skilled workers, and offer both reading and writing skills.

Compassionate leave

There is no statutory right to time off for workers with family responsibilities. Collective agreements often provide for this by treating it as compassionate leave to be granted at the discretion of management.

Trade union activities

Previous to the adoption of the new Labour Relations Act, many employers were reluctant to grant their employees time off for trade union activities. Some collective agreements, however, did provide for time off for trade union activities. In one enterprise, shop stewards collectively received 20 days' special leave of absence each calendar year to attend union or other courses or seminars with the aim of increasing their effectiveness as worker representatives.[47]

[44] Motor industry: Main agreement, op. cit., Chapter II, Part 1, Clause 7.

[45] Labour Relations Act, op. cit., Section 82(1)(s).

[46] IDS, *Employment in South Africa*, op. cit., pp. 104-105.

[47] ibid., p. 105.

Shift and night work

Law

The Basic Conditions of Employment Act limits the duration of work for employees engaged in continuous shift work to eight hours. Security guards who do not work continuous shifts may work up to 12 hours per day if they work a five-shift week, and up to ten hours per day if they work a six-shift week. Time taken for a meal break by continuous shiftworkers and security guards who do not work continuous shifts shall be regarded as working time.

For other shiftworkers who do not work continuous shifts, the daily hours on a five-shift week are limited to nine hours and 15 minutes. For those working a six-shift week, five shifts may be no longer than eight-and-a-half hours, and the remaining shift may not be longer than five hours. Meal breaks are not calculated as working time for such shiftworkers.[48]

Practice

Shift allowances tend to range between 7 and 20 per cent. Allowances for night work are at the higher end of this range. Shift allowances tend to be higher for workers in continuous process operations. Some companies are reported to pay premiums of up to 23 per cent for night work where three-shift continuous work is performed. Shift allowances increased slightly in 1994, following a greater focus by trade unions on this issue.[49]

The national agreement in the engineering sector defines a normal shift as one-fifth of ordinary five-day weekly hours, or one-sixth of normal six-day weekly hours. If three or more consecutive night shifts are worked between 18:00 on Monday and 06:00 on Saturday of the same week, this constitutes night shift work and is paid a premium of 15 per cent over the normal hourly rate. If less than six hours elapses between the end of a night shift and the start of the next day shift, overtime is required to be paid.

For two-shift work, the first shift attracts a premium of 15 per cent for hours worked before 06:00. The second shift attracts a premium of 15 per cent if the whole shift falls between 18:00 and 06:00, or 7.5 per cent until midnight and 15 per cent thereafter.

For three-shift work, the second shift attracts a premium of 7.5 per cent and the third 15 per cent.[50] Urgent call-out work that lasts six or more hours after the end of a shift, or is after midnight, is paid at time-and-a-half. Work before the normal starting time of a shift is also paid at time-and-a-half until the normal starting time of the shift, except on Saturdays. Where overtime is worked after the completion of normal hours, employees must be allowed a rest break of at least eight hours before the next normal shift starts. When the rest period overlaps

---

[48] Basic Conditions of Employment Act, op. cit., Section 5.

[49] IDS, *Employment in South Africa*, op. cit., p. 92.

[50] ibid.

into the next shift, the overlapping portion is regarded as a paid period during which the employee is not allowed to work.[51]

The motor industry agreement provides generally that shiftworkers who work the major part of their shift on a Sunday are entitled to either twice the ordinary rate for the time worked on the Sunday or, alternatively, twice the ordinary weekday remuneration, whichever is greater. The employee can also decide to receive one-and-a-third times the ordinary rate for time worked on Sunday, as well as a day of compensatory leave within seven days of the Sunday worked. For shiftworkers engaged in vehicle body building, shifts shall not be longer than nine hours and 15 minutes. Not less than eight hours shall elapse between successive shifts for any employee. Shift work between 18:00 and 06.00 entitles the worker to a 10 per cent premium. No shifts shall be worked between 12:00 on Saturday and 06:00 on Monday.[52]

---

[51] ibid., p. 90.

[52] Motor industry: Main agreement, op. cit., Chapter II, Part 1, Clause 11.

Sweden

Overview and trends

Overview

Sweden has had a 40-hour working week since 1973. In 1983, the Hours of Work Act brought together provisions regulating most working time issues, including hours of work, overtime and rest. The provisions of the Hours of Work Act may be set aside, wholly or partly, by collective agreements centrally negotiated or approved by major employer and worker organizations at the central level. Working time reductions introduced by way of collective agreements since 1973, however, have not been substantial, except for shiftworkers, where a reduction of the working week of two to four hours — depending on the type of shift work — was introduced in the late 1970s. Otherwise, agreements in the major sectors (with some variations noted below) still mandate that normal hours for employees working during the day from Monday through Friday are 40 hours. Part-time work is over 20 per cent of total employment and among the highest in Europe.

As of 1 January 1995, Sweden became a member of the European Union. In view of the Council Directive concerning certain aspects of the organization of working time,[1] a review of the present working time regulations has been undertaken. A parliamentary committee was established in January 1995 to deal, inter alia, with a range of labour issues, including the compatibility of Swedish working time regulation with the law of the European Union; its report is to be submitted before the end of 1995.

The process of change has also reached the structure of collective bargaining. In the late 1980s, a strong tendency towards decentralization of bargaining became evident. This was in marked contrast to the previous practice of conducting negotiations at the central level. Negotiations now tend to begin at the industry-wide level, with significant authority delegated to bargaining at the enterprise or plant level. The central organizations, however, have attempted to align the industry and local negotiating process through flexible framework agreements.

Trends

Flexibility in terms of individual choice of working time is especially pronounced. This is particularly evident in the health sector where a series of innovative working time arrangements, many of which emphasize individual choice, have been tested and are currently under evaluation.[2] It seems that increased flexibility in individual choice of working time is very

---

[1] Council Directive 93/104/EC concerning certain aspects of the organization of working time, dated 23 November 1993 (*Official Journal*, Vol. 36, No. L307, 13 December 1993, pp. 18-24).

[2] Landstingsförbundet (Federation of County Councils) and Hälso- och sjukvårdens utvecklingsinstitut (SPRI — Swedish Institute for Health Services Development): *Konferensrapport: En utvärdering av vårdens arbetstidsmodeller* (Preliminary report: An evaluation of working time arrangements in the health sector) (Stockholm, 1995).

popular, irrespective of gender and age, and also positively correlated with productivity. Individual choice renders personnel planning more complex, however, and computer-assisted techniques in various forms are also in development. One such project is called "Computer-assisted individual working time planning", known by its Swedish acronym "IDA — Individuell Datorstödd Arbetstidplanering". It is under way in three major hospitals.

This increased emphasis on individual planning of hours has resulted in a less clear-cut categorization of ordinary hours of work, part-time work, shift work and overtime. In the commerce and banking sectors, collective agreements permit normal working time to be "displaced" from the "traditional" nine-to-five schedule. Work during displaced hours, however, is not shift work in the traditional sense. Rather, displaced hours entitle the employee to premium pay for working inconvenient hours, although not at levels which are paid for shift work in other sectors.

Another change in working time practices concerns the scheduling of paid annual leave which traditionally took place for many workers in July, when factories would close down. There are indications that this custom may be changing. For example, in 1995, Volvo closed one of its major production lines, Torslandaverken, for two, instead of the normal four, weeks in July. This practice seems to have been followed by other industries. Trade union opposition to keeping industries operating during the summer seems to be waning.[3]

In negotiations which took place in early 1995, the reduction of working time did not seem to have been a focal point of bargaining for any sector other than manufacturing. Metall, traditionally one of the strongest trade unions within the Landsorganisationen i Sverige (LO — Swedish Trade Union Confederation), entered the negotiations with specific demands for working time reductions in a proposed exchange for relatively modest wage increases. A limit on overtime was also sought.[4] Demands for working time reductions were expressed in annual working hours (100 hours of working time reduction by the year 2000) and not in monthly or weekly working hours.[5] The opposition by employers was strong, although a compromise was eventually reached. Although the annual reduction scheme proposed by Metall was rejected, it was agreed to introduce a system of working time reduction, according to which non-shiftworking employees would earn the right to an extra 12 minutes of compensatory leave for every completed week of work.[6] A year after the entry into force of the new agreement, employees will earn another 12 minutes, i.e. 24 minutes per work-week, for every completed week of work. This amounts to a reduction of some two days in the first year of the agreement and four days in the following year. It was also agreed to introduce a right for employers to enter into individual working time agreements with employees, even if the majority of employees have a different arrangement of working time. Such agreements are

---

[3] "Industrisemester ett minne blott", in *Dagens Nyheter*, No. 127, 12 May 1995.

[4] "Sweden: Unions want working time and overtime reductions", in *European Industrial Relations Review*, No. 247, August 1994, p. 11.

[5] Another novelty was that the blue-collar (Metall) and white-collar (engineers) employees were negotiating side-by-side against the employers.

[6] Shiftworkers were excluded on the ground that reduction of the hours for work for this category of workers already is an acquired right.

not limited in time, but may be revoked after a month's notice by either party. This development was a significant departure from previous practice and represents a change towards a more deregulated labour market.[7]

It has been a concern that actual annual hours of work have been significantly lower than in many European countries because of the existence of diverse types of leave in law and high absenteeism. Although average weekly hours of work were relatively stable between 1980 and 1993, being 36.0 and 35.4 respectively,[8] measured on an annual basis actual working hours declined.

In 1991, Swedish workers in the manufacturing sector worked fewer actual hours than their fellow workers in the European countries listed in Table 1.

Table 1. Hours of work per worker in the manufacturing industry, 1991[9]

Country	Actual number of hours worked	Annual working year (= 100%)	Percentage share of actual hours
Iceland	2,048	1,792	114
United Kingdom	1,844	1,778	104
Denmark	1,625	1,665	98
Norway	1,672	1,725	97
Western Germany	1,545	1,633	95
Finland	1,604	1,716	93
France	1,617	1,740	93
Italy	1,679	1,798	93
Netherlands	1,560	1,736	90
Sweden	1,465	1,784	82

[7] Sveriges Verkstadsindustrier: "Verkstadsavtalet och industritjänstemannaavtalet1995-1998" (Industrial agreement and the agreement for employees in industry 1995-1998), in *Cirkulär arbetsgivarfrågor*, No. 9503, 8 June 1995.

[8] Sveriges officiella statistik, Statistiska centralbyrån (Swedish Central Bureau of Statistics): *Arbetsmarknaden 1970-1983: Arbetsmarknadsstatistisk årsbok 1984* (Yearbook for labour market statistics 1984) (Stockholm, 1984), p. 103.

[9] Svenska arbetsgivareföreningen (SAF — Swedish Employers' Confederation): *Facts about the Swedish economy 1993* (Stockholm, 1994), p. 12.

As a result, there has been an effort to increase actual annual working hours in recent years. The extension of different forms of leave has stopped, and in some cases leave has been reduced. An extension of the parental leave provisions was frozen in 1989. Furthermore, sick leave provisions were revised in 1990 in an effort to diminish high levels of absenteeism. Sick leave provisions had entitled most employees to up to three days' leave with full pay per illness without a medical certificate. More extended sick leave depended on a medical certificate, but provisions for paid absence were extensive. In 1990, sick pay was lowered to 75 per cent during the first three days of illness and, as of 1 January 1993, two days were introduced during which employees were not paid if on sick leave.[10] Similarly, although the Government had made a firm political commitment to gradually extend legally required paid annual leave from five to six working weeks, it was forced to back down. Although in 1991 the first step was taken by extending the paid annual leave from 25 to 27 days, economic conditions influenced the Government to reverse itself and the two extra days were taken away as of 1994.

Until very recently the predominant view appeared to be that working time reductions were not an efficient means to reduce unemployment.[11] Rather, the debate concerning working time issues had mainly focused on the social effects of working time duration and organization. Arguments in favour of a six-hour workday have been advanced, but mainly as a means to achieve increased equality between men and women and, particularly, between working couples with children. With the increase in unemployment, a possible correlation between unemployment and working time reductions is now being officially examined.[12] The Government has directed that a parliamentary committee (the same committee which also is considering the compatibility of Swedish law with the law of the European Union) examine the long-term consequences of alternative ways of reducing working time. In the terms of reference directing the committee's work, the Government referred to the fact that there are now studies which "point towards a positive correlation between working time reductions and employment", and charged the committee specifically to take into account the possibilities of using working time reductions as a means to combat unemployment.[13] The committee is also charged with examining to what extent flexible working time rules can be introduced in law. The background for the committee's work is a 1992 report of another parliamentary committee, which proposed to introduce a system of annualization of working time. The proposed ideas had a mixed reception and did not lead to any concrete changes.[14]

---

[10] "Sweden: Waiting days for sick workers", in *European Industrial Relations Review*, No. 215, December 1993, p. 13. The effect of the introduction of waiting days has resulted in a significant decrease in absenteeism. "Suède: Poursuite de la baisse de l'absentéisme", in *UIMM Social International*, No. 525, February 1994, p. 28.

[11] Official view reported in "Effekter av olika arbetstidsförändringar", in *Kommittédirektiv*, No. 6, 1995, p. 2 (terms of reference for the Committee to examine the effects of different changes in working time). See, inter alia, "Suède: Sondage du syndicat des métaux sur la durée du travail", in *UIMM Social International*, No. 519, July 1993, p. 30.

[12] "Sweden: Shorter hours debate", in *European Industrial Relations Review*, No. 239, December 1993, p. 13.

[13] "Effekter av olika arbetstidsförändringar", op. cit., pp. 5-6.

[14] Ministry of Labour: *Årsarbetstid ny lag om arbetstid och semester* (Report of the Committee to examine more flexible rules regarding working time and vacation time), document no. SOU 1992:27 (Stockholm, 1992). One of the issues that was discussed in the Parliament was the effect of these rules on overtime.

Normal hours of work

Law

Normal weekly hours of work are 40 legally, after which overtime must be paid. There are no generally applicable provisions concerning daily working hours.[15] The law does not, however, apply to work at the home of employees, employees in managerial positions, domestic work or service on board ships. With respect to the two latter categories, special legislation is in force.[16]

The Hours of Work Act lays down fundamental working time standards, but it may be overridden by collective agreements entered into or approved by central trade unions. In the absence of an agreement, certain provisions of the Act may be waived by the Arbetarskydds-styrelsen (National Board of Occupational Safety and Health). Working time can be averaged over a period of four weeks under certain circumstances, although longer periods can be provided for by collective agreement (see below under **Overtime and absolute maximum hours**).

If it is necessary in view of the nature of the work, an employee may be required to be on a "stand-by" status. Such a necessity exists, for example, in health care, social care and fire protection services. Stand-by time is defined to mean time when the employee is at the disposal of the employer at the place of work in order to perform work when needed. The legal maximum for being on stand-by is 48 hours per employee over a period of four weeks, or 50 hours per calendar month. "Stand-by" does not include time when the employee is on-call outside the working place, which is not regulated by law.

Young workers

The age of admission to employment is 16 years or after completion of compulsory schooling. As an exception, young persons 13 to 15 years old may be used to carry out light work "which is not of such a kind that it can have a detrimental effect" on their "health, development or schooling".[17]

---

[15] Hours of Work Act, Act No. 673, dated 24 June 1982 (*Svensk författningssamling*, No. 673, 1982), as amended up to Act No. 905, dated 10 June 1993 (*Svensk författningssamling*, No. 905, 1993) [LS 1982-Swe.2].

[16] Act No. 943 respecting the hours of work and other conditions of work of domestic employees, dated 20 May 1970 (*Svensk författningssamling*, No. 943, 1970), as amended up to Act No. 1988, dated 20 December 1994 (*Svensk författningssamling*, No. 1988, 1994) [LS 1970-Swe.3]; Seafarers' Hours of Work Act, Act No. 105, dated 10 April 1970 (*Svensk författningssamling*, No. 105, 1970), as amended up to Act No. 1017, dated 9 June 1994 (*Svensk författningssamling*, No. 1017, 1994) [LS 1970-Swe.1B].

[17] Work Environment Act, Act No. 1160, dated 19 December 1977 (*Svensk författningssamling*, No. 1160, 1977), as amended up to Act No. 677, dated 30 May 1991 (*Svensk författningssamling*, No. 677, 1991) [LS 1977-Swe.4; LLD 1991-SWE 2], Ch. 5, Sections 1-3.

Practice

Normal working time pursuant to collective agreements in 1994 varied between 35 and 40 hours.[18] The banking sector and public service are exceptions. In the banking sector, the daily working time is set at 38.5 hours per week. In the public service, normal hours of work are unevenly distributed over the year to allow for shorter working hours (35.5 hours) during the months of May through August, and longer hours the rest of the year (38.5 hours). Averaged over a year (not including annual leave, public holidays, and other types of leave or absence), this amounts to slightly less than 39 hours per week. Furthermore, if normal working time includes work on weekends or public holidays or nights (i.e. in the period between 24:00 and 05:00), working time is reduced by two to five-and-three-quarters hours, depending on the frequency of such inconvenient working hours. Normal hours of work for underground work are 36 hours per week.[19]

In the commercial sector, where the normal working week is 40 hours, averaging schemes are common (see below under **Overtime and absolute maximum hours**).

As can be seen from Table 2, average weekly hours have remained relatively stable over the past ten years.

Table 2. Hours of work per week by major divisions of economic activity[20]

Major division	1984	1985	1986	1987	1988	1989	1990	1991	1992	1993	1994
Manufacturing	38.3	38.4	38.4	38.4	38.4	38.4	38.5	38.3	38.5	37.2	37.8
Construction	38.9	39.2	39.4	40.2	40.1	40.2	40.2	39.6	39.5	38.2	38.6
Trades, restaurants and hotels	35.6	36.0	36.1	35.7	35.8	36.1	36.3	36.0	35.9	34.6	34.7
Transport, storage and communication	37.3	37.9	37.8	38.3	38.5	39.2	39.5	39.1	38.9	38.2	38.2
Financing, insurance, real estate and business services	36.2	36.7	37.5	37.4	37.6	38.0	38.1	38.0	38.1	36.3	36.9
Community, social and personal services	33.4	33.6	33.9	34.3	34.6	34.9	35.0	35.1	35.0	33.9	34.3
Total (all non-agricultural activities)	36.0	36.3	36.5	37.1	37.2	37.5	37.5	37.3	37.2	36.1	36.4

[18] Income Data Services (IDS): "Hours and holidays 1995", *IDS Study*, No. 590, November 1995, p. 12.

[19] Statens Arbetsgivarverk (SAV): *SA-C sektoravtal för civila statsförvaltningen* (Sectoral agreement for the state civil servants), SAV Cirkulär No. 1993 CIV 3, 14 February 1994, Division 4, Chapter 3B, Section 8.

[20] Bureau of Statistics, International Labour Office [hours actually worked; employees; labour force sample survey, including mining and quarrying, and electricity, gas and water].

Overtime and absolute maximum hours

Law

There are no generally applicable standards on absolute maximum hours of work other than those which limit recourse to overtime. The Hours of Work Act defines overtime to mean time worked in excess of ordinary working time as defined by the Act, by collective agreement, or by special authorization of the National Board of Occupational Safety and Health.[21] When there is a special need for an increase in working hours, 48 hours of overtime may be required over a period of four weeks or 50 hours during a calendar month. The yearly maximum allowed is 200 hours. Overtime may not be used in a systematic way. The overtime limits may be varied by collective agreement. In the absence of such an agreement, the National Board of Occupational Safety and Health may exceptionally grant permission for an additional 150 hours of overtime per year. Emergency overtime is limited to two days, and is only to be used during events such as a major natural disaster. If more emergency overtime is needed, the permission from the National Board of Occupational Safety and Health must be obtained.[22]

Part-time employees may have to work "additional time", which is time in excess of their normal hours. Additional time is also legally limited, on a yearly basis, to a maximum of 200 hours, but the other limitations imposed for overtime are not applicable.[23] Overtime rules apply to part-time employees when their working hours exceed normal working hours established by law or collective agreement for full-time employees.

The question whether or not employees are required to work overtime is not regulated by law, but by collective agreement. The same is true with respect to the levels of compensation for overtime and additional time.

Working time can be averaged over a maximum period of four weeks to avoid overtime "if the nature of the work and the working conditions in general so require", although a longer period can be provided for by collective agreement.[24] This exception is primarily applied in situations where work is performed on a continuous basis, i.e. shift work, health care, law enforcement and work in related security facilities, transportation, agriculture, hotels, restaurants and cafes. However, averaging also takes place in other sectors, such as commerce and manufacturing, pursuant to agreement between the social partners (see below).

[21] Hours of Work Act, op. cit., Sections 7-9 and 19.

[22] ibid., Sections 7-8.

[23] ibid., Section 10.

[24] ibid., Section 5(2).

Practice

Overtime, other premium pay and compensatory time

The legally allowed maximum limit for overtime may be overridden by collective agreement at the central level or by local agreement. In practice, union opposition to this has been very effective and there is little evidence of practice which provides for a higher number of maximum overtime hours than the legal standard.

Overtime work normally always entitles the employees to extra compensation, although the amounts vary. In the commercial sector, overtime work which occurs on weekdays from 18:15 to 20:00 is compensated with a 50 per cent premium over normal pay. After 20:00, the compensation increases to a 70 per cent premium. Overtime on Saturdays after 12:00 and on Sundays entitles employees to double regular pay. Compensation may also be offered as time off. The compensatory leave time is calculated at 1.5 hours for overtime when the premium pay rate would have been 50 per cent, 1.75 hours for overtime when the premium pay rate would have been 70 per cent, and two hours when the worker would have otherwise been paid doubletime.

When overtime work is performed in the manufacturing industry, regular pay may be exchanged for compensatory leave equivalent to the amount of overtime that has been worked, although the overtime premium must be paid. Overtime compensation is usually expressed in monetary, rather than percentage, terms. The compensation level varies depending on the day (weekday, weekend, holiday) on which overtime is performed. A special type of overtime, which is termed "collective production overtime", is overtime locally agreed to pursuant to a planned schedule of extra work for a minimum period of four weeks encompassing all employees in a workshop, department or group. Such overtime entitles the workers to higher levels of compensation than ordinary overtime.[25] Work considered to be during "inconvenient hours", defined as between 16:30 and 23:30 as well as between 23:30 and 6:30, is compensated with extra pay at different rates expressed in monetary amounts and not as a percentage of regular pay.[26]

In the municipal sector, overtime must be officially authorized. Employees in certain managerial and supervisory functions are not entitled to overtime compensation. Overtime can be "simple" or "qualified". Simple overtime is when work is performed either two hours before or after normal working hours and entitles the employee to regular pay plus an 80 per cent premium. All other overtime work is qualified overtime and entitles the employee to regular pay plus a 140 per cent premium. Overtime which starts before 5:00 is always compensated as qualified overtime. Part-time workers working over their normal working hours receive their regular pay plus a 20 per cent premium. Work by part-timers in excess of full-time hours is compensated in the same way as for full-time employees.[27]

---

[25] *Verkstadsavtalet och industritjänstemannaavtalet 1995-1998*, op. cit., Section 4:3.

[26] ibid.

[27] Landstingsförbundet: *Allmänna bestämmelser — AB 94* (Central agreement for the municipal sector) (Stockholm, 1994), Chapter IV, Section 30.

In both the commercial and banking sectors, there are special rules regarding what are termed "displaced working hours", i.e. hours which are displaced from normal hours during the day to more inconvenient times. In the commercial sector, the employer has the right to choose to compensate employees working displaced hours with either certain additions to the regular salary or by offering compensatory time off. The compensation premium in addition to normal pay for weekday work between 18:15 and 20:00 is 50 per cent, and after 20:00, 70 per cent. On Saturdays after 12:00, Sundays and holidays, the compensation premium is 100 per cent. Compensatory time, which has to be offered in full days, is one-and-a-half hours for each overtime hour at the 50 per cent premium rate of pay, one-and-three-quarters hours for each hour worked at the 70 per cent premium level, and two hours for each hour of overtime worked at the doubletime rate of pay.[28]

According to a local collective agreement on displaced working hours in the banking sector, the rules are slightly different. Normal weekly hours of work are 38.5 hours, but can be averaged over a period of four months. Working hours may be scheduled around the clock, any day of the year, subject to a daily maximum of ten hours. Work from 17:30 to 20:00 entitles an employee to normal pay plus a 35 per cent premium, while work between 20:00 and 7:00 the next day entitles the employee to regular pay plus a 60 per cent premium. Work on Saturdays, Sundays and public holidays entitles an employee to double regular pay. Alternatively, compensatory time off may be granted at the same rate (i.e. 1.35 hours for one hour worked between 17.30 and 20:00, etc.).[29]

In the period 1989 to 1992, the percentage of employees who worked overtime in relation to all employed persons went down.[30] Statistics from the Svenska Arbetsgivareföreningen (SAF — Swedish Employers' Confederation) indicate a subsequent increase in overtime expressed in percentage of normal hours worked. Between 1992 and 1993, overtime increased from 2.7 per cent to 3.8 per cent of normal time for male workers, and from 2 per cent to 2.9 per cent for female workers.[31] Comparable data in 1994 and 1995 respectively indicate that the overtime percentages for all employees were 3.9 per cent and 4.2 per cent.[32] There is an irregular use of overtime in different sectors, with overtime being particularly frequent in exporting industries. Overtime in the municipal sector is relatively low and constant, varying between 1 and 2 per cent a year. Part-time work is significant in the municipal sector and,

[28] Avtal mellan HAO Handelsarbetsgivarna och Handelsanställdas förbund 1.4.1993-31.3.1995 avscende butiks- och kontorspersonal samt lagerpersonal och chaufförer inom detaljhandeln (Agreement for the commercial sector) (Stockholm, 1993). The agreement negotiated in 1995, which succeeded this agreement, has remained unchanged with respect to the provisions discussed above.

[29] Collective agreement between Bankinstitutens Arbetsgivarorganisation (BAO) and Finansförbundet, current as of 1995.

[30] 12.8 per cent (1989), 12.5 per cent (1991) and 9.6 per cent (1992). These figures are taken from the statistical yearbooks for Sweden for the years 1992 and 1994.

[31] "Suède: Accroissement des heures supplémentaires", in UIMM Social International, No. 527, April 1994, p. 23. Fourth quarter of each year.

[32] "Övertid regel i industrin", in Dagens Nyheter, 21 April 1995, quoting recent statistics from the National Bureau of Census.

therefore, supplementary hours by these workers normally fall under the rules for "additional time" and not "overtime".

The collective agreement for civil servants states that daily work must not exceed 14 hours.[33] There are usually no such limitations in collective agreements.

Averaging schemes

Averaging of normal hours of work over a reference period of more than a week can allow employers to avoid paying overtime if such averaging is agreed to by the parties. In the commercial sector, normal hours of work are 40, although it is the usual practice that this is a yearly average unless there is a local agreement for a different, typically shorter, averaging period. Actual working time must not, however, deviate from the established average of 40 hours by more than five hours per week without overtime being paid.[34]

In the manufacturing sector, daytime and second (evening) shift employees have normal hours of work of 40 hours. It is specifically provided that, subject to local agreement at each working place, "ordinary working time of differing lengths may be unevenly distributed over the year" and that such "adjustments of the working schedules render it increasingly possible to adjust working time to suit the needs both of the enterprise and the employees".[35]

Rest

Law

Breaks

The Hours of Work Act defines a break as time during the working day when an employee is not required to be present at the workplace. Work should not continue for more than five hours without a break. The duration and frequency of breaks is established by agreement or custom. Breaks are normally not computed as working time. When a meal break must be taken at the workplace because working conditions so require, this time may be exchanged for a regular break. Work pauses are also mandated during the working day, but the employee is not allowed to leave the workplace. Contrary to a regular break, where the employee is not required to be present at the workplace, meal breaks and work pauses at the workplace are counted as working time.

Daily rest

The Hours of Work Act creates a general right for all employees to have a nightly rest which shall include, at least, the hours between 24:00 and 05:00, subject to exceptions based on the

---

[33] *SA-C sektoravtal för den civila statsförvaltningen*, op. cit., Chapter 6, paragraph 30.

[34] *Avtal mellan HAO Handelsarbetsgivarna och Handelsanställdas förbund 1.4.1993-31.3.1995*, op. cit.

[35] *Verkstadsavtalet och industritjänstemannaavtalet 1995-1998*, op. cit.

nature of the work. This is more in the nature of a prohibition of night work, however, than a minimum period of daily rest (see below under **Shift and night work**).

Weekly rest

A 36-hour consecutive period of rest is required for each seven-day period. To the extent possible, weekly rest shall be scheduled during the weekend.[36]

Practice

In the manufacturing and the municipal sectors, the provisions of collective agreements are virtually the same as the law. In the manufacturing sector, however, it has been agreed at the central level that exceptions in local agreements may be allowed.[37]

Shop-opening hours

Law

The legal regulation of shop-opening hours was abolished in 1974.

Practice

The most common opening hours are between 09:00 or 10:00 until 19:00 or 20:00. Some retail establishments have limited opening hours during the weekend, for example, from between 11:00 until 15:00 or 16:00 on Saturdays and Sundays. In the banking sector, services such as telebanking, financial counselling, insurance services, trustee services, and advice on legal affairs and business management are offered to the public at times outside normal banking hours. Collective agreements include special provisions for work performed during these inconvenient hours.[38] Earlier agreements provided that telebanking and similar activities were allowed to take place during certain hours only,[39] while the most recent agreement does not contain any such restriction. Convenience stores usually operate long hours, typically from 07:00 to 23:00 seven days a week. Large supermarkets are open most of the time until 23:00, and are closed only two or three days in the year (Christmas Day, New Year's Day and, more recently, also 1 May). Service around the clock is most frequently used for gasoline stations which carry an increasingly diverse range of goods for sale.

[36] Hours of Work Act, op. cit.

[37] *Verkstadsavtalet och industritjänstemannaavtalet 1995-1998*, op. cit.; *Allmänna bestämmelser — AB 94*, op. cit.

[38] ILO: *Recent developments affecting salaried employees and professional workers*, Report I to the Committee on Salaried Employees and Professional Workers, Tenth Session, Geneva 1994, pp. 62-63. See also the collective agreement between BAO and Finansförbundet, op. cit.

[39] Between 07:00 and 23:00 from Monday to Friday inclusive.

Public holidays

Law

There is no generally applicable legislation specifying standards for work or time off on public holidays.

Practice

The right to paid leave on public holidays is regulated by collective agreements and custom. Swedish workers typically receive 11 paid public holidays.[40] There are five public holidays which always occur on weekdays: Good Friday, Easter Monday, Ascension Day, Whit Monday and Midsummer's Eve (always a Friday by custom). There are seven public holidays which occur on fixed dates, namely New Year's Day (1 January), Epiphany (6 January), Labour Day (1 May), Christmas Eve (24 December), and Christmas Day (25 December). If they fall on a weekday, employees are given paid time off, although if they fall on a weekend, they are not.

State employees are, in addition, entitled to end their working day some hours earlier on the eve of Epiphany (four hours on 5 January), the day before Good Friday (two hours), 30 April (when it occurs Monday to Thursday, two hours, or on Friday, four hours), the day before All Saints Day (four hours) and 23 December when it falls on a Friday (four hours).[41] Similar, although not identical, practice occurs in the banking sector.[42] In the commercial sector, working hours during the weeks which include Christmas Eve, New Year's Eve, Easter Saturday, Whit Saturday and Midsummer's Eve are reduced by two hours.[43]

In many workplaces, workers are allowed to "bridge" public holidays falling on a weekday, such as Tuesday or Thursday, with the working day which falls on the Monday or Friday, respectively, to create a four-day weekend. Arrangements are made to add extra working time each day over a certain period to compensate for the time off on the "bridged" weekday taken off between the weekend and the public holiday.

Paid annual leave

Law

Annual leave is statutorily required to be a minimum of 25 days. The right to annual leave is separate from the right to receive annual leave pay. The annual leave year extends from 1 April to 31 March, and the right to annual leave pay is earned during the 12-month period

[40] IDS, "Hours and holidays 1995", op. cit., p. 12.

[41] *SA-C sektoravtal för den civila statsförvaltningen*, op. cit., Part 4, Chapter 2, paragraph 5, Section 2.

[42] Collective agreement between BAO and Finansförbundet, op. cit., Section 10, paragraph 2.

[43] *Avtal mellan HAO Handelsarbetsgivarna och Handelsanställdas förbund 1.4.1993-31.3.1995*, op. cit., Section 4(B).

preceding 1 April, although annual leave pay is not a right during the first year of service. New employees are entitled to 25 days of annual leave without pay during their first year of work, which they are not required to take. Annual leave pay constitutes 12 per cent of earnings during the qualifying year. This amounts to an employee's regular pay plus a supplementary payment while the person is on vacation. Saturdays and Sundays are not normally counted as days of annual leave, except when Saturday or Sunday would otherwise have been a working day.[44] Extended annual leave is provided for those engaged in radiological work.[45] An employee whose employment ends without taking his or her entitlement to paid annual leave is entitled to compensation. All paid annual leave days in excess of 20 days per year may be saved and carried over for a maximum of five years in order to allow the employee the chance to take a longer consecutive period of paid annual leave at a later time.

Practice

The range of paid annual leave tends to be between 25 and 30 days per year. Employees in certain supervisory functions, as well as employees with the freedom to determine the arrangement of their working time in industry, exchange the right to overtime compensation for a higher salary and/or three to five days' extra annual leave.[46]

In the public sector, state employees are generally entitled to 30 days of paid annual leave. In addition, they are entitled to extended annual leave depending on age. In the municipal sector, which covers some 1.1 million local government employees, paid annual leave is 25 days for employees up to the age of 39. Employees between 40 and 50 years of age are entitled to 31 days of annual leave, and employees above 50 years are entitled to 32 days. Days which exceed the legally required minimum of 25 can be exchanged for monetary compensation.[47]

Other types of leave

Law

Educational leave was introduced in 1975, and is available for up to a year. If the educational programme can be considered as a form of vocational training, employees may be entitled

[44] Annual Leave Act, Act No. 480, dated 9 June 1977 (*Svensk författningssamling*, No. 480, 1977), as amended up to Act No. 1688, dated 28 December 1994 (*Svensk författningssamling*, No. 1688, 1994) [LS 1977-Swe.2].

[45] Act No. 115 to provide for extended annual leave for persons employed in radiological work, dated 17 May 1963 (*Svensk författningssamling*, No. 115, 1963), as amended up to Act No. 103, dated 27 March 1990 (*Svensk författningssamling*, No. 103, 1990).

[46] IDS, "Hours and holidays 1995", op. cit., p. 12; *Verkstadsavtalet och industritjänstemannaavtalet 1995-1998*, op. cit.

[47] *Allmänna Bestämmelser -94*, op. cit., Chapter IV, paragraph 22(12).

to keep their salary, entirely or partly.[48] The right to pay has to be defined in a collective agreement. Paid leave is also a legal right for trade union-related work and training.[49] There are legal standards governing paid leave for a number of specified purposes which include, for example, nursing a relative, the participation by immigrants in Swedish language training,[50] carrying out parental responsibilities in relation to school for children,[51] or applying for a new job.[52]

Practice

In the municipal sector, additional rights to leave include leave for personal reasons for up to ten days per year. In the commercial sector, leave is typically also provided for personal reasons, which include one's own marriage, one's own 50th birthday, medical visits, and time off after the death of a close relative.

Shift and night work

Law

There is no legislation regarding shift work. With respect to night work, the Working Hours Act creates a general right for all employees to have nightly rest which shall include, at least, the hours between 24:00 and 05:00. Exceptions can be made "if the nature of the work, public needs or other special circumstances require work to be performed also during the night", or to be conducted before 05:00, or which should be continued beyond 24:00.[53] Examples include work in iron mills or pulp factories, work in hospitals, police services, postal and telecommunication services, care for animals, security and guard services, and emergency services.

---

[48] Act No. 981 respecting the right of employees to time off for training purposes, dated 13 December 1974 (*Svensk författningssamling*, No. 981, 1974), as amended up to Act No. 89, dated 24 February 1982 (*Svensk författningssamling*, No. 89, 1982).

[49] Act No. 358 respecting trade union representatives, dated 17 June 1974 (*Svensk författningssamling*, No. 358, 1974, pp. 820-823).

[50] Act No. 163 respecting the right to leave for participation in basic education in Swedish for immigrants, dated 3 April 1986 (*Svensk författningssamling*, No. 163, 1986, pp. 1-2).

[51] Act No. 1184 respecting the right to time off for certain duties in connection with school associations, etc., dated 20 December 1979 (*Svensk författningssamling*, No. 1184, 1979).

[52] Act No. 80 respecting the protection of employment, dated 24 February 1982 (*Svensk författningssamling*, No. 80, 1982), as amended up to Act No. 1496, dated 16 December 1993 (*Svensk författningssamling*, No. 1496, 1993) [LS 1982-Swe.1], Section 17.

[53] Working Hours Act, op. cit.

Practice

In the manufacturing sector, working time for intermittent shift work of three shifts per day is 38 hours per week; for continuous shift work of three shifts per day, seven days a week (but interrupted on public holidays), 36 hours per week; and for continuous shift work of three shifts seven days a week (including work on public holidays), 35 hours per week.[54]

In the municipal sector, working time for intermittent shift work of three shifts is 36 hours and 20 minutes; and for continuous shift work of three shifts, 34 hours and 20 minutes.[55]

---

[54] Sveriges Verkstadsindustrier, "Verkstadsavtalet och industritjänstemannaavtalet 1995-1998", op. cit.

[55] *Allmänna bestämmelser — AB 94*, op. cit.

United Kingdom

Overview and trends

Overview

The United Kingdom has a highly deregulated approach to working time issues. Unlike many European countries, the United Kingdom has no statutory law of general applicability which specifies normal daily or weekly hours of work, when and how overtime must be paid, or absolute maximum limits on hours of work on a daily or weekly basis. Similarly, there is no statutory regulation of daily or weekly rest of general applicability, and no legally required minimum paid annual leave.

There are few legislative restrictions on hours of work in specific industries. For example, Part VI of the Transport Act 1968 regulates the hours of driving of certain classes of vehicles.[1] Shop-opening legislation regulates the opening hours of retail establishments and, therefore, indirectly the hours of work of retail workers. Similarly, there are restrictions on work by young workers, particularly for those 16 and under.

Trends

There has been a concerted effort to substantially deregulate working time in the 1980s and 1990s. Although historically working time parameters — such as maximum hours of work, paid annual leave, minimum wages, premium payments for unsocial hours (such as work on Sundays and public holidays), and shift and night work — were regulated for a number of specific industries by tripartite wages councils first established in 1909, legislative changes have ended such regulation. The Wages Act 1986 put an end to the establishment of new wages councils, and substantially restricted the scope of those in existence. Nevertheless, in 1988, there were 26 wages councils covering 2.5 million workers, not including the agricultural wages boards. These workers were mainly women employed in retailing, catering, hairdressing and clothing manufacture. However, the Trade Union Reform and Employment Rights Act 1993 abolished the wages councils altogether.[2] The Agricultural Wages Boards were subsequently abolished as well.

Other examples of deregulation include the elimination of legal restrictions on working hours of miners below ground by Section 2 of the Coal Industry Act 1992.[3] Moreover, the Employment Act 1989 removed many limitations on the hours of work of young persons defined to be those between 16, the compulsory school attendance age, and 18. As a result,

---

[1] B.A. Hepple and C. Hakim: *Legal and contractual limitations to working time: United Kingdom* (Dublin, European Foundation for the Improvement of Living and Working Conditions, 1994), Working paper No. WP/94/46/EN, pp. 5-6.

[2] Trade Union Reform and Employment Rights Act 1993, dated 1 July 1993 (*Acts of Parliament*, Ch. 19, 1993).

[3] Hepple and Hakim, op. cit., pp. 5-6.

in certain occupations there are no maximum hours of work over which young persons are not allowed to work, no restrictions on starting and finishing times, no limits on overtime working, no prohibition of Sunday or night work, and no minimum rest periods or paid annual leave entitlements. Legal restrictions on the employment of children, i.e. those under the compulsory school age of 16, remain in force.[4]

In light of the adoption in 1994 of the Council Directive on the protection of young persons at work, the United Kingdom will have to consider changes to its regulatory framework. The Directive mandates a number of limitations on the working time of young persons, i.e. those under the age of 18, but aged 15 to 17, and no longer subject to compulsory full-time schooling, as well as limitations on the employment of children, i.e. those under 15 or still subject to compulsory full-time education. In particular, the Directive sets down limitations on daily and weekly hours of work, restrictions on night work, and mandates daily and weekly rest periods, subject to certain derogations. The transition period for the implementation of the Directive is two years from the formal date of its adoption. The United Kingdom, however, negotiated a derogation to the Directive, which allows it an additional four years for compliance with the following provisions: the limits of eight hours a day and 40 hours a week on work performed by young persons; the restrictions on night work for young persons; and the limit of 12 hours a week on work performed outside school attendance hours by children performing light work or work as part of training when school is in session.[5]

Although the domestic tendency has been to deregulate the labour market, the adoption on 23 November 1993 of the Council Directive concerning certain aspects of working time should have consequences for working time regulation and practice.[6] This Directive mandates requirements in a number of areas, such as normal and maximum daily and weekly hours of work, daily and weekly rest, and paid annual leave. The Directive can be complied with, either by changes in the regulatory framework, or by ensuring that the social partners adopt collective agreements consistent with its provisions. The British Government succeeded, however, in delaying implementation of parts of the Directive, and also obtained exceptions to many of its provisions. For example, the United Kingdom obtained an optional seven-year period for the introduction of a 48-hour maximum for weekly work, in addition to the three-year transition period granted to member states. During this period, workers can voluntarily work longer than 48 hours a week, but cannot be compelled to do so. In 2003, the Council of the European Union will review whether to continue to allow workers to voluntarily work in excess of 48 hours per week.[7]

---

[4] Children and Young Persons Act 1933, 23 Geo. 5, Ch. 12 (*Statutory Rules and Orders*, 1933), as amended up to Act, dated 16 November 1989 (*Acts of Parliament*, 1989) [LS 1933-GB.1; LLD 1989-GBR 1].

[5] Council Directive 94/33/EC on the protection of young people at work, dated 22 June 1994 (*Official Journal*, Vol. 37, No. L216, 20 August 1994, pp. 12-19). See also "Social policy state of play", in *European Industrial Relations Review*, No. 247, August 1994, pp. 26-32.

[6] Council Directive 93/104/EC concerning certain aspects of the organization of working time, dated 23 November 1993 (*Official Journal*, Vol. 36, No. L307, 13 December 1993, pp. 18-24).

[7] "'Take a break', UK workers told", in *Labour Research*, Vol. 83, No. 2, February 1994, pp. 13-14; "Council finally adopts working time Directive", in *IDS European Report*, No. 385, January 1994, pp. 20-22.

The British Government also supported measures to ensure that workers engaged in air, rail, road, sea, inland waterway and lake transport, those in sea fishing and other work at sea, and doctors in training, were exempted from the Directive. In addition, there are other derogations for certain classes of workers because of the nature of their responsibilities or the nature of their occupational tasks; because of the risk of accidents; or because of the family or religious nature of the work. Nevertheless, the Directive will affect a significant number of British workers who, for the first time, will have the right to a paid vacation of three weeks initially, and then four weeks by 1996. Another change will be that rest periods will be subject to regulation. These changes are substantial, particularly for workers in workplaces which are not unionized and which, in some cases, are characterized by long hours without rest breaks and little or no entitlement to paid annual leave.[8]

Another issue which has been subject to extensive debate in the United Kingdom concerns shop-opening hours on Sundays. After much public discussion, shop-opening hours have moved in the direction of less regulation with the Sunday Trading Act 1994.[9] However, some restrictions on the opening hours of large shops on Sunday remain after the adoption of this new law, and the Act also contains measures to protect workers who do not want to work on Sundays.

Actual working time by full-time British workers is not only the longest among the member states of the European Union, it has been increasing. In the decade 1983-1992, the time actually worked per week, i.e. normal hours of work plus average overtime, increased from 42.3 to 43.4 per week, whereas most other countries in the European Union experienced a decline, with the exception of Ireland and France, where hours of work remained stable.[10]

Overtime work tends to be performed primarily by male workers, and tends to be longer for workers doing manual rather than non-manual work.[11] High levels of overtime per individual worker have been a persistent feature of British employment and have distinguished the United Kingdom from other European countries. It has been suggested that management may view overtime as a means of extending the working day without hiring additional labour. Moreover, overtime may be considered as a way for earnings to be increased without management conceding a general wage rise, thus allowing management to cut pay levels by eliminating overtime in periods of slack demand. For some workers, overtime has come to represent a regular component of overall earnings and thus regular spending as well. Hence, overtime has traditionally been perceived by both management and employees as desirable for different reasons.[12] Although the amount of average overtime per worker has increased,

[8] ibid.

[9] "Sunday working rights for shop staff", in *Employment Gazette*, Vol. 102, No. 8, August 1994, p. 270.

[10] Eurostat: "Working time in the European Union — the average working week from 1983 to 1992", in *Statistics in focus: Population and social conditions* (Luxembourg, 1995), pp. 1-4; see also Eurostat: *Work organisation and working hours, 1983-1992* (Luxembourg, 1995), p. 28.

[11] "Council finally adopts working time Directive", op. cit., pp. 20-22; see also Income Data Services: "Hours and holidays 1993", *IDS Study*, No. 538, September 1993, p. 1.

[12] P. Blyton: "United Kingdom: The case of the metal manufacturing industry", in OECD: *Flexible working time: Collective bargaining and government intervention* (Paris, 1995), pp. 83-101.

the volume of overall overtime payment has decreased. The decrease in the absolute amount of overtime paid has been strongly influenced by the significant loss of manufacturing jobs.[13] Some commentators predict that continued reductions in the overall volume of overtime payments will continue because of the growth of part-time work and annual hours agreements, which should facilitate the scheduling of work and minimize overtime.[14]

Part-time work has increased significantly in the period 1983-1992: from 14.8 to 19.33 per cent of total employment in agriculture, from 6.81 to 8.62 per cent in industry, and from 26.12 to 29.98 per cent in services. Part-time work tends to be heavily concentrated among women workers.[15]

The 1990 Workplace Industrial Relations Survey (WIRS), a survey of management and trade union representatives across all sectors of British industry, found that working time was the key industrial relations issue after pay and an important issue for negotiation, particularly in workplaces with large numbers of manual workers. In 30 to 40 per cent of workplaces, negotiation of working hours took place at the level of the establishment. In the absence of a collective agreement, the rules concerning working time are normally determined unilaterally by the employer. Management is most likely to decide working time issues in sectors such as distribution, hotels, catering, miscellaneous services, financial services, and small manufacturing enterprises.[16]

Normal hours of work

Law

There are no generally applicable provisions.

Practice

Normal hours of work are 35 to 40 hours per week, with most workers working a 37- to 39-hour week.[17]

According to one study of approximately 500 organizations, the 39-hour week was the most common arrangement for manual workers (approximately 47 per cent of organizations surveyed). The next most frequent was hours less than 37.5 per week (approximately one-third), followed by organizations which have a 37- to 37.5-hour week (approximately 25 per cent).

---

[13] Income Data Services: "Overtime", *IDS Study*, No. 559, August 1994, pp. 4-5; see also Income Data Services: "Annual hours", *IDS Study*, No. 544, December 1993, p. 2.

[14] IDS, "Overtime", op. cit., p. 4.

[15] Eurosat, "Working time in the European Union", op. cit., p. 9.

[16] Hepple and Hakim, op. cit., pp. 7-8.

[17] Income Data Services: "Hours and holidays 1994", *IDS Study*, No. 566, November 1994, pp. 1 and 5-7.

For non-manual workers, the most common hours of work were 35 or 37 per week (26 and 23 per cent respectively), followed by 37.5 hours (17 per cent). In agreements where no distinction was made between manual and non-manual workers, weekly hours of work of 37 and 37.5 hours were evenly split among two-thirds of the organizations. A work-week of 39 hours was also found in 16 per cent of the agreements.[18]

Although a normal work day within a five-day week is generally considered to be slightly less than eight hours a day, a study by the Equal Opportunities Commission found that only 40 per cent of men worked a day starting between 08:00 and 10:00 and finishing between 16:00 and 18:00, and that just over one-half of women working full time had such a work schedule.[19]

Table 1. Hours of work per week by major divisions of economic activity[20]

Major division	1984	1985	1986	1987	1988	1989	1990	1991	1992	1993
Mining and quarrying	---	42.2	43.0	44.9	45.8	46.0	46.8	47.8	47.9	47.5
Manufacturing	43.5	43.7	43.7	43.8	44.3	44.5	44.3	42.9	43.2	43.1
Electricity, gas and water	37.9	38.0	38.4	38.2	38.0	38.2	38.4	38.4	38.2	38.1
Construction	44.3	44.4	44.4	44.6	45.3	46.0	45.9	45.3	45.0	44.7
Trades, restaurants and hotels	39.0	39.0	39.1	39.2	39.3	39.3	39.2	39.6	39.4	39.6
Transport, storage and communication	46.5	47.1	47.0	47.4	47.5	47.2	47.2	46.3	46.9	46.5
Financing, insurance, real estate and business services	36.7	36.8	36.8	36.9	37.0	37.1	37.0	36.9	36.8	36.9
Community, social and personal services	36.4	36.5	36.5	36.8	36.8	36.8	36.8	36.5	36.5	36.6
Total (all non-agricultural activities)	---	43.6	43.6	43.7	44.1	44.3	44.2	43.5	43.6	43.5

[18] Income Data Services: "Hours and holidays 1995", *IDS Study*, No. 590, November 1995, p. 1.

[19] C. Marsh: *Hours of work of women and men in Britain* (London, HMSO, 1991).

[20] Bureau of Statistics, International Labour Office [hours actually worked; full-time workers on adult rates of pay].

Table 2. Basic working hours by industry (all employees), 1995[21]

Industry	Average hours
Agriculture and forestry	39.0
Energy and water	37.0
Mining and quarrying	38.3
Bricks, pottery and glass	38.0
Oil and chemicals	37.5
Engineering and allied	37.5
Food, drink and tobacco	37.6
Textiles and leather	38.5
Clothing and footwear	38.4
Furniture and timber	38.4
Other manufacturing	37.5
Paper, print and publishing	36.9
Construction	38.4
Retail and distribution	37.5
Transport and communication	38.8
Finance and insurance	35.0
Public services	37.6
Other services	37.0
All industries and services	37.5

Overtime and absolute maximum hours

Law

There are no generally applicable provisions for overtime or absolute maximum hours.

Common law

There are common law restrictions on the maximum hours of work if the hours set by the employer could be injurious to the health and safety of the worker. In the case of *Johnstone*

---

[21] IDS, "Hours and holidays 1995", op. cit., p. 6.

v. Bloomsbury Health Authority,[22] junior doctors were hired to work 40 hours a week normally and to be available for another 40 hours. They sued the employer on the grounds that working such hours could forseeably injure their health. In allowing the claim to proceed to trial, the Court of Appeal held that a worker cannot be required to work excessive hours that could result in injury to health, and that the employer's authority to require overtime had to take into account the duty to take care of the worker's health and safety.

Young persons

There are few restrictions on work by young workers who are 16 and 17. There are significant restrictions for young persons under 16, the compulsory school age.

Transportation sector

The Transport Act 1968, Part VI, regulates the hours of driving for certain classes of vehicle.[23]

Practice

One-and-a-half times normal pay is the most widely practiced overtime pay. Some firms pay less — one-and-a-quarter or one-and-a-third times normal pay — while other firms pay one-and-two-thirds or twice normal pay. Overtime work on Sunday is frequently at double normal pay.[24]

Although there is no legal obligation to pay overtime, in practice it is usually paid to workers who earn less than a certain annual revenue which, according to one survey, varies between £13,000 and £25,000 a year. Although management personnel are generally not paid overtime, often junior management staff and sometimes middle management are eligible. While earnings cut-offs normally also apply to manual workers, their earnings normally fall below these thresholds, and around 25 per cent of all organizations surveyed had no annual revenue cut-off limits for manual workers.[25]

In the same 1994 survey, it was found that the majority of organizations paid one-and-a-half times normal pay from Monday to Friday, although a few industrial companies paid less. At approximately half of the organizations, Saturday overtime was paid at the rate of one-and-a-half times normal pay, but a number of companies paid one-and-a-half times normal pay for the first four hours of work until 12:00 and then twice regular pay. Other companies paid double normal pay for any work on Saturday. All the companies except two paid their manual workers an overtime rate of twice normal pay on Sunday.

---

[22] *Johnstone v. Bloomsbury Health Authority*, cited in *Industrial Relations Law Reports*, Vol. 20, No. 3, March 1991, pp. 118-124.

[23] Hepple and Hakim, op. cit., pp. 5-6.

[24] IDS, "Overtime", op. cit., p. 1. See also P. Blyton: *The development of annual working hours in the United Kingdom*, Working paper CONDI/T/WP.4/1995 (Geneva, ILO, 1995), pp. 3-5.

[25] IDS, "Overtime", op. cit., pp. 1-2.

Overtime work in the manufacturing sector fell from 16 million in 1977 to 8.93 million hours per week in April 1994. However, average overtime per employee actually increased, with average overtime per worker in the manufacturing sector increasing to 9.7 hours per week in 1993 from 8.7 hours in 1977. The overall decline in overtime working can be explained in part by a significant loss of manufacturing jobs in this period. Manufacturing jobs fell from 7.1 million in June 1979 to 4.2 million in April 1994.[26]

Figure 1. Percentage of all employees who work overtime, 1977-1993[27]

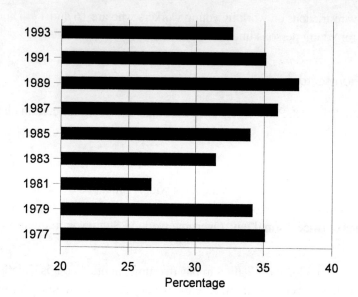

[26] ibid., pp. 4-5.

[27] IDS, "Overtime", op. cit., p. 4, citing *Employment Gazette*.

Table 3. Occupations with a high incidence of overtime working, April 1993[28]

Men*	Percentage working overtime (%)
Ambulance staff	85.5
Rail transport inspectors, supervisor, guards	81.8
Mechanical plant drivers, etc.	79.0
Rail construction/maintenance	78.4
Agricultural machinery drivers	77.1
Rail engine drivers and assistants	77.0
Bus and coach drivers	74.5
Bakery and confectionery process operatives	71.7
Cable jointers/lines repairers	69.5
Water and sewerage plant attendants	67.2
Road construction and maintenance workers	66.2
Railway station staff	65.8
Tool makers, tool fitters and markers-out	65.1
Police officers (sergeants and below)	63.8

Women*	Percentage working overtime (%)
Counter clerks and cashiers	58.4
Bank/building society and post office managers	48.3
Police officers (sergeant and below)	46.2
Road transport operatives	44.8
Telephone operators	44.6
Electric/electronic trades	44.0
Postal workers, mail sorters	41.1
Packers, bottlers, canners and fillers	39.0
Security guards and related occupations	38.9
Bakery and confectionary process operatives	38.5
Food, drink and tobacco operatives	38.2

*   Full-time employees whose pay was not affected by absence.

[28] ibid., pp. 5-6.

Rest

Law

There are no generally applicable provisions. Shop employees are to receive at least 15 minutes of rest after six hours of consecutive work. Employees of shops are normally to have one free afternoon per week in addition to another full day, and cannot be required to work on Sundays unless they are Sunday only workers.[29]

Practice

Work pauses

Paid tea breaks are customary in a number of establishments. Long working hours without breaks are reported to occur in some establishments which are not unionized.[30]

Weekly rest

Saturday and Sunday rest is the norm for weekly rest in most collective agreements, with substitution of other days when work is required on either of these days. Weekend working, especially Sunday working, increased significantly in the 1980s and the early 1990s. In the mid-1980s, approximately 25 per cent of the workforce worked on Sundays, either regularly or occasionally, and over 40 per cent on Saturdays. However, by 1992, approximately 40 per cent of the workforce worked on Sundays, either regularly or occasionally, and more than half on Saturdays. In addition, the spring 1992 Labour Force Survey indicated that 6 per cent of employees usually work seven days per week.

Shop-opening hours

Law

Shops must close by 20:00 at the latest on all but one of their working days, and by 21:00 once a week. Shops are to be closed one weekday per week by 13:00. There are no limits on small shops, and larger shops are limited to six hours on Sunday.

The Sunday Trading Act, which came into force on 26 August 1994, removed many restrictions on Sunday shop-opening hours.[31] The Act gives shop workers the right not to be dismissed, made redundant, or subjected to any other penalty for refusing to work on Sundays. With the exception of Sunday only workers, these protections apply to all employees required to work in or about a shop open on Sundays. They apply without regard to age, length of

---

[29] Shops Act 1950, 14 Geo. 6, Ch. 28, dated 28 July 1950, as amended up to Sunday Trading Act 1994, dated 5 July 1994 (*Public General Acts and General Synod Measures 1994*, Part II, Ch. 20, 1995, p. 815).

[30] "'Take a break', UK workers told", op. cit., pp. 13-14.

[31] ibid.

service, hours of work, and even if a worker has previously agreed to a contract requiring Sunday work. Workers who were employed before the Act came into force, or who were recruited after the law came into force whose contract does not specify Sunday work, are automatically protected. However, workers who have entered into a contract requiring Sunday work after the Act came into force are protected only after they have given their employer notice that they would like to "opt out" of Sunday work.[32]

Practice

According to one survey, only 18 per cent of establishments in the United Kingdom did not report any Sunday working of any kind in 1992. Non-manufacturing establishments are much more likely to undertake their main economic activity on Sunday, and there are strong economic incentives for certain types of retail establishments to operate on Sundays.[33]

Public holidays

Law

Public holidays in the United Kingdom are established by statute, Royal Proclamation or common law. There are eight such holidays.

By statute, "bank holidays" are established by Schedule 1 of the Banking and Financial Dealings Act 1971, and are applicable only to employees of banks and financial institutions. The current bank holidays are Easter Monday, the last Monday in May, the last Monday in August, 26 December (unless it is a Sunday), and 27 December (where either 25 or 26 December is a Sunday).

Public holidays designated by Royal Proclamation are New Year's Day and the first Monday in May. Christmas Day and Good Friday are common law holidays established historically by custom. For public holidays which fall on a Saturday or Sunday, a substitute day — normally the following Monday — is customarily designated in lieu of the public holiday which falls on the weekend.

Practice

There is no right to receive paid time off on any public holiday. However, most public holidays are granted to employees as paid time off by collective agreement or practice. The right to have paid time off on public holidays can be inferred into a contract of employment,

---

[32] "Sunday working rights for shop staff", in *Employment Gazette*, Vol. 102, No. 8, August 1994, p. 270.

[33] D. Bosworth: *Sunday working: Analysis of an employer survey*, Research Series No. 33 (Sheffield, Employment Department, 1994), Executive summary.

if they are customarily granted in a given industry. However, if the contract of employment specifies that time off is without pay, then there is no right to remuneration.[34]

A survey of 170 organizations found that twice regular pay plus an additional day off was the most common practice (approximately 50 per cent of the firms surveyed) when work is required on a public holiday. A number of organizations paid more for employees who work on Christmas Day, Good Friday or Easter Monday.[35]

Paid annual leave

Law

There are no generally applicable provisions.

Practice

According to one survey of approximately 500 organizations, the basic entitlement to paid annual leave was 20 to 25 days, with 25 days being most common for both manual and non-manual workers.

More than 40 per cent of the organizations granted their employees 25 days of basic entitlement to paid annual leave after one year of service. More than one-half of the organizations surveyed provided for further service-related vacation entitlement of up to four days on average.[36]

Basic entitlement to paid annual leave varies among industries. For example, according to the same survey, an average of 25 days was found in the engineering and in the paper, print and publishing sectors. In five other manufacturing sectors, and in the energy and water sector, the average was 24 days. The retail and finance sectors had the lowest entitlement, with an average of 22 and 21 days, respectively.

The autumn 1992 Labour Force Survey found that 2.2 million employees in Great Britain (10 per cent of all employees, 3 per cent of full-time employees, and 33 per cent of part-time employees) received no paid annual leave. The vast majority of these employees worked fewer than 16 hours per week and/or had worked continuously for their employer for less than one year. However, 20 per cent of this group had worked more than 16 hours a week and more than one year.[37]

---

[34] Employment Department Group: *A guide to bank and public holidays in the United Kingdom* (London, 1995); "Working on public holidays: A survey of compensation practice", in *Industrial Relations Review and Report*, No. 543, September 1993, pp. 5-8.

[35] "Working on public holidays", op. cit., pp. 5-8.

[36] IDS, "Hours and holidays 1993", op. cit., p. 1; Hepple and Hakim, op. cit., p. 20.

[37] Hepple and Hakim, op. cit., p. 20.

Other types of leave

Law

Employees have the right to leave for the following activities or in the following situations: for union duties and activities; to act as safety representatives; for public duties; for jury service and appearing as a witness; and when given notice of dismissal.[38]

Union duties and activities

Officials of an independent union, recognized by the employer for collective bargaining purposes, have the right to take time off during working hours if their duties concern matters which are subject to negotiation with the employer, or for duties that the employer has agreed that the officials may undertake on behalf of workers. Time off for training is similarly restricted to such activities. Time off is paid, although it has to be reasonable in relation to the duties to be performed.

Both union officials and members are entitled to take a reasonable amount of time off for trade union activities. Unlike time off for duties, time off for activities does not have to be paid.

Safety representatives

Safety representatives are entitled to paid time off for their duties.

Public duties

Most employees who hold the following public positions have the right to take time off to perform their duties: Justices of the Peace; members of local authorities; members of statutory tribunals; members of regional or area health authorities (England and Wales) or health boards (Scotland); members of the managing or governing bodies of local authority education establishments (England and Wales) and central institutions or colleges of education (Scotland); and members of water authorities (England and Wales) or river purification boards (Scotland). Although the employees are to be allowed reasonable time off to perform their public duties, there is no statutory requirement that this time off should be paid. A survey of 21 organizations found that it was more common for such time off to be paid than unpaid, and that requests for time off for public duties were relatively rare.

---

[38] Employment Act 1989, dated 16 November 1989 (*Acts of Parliament*, Ch. 38, 1989), as amended up to Act, dated 1 November 1990 (*Acts of Parliament*, Ch. 38, 1990) [LLD 1989-GBR1]; Employment Protection (Consolidation) Act 1978, dated 31 July 1978 (*Acts of Parliament*, Ch. 44, 1978), as amended up to Act, dated 28 June 1995 (*Acts of Parliament*, Ch. 18, 1995); Trade Union and Labour Relations (Consolidation) Act 1992, dated 16 July 1992 (*Acts of Parliament*, Ch. 52, 1992), as amended up to Act, dated 1 July 1993 (*Acts of Parliament*, Ch. 19, 1993) [LLD 1992-GBR1]. See generally Income Data Services: "Time off arrangements", *IDS Study*, No. 424, January 1989.

Jury service; appearing as a witness

Persons who are between 18 and 65 are liable to be called for jury service, unless ineligible, disqualified or exempted. Workers who serve as jurors may claim travelling and subsistence allowances, as well as loss of earning, from the court up to certain limits. There is no legal obligation for employers to pay their personnel while they are on jury service.

A survey of 21 organizations found that most top up the normal attendance allowance given by the court to normal pay, although a few organizations only granted unpaid time off. In the same survey, some establishments granted unpaid leave for a court appearance, while others topped up any court payments to normal pay. Organizations typically allowed time off if the court appearance was in connection with company business. One organization gave paid time off if the employee was required to attend, but unpaid time off if the appearance was voluntary. Another organization gave paid time off for an employee to be a witness in a criminal case, but unpaid time off in civil cases.

Redundant employees

Employees with two or more years of service who have been given notice of dismissal are entitled to reasonable time off with pay.

Practice

Based on various surveys, it was found that employees are sometimes granted leave for the following activities or in the following situations: dental and medical appointments, family illness, bereavement, marriage, activities of professional associations, sporting activities; reserve military training; and secondment to another organization.[39]

Dental and medical appointments

Most employers preferred that employees make their appointments outside working hours when possible. Of those organizations which permitted time off, approximately one-half granted paid time off, while the other half granted time off without pay.

Family illness

Practice varied among firms. Some expected employees to use their annual leave, while others granted separate paid leave. Two organizations granted up to five days off with pay, while another company granted ten days, but with the proviso that no more than five days should be used at any one time.

---

[39] IDS, "Time off arrangements", op. cit., pp. 1, 17-25.

Bereavement

Most organizations granted paid time off, usually for three days, although some establishments granted up to five days.

Marriage

Practice varied considerably, with a number of organizations preferring their workers to use their paid annual leave. Some granted unpaid leave. Others provided paid leave, although often only after the employee had worked for the establishment one or two years. Three organizations gave five days of paid leave, while one gave ten days of paid leave on the condition that the worker returned to work for the company after the marriage.

Activities of professional associations

A number of organizations granted paid time off, but on the condition that the activity had some relevance to the person's employment.

Sporting activities

Some organizations were of the view that workers should use their paid annual leave for such activities, while others granted paid time off for participation in the organization's own events or, in some cases, for inter-company competitions. The higher the level of the competition, i.e. national or international, the more likely it was that paid time off would be granted.

Reserve military training

Some employers allowed employees who were members of the Reserve Forces additional time off with pay to participate in annual military training exercises. A common arrangement was to grant an additional week of paid leave for a two-week training session, with the worker taking a week of his or her paid annual leave for the second week.

Secondment to another organization

A number of organizations allowed staff to be seconded to another organization, either as a commercial arrangement between two businesses or as a donation of the employee to a charity or voluntary organization. Many organizations which permit secondment prefer that such leave be on a full-time basis and normally for at least one year. There are some cases, however, of short-term or part-time secondment taking place as part of career development.

Shift and night work

Law

There are no generally applicable provisions for shift or night work.

The Directive concerning certain aspects of the organization of working time may have consequences for some types of shift and night work. For example, requirements for rest breaks, daily and weekly rest, as well as limitations on the duration of night work and the maximum average working week, could force certain employers to redesign their shift and night work schedules. The effect of these restrictions is most likely to be felt on rotating shift patterns, where late shifts are followed by early shifts, or other instances of double shifts. Similarly, the Directive on the protection of young people at work places a number of limitations on the employment of young persons, including requirements for daily and weekly rest breaks, and restrictions on night work and maximum hours of work per week. These restrictions place significant limitations on shift and night work by young workers, effectively excluding them from some types of such work.

Practice

According to the spring 1992 Labour Force Survey, approximately 16 per cent of the workforce was engaged in shift work. However, many part-time workers (24 per cent of all employees worked part time in 1992) effectively performed a form of shift work, although they were classified as part-time workers. For example, weekend work can be considered a type of shift work even though it may be classified as part-time work. Other forms of non-standard work, as well as increased flexibility of conventional full-time work, may also be blurring distinctions between traditional shift work and other types of work. The incidence of shift work, weekend work, and other work during non-standard hours was significantly higher in the 1990s than in the late 1970s.[40] According to another survey, the occupations with the highest rate of shift work are railway workers, postal workers, nurses and coal miners. This is followed by process workers in the rubber, chemical, gas and petroleum industries.[41]

The 1992 Labour Force Survey found that night work was relatively common among people who performed shift work, and that 7 per cent of the workforce performed shift work that included night work. The health services were a major employer of workers who are employed on night shifts. Only 1 per cent of the workforce was employed permanently on night shifts. It was also found that regular night work was most common among men.[42]

A 1994 shift pay survey of 148 collective agreements, which were effective from 1 September 1993 or later, made the following findings:[43]

---

[40] Hepple and Hakim, op. cit., pp. 21 and 28. See also Eurostat, *Labour force survey: Results 1992*, op. cit., p. 113.

[41] Income Data Services: "Shiftworking", *IDS Study*, No. 526, March 1993, p. 1.

[42] Hepple and Hakim, op. cit., p. 21.

[43] "Shift pay survey 1994", in *Bargaining Report*, No. 143, October 1994, p. 6.

— **Double-day work** (two shifts back-to-back, e.g. 06:00-14:00 and 14:00-22:00). This work had an average premium over basic pay of 15.7 per cent, with the highest premium being 40.6 per cent.

— **Night work**. Permanent night shift work paid 30.4 per cent over basic pay on average, with the highest premium paid being 81.2 per cent. The unsocial hours premium for night work was 30.8 per cent on average, and 50.7 per cent in the highest case.

— **Non-continuous 24-hour shift work**. The average premium paid was 37.4 per cent of basic pay, with the highest premium being 54.1 per cent.

— **Continuous (seven-day) 24-hour shift work**. The average premium paid was 37.4 per cent and the highest premium was 86.9 per cent.

— **Twilight shifts** (generally defined as part-time evening shifts falling between 17:00-22:00 on weekdays). These shifts frequently did not have premium payments because they were seen as convenient hours for work by women who have child-care responsibilities. Women performed approximately 66 per cent of such work, and the lack of premium payment for twilight shifts possibly reflects a traditional view that their pay is in addition to a male partner's income. Efforts by trade unions to secure premium payments for twilight hours have generally not met with success.

Table 4. Proportion of full-time employees receiving shift and similar premium payments, 1994[44]

Category of employee	Percentage of workers on shifts
Male manual	22.7
Male non-manual	6.2
All male	13.6
Female manual	16.7
Female non-manual	8.0
All female	9.5
All manuals	21.6
All non-manuals	7.0
All workers	12.1

[44] ibid., citing New Earnings Survey 1994, Part A.

United States

Overview and trends

Overview

The United States is a federal system with federal and state governments normally exercising concurrent jurisdiction over most aspects of working time. Federal law applies to federal, state, and local governments and all enterprises which are engaged in interstate commerce. The interpretation of what constitutes interstate commerce is quite broad. Activities which involve only intrastate commerce are covered only by state law. Most enterprises, however, are obligated to comply with both federal and state laws and regulations. In the event of different standards of protection or benefits between state and federal law, the law with the highest level of protection and benefits prevails.

At the federal level, the Fair Labor Standards Act (FLSA)[1] establishes the principle of a 40-hour week, after which overtime must be paid at a rate of one-and-a-half times regular pay. The FLSA is applicable to the private sector and to most federal, state and local government employees, but with numerous exceptions. The Act also has extensive provisions which are applicable to young workers under 18; it does not establish any limits on daily hours of work, nor on rest breaks, daily or weekly rest.

State law often provides more detailed regulation of working time than federal law. In addition to having limits on weekly hours of work, after which overtime must be paid, a number of states have limits on daily hours of work, beyond which overtime must be paid, as well as rules on rest breaks, daily and weekly rest.[2] All states regulate working time for young workers, in certain cases, more strictly than federal law.

In some sectors of economic activity, federal law either directly regulates or encourages the regulation of working time practices in detail. In the transportation sector, federal law prescribes rules on maximum daily and weekly hours of work, daily rest and other rest requirements for designated railway employees.[3] The rationale for this legislation, which dates back to 1907, is to ensure safety. Similar requirements are imposed by other federal laws with respect to road and civil air transportation, as well as for the maritime sector. As each sector has its own characteristics, the legal norms regarding maximum hours of work and rest are different for each type of activity.[4]

---

[1] 29 *United States Code (U.S.C.)* 201 et seq.

[2] See generally Bureau of National Affairs (BNA): "State laws", in *BNA Labor Relations Reporter* (Washington, 1995).

[3] Hours of Service Act, 45 *U.S.C.* 61 et seq.

[4] Motor Carrier Safety Act of 1984, as amended, Pub. L. 103-272, 5 July 1994; Federal Aviation Act of 1958, 49 *U.S.C.* App. 1371(k), 49 *U.S.C.* App. 1421(a)(5), 14 *Code of Federal Regulations (C.F.R.)* 121 (pp.-S); 14 *C.F.R.* 121 (5); 14 *C.F.R.* 65.47; Merchant Marine Eight-Hour Day, 46 *U.S.C.* 8104 et seq. See generally Office of Technology Assessment, Congress of the United States: *Biological rhythms: Implications for the worker* (Washington, US Government Printing Office, 1991), pp. 128 and 144-147.

Similarly, the working time arrangements of personnel employed in nuclear powerplants are strongly influenced, but not directly regulated, by the federal Nuclear Regulatory Commission (NRC). The NRC has issued a non-binding policy statement concerning working hours for nuclear powerplant personnel. If a plant voluntarily incorporates the policy statement into its technical specifications during the licensing process, the policy statement becomes enforceable. Slightly over three-fourths of licensed nuclear powerplants have incorporated the policy statement in their technical specifications and are legally bound by these working time provisions.[5]

Although the FLSA is applicable to most federal employees, additional federal legislation governs working time for the employees of the federal government in more detail.[6]

Legislation applicable to federal and federally-assisted public construction contracts and to service contracts with the federal government states that workers shall be paid wages and benefits, including paid public holidays and paid annual leave, at prevailing levels in the locality where the work is to be performed.[7] Another federal law requires payment of prevailing minimum wages to workers in the industry concerned for manufacturers or enterprises which furnish materials, supplies, articles, or equipment to the federal government.[8] This requirement, which results in industry-wide wage determination, also includes benefits such as paid public holidays and paid annual leave.

State governments and their agencies are authorized to establish the hours and conditions of work of state employees; these may provide a higher level of protection or benefits, to the extent the questions dealt with have not been preempted by federal law and the terms and conditions do not contravene any constitutional or statutory prohibitions as established in federal or state law.

Some states regulate working time issues concerning particular categories of economic activity, for example in the transportation sector (in particular, road transportation), mining or related processing industries, and certain industrial or manufacturing activities. In some states, there are legislative provisions on working time issues in connection with state public works contracts. These provisions sometimes establish daily and weekly limits on working time, and may also require comparable wages and benefits, which include paid annual leave and paid public holidays, in the locality where the work is to be performed.[9]

---

[5] Office of Technology Assessment, *Biological rhythms*, op. cit.; 47 *Federal Register (F.R.)* 23,836 (1982).

[6] 5 *U.S.C.* 6101 et seq.

[7] Davis-Bacon Act, 40 *U.S.C.* 276a et seq. (for contracts with the federal government over $2,000); a list of related federal or federally-assisted construction legislation containing similar requirements can be found at 29 *C.F.R.* 5.1; Service Contract Act, 41 *U.S.C.* 351 et seq. (for contracts over $2,500).

[8] Walsh-Healey Public Contracts Act, 41 *U.S.C.* 35 et seq.

[9] See "State laws", *BNA Labor Relations Reporter*, op. cit.

Trends

American employees work relatively long hours compared to those in other developed, industrialized countries. For full-time workers, the trend in the 1980s and 1990s has been toward slightly longer weekly hours of work. Overtime worked has been high in some years in the 1990s. Paid annual leave and other forms of leave are relatively modest by international standards. Several commentators have remarked that increased working hours have led to a decrease in leisure time during the 1980s and 1990s, and warned of the negative consequences of this development. It has been argued that workers accepted to work longer hours to have increased overtime pay because real wages declined during this period. A number of surveys in the 1990s have indicated that American workers, particularly those with higher incomes, have not been satisfied with working such long hours and would be willing to receive less income if they could have more leisure time.[10]

At the same time as some full-time workers have been increasing their working hours, there has also been a growth in part-time and other forms of non-standard work. The majority of those who work part time are women. Perhaps not surprisingly, there is a correlation between the length of working hours and income, with the result that full-time workers, often those who are skilled, have been working longer hours with more overtime pay while part-time workers, who are often unskilled or semi-skilled, have, by definition, not been working a full schedule. Short-term or contingent workers have also increasingly been used, and these workers may also not be fully employed throughout the year. These differences in the length of working time have led to wider differences in income inequality between workers and a certain polarization of the workforce.[11]

The development of part-time and other forms of non-standard work reflects another important trend towards increased flexibility. While this has taken place to some extent to accommodate workers who would prefer more flexible schedules, in particular those with child-care or other family responsibilities, enterprises have been major proponents of flexibility to increase competitiveness and to be able to respond to consumer demand more quickly.[12] The trend has not been welcomed by everyone, and some trade unions have opposed it on two grounds: on the one hand, work during unsocial hours, including the weekends, interferes with family life and is particularly difficult for single mothers; on the other, such work may be undertaken by without premium pay. Proposals have been put forth to modify the basic wage and hours law, the FLSA, so that overtime would be paid on the

[10] "Americans are working longer, enjoying it less", in *Work in America*, Vol. 17, No. 4, April 1992, p. 6; S. Rosenberg: "More work for some, less work for others: Working hours in the USA", in *Futures*, Vol. 25, No. 5, June 1993, pp. 551-560; O. Marchand: "An international comparison of working times", in *Futures*, Vol. 24, No. 5, June 1993, pp. 502-510; J.B. Schor: *The overworked American: The unexpected decline of leisure* (New York, Basic Books, 1991); "Study shows increase in hours of work, decrease in paid time off from 1969-1989", in *Labor Relations Week* (Washington), Vol. 6, No. 9, 26 February 1992.

[11] G. Burtless: "Contribution of employment and hours changes to family income inequality", in *Papers and proceedings of the Hundred and Fifth Annual Meeting of the American Economic Association, Anahiem, California, 5-7 January 1993*, pp. 131-135; "Fewer jobs filled as US factories rely on overtime pay", in *New York Times*, as reproduced in *Manpower Argus*, No. 298, July 1993, p. 2.

[12] Rosenberg, op. cit.

basis of hours worked over a two-week period of 80 hours, rather than the current standard which specifies overtime must be paid after 40 hours in a week.[13]

An interesting characteristic of the discussion of working time issues is the virtual absence of a debate over the reduction of working time in favour of the creation of additional employment. Although this has been explained by some commentators by the relatively low rate of unemployment in the 1990s, it has been pointed out that there was no debate on the issue in the economic recession during the 1980s, where workers were more prone to accept reduced wages and benefits as the price for job preservation than to negotiate reductions in working time.[14]

Normal hours of work

Federal law

Normal hours of work are 40 hours per week, although the law has numerous exceptions. There are no generally applicable limitations for daily hours of work. Special rules are applicable to young workers.[15] For federal workers, the law provides for a basic work-week of five days, on Monday through Friday when possible; basic hours of work during a work-week are the same each day; basic daily hours of work are eight; basic weekly hours are 40 for full-time workers.[16] Special rules on daily hours of work are applicable to federal workers who work compressed work-weeks or flexible schedules.[17]

The FLSA is applicable to employees engaged in interstate commerce or in the production of goods for interstate commerce, to certain agricultural workers, and to federal, state and local government workers, subject to certain exceptions. The principal exclusions under the FLSA concern persons who work in a professional, executive, or administrative capacity, and those whose work only pertains to intrastate commerce. These workers and other more specific categories are exempt from the overtime provisions of the Act and, by implication, from the standard defining normal hours of work per week (see **Overtime and absolute maximum hours** for a list of these categories).[18]

Young workers under the FLSA

Young workers who are 16 and 17 are not subject to any limitations on the number of hours per day or week they can work. However, they are prohibited from undertaking hazardous work, subject to some exceptions, as established by regulation for student learners and

---

[13] D. Kameras: "Raid on the 40-hour week goes into overtime", in *AFL-CIO News*, 17 April 1995.

[14] Rosenberg, op. cit.

[15] Fair Labor Standards Act, 29 *U.S.C.* 201 et seq.

[16] 5 *U.S.C.* 6101(a)(3).

[17] 5 *U.S.C.* 6121 et seq.

[18] 5 *U.S.C.* 6101 et seq.; 5 *U.S.C.* 5541 et seq.

apprentices. Occupations, processes, and industries which are considered as hazardous are defined in the *Code of Federal Regulations*.

Young workers who are 14 and 15 may work outside school hours, but only in non-hazardous jobs. When school is in session, hours of work are limited to three hours per day and 18 hours per week. When school is not in session, they may be employed up to eight hours per day and 40 hours per week between 07:00 and 19:00 (and until 21:00 between 1 June and the first Monday in September).

Children under 14 are not permitted to work except as actors or performers in motion pictures, theatrical production, and radio and television productions; as deliverers of newspapers; or as employees of their parents.

State law

Many states establish a 40-hour week. Some states have daily limits of eight, ten, or 12 hours; there are numerous exceptions. Special rules are applicable for young workers in all states.[19]

Although practice varies from state to state, state law is very frequently similar to federal law and establishes normal working hours as 40 per week. Some states also provide for daily limits on working time. Although an eight-hour limitation is the most frequent, some states specify ten- or even 12-hour daily limits before overtime has to be paid. These limitations, however, do not necessarily indicate that these hours are normal in the state concerned, but rather impose a higher cost on firms that employ workers in excess of these daily limits. In some cases, these limitations are applicable generally, while in other cases they may be limited to a specific occupation or to employment on public works contracts. All states which have generally applicable weekly and daily legal limits on hours of work also provide for numerous exceptions. In some cases, states do not legislate legal limitations on weekly or daily hours of work, with the result that federal law on weekly hours of work becomes the legal standard at the state level.

Young workers under state law

All states have laws on the employment of young persons. Although these laws are frequently similar to the FLSA, in some cases they are stricter. For example, many states have standards which prohibit young persons from performing hazardous work, but have more extensive standards than at the federal level. These additional standards may be based on particular local industries which have been found to be hazardous in a given state (e.g. boating and fishing in Oregon), or are based on a different appreciation of the hazards associated with certain types of work, such as work with paints, injurious amounts of dust, and other substances and chemicals which have been determined to be hazardous. Similarly, many states regulate activities which are exempt from the application of the federal law to the employment of young persons, such as the employment of young persons in the entertainment business, i.e. radio, television, and movie and theatrical productions, and in the delivery of newspapers.

---

[19] "State laws", *BNA Labor Relations Reporter*, op. cit.

Additionally, while federal law imposes limits on hours of work only for young persons who are 14 and 15, many states have hours of work limitations for those under 18.

Practice

Based on a survey of 400 collective agreements, 85 per cent of those contracts addressed the issue of work schedules and 94 per cent of those called for an eight-hour day. Five per cent provided for a standard day of less than eight hours. Only two contracts provided for normal daily hours of more than eight hours. Weekly work schedules were specified in 65 per cent of these collective agreements, and 94 per cent called for a 40-hour week, while the remainder provided for a work-week ranging from 35 to 39.5 hours. Five-day work-weeks were specified in 57 per cent of the contracts, and 40 per cent called for work Monday through Friday.[20]

Table 1 below provides an overview of average weekly hours paid for during the 1984 to 1994 period for the different economic sectors. The increase in weekly hours, which can be observed in some sectors, is due principally to an increase in overtime (see Table 2 below).

Table 1. Hours of work per week by major divisions of economic activity[21]

Major division	1984	1985	1986	1987	1988	1989	1990	1991	1992	1993	1994
Manufacturing	40.7	40.5	40.7	41.0	41.1	41.0	40.8	40.7	41.0	41.4	42.0
Mining and quarrying	43.3	43.4	42.2	42.4	42.3	43.0	44.1	44.4	43.9	44.3	44.7
Construction	37.8	37.7	37.4	37.8	37.9	37.9	38.2	38.1	38.0	38.5	38.9
Electricity, gas and water	41.5	41.7	41.8	41.5	41.5	41.9	41.6	41.6	41.9	42.3	42.4
Total (all non-agricultural activities)	35.2	34.9	34.8	34.8	34.7	34.6	34.5	34.3	34.4	34.5	34.7

Overtime and absolute maximum hours

Federal law

Overtime

Pursuant to the FLSA, overtime is payable at a rate of regular pay plus 50 per cent after 40 hours per week; there are numerous exceptions. There are no generally applicable maximum

---

[20] BNA: *Collective bargaining, negotiations and contracts: Basic patterns clause finder* (Washington, 1992), pp. 46-47.

[21] Bureau of Statistics, International Labour Office [hours paid for; private sector: production and construction workers and non-supervisory employees].

limits on the amount of overtime that may be worked. Under federal legislation applicable to most federal workers, overtime is payable after eight hours a day and 40 hours per week, subject to certain exceptions. Overtime pay for federal employees covered by separate legislation is the regular rate of pay, plus 50 per cent. There are several exceptions. There is also premium pay accorded to federal workers who work on Sunday.[22]

Exclusions

The principal exclusions under the Act concern persons who work in a professional, executive, or administrative capacity, or whose work only pertains to intrastate commerce. In addition, there are numerous exclusions — either partial or total — from the requirement to pay overtime for the following categories of economic activity: airline employees in activities relating to air transportation; certain amusement and recreational establishments; auto, farm implement, boat, and aircraft dealers; certain domestic service workers in private households; certain drivers and drivers' helpers; persons working in a foreign country; certain forestry and logging employees; employees of gas stations with limited sales; homeworkers engaged in the making of holly-wreaths; hospital and nursing home personnel; employees of motor carriers whose hours are regulated by the Department of Transportation; persons engaged in delivering newspapers to the consumer; outside salespersons; certain petroleum distributors; certain radio and television broadcasters; employees of certain railroad and steamship companies; retail commission salespersons; employees of certain establishments which engage in both production of goods and their retail sale (e.g. bakeries, ice cream shops, candy shops); sea crews; taxicab drivers employed by a taxicab company; employees of certain independently owned telephone companies; under certain conditions, substitute parents who reside in a facility for institutionalized children.

Other exclusions from the overtime provisions of the Act include specified categories of governmental employees, such as elected officials, personal staff of elected officials, policy-making appointees, legal advisors to elected officials, legislative employees, and volunteers. Law enforcement and fire protection are subject to a partial exemption, which permits a reference period for the payment of overtime to be longer than one week (see below).

Using a reference period of more than a week for overtime payment

In principal, the Act prohibits a reference period of more than one week for the payment of overtime. However, a reference period exceeding one week is permitted for a restricted number of occupations. These include:

Hospital and nursing home personnel. Such institutions may use a reference period of 14 days if employees agree in advance and if one-and-a-half times regular pay is paid for hours over eight per day, and over 80 hours during a 14-day period. Otherwise, the 40-hour week standard is applicable.

---

[22] 5 *U.S.C.* 5541 et seq.

Certain petroleum distributors. For employees of independently owned and controlled local enterprises which engage in wholesale or bulk distribution of petroleum products, it is permissible to pay such employees one-and-a-half times the statutory minimum rate for work between 40 and 56 hours per week, and one-and-a-half times the regular rate for all work in excess of 12 hours per day and 56 hours per week.

Law enforcement personnel and firefighters. Payment for overtime is based on a sliding scale reference period of between seven and 28 consecutive days. For law enforcement personnel, overtime is due after 43 hours of work in a seven-day period and after 171 hours in a 28-day period. For firefighters, overtime is due after 53 hours of work in a seven-day period and after 212 hours of work in a 28-day period. For law enforcement personnel or firefighters who have worked at least seven, but less than 28, consecutive days, overtime payment is required when the ratio of the number of hours worked to the number of days in the work period exceeds the ratio of 171 hours to 28 days for law enforcement personnel and 212 hours to 28 days for firefighters. Compensation time off in lieu of overtime payment may be granted for excess hours.

State and local government employees

Compensatory time. Pursuant to the FLSA, compensatory time off in lieu of overtime is authorized by the FLSA for state and local government employees at a rate of not less than 1.5 hours of compensation time for each hour of overtime.

Compensatory time may only be used pursuant to (1) an agreement between the government agency and the representatives of its employees; or (2) in the case of employees not covered by such an agreement, pursuant to an individual agreement arrived at before the performance of the work.

State and local government employees who perform work that is not related to public safety, emergency response, or that is not seasonal are permitted to accrue up to 240 hours of compensatory time. Employees who perform work of a public safety, emergency response, or seasonal nature are allowed to accrue up to 480 hours of compensatory time.

State and local government employees have the right to use compensatory time that is accrued and are not to be made to accept more time than an employer can, in good faith, grant within a reasonable period. Moreover, an agreement with the employer that an employee will lose all accrued compensation time not used by a certain date each year, even if negotiated as part of a collective bargaining agreement, is not legally permissible. If compensation time has not been used upon termination of employment, the employee is entitled to overtime payment for unused time.

Federal employees

Compensatory time off in lieu of overtime is also authorized for federal workers covered by separate legislation and is granted on an equal time basis for overtime worked. It can be accorded at the request of the federal employee.[23]

Maximum hours of work

Although there are no generally applicable maximum hours of work standards in the FLSA, federal law and regulations specify such norms directly in particular transportation activities, such as rail, road, and civil air transportation, as well as for the maritime sector. Maximum hours of work are strongly influenced by non-binding federal norms that are recommended for establishments engaged in the production of nuclear energy. The FLSA does specify limitations for young workers who are 14 and 15 (see above under **Normal hours of work**).

State law

Overtime

In many states, the law on overtime is frequently similar to federal law and requires that overtime must be paid after 40 hours of work in a week, subject to exceptions. Some states provide for daily limits on working time beyond which overtime must be paid. Although an eight-hour limitation is the most frequent, some states specify ten- or even 12-hour daily limits before overtime has to be paid. In some cases, these limitations are generally applicable, while in other cases they may be limited to a specific occupation or to employment on public works contracts. Where such legislation exists with respect to public works contracts at the state level, typically it specifies that overtime must be paid after eight hours of daily work, although in at least one state, Kentucky, ten hours is specified if it is agreed in advance in writing or if it is provided for by collective agreement. In some cases, states have not legislated on the question of overtime and have let federal law establish the overtime standard.[24]

Maximum hours of work

Few states address the issue of maximum hours of work outside the case of young workers, where such limits are imposed. Often the maximum hours allowed are linked to age and become progressively longer as the young worker becomes older. Special rest provisions may also be applicable to young workers. In certain sectors of economic activity, for example in motor transportation, some states impose absolute daily and weekly maximum limits on the duration of working time. There are usually exceptions to these rules in emergency situations.

---

[23] 5 *U.S.C.* 5543.

[24] "State laws", *BNA Labor Relations Reporter*, op. cit.

Practice

Based on a survey of 400 collective agreements, it was found that 97 per cent of these contracts addressed the issue of premium pay for overtime work. Daily overtime provisions were provided for in 92 per cent of the agreements, and most contracts provided for overtime pay after eight hours of work, although four per cent provided for overtime pay after seven or seven-and-a-half hours. Virtually all of these agreements specified overtime pay at the regular rate of pay plus 50 per cent. However, in 26 per cent of these agreements, doubletime was paid after a certain number of overtime hours had been worked at the regular rate of pay plus 50 per cent. The most common provision of such clauses (58 per cent) was to pay doubletime after four hours of normal overtime work, although some contracts provided shorter periods and others longer periods.

Weekly overtime benefits were provided in 72 per cent of the agreements, and, of these, 94 per cent called for overtime after 40 hours at the regular rate of pay plus 50 per cent. The other contracts — mainly agreements in the apparel industry — provided for overtime for less than 40 hours of work per week.

Premium pay provisions for work on the sixth day of work were found in 23 per cent of the collective agreements, and approximately 45 per cent of these specified that premium pay was payable only if it was the sixth consecutive day of work. All the agreements with a sixth-day clause paid the regular rate of pay plus 50 per cent.

Premium pay provisions for work on the seventh day of work were found in 26 per cent of the agreements, and, of these, 83 per cent provided for doubletime pay and 61 per cent had a seventh consecutive day of work clause.

Premium pay provisions for work on weekends were found in 67 per cent of the 400 contracts surveyed. Premium pay for work on Saturdays was called for in 51 per cent of the agreements, with most contracts providing for the payment of the regular rate plus 50 per cent, although 10 per cent provided for doubletime after a given number of hours work, usually eight. Less than 2 per cent of the contracts provided for doubletime for all work on Saturday. Premium pay for Sunday work was found in 63 per cent of the surveyed contracts, with doubletime pay being most common and provided for in 78 per cent of such agreements.

Procedures for distribution were contained in 66 per cent of the contracts surveyed: 38 per cent provided for equal distribution; 21 per cent for distribution on the basis of seniority; 14 per cent for cumulative equalization of overtime; and 9 per cent for distribution by rotating assignments. Distribution procedures also sometimes limited overtime to workers in specified job classifications (55 per cent); workers in specified departments (44 per cent); workers qualified to do the job (34 per cent); or workers who normally performed the work on a particular shift (26 per cent).[25]

Table 2 shows statistics compiled by the Bureau of Labor Statistics of the US Department of Labor. They show average weekly hours, including overtime, for different categories of economic activity of all workers in the private sector. The statistics show record levels of

---

[25] BNA, *Collective bargaining, negotiations and contracts*, op. cit.

overtime, particularly in manufacturing but also in mining, and reflect a trend to limit the hiring of new workers and to rely on more overtime even in a period of economic expansion. The low weekly hours of work in retail trade and services probably reflect substantial part-time work in these categories of economic activity.

Table 2. Average weekly hours of production of non-supervisory workers on private, non-farm payrolls by industry[26]

Industry	1992	1993	Sept. 1994
Private sector	34.4	34.5	34.6
Manufacturing	41.0	41.4	42.0
Overtime	3.8	4.1	4.7
Durable goods ①	41.5	42.1	42.8
Overtime	3.7	4.3	5.0
Non-durable goods ②	40.4	40.6	40.9
Overtime	3.8	4.0	4.3
Transportation and public utilities	38.9	39.6	39.9
Wholesale trade	38.2	38.2	38.2
Retail trade	28.8	28.8	28.8
Services	32.5	32.5	32.5

① Durable goods are defined as lumber and wood products; furniture and fixtures; stone, clay and glass products; primary metal industries, including blast furnaces and basic steel products; fabricated metal products; industrial machinery and equipment; electronic and other electrical equipment; transportation equipment, including motor vehicles and equipment; instruments and related products; and miscellaneous manufacturing.

② Non-durable goods are defined as food and kindred products; textile mill products; apparel and other textile products; paper and allied products; printing and publishing; chemicals and allied products; rubber and miscellaneous plastics products; and leather and leather products.

Rest

Federal law

There are no generally applicable provisions pursuant to the FLSA. Federal law and regulations specify norms in particular transportation activities, such as rail, road, and civil air transportation, as well as for the maritime sector. For establishments engaged in the civil

---

[26] *Monthly Labor Review*, Vol. 118, No. 1, January 1995, p. 87.

production of nuclear energy, rest requirements are strongly influenced by non-binding federal norms that are recommended by the Nuclear Regulatory Commission. Federal workers are normally entitled to two consecutive days off, on Saturday and Sunday where possible.

State law

Some states have established provisions on rest breaks, daily and/or weekly rest. In some cases, these are generally applicable while, in other cases, they are applicable to specific occupations. The examples given below are for illustration purposes only and other states not cited may have similar laws.[27]

Rest breaks

In a significant number of states, there are legal requirements concerning rest breaks for meals. The laws in California and Colorado are fairly representative, and require that employees be given an unpaid 30-minute meal break after five consecutive hours of work, except when the total working period is not more than six hours. An "on-duty" meal break is allowed only when the nature of the work prevents the person from being relieved of duty, and is counted as part of hours worked. In other states, such as Maine and Massachusetts, an unpaid meal break must be granted after no more than six hours of work.

In some states, the law on meal breaks is more precise. For example, in Connecticut and Delaware, there must be an unpaid meal break of 30 minutes when the work period is more than 7.5 hours, and this break must take place after the first two hours of work and before the last two hours of work.

In New York, the minimum meal break for workers employed in mercantile and non-factory establishments is 30 minutes, and is due to an employee who works more than a six-hour period that extends over the noon period, and the meal break should take place between 11:00 and 14:00. An additional 20-minute meal period, between 17:00 and 19:00, is required for those whose work periods starts before 11:00 and continues after 19:00. Persons employed in mercantile and non-factory establishments for a shift of more than six hours between 13:00 and 06:00 the next day shall be given a 45-minute meal break. For factory workers, meal breaks shall be at least 60 minutes for both the noon meal break and those working an evening or night shift.

Work pauses

Standards on work pauses are rare, although they do exist in some states. For example, in Colorado, in addition to providing for a meal break, the law also provides for work pauses of at least ten minutes for each four hours of work.

[27] "State laws", *BNA Labor Relations Reporter*, op. cit.

Daily rest

Generally applicable provisions concerning daily rest are relatively rare in state legislation. Illinois, for example, mentions that workers should benefit from regular rest at the close of business each day. However, some states, such as Florida, Iowa and Massachusetts, provide for daily rest requirements for particular occupations in designated areas of economic activity, such as road and rail transportation.

Weekly rest

The question of weekly rest is dealt with in a number of states, and the approach is far from uniform. In a number of states, such as Alabama, Alaska, Arizona, California and Florida, Sunday is designated as a holiday, although this designation does not necessarily mean workers cannot be asked to work on Sunday. In other states, such as Illinois, Massachusetts and New York, it is specified that workers should have at least 24 hours of consecutive rest per week. In some states, such as Louisiana and Maryland, the law is worded in the negative and mandates that no business opposed to being open on Sundays may be required to be open on this day, subject to certain exceptions. A significant number of states do not address the issue.[28]

Practice

Rest breaks for meals

In one review of collective agreements, it was found that meal breaks typically ranged from 15 minutes to one hour, and contracts specified whether they were unpaid or paid. Unpaid meal breaks were more common on regular shifts and tended to be longer, that is between 30 minutes to one hour. Paid meal breaks tended to be shorter, and these typically were given either for 15, 20 or 30 minutes. Paid meal breaks appeared to have been more common for shift work.[29]

Statistics compiled by the Bureau of Labor Statistics of the US Department of Labor for the period 1980-1991 indicate that paid meal breaks were given by only a minority of establishments in the private and public sectors. Only 8 to 11 per cent of workers in medium and large establishments participated in employer-provided paid lunch programmes between 1980 and 1991, and the average duration of the break was around 30 minutes, with some small variations.

Work pauses

In one survey of collective agreements, it was found that frequently contracts specified two breaks per shift, one in the first part of the shift and the second in the latter part. Additional

---

[28] ibid.; *Monthly Labor Review*, January 1995, op. cit., p. 48.

[29] BNA, *Collective bargaining, negotiations and contracts*, op. cit.

rest periods during overtime hours were also frequently required. Some agreements imposed restrictions on the use of work pauses. In one agreement, for example, it was stated that such work pauses could not be used to permit late arrival, early departure, or an extended lunch period.[30]

In statistics compiled by the Bureau of Labor Statistics of the US Department of Labor for the period 1980-1991, it was found that the majority of establishments in the private and public sectors normally gave paid work pauses each working day, and that the average total time granted for work pauses varied between 25 to 29 minutes.

Daily rest

Some collective agreements in one survey specified absolute maximum hours of daily work, for example fixing ten or 16 hours, or another figure. These limits were normally subject to certain exceptions.[31] However, most agreements usually addressed the question of daily rest indirectly by fixing daily overtime and, in some cases, by either placing limits on overtime or providing for higher premium pay after a specified number of overtime hours in a given day.

Weekly rest

Collective agreements usually indicate that normal hours of work are five days a week, and frequently indicate a Monday through Friday schedule. Often there is an overtime premium for the sixth and seventh days of work to penalize work on what would normally be considered weekly rest days. The overtime premium tends to be particularly high for work on the seventh consecutive day in many collective agreements (see above under **Overtime and absolute maximum hours**).

Shop-opening hours

Federal law

No generally applicable provisions.

State law

The issue is normally addressed at the local level of government.

---

[30] BNA, *Collective bargaining, negotiation and contracts*, op. cit.

[31] BNA, *Collective bargaining, negotiations and contracts*, op. cit.

Practice

Merchants and businesses are free to set their own shop-opening hours in many states, where a number of retail establishments, including some supermarkets, gas stations and convenience stores, operate 24 hours a day, seven days a week. Many retail establishments are closed on Sundays, however, and a number of these may have only limited operating hours on Saturday.

Public holidays

Federal law

There are ten federal public holidays: 1 January, New Year's Day; 15 January, Martin Luther King Jr.'s Birthday; the third Monday in February, President's Day; the last Monday in May, Memorial Day; 4 July, Independence Day; the first Monday in September, Labor Day; 11 November, Veteran's Day; the fourth Thursday in November, Thanksgiving; and 25 December, Christmas.

There is no obligation for private employers to grant paid time off for federal public holidays or to provide premium pay for work undertaken on these days. Most federal workers are granted paid time off and, if they are required to work, they are paid double their basic rate of pay. They are also paid for a minimum number of hours worked, even if they actually worked less.[32] For workers who must be paid wages and benefits at prevailing levels in the industry or in the locality where the work is performed, the concept of prevailing wages includes benefits such as paid public holidays (see above under **Overview and trends**).

State law

Each state establishes its own public holidays. In most cases, there is considerable overlap with federal public holidays, but most states have one or more public holidays which reflect the local history and traditions. In some states, there may be public holidays only for some localities. In general, many states have between ten and 13 public holidays, but some states have less or more (e.g. at least one state has as few as nine and another 17 public holidays.) There is no obligation for private employers to grant paid time off on state public holidays. Some states, such as Illinois and Maryland, have legislation with respect to state public works contracts, which contains provisions that are similar to federal law and which mandate the payment of prevailing wages and benefits, including paid public holidays, in the locality in which the work is to be performed.[33]

Practice

In one survey of 400 collective agreements, it was found that 99 per cent of contracts had provisions for public holidays, and that all or some of these were paid. Ten or more public

---

[32] 5 *U.S.C.* 5546.

[33] "State laws", *BNA Labor Relations Reporter*, op. cit.

holidays were recognized in 72 per cent of the contracts. Thirty-one per cent provided 12 or more public holidays, and 8 per cent provided 14 or more public holidays. The median number of public holidays provided for in the total survey was 11 days.

Six public holidays — Christmas Day, Memorial Day, Independence Day, Labor Day, Thanksgiving, and New Year's Day — were found to be granted in 92 per cent of the contracts surveyed. Three other days — the day after Thanksgiving, a full day on Christmas Eve, and part or all of Good Friday — were the next public holidays most frequently granted. Other federal, state, local, religious and personal days (such as an employee's birthday) appeared in lesser frequency.

Eligibility for holiday pay provisions appeared in the great majority of the contracts surveyed. Length of service requirements were provided for in 54 per cent of those agreements, with four weeks of employment being the most common requirement in 39 per cent of the survey sample. Almost all contracts surveyed which had length of service conditions required more than four weeks, and had requirements that ranged from six weeks to six months. Periods of service of three months (21 per cent) and two months (slightly less than 20 per cent) were most common. Work requirements appeared in 85 per cent of the contracts surveyed. In approximately 80 per cent of these provisions, the employee was required to work both the day before and the day after the holiday to receive holiday pay.[34]

According to statistics compiled by the Bureau of Labor Statistics of the US Department of Labor for the period 1980-1991, it was found that between 94 and 99 per cent of workers in private sector establishments were granted around ten paid public holidays per year. A substantial majority of state and local governments granted between 13 and 14 paid public holidays per year.

Paid annual leave

Law

There are no generally applicable provisions at the federal or state level. For workers who must be paid wages and benefits at prevailing levels in the industry or in the locality where the work is performed, the concept of prevailing wages includes benefits such as paid annual leave (see above under **Overview and trends**).

Some states, such as Illinois and Maryland, have legislation with respect to state public works contracts which contains provisions that are similar to federal law and which mandate the payment of prevailing wages and benefits, including paid annual leave, in the locality in which the work is to be performed.[35]

[34] BNA, *Collective bargaining, negotiation and contracts*, op. cit.

[35] "State laws", *BNA Labor Relations Reporter*, op. cit.

Practice

In one survey of 400 collective agreements, it was found that there were vacation provisions in 91 per cent of the contracts surveyed. This figure rose to 98 per cent when the construction industry was excluded. In 89 per cent of the contracts surveyed, the amount of vacation was tied to length of service. The median service requirements for vacation were one year for one week of vacation, two years for two weeks, eight years for three weeks, 15 years for four weeks, 20.5 years for five weeks, and 28 years for six weeks. In 87 per cent of the contracts surveyed, the basis for vacation pay was elaborated. In 53 per cent of those contracts, it was stated that vacation pay was to be calculated at base rates; in 32 per cent, at a worker's average earnings; in 8 per cent, at a worker's base pay or average earnings, whichever was greater; and in 7 per cent, on base rates or average earnings, depending on the classification of the employee. Seven per cent of these contracts stated that there should be a vacation pay bonus, with some contracts specifying a flat amount and others indicating an amount for each week of vacation taken.

According to statistics compiled by the Bureau of Labor Statistics of the US Department of Labor for the period 1980-1991, it was found that virtually all medium and large-scale private establishments provided paid annual leave, and that the great majority of small private establishments and state and local governments also granted paid annual leave.

Other types of leave

Federal law

No generally applicable conditions.

State law

There are few types of leave or justified absence which are provided for by law in most states. Generally, the types of leave granted can be grouped into leave for reserve military service, voting, jury service, performance of public functions, and humanitarian activities.[36]

Military service

Virtually all states provide for an unpaid leave of absence to undertake duties associated with being in a state or federal reserve military unit. These provisions vary, but generally state that a worker should be granted an unpaid leave of absence for a defined period of time to undertake such duties and should not be penalized in his or her employment for taking such leave. Many states also have provisions to facilitate the re-employment of veterans who had previously worked in an establishment, although typically these provisions are qualified.

---

[36] "State laws", *BNA Labor Relations Reporter*, op. cit.; R. Nelson: "State labor legislation enacted in 1993", in *Monthly Labor Review*, Vol. 117, No. 1, January 1994, p. 38.

Voting

A significant number of states provide that the employer should grant two or three hours off from work so that employees can vote in elections. Sometimes this language is qualified to state that this time off should only be granted if the person would not have adequate time to vote before or after working hours.

Jury service

Some states have provisions on jury service, which state whether it is paid or unpaid and the obligations of the employer.

Other civic duties

In at least one state, Illinois, an elected official of a unit of local government or school district may be permitted to have an unpaid leave of absence to attend an official meeting of such a public body, and shall not be penalized by the employer for such absence.

Humanitarian activities

In some states, such as Kansas, Nebraska and North Carolina, state employees who are American Red Cross certified disaster service volunteers are granted paid leave.

Practice

Military service

In a survey of 400 collective agreements, long-term military leave was mentioned in 66 per cent of the contracts. Provisions for disabled veterans returning from long-term military leave were specified in 14 per cent of the long-term military leave provisions. Educational leave for veterans was also specified in 9 per cent of the contracts. Short-term military leave was mentioned in 38 per cent of the contracts, with pay provisions being contained in 83 per cent of these clauses. In 91 per cent of the pay clauses, the employee was paid the difference between military pay and regular pay at the establishment while on short-term military leave. The length of leave was also specified in 81 per cent of these provisions, with two weeks' leave being the most typical period allowed.[37]

Voting

Although many states provide for time off for voting in at least general elections, a review of collective agreements also found that some contracts specify time off to vote. In some cases, the contracts stated that the day of general elections was a paid holiday, while other

---

[37] BNA, *Collective bargaining, negotiations and contracts*, op. cit.

contracts provided a limited amount of time off, normally with pay. Time off was also sometimes given for voting in primaries and local elections.[38]

Jury service

In a review of collective agreements, it was found that pay for jury duty was sometimes provided for. Usually the pay granted was the difference between the amount provided by the state and the worker's basic pay. Sometimes this payment was limited to a maximum period of jury duty.[39]

Other civic duties

One review of collective agreements found that these contracts sometimes have provisions for leave to serve as a witness in court. Leave without pay was provided for in some cases when an employee was elected to public office, as well as for an employee who assumed other public functions, such as working at the polls on election day, or serving as a volunteer firefighter, as a member of a rescue squad or an ambulance team, as a member of the Civil Air Patrol Group involved in air search and rescue missions, as a participant in civil defence activities as a credit union officer, or in the Peace Corps (an overseas foreign assistance programme).[40]

Union leave

One review of collective agreements found that these agreements often contain provisions for leave to participate in union affairs. This may involve long-term leave to assume union office, or short-term leave to attend conventions and conferences, or time off for contract negotiations. Long-term leave was sometimes granted for the duration of the term of office. In the case of short-term leave to attend meetings, the amount of time was specified — usually 30 days or less. Normally long-term and short-term union leave was without pay. With respect to time off for contract negotiations, pay was sometimes granted, but the agreements normally put limits on the number of employees eligible or on the total number of compensable hours for this activity.[41]

Personal leave

In a survey of 400 collective agreements, provisions for leave for personal or unspecified reasons were provided for in 76 per cent of the contracts. Some agreements stated that leave would be granted for "good" or "sufficient" reasons, while others stated that leave would be

---

[38] BNA: *Documentation on leaves of absence based on a review of collective agreements* (Washington, 1991).

[39] ibid.

[40] ibid.

[41] ibid.

granted for specific reasons, such as family illness or personal business. Time off to marry or to further one's education were also typical reasons for the taking of personal leave. The duration of such leave was mentioned in 81 per cent of these provisions, and ranged from one week to one year, with one month (33 per cent) and three months (21 per cent) being most common. Extension of the leave was provided for in 50 per cent of these provisions. Normally personal leave was unpaid.[42]

Funeral leave

In a survey of 400 collective agreements, this types of leave was provided for in 85 per cent of the contracts. Three days' paid leave was permitted in 83 per cent of these provisions; five days in 9 per cent; and four days in 4 per cent. Only five of the contracts charged funeral leave against paid annual leave or paid sick leave. According to statistics compiled by the Bureau of Labor Statistics of the US Department of Labor, 80 per cent of medium and large private establishments provided funeral leave in 1991, and the average paid leave was 3.3 days. For small private establishments with fewer than 100 workers, in 1990 only 47 per cent of these employers offered paid funeral leave, and the average number of days granted was 2.9.[43]

Shift and night work

Federal law

Shift and night work

There are no generally applicable provisions on shift or night work. Shift work, however, is regulated by federal statute or regulation for employees engaged in rail, road and civil air transportation, as well as in the maritime sector. Shift work in the civilian nuclear industry is strongly influenced by non-binding federal standards (see above under **Overview and trends**). Legal restrictions under these statutes and regulations is often indirect, however, specifying maximum hours of work per day, week or another period, as well as rest requirements, which effectively place limitations on how shift work can be organized. Pursuant to the FLSA, young workers who are 14 and 15 may not undertake night work.

State law

Shift and night work

There are no generally applicable provisions to shift and night work. Similar to federal regulation of specific industries, state regulation of selected industries, for example motor and rail transport, places restrictions on the organization of shift work because of restrictions on maximum hours of work per day or week or other time period, and because of rest

---

[42] BNA, *Collective bargaining, negotiation and contracts*, op. cit.

[43] ibid.

requirements. Virtually all states restrict or ban night work for young workers who are under 18.[44]

Practice

Shift and night work

Shift work, broadly defined to cover all workers who do not work a standard day-time shift, that is employees who work evenings, nights, a split or extended shift, or rotating shifts, has been estimated to include one in five working Americans.[45] In some establishments, premiums may be paid for shift work, and higher rates of overtime may be applicable when a worker is required to work beyond his or her regular shift. In some cases, a worker may be paid for a full eight hours' work, even though he or she is required to work fewer than eight hours on the second (evening) or third (night) shifts.[46]

[44] "State laws", *BNA Labor Relations Reporter*, op. cit.

[45] Office of Technology Assessment, *Biological rhythms*, op. cit., p. 9.

[46] BNA, *Collective bargaining, negotiation and contracts*, op. cit.

The regulation of working time

Contents of the tables

Part III of the *Digest* contains the basic regulations on working time of 151 countries. Apart from a few exceptions, which are specifically mentioned, all information is based on the latest legislation of the country concerned. Only the generally applicable provisions are given and no mention is made of the many exceptions which exist in a number of countries for different categories of workers and special circumstances. For countries which do not have such basic legal provisions or where the legislation has not been updated for many years, reference is sometimes made to practice. This is based on information sent to the ILO, usually by the Ministry of Labour of the country concerned. In some countries where there is no labour code which is applicable to all workers, legislation for major categories of workers, such as workers in industry, in establishments or in agriculture, has been used. Public service workers have not been mentioned as a category. In addition, special provisions applicable to workers in hazardous occupations, young workers and women have been mentioned wherever such provisions were found.

The information is divided into four sets of tables and a list of sources. The first table contains information on normal hours of work, paid annual leave and public holidays.

The normal hours of work indicated concern full-time workers only. Information concerning part-time work, special working time arrangements, such as flexitime, compressed work weeks and averaging schemes, have been dealt with in previous issues of the *Digest*.[1] Regulations establishing shorter hours of work for shift- and night workers, which tend to be rather complex, were treated as exceptions and were not included. However, provisions which applied generally to all workers in hazardous occupations, for example, have been mentioned when they were included in the basic legislation.

The amount of paid annual leave to which all workers have a right after one year of service is the first figure indicated in this column. Increases after a certain number of years of service are then added, if this is indicated in the same legislation. Special provisions for young workers, in some cases for women with children and workers in hazardous occupations, are sometimes included.

The information concerning the number of days of paid public holidays to which all workers are entitled, which is often established by a separate Act, was not available for all countries. The legislation on public holidays often regulates whether or how public holidays falling on the weekly rest day are to be compensated, or whether the hours of work on the day preceding the public holiday should be shorter. It was not possible to include all this information in the table. However, if in some cases public holidays are not paid, this was specifically mentioned.

---

[1] Previous issues of the *Conditions of Work Digest* on working time include "Flexibility in working time", Vol. 5, No. 2, 1986; "Part-time work", Vol. 8, No. 1, 1989; and "The hours we work: New work schedules in policy and practice", Vol. 9, No. 2, 1990.

The second table contains information on overtime regulations, premium pay and compensatory rest. Under the column on overtime, the first information often concerns the maximum hours that a worker may work on one day or week, including overtime, and, in some cases, obligatory rest periods. The second amount concerns the overtime hours that workers may work in addition to their normal hours of work. This amount may be per day, per week or per year. It was not possible to include the many conditions under which overtime hours are allowed and the exceptional cases under which even the maximum hours may sometimes be exceeded.

Three types of premium pay are usually indicated under the second column. The first figure and, in some cases, the only figure, concerns the basic overtime pay, i.e. the percentage of their normal pay that workers receive in addition to their normal wage for the overtime hours worked. Sometimes this percentage increases when the overtime exceeds a set number of hours. The second and third set of percentages concern work on the weekly day of rest and on public holidays. In some rare cases, the amount increases, or even doubles, when overtime on such days exceeds normal hours of work.

The column on compensatory time off complements premium payments for overtime or work on weekly rest days and public holidays. In many cases, overtime can be compensated by either premium pay or compensatory rest of equal value or at a premium rate. Sometimes both compensatory time off and a smaller amount of premium pay is due. However, not many countries have detailed provisions on this.

The third table concerns rest periods during the working day, between working days and between working weeks. In several countries, the hours of daily rest were not indicated, but could have been deducted from the maximum hours per day. This was not done, as the information in the table strictly reflects what is in the legislation. With regard to weekly rest, quite a number of countries had provisions which allowed for longer periods of rest. This column should be interpreted as being the basic entitlement to weekly rest.

The fourth table on special types of leave presents the entitlement of workers to be absent from work for personal or other reasons. In some cases, such absences are paid; in others, they are not. Although many practices may exist in this respect, only provisions in legislation have been listed. It should be pointed out that maternity protection and parental leave have not been mentioned, as this was the topic of a previous issue of the *Digest*.[2] Sick leave and leave for military service have also been excluded, as this would be outside the scope of this *Digest*.

Finally, the list of sources indicates for each country all the legislation and the sections on which the information in the tables is based. If additional sources were used, this is also indicated. This permits anyone doing research in this area to look for further details concerning the exceptions and special provisions concerning each point, which it was not possible to include in the tables.

These tables represent perhaps the first attempt ever to synthesize working time regulations on a world-wide basis. As can be seen from the list of sources, there are many relatively new labour codes which regulate working time along very similar lines. This could be a sign that

---

[2] *Conditions of Work Digest* on "Maternity and work", Vol. 13, 1994.

trends in working time are converging and that workers' basic protection in this regard is spreading throughout the world.

Summary of provisions

Normal hours of work, paid annual leave and public holidays

Most of the countries surveyed regulate normal weekly hours as well as, in many cases, daily hours. The same applies to paid annual leave and, to some extent, public holidays. Only in a few countries are there no generally applicable provisions.

Normal hours of work

Normal hours of work range from 54 per week in Thailand (for commercial work), 52 per week in Kenya (although, in practice, 44 hours per week are worked), or 50 in Switzerland (where, however, normal weekly hours are 45 in several branches of economic activity) to 38 per week on average in Australia. France, with 39 hours per week, is the only other country where statutory weekly hours are below 40. Spain is the only country where the concept of an annual averaging of hours is set out in the legislation.

The 40-hour week is the norm in 42 countries, 16 of which provide also for normal daily hours of work (eight hours in 14 cases, nine hours in one case and seven in another). However, the largest group of countries (53) still provides for a 48-hour week; 43 countries set normal daily hours. While the bulk uses the eight-hour day as the norm, in three countries the normal working day is of nine hours and, in one, it is of eight-and-a-half hours. The next most important group of countries (17) uses a 44-hour week; 12 combine this with an eight-hour day, while one provides for a nine-hour day. One country has a 47-hour week and two have a 46-hour week, one of them with an eight-hour day. Thirteen countries have a 45-hour week; three also provide for a nine-hour day (in one of these, this applies to the five-day week; daily hours are fixed at seven-and-a-half for a six-day week), while five use the eight-hour day. One country has a 43-hour week and four have a 42-hour week (one of these combined with an eight-hour day). Finally, three countries use the 41-hour week, one of these in combination with a seven-hour day.

Several countries provide for different normal hours of work for different sectors, occupations or groups of workers. The sector most commonly regulated differently is agriculture, where normal hours are often expressed over the year, rather than the day or week, in view of the very long hours needed at such times as planting or harvesting. In addition, a few countries provide for different hours in factories and shops or establishments, or for salaried employees and manual workers. Dangerous or arduous work often entitles the workers engaged in such work to shorter hours than workers in occupations that do not threaten their health and safety. Young workers also work shorter hours; frequently, two sets of limits are set for the ages of 14 to 16 and 16 to 18. Finally, some of the Muslim countries provide for a shorter working day or week during the month of Ramadan.

Figure 1. Normal weekly hours of work

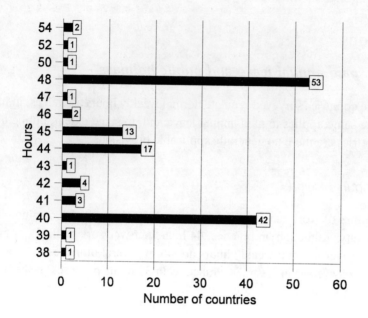

Note: Daily limits only: six countries. No generally applicable provisions/no information: one country. Two entries for six countries which have two limits. Total 151 countries.

Paid annual leave

Two main systems are used to compute the paid annual leave to which workers are entitled.

The most common approach is to state the number of days, weeks or months which accrue to workers after a qualifying period, which is usually one year of service (six months in Nicaragua). Sometimes, the law states whether these days or weeks are calendar or working days or weeks, but sometimes not. The second approach is to state that workers are entitled to so many days of leave per month (e.g. one day per month in Zaire, 1.25 days per month in Botswana, 1.5 days in Cameroon, two days in Zambia), or that they are entitled to one day of paid annual leave after so many days of work (e.g. in Bangladesh, one day for every 18 days worked in establishments or for every 22 days worked in factories; India, one day for every 20 days worked; Indonesia, one day for every 23 days worked).

Brazil has a an original system designed to discourage absenteeism: a person who has been absent from work for up to five days during the qualifying period receives 30 calendar days of leave, and one who has been absent between 24 and 32 days only receives 12 calendar days.

The basic leave entitlement varies from a few days (e.g. five or six, or a week) to five or six weeks. These two extremes are to be found in the legislation of a few countries only. More common durations are two and three weeks.

In many countries, the basic entitlement increases with length of service. Again, two approaches are used. One consists of increasing the leave by one day each year, up to a maximum. The other consists of granting three, four or five more days after a certain number of years of service (e.g. three, five, ten years), usually also with a maximum.

Except for a very few countries where it varies according to the sector of economic activity, the duration of paid annual leave is the same for all adult workers, with the exception of workers undertaking dangerous or arduous work, who are sometimes entitled to a longer period of leave. Mothers of children below a certain age also enjoy one more day of leave for each child in a number of countries. Very often, the basic entitlement is increased for young workers.

Public holidays

In about one-fifth of the countries surveyed (34), the law does not regulate the number of public holidays, although in most of these, such days are in fact granted through custom.

The number of statutory public holidays available to workers ranges from two to 18 per year. Relatively few countries grant such extreme numbers: one country has two days, one has three, one has five, two have six and six have seven, while four countries have 15 days, one has 17 and three have 18. The most frequent numbers are ten days (17 countries), 11 days (16 countries), nine days (15 countries) and 13 days (14 countries), closely followed by eight days (13 countries) and 12 days (12 countries). Nine countries grant 14 days and seven have seven days. In a few countries, extra days are granted on special occasions; for example, when the elected President takes up office or when the newly elected Parliament meets for the first time.

Overtime hours

Two ways in which national legislation provides for employees to work additional hours beyond the legal normal working hours are, first, by stipulating the number of hours that may be worked per day, per week, per month and/or per year. Countries vary considerably in the use of these time reference periods, limiting overtime according to any one period or a combination, as for example, stipulating both daily and yearly limits. The second approach is for national laws to fix the number of maximum hours that may be worked per day or per week. This is common for limiting the number of hours that may be worked in a day, though in some cases, limits are also set for maximum hours that may be worked in a week. In some countries, overtime and obligatory rest periods are included in the maximum hour limits. By subtracting the number of legal normal hours from the maximum limits, the amount of overtime per day or week can be estimated.

In many instances, national laws specify the conditions under which overtime or maximum hours may be worked. These usually relate to urgent needs, such as ensuring services to the public, guaranteeing timely delivery of products, and unforeseen events by which goods or property would perish or be damaged if additional hours were not worked. Often either prior permission must be obtained or notice afterwards must be given to the relevant authorities.

In cases of *force majeure* (e.g. accidents, natural disasters), legal limits may be waived or higher limits set.

Around 60 countries stipulate daily limits on the amount of overtime which may be performed. The number increases to almost 100 countries when taking into account the difference between normal hours of work and maximum hours permitted.

The most common daily limit on overtime is two hours set by 26 countries and around 40 countries when maximum hours are considered. About 18 countries specify four-hour daily limits, which rises to 30 countries when maximum hours are taken into account. Daily limits of three hours are set by 14 countries and 19 countries in total, including those fixing maximum hours. Around five countries have one-hour daily limits using both maximum hours and specific daily limit methods of calculation (see Figure 2).

Figure 2. Daily overtime limits
(Total: 96 countries)

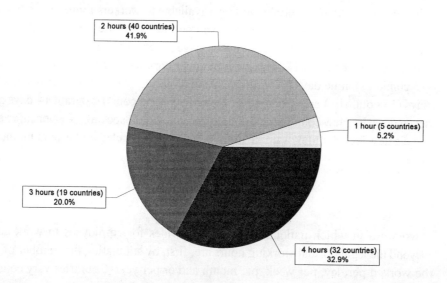

Weekly overtime limits are set by 31 countries and, when including maximum weekly hours, the number of countries rises to 43. The range is between two and 24 hours. The most common weekly overtime limit is 12 hours (nine countries) and ten hours (seven countries). Three countries have as little as two hours a week and seven countries between 20 and 24 hours weekly (see Figure 3).

Figure 3. Weekly overtime limits
(Total: 43 countries)

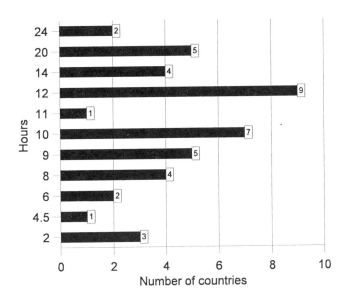

Monthly overtime limits are also fixed by around 11 countries and these range between 20 and 104 hours. Two countries, however, were identified as setting overtime limits over a two-week period (four hours in Latvia and 20 hours in Finland). Just one country — the Dominican Republic — fixes a quarterly (three-month) overtime limit, which is 80 hours.

A good number of countries (41) fix yearly overtime limits. Most of these are in addition to daily, weekly or monthly limits. The latter are thus offset by the limits on the extra number of hours which may be worked in a year. In this way, individual workers are not able to work overtime on a regular basis. Four countries were identified as only having yearly limits which allow for maximum flexibility in the performance of overtime when required, but also prevents excessive use of overtime over a year. These countries are Guinea (100 hours), Poland (120 hours), Spain (80 hours) and Sweden (200 hours). The yearly limits range from 60 to 320 hours, with most countries (32 out of the 41) having 100 to 200 hours (see Figure 4).

Often different overtime limits are set for different economic sectors or categories of workers, or for night work. In agriculture, limits may be higher and may be permitted for limited periods of time. For example, in Austria, agricultural workers may work overtime for two hours a day and 12 hours a week, but overtime of four hours daily or 18 hours weekly may be performed during 13 weeks per year.

Figure 4. Yearly overtime limits
(Total: 41 countries)

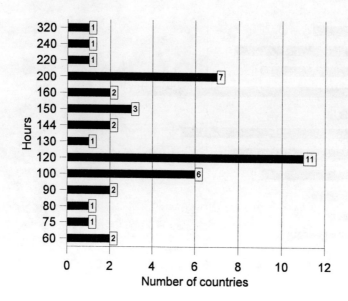

Overtime is prohibited for young people in 25 countries out of the total number of countries (118) for which information on overtime hours was available. In a further 13 countries, lower limits are set for young workers. The defined age limit for "young workers" ranges from 15 to 18 years. Overtime is also prohibited for pregnant women and women with young children in ten countries and, in Mongolia, single fathers with young children are also prohibited from working overtime. Lower overtime limits are set for women in about four countries and prohibited in one other. For dangerous work, overtime is prohibited in nine countries and lower limits are set in two other countries.

Overtime premium pay

From the legislative information available on overtime premium payments for 122 countries, around 50 countries fix the premium for overtime work on normal working days at 50 per cent above the usual wage. This is followed by 23 countries with 25 per cent premium payments. A handful of countries (eight) provide for premium wages of 100 per cent for overtime work on normal working days.

Around 16 countries stipulate a certain premium for the first hour of overtime or the first two or three hours of overtime and, thereafter, higher premiums are paid. For example, a 50 per cent premium is payable for the first hour or first two hours of overtime and thereafter 75 or 100 per cent is payable. For a few countries (six), the number of hours for which a lower premium is payable is considerably higher. For example, in France, an overtime premium of 25 per cent is payable for the first eight hours of overtime and 50 per cent thereafter. In Zaire, a 30 per cent premium is payable for the first six hours and 60 per cent thereafter. In Greece, the premium for the first 50 hours of overtime is 25 per cent, and from 51 up to 120 hours it increases to 50 per cent and thereafter to 75 per cent.

The remaining countries do not fit within these common patterns for overtime premiums. For example, the Islamic Republic of Iran and Norway provide for premium payments of 40 per cent for overtime work on normal working days. In South Africa, the premium is one-third of the normal wage and, in Italy, 10 per cent. In Guatemala, an overtime premium of 50 per cent above the minimum wage is payable, or as otherwise agreed by the parties.

A small number of countries (three) provide for premiums to be paid for overtime only on public holidays and rest days, while normal rates for wages are applied to ordinary overtime. For a number of countries, the legislation provides that overtime premiums are to be fixed through collective agreements.

For work performed on public holidays or weekly rest days, the large majority of countries (65) stipulate a 100 per cent overtime premium. Eighteen countries provide for a 50 per cent premium on these days, and there is a 25 or 35 per cent premium in three countries. A number of countries grant a considerably higher premium of 150 per cent (seven countries) or 200 per cent (six countries). For the rest of the countries, information was available for premiums for overtime on normal working days but not on public holidays and rest days. A number of countries (ten) provide for higher premium rates for work on public holidays than on weekly rest days. For example, in Ethiopia, the premium for work on weekly rest days is 100 per cent, and on public holidays it is 150 per cent. In El Salvador, a 50 per cent premium is payable for work on weekly rest days and 100 per cent on public holidays. A few countries differentiate between work on public holidays and weekly rest days and overtime on these days, a higher premium being paid for the latter. For example, in Guinea-Bissau, a 100 per cent premium is payable for work on public holidays and weekly rest days and 200 per cent for overtime on these days. Similarly, Mauritius provides for the same premiums. In Indonesia, a 200 per cent premium is payable for the first hour after seven hours of work on public holidays and weekly rest days, and 300 per cent for the second hour. In Thailand, a 100 per cent premium is payable for work on public holidays and 200 per cent for overtime on these days.

Finally, around 15 of the 122 countries specify premiums ranging from 50 to 150 per cent for overtime work which takes place at night. Several countries also provide for premiums for evening overtime work.[3]

Compensatory time off

For the 50 countries for which legislative information was available on compensatory rest, many (20 countries) provided the same amount of time off for overtime performed on normal working days or public holidays and weekly rest days. One country provides for one-and-a-quarter time off for overtime work on normal working days and three countries grant one-and-a-half time off for overtime work on normal working days. Israel gives one-and-a-quarter time off for the first two hours and thereafter one-and-a-half time. Lebanon gives one-and-a-half time off after 12 hours. Around five countries provide one-and-a-half time off for work on public holidays and weekly rest days, and a similar number give twice the time off for work

---

[3] N.B. This information may not be complete because special provisions on night work were not examined.

on these days. In some cases, compensatory rest must be taken within certain time limits. Several countries specify one week, and a few others, three days for overtime on normal working days. For public holidays and weekly rest, the time periods specified are longer, from two to eight weeks.

A few countries do not allow for time off. In one country —Bulgaria — it is prohibited to compensate overtime by rest; that is, it must be paid. A number of countries (five) provide for compensatory rest but do not specify the amount. In other countries, the legislation provides that compensatory rest may be taken by mutual agreement (Czech Republic) or is regulated by collective agreement (Sweden). In some countries, such as the United Kingdom and the United States, there are no statutory provisions for compensatory rest, which is left up to collective bargaining. In a few countries, the legislation provides that compensatory rest is in addition to premium pay for overtime. For example, in France, compensatory rest is in addition to paid overtime after 42 hours of weekly work (normal hours are 39), and is 150 per cent of the overtime worked. The rest must be taken within two months of the overtime worked. In South Africa, more than four hours of work on Sundays or public holidays is compensated by one day off plus one-third overtime premium. In the United Arab Emirates, equal time off is given for overtime on weekly rest days and work on public holidays, plus 50 per cent premium pay.

Rest periods

Rest breaks

Out of 101 countries for which legislative information was available for rest breaks during the working day, the most common length of break is 30 minutes (38 countries). The length of periods of work after which the 30-minute break has to be taken varies from four to six hours, with five hours being the most frequent (14 countries). In 13 countries, however, the period of work after which a 30-minute break must be taken is not specified. In a few countries, a 30-minute break is required during the period of a workday of seven or eight hours.

A one-hour rest break is stipulated in 28 countries. The range of work periods after which the break must be taken is from three to six hours, the most frequent being after five hours (ten countries). In six countries, however, the work interval is not specified. In a few countries, the one-hour break must be taken during workdays of seven to ten hours.

In three countries, 45 minutes is the required length for the rest break, and in 13 countries, the rest break is a maximum of two hours. Six countries stipulate that there be a rest break, but the length is not specified (see Figure 5).

Figure 5. Length of rest breaks
(Total: 90 countries)

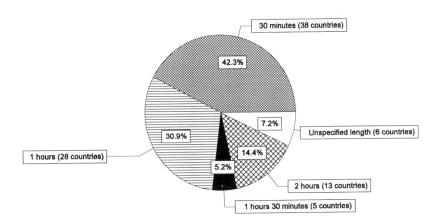

Eighty-six countries specify that breaks be taken after a certain work interval. These periods usually range from three to six hours and, in some cases, rest breaks must be taken at some point during the working day, which can be from seven to ten hours. The most common requirements are for a break to be taken after five hours of work (31 countries) or six hours (14 countries). Seven countries require a break after four hours of work and nine countries stipulate that a break (ranging from 30 minutes to two hours) be taken during the working day (seven to ten hours) (see Figure 6). A further 25 countries require rest breaks to be taken without specifying the length of the work interval.

Figure 6. Work intervals for rest breaks
(Total: 86 countries)

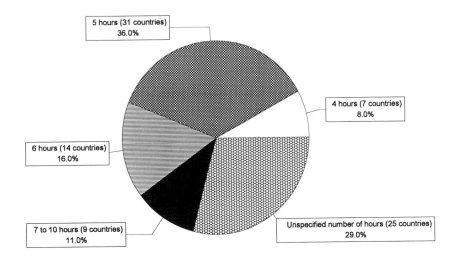

Some countries stipulate different lengths of rest breaks according to the number of hours worked. For example, in Turkey, 15 minutes of rest must be taken for work intervals of not more than four hours of work; 30 minutes for more than four hours of work; and one hour for intervals of more than seven-and-a-half hours. In the Netherlands, a 30-minute break must be taken after five-and-a-half hours, and there is a one-hour break for working days of ten hours or more.

For countries with rest breaks lasting up to two hours, this usually represents a maximum and there is a minimum period also specified. For example, in Angola and Panama, the rest break can be from 30 minutes to two hours.

A number of countries (around 23) stipulate longer rest periods and at shorter intervals for young workers. In six of these countries, provisions on rest breaks exist exclusively for young workers. In most of the countries, the length of the rest period is the same as for adult workers, but the work intervals after which a break is required are shorter. For example, in Botswana, Iraq, Kuwait, Lesotho, Portugal, the Syrian Arab Republic and the United Arab Emirates, the work interval is reduced from five to four hours for young workers. In a few countries (India and Nepal) and for very young workers (Botswana and Malaysia), the work interval is reduced further from five to three hours. Work intervals of six hours are commonly reduced to four or four-and-a-half for young workers (Austria, Lebanon, the Libyan Arab Jamahiriya and Singapore). In only two countries (India and the Sudan) are rest breaks actually longer in addition to the work intervals being shorter than for adult workers. Finally, a few countries also stipulate shorter work intervals for women (Guyana, Lebanon and the Sudan).

Whether rest breaks are paid is not always clearly indicated in national laws. From the information available, rest breaks are clearly stated in the legislation as being paid in about 13 countries and unpaid in around 20 countries. In 60 countries, the legislation does not indicate whether the rest breaks are paid or counted as working hours. In some cases, such as Finland and Norway, the law states that the rest breaks are considered as hours worked as long as the employee does not leave the workplace.

Daily rest

Seventy-seven countries were identified as having statutory provisions for periods of daily rest (see Figure 7). Of these, 24 countries had provisions only for young workers or women, and a further three countries had provisions for young people in addition to those for workers in general (see Figure 8). The most common daily rest period (excluding young workers and women) was for 12 hours (27 countries) (see Figure 9). Nine countries had a ten-hour daily rest requirement and six had 11 hours. Six countries stipulated between 13- and 16-hour daily rest breaks. The most common provision for young persons was 12 hours (18 countries), followed by seven countries with 11 hours. One country had 13 hours and another 15 hours. For women, nine countries stipulated an 11-hour break and six others, a 12-hour rest period.

Figure 7. Daily rest for young workers and adult workers
(Total: 77 countries)

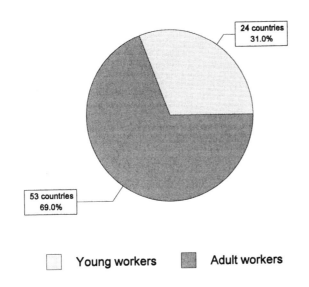

Figure 8. Daily rest for young workers
(Total: 27 countries)

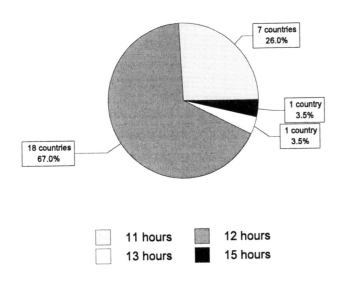

Figure 9. Daily rest for adult workers
(Total: 54 countries)

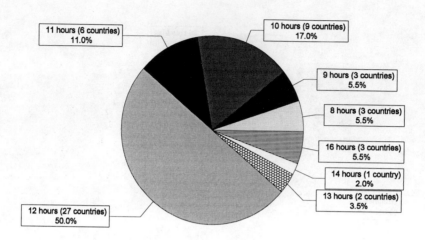

11 hours (6 countries) 11.0%

10 hours (9 countries) 17.0%

9 hours (3 countries) 5.5%

8 hours (3 countries) 5.5%

16 hours (3 countries) 5.5%

14 hours (1 country) 2.0%

13 hours (2 countries) 3.5%

12 hours (27 countries) 50.0%

Weekly rest

From the legislative information available on 145 countries, the majority of countries (115) provide for a weekly rest period of 24 hours. For 56 of these countries, this period coincides, in principle or normally, with a Sunday. For nine countries, the 24-hour period is on a Friday. Other countries stipulate longer weekly rest periods: 30 hours (one country); 32 hours (one country); 36 hours (12 countries, of which five countries include a Sunday); 42 hours (12 countries, of which one country includes a Friday and three countries include a Sunday); 44 hours (one country); 48 hours (three countries). In many countries, the weekly rest period is stipulated as one day and the exact number of hours is not stated. However, when the number of hours are indicated, such as 24 or 36, these are in most cases stipulated as being consecutive hours. In Norway, the law states that the weekly rest be at least 36 hours, including one full 24-hour day. In Poland, the law provides for the possibility for longer weekly rest periods over longer reference periods — at least 48 hours during 38 weeks or 24 hours during 14 weeks (see Figure 10).

Figure 10. Weekly rest
(Total: 145 countries)

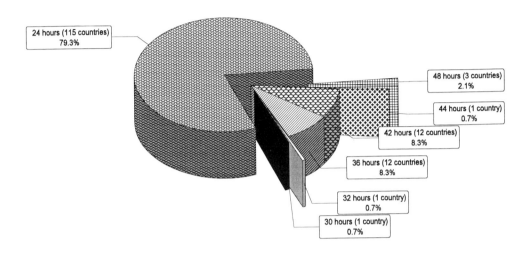

24 hours (115 countries)
79.3%

48 hours (3 countries)
2.1%

44 hours (1 country)
0.7%

42 hours (12 countries)
8.3%

36 hours (12 countries)
8.3%

32 hours (1 country)
0.7%

30 hours (1 country)
0.7%

Special types of leave

Special types of leave can be paid or unpaid. In some cases, a relatively short paid leave is supplemented by a more extensive period of unpaid leave. The most common special types of leave available in the 87 countries where relevant statutory provisions were found include leave for personal reasons and for religious reasons, educational leave, and leave for public, civic or trade union activities. Other types of leave exist only in a few countries.

Leave for personal reasons, also called urgent leave, casual leave, special leave or leave for family reasons, is granted in 70 countries to enable workers to cope with illness in the family or devote time to such family events as births, marriages and deaths. Two of these countries restrict personal leave to cases of death in the worker's family (bereavement leave), while one grants paid mourning leave when, according to family custom, a worker must remain in mourning. In another, the only grant for personal leave is for marriage. When a certain number of days are reserved for specific events, the leave is often longer when the event concerns the worker or his immediate family (e.g. spouse, child, parent) than when it concerns less immediate family members. In several countries, the reasons for taking such leave are not specified, so that leave could be used for purposes for which a specific type of leave exists in other countries (e.g. public or civic duties). In such cases, workers are entitled to a certain number of days, for example ten a year in several countries.

Also closely linked to the personal sphere is leave for religious reasons, found in nine countries, where workers are entitled, once in the course of their employment, to take time off for a pilgrimage.

Twenty-one countries provide for some form of statutory educational leave, which can be for a few days, a year or for a long period after a certain number of years of service (sabbatical leave). The shorter type of educational leave is foreseen either for general or vocational training or to attend workers' education programmes, or both.

In seven countries, trade union duties is a separate ground for obtaining leave. Eleven countries provide for leave for civic duties. One country combines these two grounds for obtaining leave.

Sixteen countries provide for leave for miscellaneous reasons, including time off for house-work, creative leave, home leave, long service leave or special leave. Leave to start a business, currently available in France and Italy, was introduced much more recently than any other type of leave, in response to macro-economic trends.

Figure 11. Special types of leave in selected countries
(Total: 87 countries)

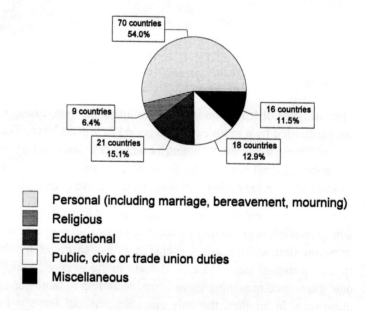

Personal (including marriage, bereavement, mourning)
Religious
Educational
Public, civic or trade union duties
Miscellaneous

Table 1. Normal hours of work, paid annual leave and public holidays

Country	Normal hours of work	Paid annual leave	Public holidays
Afghanistan	40 per week. 30 for youths under 16 years. 35 for youths aged 16-18 and underground workers doing work injurious to health.	20 days. 30 days for persons under 18 years. 20 to 30 days for underground, heavy or arduous work and work harmful to health.	5
Albania	8 per day and 48 per week. 6 per day for workers under 18 years.	3 calendar weeks	---
Algeria	44 a week. 2,000 a year in agricultural undertakings.	Up to 30 calendar days. 10 additional days in the southern regions.	---
Angola	9 a day and 44 a week. 6 a day and 34 a week for persons aged 14 to 16 years. 7 a day and 38 a week for persons between 16 and 18 years.	10 minimum. 30 calendar days maximum.	---
Antigua and Barbuda	8 a day and 48 a week.	12 working days	11
Argentina	8 per day or 48 per week. 6 per day or 36 per week for unhealthy or dangerous work.	14 consecutive days for up to 5 years of service; 21 days for 5-10 years of service; 28 days for 10-20 years of service; and 35 days for more than 20 years of service.	8 national public holidays
Australia	38 per week on average.	4 weeks or 20 working days on average.	10 national and up to 3 additional state holidays.
Austria	8 per day and 40 per week.	30 working days; 36 working days after 25 years of service.	13

Part III: The regulation of working time

Country	Normal hours of work	Paid annual leave	Public holidays
Azerbaijan	41 per week. 24 for workers aged 15 to 16. 36 for workers aged 16 to 18 and workers engaged in work detrimental to health.	15 working days. 1 calendar month for workers under 18 years. Additional leave for certain categories of workers.	10
Bahamas	8½ hours a day or 48 a week.	1 week	—
Bahrain	8 per day or 48 per week. 6 per day or 36 per week during the month of Ramadan, except for non-Moslem workers.	21 days. At least 28 days after 5 continuous years of service. 1 month minimum for young persons aged 14 to 16.	12
Bangladesh	48 a week. 5 a day for persons between 14 and 16 years in any factory. 7 a day and 42 a week for persons between 16 and 18 years in any establishment.	In factories, 1 day for every 22 worked (every 15 days for young persons under 16 years). In establishments, 1 day for every 18 worked (every 14 days for young persons under 18 years).	10
Belarus	7 per day and 41 per week. 4 a day and 24 a week for persons aged 14-16. 6 a day and 36 a week for young persons 16-18 and workers engaged in harmful employment.	15 working days, increasing progressively. 1 calendar month for persons under 18 and disabled persons.	11
Belgium	8 per day and 40 per week.	24 days per year	10
Belize	9 a day or 45 a week.	6 working days. 14 days in practice.	13
Benin	40 a week. 2,400 a year in agricultural undertakings.	24 working days. Increased leave period in view of length of service, mothers with families and persons under 18 years.	12
Bolivia	8 per day and 48 per week. 40 per week for women.	15 working days. 20 working days after 5 years and 30 days after 10 years of service.	8, plus provincial festivities.

302

Country	Normal hours of work	Paid annual leave	Public holidays
Botswana	8 a day or 48 a week. 7 a day for persons under 18 years.	1.25 days for every month of continuous employment.	9
Brazil	8 per day and 44 per week.	System of gradual paid annual leave, depending on days absent from work, starting with 12 calendar days of leave for 24-32 days of absence per year and up to 30 days of leave for 5 absences during the year.	9 civil holidays (fixed by federal law) and 6 religious holidays (fixed by municipal law).
Bulgaria	8 a day and 40 a week for a 5-day working week (46 for a 6-day working week). 7 a day and 35 a week, or 6 a day and 36 a week, for employees under 18 years.	14 working days. 16 after 10 and 18 after 15 years of service. 26 working days for young employees. 5 additional working days for work under unhealthy conditions.	9½
Burkina Faso	40 per week. 2,400 per year in agriculture.	2.5 working days per month of work, increasing up to 6 additional days after 30 years of service. 30 working days for young persons under 18. 24 working days for young persons aged 18 to 21.	3
Burundi	8 a day and 45 a week.	20 working days.	---
Cambodia	8 per day or 48 per week.	18 working days. 1 additional day for every 3 years of service.	---
Cameroon	40 per week. 48 per week and 2,400 per year in agriculture.	1.5 working days for each month of actual service (4 weeks or 24 working days shall be deemed to be 1 month of effective service). 2.5 days for young persons under 18.	11
Canada	8 per day and 40 per week at federal level and in half of the provinces and territories.	2 weeks at federal level and all provinces and territories, except Saskatchewan, where it is 3 weeks. 1 additional week after 5 or 6 years of service.	9 at federal level and between 5 and 9 in different provinces.

Country	Normal hours of work	Paid annual leave	Public holidays
Cape Verde	8 per day and 44 per week. 7 per day and 38 per week for workers under 18 years.	Between 21 and 30 consecutive days.	---
Central African Republic	40 per week. 48 in agricultural undertakings.	18 working days, increasing with length of service. 1 additional day per child under 14 for mothers with families. 24 days for young persons under 18.	13
Chad	40 per week. 2,400 per year in agricultural and assimilated establishments.	18 working days.	15 days, of which 3 days are paid.
Chile	8 per day or 48 per week.	15 days per year. After 10 years of service, 1 additional day for every 3 years of service.	14
China	8 per day and 40 per week.	---	7
Colombia	8 per day and 48 per week.	15 consecutive working days	18 days of civil or religious holidays
Comoros	40 per week. 2,400 per year in agricultural enterprises.	30 days, with increases for mothers with families, young workers under 18 and workers with longer length of service.	---
Congo	40 per week. 2,400 per year in agricultural undertakings.	26 working days, increasing with length of service.	9
Costa Rica	8 per day and 48 per week.	15 calendar days for every 50 weeks of continuous work in the service of the same employer. 20 days after 5 years of employment. 30 days after 10 years of employment.	14 days, of which 5 are paid holidays and 9 unpaid.
Côte d'Ivoire	40 per week. 2,400 per year in agricultural and equivalent undertakings.	24 working days, increasing at the rate of 2 additional days for every 5 additional years of service. 26.4 days for workers under 18 years.	National Day and Labour Day are paid.

Country	Normal hours of work	Paid annual leave	Public holidays
Croatia	42. Shorter hours for employees engaged in harmful employment.	18 working days. 24 for young persons. 30 for employees engaged in harmful employment.	---
Cuba	8 per day and 44 per week.	30 calendar days for a period of 11 months actually worked.	6
Cyprus	8 per day and 44-54 per week.	---	13 to 18
Czech Republic	43 per week. 33 per week for persons under 16 years.	21 calendar days. 28 for 15 years of service and workers engaged in work especially hard or hazardous to health.	---
Denmark	No legislation. 37 hours common norm.	25 working days or 5 weeks minimum.	No legislation. Customarily 9½-10½ days.
Djibouti	40 per week. 2,400 per year in agricultural undertakings.	30 calendar days. 2 additional working days after 20 years of service, 4 days after 25 years and 6 days after 30 years. 2 additional days for mothers per child under 21 years of age.	11
Dominica	8 a day and 40 a week.	2 weeks. 3 weeks after 5 years of service.	12
Dominican Republic	8 per day and 44 per week. 6 per day and 36 per week for hazardous or unhealthy work.	14 days. 18 days after 5 years of service.	11
Ecuador	8 per day and 40 per week. 35 per week and 7 per day for young persons between 15 to 18 years old. 6 per day and 30 per week for persons under 15.	15 days. One additional day for each year of service in excess of 5 (not exceeding 15 days), or a sum of money for the additional days. 20 days for employees under 16 years. 18 days for those over 16 but under 18.	11

Country	Normal hours of work	Paid annual leave	Public holidays
Egypt	8 a day or 48 a week. 7 a day for certain categories of workers or in certain industries or activities. 6 a day for persons under 17.	21 days; 30 after 10 years of continuous service or for persons over 50 years. Up to 7 additional days for workers in arduous or dangerous jobs or in remote areas.	13
El Salvador	8 per day and 44 per week. 7 per day and 39 per week for dangerous or unhealthy work. 6 a day and 34 per week for young persons under 16.	15 days' leave after 1 year of uninterrupted service for the same employer.	10, plus 1 day, depending on local custom and festival days.
Equatorial Guinea	8 a day or 48 a week. 6 per day for young persons under 18 years.	1 month; after 10 years of service, 1 additional day for every 2 additional years of service.	—
Ethiopia	8 a day or 48 a week. 7 a day for workers under 18 years.	14 working days in the first year; 1 more day for every additional year of service.	14
Fiji	No generally applicable provisions. 45 to 48 hours per week, depending on sector; determined in general by wages regulations.	8 working days	9 or 12 days, depending on sector.
Finland	8 per day and 40 per week, or on average 120 hours in 3-week period or 80 hours in 2-week period.	2½ days per month after 1 year of service.	10
France	39 per week and not exceeding 10 per day.	5 weeks	11, with only one legally paid.
Gabon	40 a week. 2,400 a year in agricultural and equivalent undertakings.	24 working days. 1 additional day for mothers with families for every dependent child under 16 years. 30 days for persons under 18.	—
Germany	8 per day. 40 a week for young persons under 18 years.	24 working days a year. 30 working days for persons under 16; 27 for persons aged 16 to 17; 25 for persons aged 17 to 18.	9 to 13 days, depending on the state.

Country	Normal hours of work	Paid annual leave	Public holidays
Ghana	8 a day or 45 a week. Shorter hours for work injurious to health.	14 working days	10
Greece	8 per day and 48 per week. By national collective agreement: 40 per week. 6 a day or 30 a week for persons under 16 years.	4 weeks (20 working days on a 5-day week basis). 2 additional days after 3 years of service.	5 obligatory and 1 optional to the employer. 5 extra holidays per year may be granted by Ministerial decree.
Guatemala	8 per day or 48 per week. 45 per week of actual work, which shall be deemed to be 48 hours for the payment of wages.	15 days after 1 year of continuous work (minimum of 150 days of work).	8
Guinea	40 per week. 42 in the agricultural sector, commerce and pharmacies, hospitals, restaurants and the like.	30 working days	11
Guinea-Bissau	8 or 9 per day and 45 per week.	30 consecutive days	---
Guyana	8 a day or 48 a week in factories. 8 a day or 44 a week for persons under 16 and women in factories.	12 working days.	13
Haiti	8 per day and 48 per week.	15 consecutive days after 1 year of service, consisting of 13 working days and 2 Sundays.	14 days, of which 3 are half-days (from 12:00 on).
Honduras	8 per day and 44 per week.	10 to 20 working days for 1 to 4 years of service.	11
Hungary	8 per day and 44 per week. 2,500-3,000 hours annually in agriculture and manufacturing. 6 per day in hazardous work.	20 working days, increasing to 30 days according to age. 5 additional days for workers under 18 years.	9
Iceland	40 per week	1 to 2 days per working month.	7

Country	Normal hours of work	Paid annual leave	Public holidays
India	9 per day or 48 per week. 4½ per day for persons under 15 years in factories.	1 day for every 20 days of work (every 15 days for persons under 15 years).	--
Indonesia	7 a day and 40 per week. 6 a day and 35 a week for work dangerous or injurious to health.	1 day for every 23 days of work, up to 12 days per year.	13
Iran, Islamic Republic of	8 per day and 44 per week. 6 per day or 36 per week for arduous, unhealthy or underground work. 6½ for persons aged 15 to 18.	1 month, including 4 Fridays and excluding other holidays. 5 weeks for arduous work.	--
Iraq	8 per day. 7 per day for persons under 16 years.	20 days. 2 additional days for every 5 years of continuous service. 30 days for persons under 18 years and for work arduous or harmful to health.	--
Ireland	48 per week. 40 per week for persons over 16 years; 37½ if aged 15.	3 working weeks	8
Israel	8 per day and 47 per week.	14 calendar days after 1 year of service, gradually increasing to 28 days after 14 years of service.	9
Italy	8 per day and 48 per week.	4 to 6 weeks	4 paid and 11 unpaid holidays
Jamaica	8 a day or 40 a week.	2 working weeks. 3 weeks after 10 years of service.	10
Japan	8 per day and 40 per week, to be fully implemented by 1997.	10 days, increasing by 1 day a year of service to a maximum of 20 days.	14
Jordan	8 per day and 48 per week. 9 per day and 54 per week in hotels, bars, restaurants, cinemas and similar undertakings. 6 a day for persons under 16 years.	3 weeks	--

Country	Normal hours of work	Paid annual leave	Public holidays
Kenya	52 a week (45 a week in practice). 46 a week in agricultural industry. 6 a day for persons under 16 years.	21 working days	10
Korea, Republic of	8 per day and 44 per week. 6 a day and 34 a week for dangerous and underground work. 7 per day and 42 per week for persons aged 13-18 years.	10. One additional day for each consecutive year of service.	18. Only one is paid.
Kuwait	8 per day or 48 per week. 6 per day for persons between 14 and 18 years.	14 days. 21 days after 5 years of continuous service.	9
Kyrgyzstan	41 per week. 24 per week for persons between 15 and 16 years. 36 for young persons aged 16 to 18 and for employees working under hazardous conditions.	15 working days. 1 calendar month for persons under 18. Additional days for workers working under difficult conditions.	7
Lao People's Democratic Republic	8 per day or 48 per week. 6 per day or 36 per week for persons aged 15-18 and for dangerous or unhealthy work.	15 days. 18 days for work arduous or damaging to health.	---
Latvia	40 a week. 24 a week for persons under 16 years. 35 for employees aged 16-18 years, workers in hazardous or heavy work, and women with children under 3 years.	4 calendar weeks. 1 calendar month for persons under 18. Additional 3 working days for women with 3 or more children under 16 or a disabled child.	11
Lebanon	48 per week. 7 per day for persons under 16 years.	15 days	---
Lesotho	45 a week. Maximum of 8 a day for persons under 16 years.	Minimum of 12 working days.	13

Country	Normal hours of work	Paid annual leave	Public holidays
Libyan Arab Jamahiriya	8 a day. 6 a day for persons under 18 years.	16 working days; 24 after 5 years of continuous service and for senior employees. 24 working days for persons under 18.	---
Lithuania	---	28 calendar days. 35 for employees under 18 years. Up to 58 days for work with greater nervous, emotional or mental strain or professional risk.	---
Luxembourg	8 per day and 40 per week.	25 working days. 3 additional days in mines and quarries.	10
Madagascar	40 per week. 2,200 per year or 42½ per week in agriculture.	2.5 calendar days for every month of actual service. Entitlement after 12 months of actual service.	2 paid and 7 unpaid public holidays.
Malaysia	8 per day or 48 per week. 6 per day, including school hours, for persons under 14 years. 7 for persons under 16 years.	8 days. 12 days for service between 2 and 5 years. 16 days thereafter.	17
Mali	40 per week	2½ days per month or 30 days per year, increasing 2 days after 15 years of service, 4 days after 20 years, and 8 days after 25 years of service.	---
Malta	No generally applicable provisions. Hours of work are governed by wage regulation orders.	4 working weeks and 4 working days.	12
Mauritania	40 a week. 2,400 a year in agricultural undertakings. 8 a day of actual work for young persons under 18 years and women.	18 working days. 1 additional day for mothers with children in respect of each child under 14 years. 24 days for workers under 18 and for workers under special climatic conditions.	7

Country	Normal hours of work	Paid annual leave	Public holidays
Mauritius	8 per day. 6 per day including breaks or 36 per week for persons under 18.	12 working days after 12 months of employment.	---
Mexico	8 per day.	6 working days. 2 more working days for every additional year of service, up to 12 days. 2 extra days for every 5 years of service thereafter.	7. The day of national or local elections is also a public holiday.
Moldova, Republic of	40 per week. 24 for persons aged 15 to 16 years. 36 for persons aged between 16 and 18 and for hazardous work.	24 working days. 1 calendar month for persons under 18. Additional days for hazardous work.	8
Mongolia	8 per day and 46 per week. 30 per week for persons aged 14-15 years. 36 for persons aged 16-18.	21 working days. 3 to 14 additional days, depending on the length of service. 26 to 35 days for heavy, hazardous and arduous work. 31 to 39 days for underground work. 30 days for young persons under 18.	8
Morocco	8 per day and 48 per week.	21 days (18 working days at least) after 12 months of continuous employment.	12
Mozambique	8 per day or 48 per week. 7 per day or 38 per week for minors aged 15 to 18.	15 days; 20 days during the third calendar year; 30 days thereafter.	---
Namibia	45 a week (9 a day for a 5-day working week or 7½ for a 6-day week).	24 consecutive days	---
Nepal	8 per day or 48 per week. 6 per day and 36 per week for persons aged 14-16.	1 day for every 20 days of work.	13

Country	Normal hours of work	Paid annual leave	Public holidays
Netherlands	8½ per day and 48 per week. 8 per day for young persons under 18.	4 weeks	7 working days, plus National Liberation Day (once every 5 years).
New Zealand	8 per day and 40 per week.	3 weeks minimum.	11
Nicaragua	8 per day and 48 per week. 6 per day in unhealthy work and for persons aged 12 to 16.	15 days after 6 months of continuous work.	8
Niger	40 per week. 2,400 per year in agricultural undertakings.	18 working days; 2 additional working days after 20 years of service; 4 days after 25 years; 6 days after 30 years. 2 additional days for apprentices under 21 years, and for women workers in respect of every child. 24 working days for persons under 18.	—
Nigeria	No general legislation. 8 a day for young persons under 16. Fixed by mutual agreement, collective bargaining or an industrial wages board. In practice, 8 a day and 40 a week.	6 working days (12 for persons under 16) by law. In practice, ranges from 12 days in the early years of employment to 21 or more after 10 years of service. 30 days on average for non-manual employees.	9
Norway	9 per day and 40 hours per week.	4 weeks and 1 day	12
Pakistan	9 per day and 48 per week in factories with 10 or more workers and in establishments. 8 per day or 48 per week in mines and road transport. 7 per day and 42 per week for young persons.	14 calendar days in factories and establishments. 1 day for every 30 days of work in tea plantations. 1 day for 17 days of work in underground mines. 1 day for 20 days of work for mines above ground, road transport and for persons under 17 years in tea plantations.	At least 5 days in tea plantations, 10 in establishments, 12 in road transport.
Panama	8 per day or 48 per week.	30 days for every period of 11 continuous months of service.	10 paid days, plus the day the titular President of the Republic takes up office.

Country	Normal hours of work	Paid annual leave	Public holidays
Papua New Guinea	8 per day and 44 per week.	21 calendar days; 14 in agriculture.	10 nationally and 1 additional day in provinces.
Paraguay	8 per day and 48 per week. 6 per day or 36 per week for dangerous or unhealthy work.	12 consecutive days; 18 after 5 years of service; 30 days after 10 years of service.	10
Peru	8 per day and 48 per week.	30 consecutive days.	12 national days, plus others not specified by law.
Philippines	8 per day and 48 per week.	5 days	10, plus 2 nationwide special days.
Poland	8 per day or 42 per week. 6 a day for persons under 16 years.	14 working days, 17 after 3 years, 20 after 6 years, 26 after 10 years of employment. Additional 6 to 12 days for workers in arduous or unhealthy conditions, depending on risk.	---
Portugal	8 per day or 44 per week. For young workers under 16 years, 7 per day or 35 per week.	22 working days. In agriculture, 21 days.	12
Qatar	8 per day and 48 per week. 6 per day and 36 per week during Ramadan. 6 per day and 36 per week for persons aged 15 to 18 (4 per day and 24 per week during Ramadan).	2 weeks for less than 5 years of continuous service; 4 weeks thereafter.	10
Romania	8 a day and 40 a week in manufacturing. Reduced daily hours for harmful, difficult or dangerous work.	18 working days. 3 additional working days for difficult, dangerous or harmful work. 24 working days for persons up to 18 years.	8
Russian Federation	40 per week. 24 for workers between 15 and 16 years. 36 for workers aged 16 to 18 and workers employed under hazardous working conditions.	24 working days. 1 calendar month for workers under 18. Additional leave for workers engaged in unhealthy work.	9

Country	Normal hours of work	Paid annual leave	Public holidays
Rwanda	8 per day or 45 per week.	18 working days; 1 additional day per every 3 years of service. 24 working days for persons under 18 years.	12
Saint Vincent and the Grenadines	8 a day	14 working days. For agricultural workers, 10 working days.	--
San Marino	8 a day and 48 a week for all workers. 44 for salaried employees.	For wage-earners, 10 days, increasing to 20 days after 15 years of service. For salaried employees and intermediary staff, 12 days, increasing to 30 days after 12 years of service.	8
Sao Tome and Principe	8 or 9 per day and 45 per week. In agriculture, 7 consecutive hours a day or maximum of 42 per week.	30 consecutive days, excluding weekly rest days.	--
Saudi Arabia	8 a day or 48 a week (6 a day or 36 a week during Ramadan). 6 per day for persons aged 15 to 18 years.	15 days. 21 days after 10 years of continuous service.	10
Senegal	40 per week. 2,352 per year in agriculture.	1.5 days per month actually worked after 12 months of employment. 2 days for young persons under 18.	2 paid holidays, 12 unpaid.
Seychelles	In practice, 8 per day, 40 per week or 160 per month.	21 days	13
Singapore	8 per day or 44 per week. 6 per day for children aged 12-14 and 7 for young persons aged 14-16.	7 days. 1 additional day for every year of service, up to 14 days per year.	11
Slovenia	42 a week. Shorter hours for work particularly arduous, strenuous or harmful to health.	18 working days. 25 for persons under 18 years.	--
Solomon Islands	9 a day and 45 a week.	--	--
Somalia	8 a day or 48 a week. 10 a day and 60 a week for intermittent work.	15 days	9

314

Country	Normal hours of work	Paid annual leave	Public holidays
South Africa	46 per week.	14 days per year.	12 paid days
Spain	40 per week when annually averaged.	30 calendar days	14
Sri Lanka	8 a day and 48 a week in industries. 8 a day and 45 a week in shops and offices.	14 days in industries and in shops and offices.	15, of which 6 paid. 8 paid days in shops and offices.
Sudan	8 per day or 48 per week. 7 per day for fasting workers during the month of Ramadan.	15 days; 20 after 4 to 8 years of service; 25 after 9 to 15 years; 30 thereafter.	---
Swaziland	No generally applicable provisions. Specified by Wages Orders. 48 a week in manufacturing. 57 a week in agriculture. 6 a day and 33 a week for persons aged 15 to 18.	Not less than 2 weeks.	9
Sweden	40 per week.	25 days	12 days according to custom and collective agreement.
Switzerland	45 per week for workers in industry, office workers, technical personnel and other employees. 50 for all other workers.	4 weeks a year. 5 weeks for young workers up to 20 years.	8
Syrian Arab Republic	8 a day or 48 a week. 7 a day for dangerous or unhealthy work. 6 per day for persons under 15.	14 days. 21 days after 10 years of continuous service.	9
Tanzania, United Republic of	8 a day and 45 a week.	28 days	15
Thailand	48 per week for industrial work and 54 for commercial work. 7 per day and 42 per week for work detrimental to health.	6 working days	13

Country	Normal hours of work	Paid annual leave	Public holidays
Togo	40 per week. 46 in agricultural undertakings.	30 days	13
Tunisia	9 a day and 48 a week. 40 in certain branches of activity. 2,700 a year for a total 300 days of actual work in agricultural undertakings.	12 working days. 1 additional day per 5 years of service, up to 18 days. 24 working days for employees under 18 years. 18 working days for employees aged 18 to 21.	14
Turkey	45 a week. 7½, including school hours, for children aged 15 to 18 years.	12 days. 18 days for between 5 and 15 years of service; 24 days thereafter. 18 days for workers aged 18 or under.	12½
Uganda	48 a week. In practice, 8 a day, 40 a week and 176 a month.	18 working days. In practice, 28 calendar days.	13
Ukraine	40 per week. 24 per week for persons between 15 and 16 years. 36 for persons aged 16 to 18 and workers working under harmful conditions.	15 working days. Additional days for work under difficult conditions. 1 calendar month for persons under 18.	9
United Arab Emirates	8 a day or 48 a week in industry. 9 a day in commercial establishments, hotels and cafés. Reduced by 2 hours during Ramadan. 6 a day for young persons.	30 days	10
United Kingdom	No generally applicable provisions. Practice: 35 to 40 per week.	No generally applicable provisions. Practice: 20 to 25 days.	8. No legal obligation for payment, but in practice paid.
United States	8 per day and 40 per week at federal level and in many states.	No generally applicable provisions at federal or state level.	10 federal public holidays. No obligation for employers to grant paid time off. Between 10 and 13 at state level.

Country	Normal hours of work	Paid annual leave	Public holidays
Uruguay	8 per day of actual work and 48 a week in industry. 44 a week in commerce.	20 working days, plus 1 day for every 4 years of service.	11 public holidays (5 days paid by law).
Venezuela	8 per day and 44 per week.	15 days, increasing 1 day per year up to a maximum of 15 additional days.	13
Viet Nam	8 per day or 48 per week. 7 per day or 42 per week for persons aged 15 to 18 years. 1 to 2 hours less per day for hard, harmful or dangerous work.	12 working days. 14 for persons in harmful work and young persons. 16 for persons in especially harmful work. 1 additional day for every 5 years of service.	8
Yemen	8 per day or 48 per week. 6 per day or 36 per week during the month of Ramadan. 6 per day for persons between 15 and 18 years.	21 days	Maximum of 10 days
Yugoslavia	42 per week. Reduced hours of work for workers under 18 and those performing arduous tasks.	18 working days in manufacturing.	7
Zaire	8 per day and 48 per week.	1 working day for every full month of service. 1.5 days in the case of a worker under 18 years of age.	8
Zambia	48 per week.	Not less than 2 days for each completed month of service.	---
Zimbabwe	No generally applicable provisions. Governed by labour relations regulations and collective agreements. Range from 44 to 48 hours per week according to industry.	No generally applicable provisions. 15 to 18 working days for a 5-day week, and 18 to 21 for a 6-day week, depending on industry.	11

Table 2. Overtime

Country	Overtime	Premium pay	Compensatory time off
Afghanistan	---	25% during working days and 100% on holidays.	---
Albania	2 hours per week.	25% on normal working days and 50% on Sundays and public holidays.	Overtime to be compensated by time off at the rate of time-and-a-quarter. Work on Sundays or public holidays to be compensated by time off at the rate of time-and-a-half.
Algeria	Maximum daily hours: 12, including overtime. 20% of 44 hours a week.	25% for overtime and for work on a statutory day of rest.	For work on a statutory day of rest, compensatory rest of equal length and 50% supplement.
Angola	20 or 40 hours as a monthly average over any year, depending on the nature of the work. 2 a day or 30 a year for persons aged 16 to 18 and only in the case of *force majeure*.	50% between 06:00 and 20:00; 100% between 20:00 and 24:00; 150% between 24:00 and 06:00.	For work on weekly rest days, half a day of compensatory rest for between 3 and 5 hours; a full day thereafter.
Antigua and Barbuda	Maximum of 12 hours in any 24-hour period or 72 hours in any 168-hour period.	50% for overtime and for work on public holidays.	---
Argentina	Maximum 12 hours a day, including overtime.	50% during working days, 100% on Saturday after 13:00 and on weekly rest days and public holidays.	Work done on regular weekly rest days may be compensated as from the first working day of the following week.
Australia	No limits at the federal level.	Common practice: 50% for the first 3 (or 2) hours and 100% thereafter. Overtime on weekends and public holidays 100% throughout	---

Country	Overtime	Premium pay	Compensatory time off
Austria	10 hours per week, not exceeding total working time of 10 hours daily. 60 hours per year. In agriculture, 2 hours daily and 12 hours weekly. During 13 weeks per year, 4 hours daily or 18 hours weekly. 3 hours a week for young persons over 16.	50%. Extra pay for work on public holidays.	50% extra time off. 1 full day or 36 hours for work on a public holiday or during weekly rest.
Azerbaijan	4 hours on any 2 days in succession and 120 per year. Prohibited for pregnant women, nursing mothers, mothers of children under 2 years, workers under 18 years, and workers attending training courses.	50% for the first 2 hours; 100% thereafter.	No compensatory time off for overtime.
Bahamas	--	50% on normal working days; 100% on public holidays or weekly rest days.	--
Bahrain	Maximum 60 hours per week, including overtime. No overtime for persons between 14 and 16 years.	25% during working days and 50% between 19:00 and 07:00. 150% for work on weekly rest day.	Compensatory day off for work on weekly rest day.
Bangladesh	Maximum 10 hours per day and 60 hours a week in factories and in establishments, both including overtime. 52 hours a week for persons under 18 years.	100% in factories and establishments.	--
Belarus	4 hours during 2 successive days and 120 a year. Prohibited for pregnant women, women with children under 3 years and persons under 18 years.	100% for overtime and for work on days of rest and public holidays.	A day off by agreement with the employer.
Belgium	Maximum: 11 hours per day and 50 hours per week, including overtime.	50% for work beyond 9 hours per day or 40 hours per week. 100% for work on Sundays and public holidays.	Overtime reaching the limit of 65 hours must be compensated for in time off during the following 3 months.

Country	Overtime	Premium pay	Compensatory time off
Belize	---	50% during working days, work on Sundays and on public holidays. 200% on Christmas Day, Good Friday and Easter Monday.	---
Benin	---	On working days: 12% supplement from 40 to 48 hours; 35% thereafter. 50% on Sundays and public holidays.	---
Bolivia	2 hours per day.	100% for working days and public holidays, and 200% on Sundays, if 48-hour limit has been exceeded.	---
Botswana	14 hours per week	50%. 100% for work on public holidays and weekly day of rest.	Another day off in lieu of public holidays within 19 days or for a weekly day of rest before next weekly rest.
Brazil	2 hours per day over 45 days a year.	50% during working days, 100% during public holidays and on weekly rest days.	Extra hours worked may be compensated by reduced hours on another workday.
Bulgaria	150 hours per year. 30 hours of day work or 20 of night work a month; 6 of day or 4 of night a week; and 3 of day or 2 of night in 2 consecutive days. Prohibited for employees under 18, pregnant women and mothers with children under 6 or disabled children.	50% on working days, 75% on weekends and 100% on official holidays.	Prohibited to compensate by rest.
Burkina Faso	20 hours per week.	To be determined by law or collective agreement.	---
Cambodia	Maximum 10 hours per day, including overtime. 2 hours per day.	---	Compensatory day off for work on weekly rest day.

Country	Overtime	Premium pay	Compensatory time off
Canada	Maximum: 48 hours per week, including overtime, at federal level; 10 to 12 hours per day in some provinces.	50% at federal level and in most provinces and territories. 150% for work on public holidays.	Compensatory rest possible in lieu of overtime pay in some provinces.
Cape Verde	2 hours per day, 160 hours per year. 4 hours per day in case of shift work.	50%. 100% for work on weekly rest day or on public holidays.	---
Chad	24 hours per week	---	---
Chile	2 hours per day.	50% during working days and 100% during night, on Sundays and public holidays.	Compensatory time off for work on weekly rest days.
China	1 hour a day. 3 hours a day or 36 a month in special circumstances.	50% during working days. 100% on weekly rest day if impossible for compensatory time off. 200% on public holidays.	Compensatory time off for work on weekly rest day.
Colombia	2 hours per day and 12 per week for day or night work.	25% for working days, 75% for night work, and 100% for work during public holidays.	Compensatory time off for work on Sunday.
Congo	Maximum permissible length of overtime and rates are fixed by decree for each branch of activity and occupational category.	---	---
Costa Rica	4 hours a day and not more than 4 times a week, except in the event of a catastrophe or imminent danger. Not permitted in the case of work which is dangerous or unhealthy.	50%. 100% for work on weekly rest day.	---
Croatia	10 hours a week. Prohibited for young persons and employees engaged in harmful employment.	---	---

Country	Overtime	Premium pay	Compensatory time off
Cuba	4 hours in 2 consecutive days. 160 hours per year.	At the same rate as normal hours of work. 100% for work on public holidays.	Equivalent periods of compensatory time off.
Cyprus	2 hours per day in commerce, offices and retail shops. 8 to 10 hours per week in services.	50% on working days and for night work; 100% on weekly rest days and public holidays.	---
Czech Republic	8 hours a week, 150 a year. Forbidden for young persons.	25% on working days, 50% on weekly rest days or at night.	Possible for compensatory time off within 3 months, by mutual agreement.
Dominica	---	50% on normal working days; 100% on rest days and public holidays.	---
Dominican Republic	Daily maximum hours are 10 in commerce and 9 in industry, including overtime. 80 hours per quarter.	35% during working days, 100% for work exceeding 68 hours a week, and for work on statutory holidays and during weekly rest days.	Compensatory rest period the following week for work performed during weekly rest days.
Ecuador	4 hours per day.	50%. 100% for night work and for work on Saturdays and Sundays.	---
Egypt	Maximum: 11 hours a day, including rest period and overtime, for 15 days to 2 months a year, depending on the circumstances. Prohibited for persons under 17 years.	25% during the day, 50% at night, 100% on weekly rest days and public holidays.	Another day off in the following week for work on weekly rest days.
El Salvador	2 hours for young persons under 16.	100%. 50% for first 4 hours, 100% thereafter. 50% for work on weekly rest days. 100% for work on public holidays.	Work on weekly rest days or public holidays must be compensated by another day off in the following week.
Equatorial Guinea	2 hours a day. Maximum of 200 hours per year.	25% for overtime worked during the day; 50% for overtime worked after 18:00 and for work on weekly rest days and public holidays.	A compensatory day of rest for work on weekly rest day.

Country	Overtime	Premium pay	Compensatory time off
Ethiopia	2 hours per day, 20 per month or 100 per year. Prohibited for workers under 18 years.	25% between 06:00 and 22:00, and 50% between 22:00 and 06:00 on normal working days. 100% on weekly rest days. 150% on public holidays.	---
Fiji	No generally applicable provisions.	In most sectors, 50% for the first 4 hours on normal working days, 100% thereafter. 100% for work on Sundays and public holidays.	---
Finland	20 hours in any 2-week period. 200 hours in any calendar year.	50% for first 2 hours; 100% thereafter.	---
France	Maximum, including overtime: 12 hours per day; 48 hours per week. 130 hours per year, without authorization of Labour Inspectorate. 8 hours per day and 39 hours per week for young workers under 18 years.	25% for the first 8 hours of overtime in a week; 50% thereafter.	Compensatory rest is in addition to paid overtime after 42 hours of weekly work. Compensatory rest is 50% of overtime worked. After annual limit of 130 hours, compensatory rest is 100%. In enterprises with no more than 10 workers, compensatory rest after 130 hours of overtime (50%). Must be taken within 2 months of overtime worked.
Germany	Maximum 10 hours of work per day, including overtime. 2 hours a day and 60 days a year.	No generally applicable provisions. In practice on average: 27-42% for overtime, 62% on Sundays and 139-149% on public holidays.	Compensatory time off for work on Sunday within 2 weeks; for work on public holidays, within 8 weeks.
Ghana	Prohibited for pregnant women and mothers with children below the age of 8 months.	Fixed by undertakings.	---
Greece	3 hours per day, 120 hours a year.	25% for the first 50 hours; 50% up to 120 hours; 75% thereafter. 75% for work on Sundays and public holidays.	---

Country	Overtime	Premium pay	Compensatory time off
Guatemala	4 hours per day.	50% above the minimum wage or other agreed by the parties.	---
Guinea	100 hours per calendar year.	30% for day work and 50% for night work for first 4 hours; 60% for day work and 80% for night work thereafter. 60% for day work and 100% for night work on public holidays.	---
Guinea-Bissau	2 hours per day, 120 a year. Prohibited for young persons under 18.	50% for first overtime hour; 75% thereafter. 100% for work on public holidays and weekly rest days. Overtime on public holidays and weekly rest days is paid at double overtime rates.	1 day off for work on a weekly rest day, to be taken within the following 3 days.
Guyana	2 hours a day or 20 a month in commerce and offices. 1 hour a day and 100 a year for persons under 16 and women in factories.	50% on normal working days. 100% on public holidays.	---
Haiti	Daily maximum hours are 9 in industry and 10 in commerce, including overtime. 80 hours per quarter for industry. 2 per day up to 320 hours per year in commerce. Not permitted in dangerous or unhealthy jobs.	50%	---
Honduras	Maximum of 12 hours per day, including overtime.	25% for work performed by day; 50% for work at night; 75% more than the night-time wage when overtime is done in addition to night work; 100% during weekly rest days and on public holidays.	---

Country	Overtime	Premium pay	Compensatory time off
Hungary	Maximum: 12 hours a day, including overtime. 8 hours over 4 consecutive days or 144 hours annually. Prohibited for workers under 18 years and in hazardous work.	50%; 100% on weekly rest day and public holidays.	Another day of rest and 50% supplement for work on weekly day of rest.
India	6 hours a week in public entertainment. Prohibited for persons under 15 years.	100% in factories, mines, and beedi and cigar industry.	---
Indonesia	Maximum 54 hours per week, including overtime. Prohibited in work dangerous to health.	50% for the first hour on working days, 100% thereafter and on weekly rest day and public holidays, up to 7 hours. 200% for the first hour over the limit and 300% for the second hour.	---
Iran, Islamic Republic of	4 hours per day. In exceptional cases and subject to agreement, maximum of 8 per day. Prohibited for workers aged 15-18 and those performing night work or dangerous work.	40% for overtime and for work on weekly rest day.	---
Iraq	4 hours per day. Prohibited for persons under 17 years in certain types of work.	50% during working days. 100% at night for arduous and harmful work and for work on weekly rest day and public holidays.	---
Ireland	2 hours per day, 12 hours per week and 240 hours per year, or 36 hours in any period of 4 consecutive weeks. For young persons: 2 hours per ordinary day, 10 a week, 200 a year, or 30 in any period of 4 consecutive weeks.	25%	Work on weekly rest days must be compensated by 24 consecutive hours of rest before the following Sunday.

Country	Overtime	Premium pay	Compensatory time off
Israel	4 per day or 100 hours per year.	25% for the first 2 hours on the same day; 50% for each additional hour and on weekly rest days.	1¼ hours for each of the first 2 hours of overtime worked on the same day and not less than 1½ hours for each additional hour of overtime.
Italy	2 per day and 12 per week.	10%	Sunday work may be compensated the following week.
Japan	No generally applicable limits. 2 hours per day for dangerous work. 6 to 12 hours per week and 150 hours per year for women, depending on occupation.	25%. 35% for work on rest days and public holidays.	---
Jordan	Maximum 11 hours per day, including rest period and overtime. 2 or 3 hours per day.	25% for overtime and work on weekly rest day.	Compensatory day off for work on weekly rest day, plus premium pay.
Kenya	Maximum 116 hours in 2 consecutive weeks.	50% on working days and 100% on rest days and on public holidays.	---
Korea, Republic of	12 hours a week for men. 2 a day 6 a week and 150 a year for women. 1 a day and 6 a week for persons aged 13-18.	50% for overtime and work on public holidays.	Compensatory time off corresponding to time worked.
Kuwait	2 hours per day.	25%. 50% for work on weekly rest days. 100% for work on public holidays.	---
Kyrgyzstan	4 hours on any 2 days in succession and 120 per year. Prohibited for young persons, nursing mothers and pregnant women.	50% for the first 2 hours, 100% thereafter. 100% when worked during weekly rest days and on public holidays.	No compensatory time off for overtime. A day off for work on weekly rest day.

Part III: The regulation of working time

Country	Overtime	Premium pay	Compensatory time off
Lao People's Democratic Republic	30 hours a month. Maximum 3 hours overtime at a time.	50% and 100% at night on working days. 150% and 200% at night on weekly rest days and public holidays.	---
Latvia	4 hours in 2 successive weeks and 120 a year. Prohibited for pregnant women, women with children under 14 and persons under 18.	100% for overtime and for work on weekly rest days and public holidays.	Work on public holidays or weekly rest days may be compensated by an additional day off.
Lebanon	Maximum 12 hours per day, including overtime. Increased in urgent work.	50%	36 hours of rest for work beyond 12 hours a day.
Lesotho	11 hours a week.	25%. 100% when worked on weekly rest days and public holidays.	Another day off for work on public holidays.
Libyan Arab Jamahiriya	3 hours a day. Prohibited for persons under 18 years. Maximum 48 hours a week for women.	50% during weekdays. 100% on a weekly rest day or a public holiday.	For work on weekly rest day, another day off within the next 3 days.
Lithuania	---	50%. 100% for work on public holidays and on days off in lieu of compensatory time off.	An additional day off for work on public holidays or on weekly day off, to be taken within 1 month.
Luxembourg	Maximum 10 hours a day, including overtime. 2 hours per day.	50%. 70% for work on Sunday and 100% on public holidays.	One day of compensatory rest for 4 hours of work on Sunday; half a day for less than 4 hours of work.
Madagascar	20 hours per week.	30% for the first 8 overtime hours; 50% thereafter and for work on public holidays. 40% for work on weekly rest day.	---
Malaysia	Maximum 12 hours a day, including overtime. 4 per day and 104 per month.	50% during working days. 200% on weekly rest days and public holidays.	---

328

Country	Overtime	Premium pay	Compensatory time off
Mali	---	10% from the 41st to the 48th weekly hours; 25% thereafter. 50% for day work and 100% at night for non-working days.	---
Malta	No generally applicable provisions.	No generally applicable provisions.	---
Mauritania	---	Fixed by collective agreement or by order of the Minister of Labour.	---
Mauritius	Maximum of 10 hours a day, including overtime, for women and young workers.	50% on weekdays. 100% for work on public holidays during stipulated hours; 200% thereafter.	---
Mexico	3 hours per day, but not more than 3 times per week.	100% during working days and on public holidays. 200% for hours exceeding the 9-hour weekly overtime limit.	---
Moldova, Republic of	4 hours on 2 consecutive days; 120 per year. Prohibited for nursing mothers, pregnant women and persons under 18 years.	50% for the first 2 hours, 100% thereafter. 100% for work on weekly rest days and public holidays.	No compensatory time off for overtime. Compensatory day off for work on weekly day of rest.
Mongolia	4 hours on 2 consecutive working days. Prohibited for women and single fathers with children below 1 year and for persons under 18 years.	100% for overtime and work on weekly rest day.	Work on weekly rest day compensated by another day off, an additional day of annual leave or premium pay.
Morocco	---	Agreed in the contract by the employer and the employee.	Equal amount of compensatory time off.
Mozambique	2 hours per day. 100 hours per year.	---	For work on weekly rest days and public holidays, 1 half-day of rest as compensation for less than 5 hours of work; 1 day thereafter.

Country	Overtime	Premium pay	Compensatory time off
Namibia	3 hours per day or 10 a week.	50% on working days and 100% when worked on weekly rest days and public holidays.	For work on weekly rest days and public holidays, compensatory rest of equal length and 50% supplement.
Nepal	4 hours a day and 20 a week.	50%	--
Netherlands	Maximum 11 hours a day, 62 hours a week, including overtime.	25% during the working day, 50% for night work, 75% on Saturdays, 100% on Sundays and public holidays.	--
New Zealand	--	No general provisions. Common practice: 50% for the first 3 hours and 100% thereafter.	--
Nicaragua	3 hours per day, not more than 3 times per week. Prohibited for women and young persons under 16.	100% for overtime and for work on weekly rest day.	--
Niger	8 per week in all kinds of activities. 1 hour per day and 75 hours per year in non-agricultural undertakings. 2 per day and 150 per year in agricultural undertakings.	In non-agricultural undertakings: 10% for the first 8 hours and 25% thereafter for day work; 50% at night. In agricultural undertakings: 10% for day work and 50% at night on normal working days. For all: 25% for day work and 100% at night on weekly rest days and on public holidays.	For work on weekly rest days, compensatory rest of equal length.
Nigeria	--	50% on working days and 100% on weekly rest days and on public holidays.	--
Norway	Maximum 14 hours per day, including overtime. 10 hours per week or 25 hours per 4 consecutive weeks, or 200 per year.	40% minimum	--

330

Country	Overtime	Premium pay	Compensatory time off
Pakistan	Daily maximum, including breaks: 10½ hours in factories (7½ for persons under 15 years); 8 for underground mines and 12 for mines above ground. 150 hours per year in establishments (100 for persons under 17 years).	100%	Compensatory time off equivalent to hours worked for weekly rest day.
Panama	3 hours per day and 9 hours per week. Prohibited for dangerous or unhealthy work and for young persons under 16.	25% during working days; 50% at night or on weekly rest days and public holidays. 75% for overtime beyond legal limits or following night work.	A compensatory day off for work on weekly rest days and public holidays.
Papua New Guinea	Maximum 12 hours daily, including overtime.	50% during working days. 100% on Sundays.	Compensatory time off equal to the overtime worked.
Paraguay	3 hours per day. Maximum 57 per week, including overtime.	50%. 100% for work at night or on public holidays.	---
Peru	---	50% on working days; 100% on weekly rest days and public holidays.	---
Philippines	---	25% during working days. 30% on weekly rest days. 100% on public holidays.	---
Poland	120 hours per year	50% for the first 2 hours; 100% for additional hours.	---
Portugal	Maximum 2 hours per day, 200 per year. Prohibited for young persons.	50% for the first hour on working days; 75% thereafter. 100% on weekly rest days.	A compensatory day off for work on weekly rest days, to be taken within 3 days of overtime worked.

Country	Overtime	Premium pay	Compensatory time off
Qatar	2 hours per day. 14 per week or 60 per month. Prohibited for persons aged 15 to 18.	25% for overtime. 150% for work on weekly rest days and public holidays.	Another paid day off for work on weekly rest day or premium pay. No work on more than 2 consecutive Fridays.
Russian Federation	4 hours on any 2 days in succession and 120 per year. Prohibited for pregnant women, nursing mothers, mothers of children under 3 years and workers under 18..	50% for the first 2 hours, 100% thereafter. 100% for work on weekly rest days and public holidays.	No compensatory time off in lieu of overtime pay. Compensatory day off for work on weekly rest day.
Rwanda	2 hours a day during a maximum of 60 working days per year.	50% for the first 2 hours; 70% thereafter; 70% at night on normal working days. 100% for day work and 120% at night during non-working days.	---
Saint Vincent and the Grenadines	---	50% on normal working days. 100% on Sundays and public holidays.	---
San Marino	2 hours a day	25%. 100% for work on weekly rest days. 200% for work on national holidays.	---
Sao Tome and Principe	Maximum of 10% of normal hours of work per week or year.	25% for first hour; 50% thereafter. 100% for work performed on weekly rest days and public holidays, plus overtime premium for work beyond normal daily hours.	1 day if work performed on weekly rest day.
Saudi Arabia	Maximum 11 hours a day, including overtime. 2 hours a day.	50% for overtime and for work on weekly rest days and public holidays.	---

Country	Overtime	Premium pay	Compensatory time off
Senegal	---	10% for the first 8 overtime hours per week; 35% above 48 hours per week. 50% for overtime hours during night work and during weekly rest periods. 100% for overtime work at night during weekly rest period.	---
Seychelles	Maximum 60 hours a week, including overtime. 60 hours per month.	50% on working days and 100% on official holidays and weekly rest days.	For work on weekly rest day, another day off at the option of the employer.
Singapore	Maximum 12 hours a day, including overtime. 72 hours a month.	50%	---
Solomon Islands	Maximum 57 hours a week or 228 hours a month, including overtime.	50% during working week and weekly rest days. 100% on public holidays.	---
Somalia	12 hours a week	25% on working days. 50% or 100% on public holidays.	---
South Africa	Maximum 3 hours per day and 10 hours per week.	One-third the hourly wage for overtime on ordinary working days and weekly day of rest (up to 4 hours). 100% for work on weekly rest day after 4 hours of work and on public holidays.	4 hours worked on Sunday can be compensated by 1 full day during the week. More than 4 hours on Sunday or work on public holidays can be compensated by 1 day plus one-third premium pay.
Spain	80 hours per year.	No less than the amount corresponding to a normal hour of work.	Equivalent periods of remunerated rest.
Sri Lanka	Maximum 12 hours daily in industries and in shops and offices.	50%. 100% for work on public holidays.	Another day off for work on a public holiday or on a weekly rest day.

Country	Overtime	Premium pay	Compensatory time off
Sudan	4 hours a day and 12 per week. Prohibited for persons under 15.	50% on normal working days. 100% for work at night, on weekly rest days and public holidays.	---
Swaziland	No generally applicable provisions.	No generally applicable provisions. 50% on normal working days and 100% on weekly rest days and public holidays in manufacturing and agriculture.	---
Sweden	Maximum: 48 hours per 4 weeks or 50 hours per calendar month and 200 hours per year.	Determined by collective agreement.	Determined by collective agreement.
Switzerland	Maximum 14 hours a day, including overtime and breaks. 2 hours per day and 200 hours per calendar year, of which 60 may be worked without a special permit.	25%. 50% for work on Sundays and public holidays.	Compensatory time off equal to the overtime worked if the worker agrees. 1 day off for any Sunday work of 5 hours or more.
Syrian Arab Republic	Maximum 11 hours a day, including breaks and overtime. 8 hours in mines and quarries. Prohibited for young persons.	25% during day and 50% at night on working days. 100% during weekly rest days and public holidays.	---
Tanzania, United Republic of	---	50% on working days and 200% on weekly rest days and public holidays.	---
Thailand	---	50% during working days. 100% for work on public holidays. 200% for overtime on public holidays.	---
Togo	To be established by Ministerial decree.	---	---

Country	Overtime	Premium pay	Compensatory time off
Tunisia	Maximum hours: 10 a day and 60 a week. 100 hours per year.	25% for the first 8 hours, 50% thereafter, for a 40-hour workweek. 75% in a 48-hour workweek. 25% in agricultural undertakings.	For overtime work and urgent work on weekly rest days, compensatory rest of equal length.
Turkey	3 hours a day and 90 days a year.	50%. 100% for work on public holidays.	Another day of rest for work on weekly rest day.
Uganda	Maximum 9 hours of work a day in industrial undertakings and 10 in any other employment.	50% on working days.100% on weekly rest days and public holidays.	---
Ukraine	4 hours in 2 consecutive days; 120 per year.	50% for the first 2 hours, 100% thereafter. 100% for work on weekly rest days or public holidays.	A day off for work on weekly rest day.
United Arab Emirates	2 hours a day. 1 hour a day for young persons. Prohibited for persons under 15 years.	25% during working days. 50% between 21:00 and 04:00. 150% for work on weekly rest day and on public holidays (if time not compensated).	Equal time off on weekly rest day and for work on public holidays, plus 50% premium pay.
United Kingdom	No generally applicable provisions.	No generally applicable provisions: Practice: 50%; 100% for Sunday work.	No generally applicable provisions.
United States	No generally applicable provisions.	50% after 8 hours a day and 40 hours a week at federal and frequently at state level; after 10 to 12 hours a day in some states.	No generally applicable provisions.
Uruguay	Maximum 10 hours a day, including overtime. 8 hours per week with the agreement of the employee.	100% during the working day and 150% on public holidays and weekly rest days.	---
Venezuela	Maximum 10 hours a day, including overtime. 10 hours per week and 100 per year.	50% on normal working days and public holidays.	---

Part III: The regulation of working time

Country	Overtime	Premium pay	Compensatory time off
Viet Nam	4 hours per day or 200 per year.	50% during working days. 100% on weekly rest days and public holidays.	Compensatory rest for additional hours worked plus additional wage beyond the normal wage.
Yemen	Maximum 10 hours a day, including overtime; 30 days per year. Prohibited for persons under 15.	50%. 100% for work on weekly rest days and public holidays.	---
Yugoslavia	10 hours per week. Prohibited for pregnant women or women who have a child of up to 2 years. Prohibited for workers under 18.	---	---
Zaire	3 hours per day, 8 hours per week. With special authorization of 12 per week and 144 per year.	30% for first 6 hours of work, 60% for following hours. 100% during the weekly rest.	---
Zambia	---	50% on normal working days; 100% on weekly rest days and public holidays.	---
Zimbabwe	No generally applicable provisions. 4 hours a day or 7 to 21 a week, according to industry and job grades.	100% for work on public holidays.	---

Table 3. Rest periods

Country	Rest breaks	Daily rest	Weekly rest
Afghanistan	Not more than 1 hour of breaks for meals and prayers, not included in the working time.	---	At least 42 consecutive hours, including Friday.
Albania	---	11 consecutive hours	36 consecutive hours, including Sunday.
Algeria	1 hour for continuous work, of which 30 minutes considered as working time.	12 hours	1 day, normally Friday.
Angola	One or more rest breaks between 30 minutes and 2 hours. No work for more than 5 consecutive hours without a break.	10 hours	24 consecutive hours, usually Sunday.
Antigua and Barbuda	15 minutes or more for rest, meal or break.	11 hours for young persons.	24 consecutive hours
Argentina	---	12 hours between two regular working days.	From 13:00 on Saturday to 24:00 on Sunday.
Australia	No federal legislation. Common practice: a meal break of 30-60 minutes per 5 hours of work.	No legislation. Common practice: 8 (10) hours minimum rest between 2 shifts.	No legislation. Common practice: weekly rest on Saturdays and Sundays.
Austria	30 minutes for working time exceeding 6 hours. Breaks do not count as working time. 1 hour per day in agriculture. 30 minutes after 4½ hours for young persons.	11 consecutive hours per day. 10 hours in agriculture. 12 hours for young workers.	36 consecutive hours, including normally Sunday. 1 day in agriculture. 43 consecutive hours for young workers.
Azerbaijan	A break for rest and meals not exceeding 2 hours. Not counted as working hours.	---	42 consecutive hours

Country	Rest breaks	Daily rest	Weekly rest
Bahamas	--	--	1 day
Bahrain	At least 30 minutes for rest or meal after maximum of 6 consecutive hours of work. Not counted as hours of work.	--	Friday
Bangladesh	30 minutes for rest or meal after 5 hours of work; 1 hour after 6 hours.	--	Sunday or Friday in factories. One-and-a-half day's consecutive rest in establishments.
Belarus	2 hours for rest and meal after 4 hours of work.	--	42 hours
Belgium	No generally applicable provisions. Practice: 30 minutes after 4½ hours of work. 1 hour if work exceeds 6 hours for young workers.	No generally applicable provisions. 12 hours for young workers.	General prohibition to employ workers on Sundays.
Belize	1 hour for more than 6 hours of work, not included in the actual hours of work.	9 consecutive hours	1 day
Benin	--	12 consecutive hours for women and young persons under 18 years.	24 consecutive hours, usually Sunday.
Bolivia	1 or more breaks of no less than 2 hours in total. No more than 5 hours of work without a break.	--	Sunday
Botswana	30 minutes for 5 consecutive hours of work. 30 minutes after 3 consecutive hours of work for persons under 15 and after 4 hours for persons aged 15 to 18.	12 hours	24 consecutive hours

Country	Rest breaks	Daily rest	Weekly rest
Brazil	In any period exceeding 6 continuous hours, a break for meals and rest of at least 1 hour, but not more than 2 hours. In periods not exceeding 6 hours, 15-minute break after 4 hours, not counted as working time.	At least 11 hours.	24 consecutive hours coinciding totally or partially with Sunday.
Bulgaria	1 or several breaks, including 1 meal break of 30 minutes, not included in working time.	12 uninterrupted hours	At least 24 hours or 48 hours in a 5-day working week, in principle including Sunday.
Burkina Faso	30 minutes during the 8-hour working day.	16 hours	24 consecutive hours per week minimum, normally on Sunday.
Burundi	---	12 consecutive hours for persons under 18 years.	24 consecutive hours, in principle on Sunday.
Cambodia	---	---	24 consecutive hours
Cameroon	---	---	24 consecutive hours minimum, as a general rule on Sundays.
Canada	30 minutes or 1 hour after 5 hours of work in many provinces.	8 consecutive hours of work in some provinces.	1 full day, on Sunday if possible, at federal level and in most provinces and territories.
Cape Verde	1 hour after 5 hours of work.	12 consecutive hours minimum.	24 consecutive hours, normally on Sunday.
Central African Republic	---	11 consecutive hours for women and young persons.	24 consecutive hours, on Sunday.
Chad	---	12 consecutive hours for women and young persons.	24 consecutive hours, as a rule on Sunday.

Country	Rest breaks	Daily rest	Weekly rest
Chile	At least 30 minutes, usually at noon, not included as working time.	14 hours	1 day (24 consecutive hours), which is Sunday.
China	--		Two days
Colombia	Working day divided into two periods with a rest break of unspecified length in between.	--	24 hours on Sundays.
Comoros	--	12 consecutive hours for women and young persons.	24 consecutive hours, in principle on Sunday.
Congo	--	11 consecutive hours for women.	24 consecutive hours, in principle on Sunday.
Costa Rica	30 minutes to 1 hour paid meal breaks.	No less than 12 hours for all economic sectors.	1 full day's rest per week.
Côte d'Ivoire	--	At least 12 consecutive hours for persons under 18 years.	24 consecutive hours, in principle on Sunday.
Croatia	30 minutes, included in the working hours.	12 consecutive hours	24 consecutive hours
Cuba	30 minutes during the 8-hour working day.	16 hours in all sectors of industry.	24 uninterrupted hours per week at least, normally on Sunday.
Cyprus	30-minute break every 4½ hours for young persons.		--
Czech Republic	30 minutes for meal and rest after a maximum of 5 hours of continuous work.	12 consecutive hours. 8 hours for men and 11 for women in special cases.	32 hours. 24 hours in exceptional cases.
Denmark	--	11 consecutive hours	24 hours of rest immediately after a daily rest period, preferably on a Sunday.

Country	Rest breaks	Daily rest	Weekly rest
Djibouti	---	11 consecutive hours for women and young persons.	24 consecutive hours, as a rule on Sunday.
Dominica	30 minutes after 5 hours of work.	---	1 day, normally Sunday.
Dominican Republic	1 hour after 4 uninterrupted hours of work, or 1½ hours after 5 uninterrupted hours of work.	---	Uninterrupted weekly rest of 36 hours, usually starting on Saturday at noon.
Ecuador	---	12 hours	2 days' compulsory rest, which must be taken on Saturday and Sunday. 42 consecutive hours at least of compulsory rest.
Egypt	One or more meal and rest breaks totalling at least 1 hour. No work for more than 5 consecutive hours without a break, not included in normal hours of work.	13 hours	1 day
El Salvador	30 minutes	8 hours	1 day of rest with pay for every week of work. In absence of agreement, the rest day shall be Sunday.
Equatorial Guinea	1 hour after a maximum of 5 hours of work.	12 consecutive hours	1 full day if at least 4 days have been worked, preferably Sunday.
Ethiopia	---	---	24 uninterrupted hours
Fiji	No generally applicable provisions.	---	1 day
Finland	1 hour if daily working time exceeds 7 hours. Permission to leave workplace, in which case rest is not considered as working time.	At least 9 hours.	30 hours per week, including Sunday if possible.

Country	Rest breaks	Daily rest	Weekly rest
France	No generally applicable provisions. A break after 4½ hours for young workers under 18 years.	No generally applicable provisions.	24 hours on Sunday
Gabon	–	At least 12 consecutive hours for women and young persons.	24 consecutive hours, in principle on Sunday.
Germany	30 minutes for between 6 to 9 hours of work; 45 minutes thereafter. For persons under 18 years, 30 minutes for between 4½ and 6 hours of work; 1 hour thereafter.	11 consecutive hours. 12 consecutive hours for young persons under 18 years.	24 hours, in principle on Sunday. 48 hours for young persons under 18 years.
Ghana	30 minutes in case of continuous work, counted as working time. 1 hour if the normal hours of work are in two parts, not counted as working time.	12 consecutive hours	36 consecutive hours
Greece	–	12 consecutive hours for young persons under 18.	24 hours, in principle on Sunday.
Guatemala	–	12 hours	1 rest day after every 6 days of continuous work or after a week of normal work.
Guinea	–	12 consecutive hours for women and young workers under 18 years.	24 consecutive hours, as a rule on Sunday.
Guinea-Bissau	At least 1 hour, but not more than 3, after a maximum of 5 hours of work.	10 consecutive hours	1 day, in principle on Sunday.
Guyana	30 minutes for meal or rest after 4½ hours of continuous work and for persons under 16 and women in factories. Practice: 1¼ hours for rest and meal.	10-12 hours, depending on sector.	1 day in factories

Country	Rest breaks	Daily rest	Weekly rest
Haiti	1 rest break of at least 1½ hours towards the middle of the working day, not included as working time.	---	24 paid hours, preferably on Sundays, after each period of 6 consecutive working days.
Honduras	30-minute rest break in the course of the day, to be counted as actual working time.	10 consecutive hours	1 rest day of 24 hours for every 6 days of work.
Hungary	One break if working day exceeds 6 hours. In practice, 30 to 60 minutes.	11 hours	2 days, including Sunday, or 42 hours per week.
Iceland	30 minutes, not included in the working hours.	---	2 days
India	30 minutes for rest after 5 hours of work in factories (1 hour after 3 hours for a child under 15 years). 30 minutes after 4 hours in mines and in beedi and cigar industry.	---	1 day
Indonesia	30 minutes after 4 hours of continuous work, not counted as working hours.	---	1 day
Iran, Islamic Republic of	---	---	1 day
Iraq	1 or more periods totalling between 30 minutes and 1 hour for rest and meals, not considered as working hours. No work for more than 5 hours without a breaks (4 hours for persons under 16).	11 hours for women	1 day
Ireland	30 minutes for each 5 hours worked and between normal hours and overtime if more than 1½ hours of overtime are to be worked.	12 hours for young persons between 15 and 18 years.	24 consecutive hours

Country	Rest breaks	Daily rest	Weekly rest
Israel	Not less than 45 minutes for a working day of 6 hours or more, including an uninterrupted break of 30 minutes for a meal.	Not less than 8 hours.	Not less than 36 consecutive hours.
Italy	--	--	24 hours, usually on Sunday.
Jamaica	--	--	1 day
Japan	45-minute breaks for working time exceeding 6 hours. Not counted as working time.	--	1 day
Jordan	30 minutes after 5 hours of continuous work, or 1 hour after 6 hours.	13 hours	Friday
Kenya	--	--	1 day
Korea, Republic of	30 minutes for every 4 hours of work and 1 hour for every 8 hours, excluded from working hours.	--	One or more days off.
Kuwait	1 hour after 5 hours of consecutive work, excluded from hours of work. 1 hour after 4 hours for persons aged 14-18.	--	1 day
Kyrgyzstan	A break for rest and meals not exceeding 2 hours after 4 hours of work, not considered as working hours.	--	42 consecutive hours
Lao People's Democratic Republic	5-10 minutes after 2 hours of work, to be counted as hours of work.	11 hours for women	1 day

Country	Rest breaks	Daily rest	Weekly rest
Latvia	Not more than 2 hours for rest and meals after a maximum of 4 hours of work, not included in working time.	---	42 consecutive hours
Lebanon	1 hour after 6 hours of work for men; after 5 hours for women; and after 4 hours for persons under 16.	9 hours	36 hours
Lesotho	1 hour for a maximum of 5 hours of work (for 4 hours of work for persons under 16).	---	24 continuous hours
Libyan Arab Jamahiriya	One or more breaks for rest and meals totalling at least 1 hour. No work for more than 6 hours (4 hours for persons under 18) without a break.	12 hours (15 for persons under 18).	1 day, on Friday.
Luxembourg	A pause of 30 minutes after 4 hours of work for persons aged 15 to 18.	10 hours. 12 hours for persons aged 15 to 18.	44 consecutive hours
Madagascar	30 minutes paid break for lunch in administration.	11 consecutive hours minimum for women and children.	24 consecutive hours, normally on Sundays.
Malaysia	30 minutes after 5 consecutive hours. 45 minutes within 8 hours continuous work for meal. 30 minutes after 3 consecutive hours for children and 30 minutes after 4 consecutive hours for young persons.	12 hours	1 day. 30 hours for shiftworkers.
Mali	---	---	24 consecutive hours, usually on Sundays.
Malta	No generally applicable provisions.	---	1 day
Mauritania	One or more rest breaks of not less than 1 hour for women and young persons.	11 consecutive hours for women and young persons under 18.	24 consecutive hours, on Sundays.

Country	Rest breaks	Daily rest	Weekly rest
Mauritius	1 hour for a meal. 20 minutes for a tea break.	--	24 hours
Mexico	At least 30 minutes for each ordinary working day.	--	1 day for 6 days of work, preferably on Sunday.
Moldova, Republic of	A break for rest and meals of not more than 2 hours, not considered as working hours.	--	42 consecutive hours
Mongolia	Unspecified break for rest and meal.	At least 12 hours.	At least 42 hours, including Sunday.
Morocco	--		24 consecutive hours on either Friday, Saturday, Sunday or on the market day (the same day for all employees of an establishment).
Mozambique	A period of rest between 30 minutes and 2 hours after a maximum of 5 hours of consecutive work.	--	24 consecutive hours, on Sunday.
Namibia	A meal break of 1 hour for 5 consecutive hours of work.	12 hours	1 day, on Sunday.
Nepal	At least 30 minutes for refreshment after 5 hours of consecutive work, and after 3 hours for persons below 16 years. Regarded as working hours.	--	1 day
Netherlands	30 unpaid minutes after 5½ hours. 60 minutes for a day of 10 hours or more.	12 hours	42 consecutive hours in industry. 36 hours in commerce and offices.
New Zealand	To be agreed between the parties.	To be agreed between the parties.	--
Nicaragua	1½ hours' unpaid break during the working day.	--	1 rest day after every 6 days of continuous work, normally on Sunday.

Country	Rest breaks	Daily rest	Weekly rest
Niger	---	11 consecutive hours for women and young persons.	24 consecutive hours, in principle on Sunday.
Nigeria	One or more rest intervals of not less than 1 hour in total for 6 hours or more of work. No work for more than 4 consecutive hours of work for persons under 16 years.	---	24 consecutive hours
Norway	At least 1 break when working time exceeds 5½ hours. Breaks are counted as working time if the employee must remain at the workplace.	Minimum of 10 hours.	At least 36 hours, including 1 full 24-hour day.
Pakistan	In factories, 30 minutes after 5 hours of work, or 1 hour after 6, or two 30-minute intervals during an 8½-hour period. 1 hour after 6 hours of work in establishments (1 hour after 3½ hours for persons under 17 years) and mines above ground.	---	1 day
Panama	No less than 30 minutes and no more than 2 hours.	12 consecutive hours	1 day, preferably on Sunday.
Papua New Guinea	1 or more meal or rest breaks totalling at least 50 minutes for 8 or more hours of work. 30 minutes after 5 hours if an employee has taken a 10-minute rest during that period.	---	24 consecutive hours
Paraguay	1½ hours during the working day.	10 hours	1 day, normally on Sunday.
Peru	---	---	24 consecutive hours in a 7-day period.
Philippines	1 hour for meals.	---	24 consecutive hours

Part III: The regulation of working time

Country	Rest breaks	Daily rest	Weekly rest
Poland	15 minutes of paid meal break.	At least 12 hours.	At least 48 consecutive hours during 38 weeks, or 24 hours during 14 weeks.
Portugal	1- to 2-hour break after a maximum of 5 hours of continuous work. 1-hour break after a maximum of 4 hours of continuous work for young workers under 16 years.	---	1 day, normally Sunday. Two days for young workers under 16 years.
Qatar	1 or more intervals for rest, food or prayer after 5 hours of continuous work (3 for persons under 18), except during the month of Ramadan. Not counted as working hours.	---	Friday, except shiftworkers.
Russian Federation	A break for rest and meals not exceeding 2 hours after 4 hours of work, not considered as working hours.	---	42 consecutive hours
Rwanda	---	12 consecutive hours for women and minors.	24 consecutive hours, as a rule on Sundays.
San Marino	---	---	24 consecutive hours, as a rule on Sunday.
Sao Tome and Principe	1- to 2-hour break after a maximum of 5 hours of continuous work.	10 consecutive hours	1 day, normally Sunday.
Saudi Arabia	30 minutes for rest, prayer and meals after 5 consecutive hours of work, or 1½ hours during the total working hours.	---	Friday
Senegal	---	---	24 consecutive hours per week, normally on Sunday.
Seychelles	30 minutes	12 hours	36 consecutive hours

348

Country	Rest breaks	Daily rest	Weekly rest
Singapore	Unspecified break after 6 hours of consecutive work. 30 minutes after 3 hours for children and after 4 hours for young persons.	---	1 day
Slovenia	To be laid down in proportion to the length of the working day.	---	---
Solomon Islands	30 minutes after 5 hours of continuous work.	12 hours	24 continuous hours, including Sunday.
Somalia	---	---	24 consecutive hours, normally on Friday.
South Africa	1-hour meal break after 5 hours of work.	12 hours	Sundays
Spain	15 minutes after 6 hours.	12 hours of uninterrupted periods.	1.5 consecutive days, which shall comprise the whole of Sunday.
Sri Lanka	In industry, 1 hour for meals or rest after 3 hours of work. 30 minutes for 4 hours of continuous work in shops and offices.	12 hours in industries and in shops and offices.	1 day in industries and 1.5 days in shops and offices.
Sudan	An interval of 30 minutes with pay for meal or rest. One hour for women after 5 consecutive hours (after 4 for persons under 15).	---	1 day
Swaziland	No generally applicable provisions. 1 hour for meal or rest after a maximum of 4 hours of work for persons aged 15 to 18.	No generally applicable provisions. 13 consecutive hours for persons under 18.	1 to 2 days, depending on industry.
Sweden	A break after 5 hours.	Must be provided for and include the times between 24:00 and 05:00.	Minimum of 36 hours consecutive rest period per 7 days, if possible during week-ends.

Country	Rest breaks	Daily rest	Weekly rest
Switzerland	15 minutes for more than 5½ hours of work, 30 minutes for 7 hours and 1 hour for more than 9 hours, counted as working time if the worker stays at the workplace.	12 consecutive hours for women and young persons aged 15 to 18 years.	1 day, in principle on Sunday.
Syrian Arab Republic	One or more breaks for rest and meals, totalling at least 1 hour, included in hours of work. No work for more than 5 consecutive hours without a break (4 for persons under 15 years).	—	24 consecutive hours
Tanzania, United Republic of	—	16 hours	1 day
Thailand	1 hour for rest after 5 hours of work.	—	1 day
Togo	—	11 consecutive hours for women and young persons.	24 consecutive hours, in principle on Sunday.
Tunisia	One or more rest periods totalling at least 1 hour. A break of 30 minutes after maximum of 6 consecutive hours of work.	10 consecutive hours	24 consecutive hours, on Friday, Saturday or Sunday.
Turkey	15 minutes for not more than 4 hours of work; 30 minutes for work more than 4, but less than 7½, hours; 1 hour thereafter. Not counted as the hours of work.	—	1 day
Uganda	One or more breaks totalling 30 minutes for more than 6 hours of work. No work for more than 5 continuous hours without a break.	12 hours	24 consecutive hours, wherever possible including Sunday.

Country	Rest breaks	Daily rest	Weekly rest
Ukraine	A break for rest and meals of not more than 2 hours (not considered as part of working hours) after 4 hours of work.	--	42 consecutive hours
United Arab Emirates	1 hour for rest, meals and prayer. No more than 5 consecutive hours of work without breaks (4 for young persons). Not counted as hours of work.	--	Friday. May not work for more than 2 successive Fridays.
United Kingdom	No generally applicable provisions. Practice: paid tea breaks.	No generally applicable provisions.	No generally applicable provisions. In practice: Saturdays and Sundays.
United States	No generally applicable provisions. Unpaid 30-minute meal break after 5 consecutive hours of work in many states. Some states require work pauses of 10 minutes for each 4 hours of work.	No generally applicable provisions.	No generally applicable provisions. 24 consecutive hours or designation of Sunday as a holiday in some states.
Uruguay	2 hours after 5 hours of work, or 1½ hours if the employee works 4 hours at a time.	--	24 hours minimum, normally Sunday, for 6 days of work.
Venezuela	30 minutes minimum after 5 hours of work.	--	Sundays
Viet Nam	Minimum of 30 minutes to be included in 8 hours of consecutive work.	12 consecutive hours	1 day
Yemen	An interval or intervals of not less than 1 hour for rest, prayer and meals.	--	1 day
Yugoslavia	A rest of 30 minutes, counted as working time.	12 consecutive hours	24 consecutive hours
Zaire	--	12 uninterrupted hours	24 consecutive hours
Zambia	--	--	24 consecutive hours, usually on Sunday.

Part III: The regulation of working time

Country	Rest breaks	Daily rest	Weekly rest
Zimbabwe	No generally applicable provisions. 30 minutes after 5 or 6 hours of continuous work, depending on industry.	---	1 day in most industries.

Table 4. Special types of leave

Country	Type of leave
Afghanistan	*Essential (urgent) leave*. Ten paid days per year. *Leave for religious reasons*. 45 paid days, once during the entire service.
Albania	*Leave for personal reasons*. Five paid days on marriage or in the event of the death of a family member. *Unpaid leave for personal reasons*. Ten days maximum per case in the event of serious illness of a family member.
Algeria	*Leave for personal reasons*. Three working days on the wedding of a worker or one of the worker's descendants, the birth of a child, the death of the spouse or a relative in the ascending or descending line or a first cousin of the worker or his spouse.
Angola	*Time off for housework*. One day off with pay each month for working women who have an established household if they run their own homes or look after one or more children.
Argentina	*Leave for personal reasons*. Ten paid days in case of marriage. Three days for the death of a spouse or of a person living with the employee, or in case of the death of a child or parent. Two days for the birth of a child. One paid day for the death of a brother or sister. *Educational leave*. Two paid days for each examination, subject to a maximum of ten days in any calendar year.
Australia	*Long-service leave*. Most states provide for a right to 13 weeks of leave after 15 years of qualifying service.
Austria	*Paid leave for personal reasons*. One week per year to look after a close relative who is ill living in the same household. One additional week in case of sickness of a child below 12 years. *Unpaid leave for personal reasons*. One week.
Azerbaijan	*Unpaid leave*. Unspecified duration of unpaid leave for family reasons or other valid reasons.
Bahrain	*Leave for personal reasons*. Three paid days in case of marriage, the death of the worker's wife or any relatives to the fourth degree of relationship. One paid day upon the birth of a child. *Leave for religious reasons*. Four unpaid weeks for Moslem workers, once during their working life, to perform pilgrimage obligation.
Bangladesh	*Casual leave*. Ten paid days each year in factories and in shops, commercial and industrial establishments.

Country	Type of leave
Belgium	*Paid leave for personal reasons.* One day for the marriage of a child, grandchild, sibling, parent, or for the sibling of a spouse or parents-in-law, or second marriage of parents or parents-in-law. One day for the death of a sibling, a sibling of a spouse, grandparent or grandchild. One day for the ordination or entry into a convent of a child, a sibling or sibling of a spouse. One day for communion of a child; the name day (*fête*) of a child; a family counselling meeting convoked by a Justice of the Peace. Two days for the worker's own marriage. Three days for the birth a child, to be taken within 12 days of the birth; the adoption of a child; the death of a spouse, child, parent, parent-in-law or the second spouse of a parent. *Paid leave for civic duties.* Three days for recruitment and selection for military service or for duties of conscientious objectors at state health services institutions. Five days for jury service in labour courts and for vote counting in government elections.
Benin	*Leave for personal reasons.* Three days in the event of marriage of the worker, birth of a child, or death of the worker's spouse, father, mother or child. Two days in the case of death of a brother, sister, father-in-law or mother-in-law. One day in the case of marriage of a child, brother or sister. *Leave for trade union activities.* Three paid days a year for trade union representatives for trade union congresses. In addition, unpaid leave for trade union activities.
Bulgaria	*Leave for personal reasons.* Two working days on marriage and in the event of the death of a parent, child, spouse, brother or sister, other relatives in direct lineage without restriction, and first and second cousins. *Leave for civic and public duties.* Two days for blood donation, including the day of medical check-up and donation. *Leave for trade union activities.* 25 hours with pay each calendar year for the unpaid members of national, sectoral and regional leadership of trade union organizations, as well as the unpaid chairpersons of the trade union leadership in the enterprises. *Unpaid leave.* Up to 30 working days without pay each calendar year, which is included in the length of service. *Official and creative leave.* A paid or unpaid official or creative leave of up to one year for the accomplishment of important tasks of public significance, or of creative tasks, under terms and procedures to be established by the Council of Ministers, the collective agreement, or an agreement between the parties to the employment relationship. *Paid educational leave.* Up to 30 working days for workers attending higher or secondary schools, and reading and sitting for a matriculation or university final examination. Six months for preparing a M.Sc. degree and 12 months for a Ph.D. degree.

Country	Type of leave
Burkina Faso	*Leave for personal reasons.* 20 days a year to attend family events. *Special leave.* Up to 15 working days' unpaid leave for different reasons: cultural or sports education course; representing Burkina Faso in an international sports competition; attending labour union meetings or training; representing a public association.
Burundi	*Special leave.* 15 days with pay per year. *Educational leave.* Unspecified period of leave with pay for attending classes of workers' education or trade union training.
Cambodia	*Special leave.* A maximum of ten days' paid special leave each year during a public protest or an event harming the employee's family.
Cameroon	*Leave for personal reasons.* A maximum of ten days per year of paid special leave on the occasion of family events directly concerning the worker's own home. *Educational leave.* A maximum of 18 working days' unpaid leave for a worker or apprentice who wishes to attend a course devoted to workers' education or trade union training.
Canada	*Bereavement leave.* Three days of paid leave (federal); three days of unpaid leave in several provinces; one day with pay and two unpaid in one province; and five days without pay in another province. *Leave for civic duties.* Leave for jury duty in eight provinces, usually unpaid. *Marriage leave.* In Quebec, one day of paid leave for worker's own marriage. One day of unpaid leave for marriage of a child, mother, father, brother, sister or child of consort.
Cape Verde	*Leave for personal reasons.* Up to five days maximum in case of need to provide urgent assistance to members of the immediate family. Three days in case of marriage or death of spouse or first-degree relative in direct line. Two days for the death of other relatives in direct line or second-degree relatives or in-laws. *Leave for trade union activities.* One day per month.
Central African Republic	*Leave for personal reasons.* Up to ten days per year in the case of family events.
Chile	*Leave for personal reasons.* One paid day in case of death of a child or spouse, to be taken within three days of the event. *Leave for trade union activities.* Six paid hours per week for union leaders and eight paid hours when the enterprise has more than 250 employees.

Country	Type of leave
China	*Leave for personal reasons.* For workers in state enterprises: one to three paid days in cases of marriage or death of a parent, spouse or child. *Paid home leave.* For regular workers in government offices, mass organizations, state enterprises and public institutions, who have worked separated from their spouse or parents for at least one year: 30 calendar days a year to visit a spouse; 20 calendar days a year or 45 calendar days every two years for unmarried workers, and 20 calendar days every four years for married workers to visit parents.
Colombia	*Leave for personal reasons.* Domestic problems; bereavement of a workmate (without affecting the normal functioning of the establishment). *Leave for civic duties.* To vote or to take up temporary public duties.
Comoros	*Leave for personal reasons.* Ten days per year.
Congo	*Leave for personal reasons.* Up to ten days per year on the occasion of family events.
Croatia	*Leave for personal reasons.* Seven working days with pay each calendar year in the event of marriage, childbirth, serious illness or death of a member of the immediate family. *Educational leave.* Paid leave for professional or general schooling, training or advanced training, as well as schooling for the needs of the employees' council or union work, under the conditions, for the duration and for an additional amount determined by a collective agreement, an agreement made between the employees' council, and the employer or the employment by-laws.
Cuba	*Leave for personal reasons.* Two days in case of death of a spouse, father, mother, children or other first-degree relatives. Three days if it involves travel to another province.
Denmark	*Educational leave and sabbatical leave.* Both types of leave are available to people over 25 years who are members of the unemployment insurance fund and who have been employed for at least three of the last five years. Educational leave can be granted from one week to one year, and can only be used once in a five-year period. Sabbatical leave is granted from 13 to 52 weeks. The employee is paid through the unemployment insurance fund. Those on educational leave receive full benefits from the unemployment insurance fund, and those on sabbatical leave, 70 per cent.
Dominican Republic	*Leave for personal reasons.* Five days for marriage. Three days in case of the death of a grandparent, parent, child, and spouse or companion (if registered).

Country	Type of leave
Ecuador	*Leave for personal reasons.* Three days' paid leave for the death of a spouse or a second-degree relative by blood or marriage. *Leave for civic duties.* Four hours for judicial requirements and the exercise of the right to vote in public elections established by law. *Educational leave.* One year or more for studies abroad. Two hours per day to attend school for employees under 18 years who have not completed their elementary education.
Egypt	*Leave for religious reasons.* For workers with three years of continuous service in the private sector, a maximum of one month of leave on half-pay for a pilgrimage or to visit holy places once during the worker's employment.
Ethiopia	*Leave for personal reasons.* Three working days in the event of marriage, death of the spouse, descendants or ascendants, or another relative. Up to five consecutive days without pay in the case of exceptional and serious events.
Finland	*Study leave.* Nine months per three-year period. Includes training for trade union activities. Whether the leave shall be paid or not is determined by collective agreement.
France	*Paid leave for family reasons.* Four days for marriage. Three days for birth or adoption of a child. Two days for the death of a spouse or child. One day for the marriage of a child. One day for the death of a mother or father. *Unpaid leave for civic duties.* 1,014 hours per year for locally elected officials. Up to ten hours per month for employee representation of a union in a Labour Court; for meetings and functions of social security organizations, family associations and organizations dealing with problems of immigrants, employment and training. Twenty days per year to participate in humanitarian organizations assisting natural disaster victims. Nine days per year to represent an association or mutual benefit organization. *Leave for trade union training.* Up to 12 days of unpaid leave per year. *Educational or vocational training leave.* Up to six weeks of paid leave for training to participate in Labour Court functioning. Up to 200 hours of paid leave during the first two years of employment for young workers under 25 years with no vocational training. Unpaid leave for up to six days for young persons under 25 years to be trained as youth leaders or coordinators. *Sabbatical leave.* Six to 11 months for employees with total employment of six years, and three years with the same enterprise. Up to one year of unpaid leave for teaching and research. Can be taken on a part-time basis of four hours per week or 18 hours per month. *Leave to start or take over a business.* One year of leave of absence for workers with 36 months of service. Renewable once for a maximum leave of two years.
Gabon	*Leave for personal reasons.* Maximum of ten days per year on the occasion of family events.

Country	Type of leave
Germany	*Leave for personal reasons.* Workers have a right under the Civil Code to be absent from work for relatively short periods of time for personal reasons, provided that the absence was not caused by a fault of the worker.
Greece	*Leave for personal reasons.* Six working days per year to look after a sick dependent child or other member of the family. This leave may be increased to eight working days if the worker has two dependent children, or up to ten days if the worker has more than two dependent children. *Education leave.* Employees under the age of 25 years, who take courses at schools, are entitled to 14 days of leave with pay for taking examinations.
Guatemala	*Leave for personal reasons.* Five days in case of marriage. Three days for the death of a spouse or the person living with the worker, parents or children. Two days in case of birth; other expressly provided by the employer. Half a day or one day for judicial summons, depending on the location of the district court. The necessary time for the accomplishment of trade union functions. In all other cases, provided by collective agreements or in working conditions regulations.
Guinea-Bissau	*Leave for personal reasons.* Seven working days for the worker's wedding. Seven consecutive days upon the death of a spouse, child, father, mother (including in-laws). Three consecutive days upon the death of second-degree relatives (brother, sister, grandfather, grandmother). *Educational leave.* The days necessary to sit for exams.
Hungary	*Leave for family reasons.* One of the parents or a single parent is entitled to two to seven days of supplementary paid leave, depending on the number of children under 16 years old. Unpaid leave to care for a child under 3 years of age or under 10 years of age, if chronically ill or seriously disabled. Up to a maximum of two years of unpaid leave for nursing a close relative. *Educational leave.* Four paid workdays to study for exams for each subject studied, and ten paid workdays for the completion of a thesis. *Leave for personal reasons.* Two days of paid leave for fulfilling a public duty or for the death of a close relative. Up to a maximum of one year of unpaid leave for building one's own house out of private resources.
Indonesia	*Leave for personal reasons.* One paid day for birth of child, circumcision, baptism. Two paid days for the employee's or his/her children's wedding, death of spouse, child, parents or parents-in-law. *Leave for religious reasons.* Up to three months.
Iran, Islamic Republic of	*Leave for personal reasons.* Three paid days in the event of the worker's marriage, the death of spouse, father, mother or a child. *Leave for religious reasons.* One month of unpaid leave once during the working life to perform the pilgrimage to Mecca.

Country	Type of leave
Italy	*Leave for personal reasons.* Four days for marriage. Three days for birth or adoption of a child. Two days for the death of a spouse or child. One day for the marriage of a child. One day for the death of a father or mother. *Educational leave.* 150 to 250 hours per year to obtain a basic degree of compulsory education (half the number of hours are generally paid). Paid vocational training leave during the first two years to a maximum of 200 hours for young workers under 25 years old. *Leave for social or civic activities.* Unpaid leave of not more than ten days for judicial activities. Not more than 20 days for activities concerning immigrants, unemployed and training, and humanitarian organizations. Nine days for workers appointed to an association or mutual benefit organization linked to public authority at the national, regional or local level. *Sabbatical leave.* Eleven months of leave after three years of employment in the same firm and six years of work altogether. Up to one year (after at least one year of service) for teaching or research can be taken on a part-time basis or for four hours per week. *Business leave.* One year to start or take over a business if the employee has worked at least 36 months.
Japan	*Leave for personal reasons.* No statutory provision. Common practice: leave for marriage, birth of a child or death of a close relative. Three months to care for elderly parents or other family members (to come into force in April 1997).
Kyrgyzstan	*Leave for personal reasons.* Unspecified duration of unpaid leave for family reasons or other valid reasons.
Latvia	*Leave for civic reasons.* Employees who are blood donors will be given a day off with pay on the day of the check-up, the day when they donate blood and the day after.
Lebanon	*Leave for personal reasons.* Two paid days on the death of a father, mother, spouse, child, grandchild or relative in the ascending line.
Lesotho	*Educational leave.* An unspecified reasonable amount of time off work with pay during normal working hours for receiving education or training, with the consent of the employer.
Libyan Arab Jamahiriya	*Leave for religious reasons.* 25 days of special pilgrimage leave with pay, once in the worker's lifetime, for workers who have been in continuous service for three years.
Lithuania	*Educational leave.* Two to six days for preparing and taking examinations in educational institutions, depending on the nature of the examination. As many days as required in educational projects and schedules for performing laboratory work and consultations. 30 calendar days for finishing and defending graduation theses.

Country	Type of leave
Luxembourg	*Leave for personal reasons.* One day on the death of a second-degree relative by blood or marriage. Two days on the wife's confinement, a child's marriage or a change of domicile. Three days on the death of the spouse or a first-degree relative by blood or marriage. Six days on the employee's marriage. *Paid educational leave.* 20 days over a period of two years or 60 days during the course of working life for persons under 30 years for the purposes of (a) civic and social training; and (b) training and further training of youth leaders and officers of youth movements.
Mali	*Leave for personal reasons.* Ten days.
Mauritania	*Leave for personal reasons.* Maximum of ten days per year on the occasion of family events. *Leave for trade union activities.* Maximum of 15 unpaid working days per year to attend a trade union congress and to follow courses organized by the worker's trade union.
Moldova, Republic of	*Unpaid leave.* Unspecified duration of unpaid leave for family reasons or other valid reasons.
Mozambique	*Unpaid leave.* Maximum of 60 calendar days per year.
Nepal	*Paid mourning leave.* A maximum of 13 days per year if workers or employees must remain in mourning themselves according to their family custom. *Special leave.* A maximum of 30 days' unpaid leave for special reasons a year for permanent workers or employees who have no leave due. Total duration not more than 6 months during entire period of service.
New Zealand	*Special leave.* Five days after six months of service.
Niger	*Leave for personal reasons.* Maximum of ten days per year on the occasion of family events.
Nigeria	*Compassionate leave.* Three to five days a year.
Pakistan	*Casual leave.* Ten paid days a year.
Papua New Guinea	*Leave for personal reasons.* 14 unpaid days per year. *Long-service leave.* Six months' paid leave after 15 years of continuous service.
Paraguay	*Leave for personal reasons.* Four days in case of death of a spouse, a child, parents, grandparents or other first-degree relatives. Three days in case of marriage. Two days for the birth of a child.
Peru	*Leave for personal reasons.* Eight paid days in case of the death of a spouse, parent, child (in the same province where the employee works); 15 paid days if the employee works in a different province.

Country	Type of leave
Poland	*Leave for personal reasons.* Two paid days in case of marriage; death of parents, spouse or child; birth. One day for marriage of a child or death of a sister, brother, mother-in-law or father-in-law.
Portugal	*Leave for personal reasons.* Two days on the birth of a child. Fifteen days in case of illness of spouse or relatives in ascending or descending line who are older than 10 years. Thirty days to attend to a child under 10 years (including adopted or step-children) in the event of illness or accident. If the child is hospitalized, the leave is extended throughout the stay in hospital. Eleven consecutive workdays for marriage. Five consecutive workdays for death of a spouse, a member of the family or a direct relative, including in-laws. Two consecutive workdays for death of a second-degree relative (including in-laws) or anyone living with the worker as part of his family. *Educational leave.* Up to 60 unpaid days for vocational training.
Qatar	*Leave for personal reasons.* Three days in case of the death of a close relative. *Leave for religious reasons.* Four weeks' unpaid leave for the worker's pilgrimage.
Romania	*Leave for personal reasons.* Unspecified period of paid leave in the case of special family events. *Unpaid leave.* Unspecified period of unpaid leave for solving certain private affairs.
Russian Federation	*Unpaid leave.* Unspecified duration of unpaid leave for family reasons or other valid reasons.
Rwanda	*Leave for personal reasons.* Five working days in the case of marriage of the worker; four days in the case of marriage of an ascendant or a descendant on direct line, and of a brother or a sister. Ten working days in the case of death of a spouse; four days in the case of death of an ascendant or descendant on direct line, of a brother or a sister, of a father-in-law or mother-in-law, and of a brother-in-law or sister-in-law. Four working days for spouse's confinement. Three working days for transfer of the worker.
San Marino	*Leave for personal reasons.* 15 days of paid leave on the occasion of the worker's marriage.
Sao Tome and Principe	*Leave for personal reasons.* Seven days for marriage. One day for birth of a child. Seven days for death of a spouse or first-degree relative in direct line. Three days for death of other relatives in direct line or second-degree relative in-law.
Saudi Arabia	*Leave for personal reasons.* Three paid days on marriage. One paid day in cases of birth of a child, the death of the spouse or any of the ascendants or descendants. *Unpaid leave.* Ten days a year, subject to the employer's approval.

Country	Type of leave
Seychelles	*Leave for personal reasons.* Four paid days in a period of 12 months in the event of the death of a very close relative of the worker or other compassionate reasons. Leave exceeding four days is unpaid or deducted from annual leave, at the discretion of the employer. *Educational leave.* For workers who have never attended a training programme approved by the Minister for Manpower, six months with pay in case of a full-time training programme or the duration of the programme in case of a part-time one. If a full-time training programme lasts for more than six months, two-thirds of the salary during the training period and one-third of the salary on successful completion of the programme. *Leave for civic duties.* 14 days of paid leave in any 12-month period for the purpose of fulfilling, or in connection with, any civic duties approved by the Minister.
Slovenia	*Special leave.* Up to seven working days with pay a year in special circumstances in the cases and under the conditions laid down in a collective agreement or general act. Possible for more than seven days if the employer directs a worker to training.
Spain	*Leave for personal reasons.* 15 days for a worker's marriage. Two days on the birth of a child. One day for moving to a new house.
Sweden	*Educational leave.* Available to all employees for up to one year. For professional training, employees may be entitled to keep their salary entirely or partly. *Special leave.* Various leaves are available to employees, such as leave for carrying out trade union work, leave to nurse a sick relative, leave to participate in Swedish-language training for immigrants, leave to carry out duties in schools, and leave to apply for a new job.
Switzerland	*Leave for personal reasons.* The employer has to grant the necessary leave for family events, such as marriage, death of a relative, birth of a child, moving, or for public or trade union activities, provided that the total absence does not exceed one month per year and was not caused by a fault of the employee. As a rule, collective agreements determine the types and duration of the so-called "justified" leaves.
Syrian Arab Republic	*Leave for religious reasons.* Unspecified period of paid special leave for the holy pilgrimage once during the entire career for employees in public organizations.
Togo	*Leave for personal reasons.* Up to ten days per year on the occasion of family events.
Turkey	*Leave for personal reasons.* Up to three days' leave of absence in the event of the worker's marriage. Up to two days' leave in the event of the death of the worker's mother, father, spouse, brother, sister or child.
Ukraine	*Unpaid leave.* Unspecified duration of unpaid leave for family reasons or other valid reasons.

Country	Type of leave
United Arab Emirates	*Leave for religious reasons.* A maximum of 30 unpaid days for making the pilgrimage once in the course of the working life.
United Kingdom	*Leave for personal reasons.* No statutory provisions, but many employers grant paid leave for bereavement (two to five days); marriage (varying amounts, paid or unpaid); and family illness (varying amounts, paid or unpaid). *Leave for trade union duties and activities.* Reasonable amount of paid time off for duties concerning matters subject to negotiation or duties agreed to by the employer and for training related to these. Reasonable amount of unpaid time off for union officials and members for union activities. Paid time off for duties of safety representatives. *Leave for civic duties.* Time off for jury service, with costs and subsistence allowances paid by the court. Though not legally obliged, many employers top up court payments to normal pay.
Viet Nam	*Leave for personal reasons.* Three days for a worker's marriage. One day for the marriage of a child of the worker. Three days in the event of the death of a parent (including the spouse's parents), spouse or child.
Yugoslavia	*Leave for civic reasons.* Two consecutive working days in respect of each donation of blood.
Zaire	*Leave for personal reasons.* Two working days upon marriage and the birth of a child. Four working days in case of death of a spouse or a relative by blood or marriage within the first degree (two days in case of second-degree relatives). One working day upon marriage of a child.
Zambia	*Special leave.* Three days on the occasion of the employee's marriage. Seven days on the death of the employee's spouse, child, mother or father.

Legislative sources

Afghanistan

— Ordinance No. 103 of the Presidium of the Revolutionary Council of the Democratic Republic of Afghanistan adopting the Labour Code of the Democratic Republic of Afghanistan, dated 11 June 1987 (*Official Gazette*, No. 645, Special Number, 23 August 1987). Sections 48-71.

— Decree No. 230 of the Council of Ministers on regulations concerning overtime work of the personnel, dated 10 November 1987 (*Official Gazette*, No. 655-1366/18, 1987). Sections 11-16.

Albania

— Act No. 7961 to promulgate a Labour Code, dated 12 July 1995 (*Fletorja Zyrtare*, No. 16, September 1995, pp. 660-705). Sections 76-96.

Algeria

— Act No. 91-11 respecting labour relations, dated 21 April 1990 (*Journal Officiel*, No. 17, 25 April 1990, pp. 488-501), as amended up to Act No. 91-29, dated 21 December 1991 (*Journal Officiel*, No. 68, 25 December 1991, pp. 2167-2168) [LLD 1990-DZA4]. Sections 2-4 and 22-54.

Angola

— Decree No. 61 to regulate hours of work, dated 3 August 1982 (*Diário da República*, No. 181, 3 August 1982, p. 1009) [LS 1982-Ang.2]. Sections 1-14 and 32-42.

— Decree No. 30 to approve annual leave, dated 25 September 1987 (*Diário da República*, No. 59, 25 July 1987, pp. 273-276). Section 3.

— General Labour Act, Act No. 6, dated 24 August 1981 (*Diário da República*, No. 199, 24 August 1981; errata: ibid., No. 24, 29 January 1982) [LS 1981-Ang.1]. Sections 122 and 155.

Antigua and Barbuda

— Labour Code 1975, Act No. 14, dated 19 September 1975 (*Official Gazette*, 1975), as amended up to Act No. 3, dated 19 June 1976 (*Official Gazette*, 1976). Sections A6, C3, C14-C28 and E2-E3.

— Information provided to the ILO by the Ministry of Labour, April 1995.

Argentina

— Act No. 11,544 respecting the eight-hour day, dated 12 September 1929 (*Boletín Oficial*, No. 10,614, 17 September 1929, p. 501), as amended up to Resolution No. 276, dated 28 May 1976 (*Boletín Oficial*, 1976) [LS 1929-Arg.1A; 1933-Arg.1].

— Decree No. 390 to approve the code governing contracts of employment, dated 13 May 1976 (*Boletín Oficial*, No. 23,410, 21 May 1976, p. 2), as amended up to Act No. 24,465, dated 23 March 1995 (*Boletín Oficial*, No. 28,112, 28 March 1995, pp. 1-2). Sections 150, 159, 197 and 201-206.

— See also country study in Part II for additional sources.

Australia

— Queensland Industrial Relations Act 1990, Act No. 28, dated 15 June 1990 (*Queensland Government Gazette*, 1990), as amended up to Act No. 14, dated 11 April 1995 (*Queensland Government Gazette*, 1995). Sections 221-222.

— New South Wales Industrial Relations Act 1991, Act No. 34, dated 11 November 1991 (*Statutes of New South Wales*, 1991), as amended up to Act No. 11, dated 9 June 1995 (*Statutes of New South Wales*, 1995). Section 23.

— Northern Territory Public Holidays Act 1981, Act No. 71, dated 11 December 1981 (*Northern Territory Gazette*, 1981), as amended up to Act No. 28, dated 30 June 1993 (*Northern Territory Gazette*, 1993). Section 11.

— Information provided to the ILO by the Government of Australia, May 1995.

— See also country study in Part II for additional sources.

Austria

— Federal Act to regulate hours of work, dated 11 December 1969 (*Bundesgesetzblatt*, No. 114, Text 461, 31 December 1969), as amended up to Federal Act, dated 14 June 1994 (*Bundesgesetzblatt*, No. 132, Text 446, 14 June 1994, p. 3765). Sections 3-12.

— Federal Act on the employment of children and young persons, dated 1 July 1948 (*Bundesgesetzblatt*, No. 146, Text 599, 14 August 1948), as amended up to Federal Act, dated 31 March 1992 (*Bundesgesetzblatt*, No. 68, Text 175, 31 March 1992, pp. 819-822) [LS 1948-Aus.3]. Sections 11-19.

— Federal Act respecting weekly rest and public holidays, dated 3 February 1983 (*Bundesgesetzblatt*, No. 59, Text 144, 8 March 1983, pp. 721-720), as amended up to Ordinance, dated 28 February 1995 (*Bundesgesetzblatt*, No. 48, Text 143, 28 February 1995). Sections 3-4, 7 and 9.

— Agricultural Labour Act, dated 2 June 1948 (*Bundesgesetzblatt*, No. 140, 12 August 1948, p. 515), as amended up to Federal Act, dated 4 August 1992 (*Bundesgesetzblatt*, No. 165, 4 August 1992, pp. 1929-1932). Sections 61-65.

— Information provided to the ILO by the Ministry of Labour and Social Affairs, June 1995.

Azerbaijan

— Fundamental principles governing the labour legislation, dated 10 December 1971, as amended up to 1 November 1993 [*Kodeks Zakonov o Trude Azerbaidjanskoy SSR (s izmeneniyami i dopolneniyami na 1 noyabrya 1993 goda), Azerbaidjanskoye gosudarstvennoie izdatel'stvo, Azerbaijan, 1987-1993*, pp. 1-120]. Sections 46-74, 96, 176-177, 198 and 213.

Bahamas

— Fair Labour Standards Act 1970, Act No. 13, dated 17 July 1970 (*Official Gazette*, Supplement, Part I, No. 30, 30 July 1970), as amended up to Act No. 32, dated 14 April 1971 (*Official Gazette*, 1971). Sections 3-7 and 20.

Bahrain

— Amiri Decree-Law No. 23 to promulgate the Labour Law for the private sector, dated 16 June 1976 (*Official Gazette*, No. 1184, Supplement, 15 July 1976), as amended up to Amiri-Decree No. 3, dated 25 February 1984 (*Official Gazette*, 1984) [LS 1976-Bah.1]. Sections 49-58 and 78-89.

Bangladesh

— Factories Act 1965, Act No. 4, dated 1 September 1965 (*Dacca Gazette*, Extraordinary, 1 September 1965, p. 1535) [LS 1965-Pak.1]. Sections 2, 50-53, 70 and 78-80.

— Shops and Establishments Act 1965, Act No. 7, dated 1 September 1965 (*Dacca Gazette*, Extraordinary, 1 September 1965, p 1641). Sections 8-15.

Belarus

— Labour Code of the Republic of Belarus, dated 23 June 1972, as modified and amended up to 15 December 1992 (*Vedomosti Verkhounogo Soveta*, 1992) [DDS 1992-BLR1]. Sections 2, 42-67, 88, 162 and 177.

Belgium

— Labour Act, dated 16 March 1971 (*Moniteur Belge*, No. 62, 30 March 1971, p. 3931), as amended up to Act, dated 21 March 1995 (*Moniteur Belge*, No. 81, 21 April 1995, pp. 10,310-10,313) [LS 1971-Bel.2]. Sections 19-29.

— Coordinated laws on annual leave of salaried workers, dated 28 June 1971 (*Moniteur Belge*, 1971), as amended up to Act, dated 10 June 1993 (*Moniteur Belge*, 1993). Section 3.

— Act concerning public holidays, dated 4 January 1974 (*Moniteur Belge*, 31 January 1974), as amended up to Act, dated 23 March 1994 (*Moniteur Belge*, 1994). Section 1.

— Royal Order concerning leave days for family events or for public duties, dated 28 August 1963 (*Moniteur Belge*, 11 September 1963), as amended up to Royal Order, dated 7 February 1991 (*Moniteur Belge*, 16 February 1991). Section 2.

— Information provided to the ILO by the Ministry of Labour and Employment, May 1995.

Belize

— Labour Act 1960, Ordinance No. 27, dated 1 August 1960 (*Official Gazette*, Ch. 234, 1960), as amended up to Act No. 31, dated 31 January 1989 (*Government Gazette*, No. 6, 4 February 1989, pp. 209-210). Sections 2, 115-122 and 169.

— Information provided to the ILO by the Ministry of Home Affairs and Labour, June 1995.

Benin

— Ordinance No. 33-PR/MFPTT to promulgate a Labour Code, dated 28 September 1967 (*Journal Officiel*, No. 27, 15 December 1967, p. 831), as amended up to Ordinance No. 74-38, dated 9 May 1974 (*Journal Officiel*, No. 11, 1 June 1974, p. 570) [LS 1967-Dah.1; 1974-Dah.1]. Sections 101-111.

— General collective labour agreement applicable to undertakings in Dahomey in the private sector, dated 17 May 1974 (*Journal Officiel*, No. 20, 1 October 1974, p. 969) [LS 1974-Dah.2]. Sections 36 and 46.

— Ordinance No. 79-33 to prescribe legal public holidays in the People's Republic of Benin, dated 2 July 1979 (*Journal Officiel*, No. 15, 1 August 1979, p. 206). Section 1.

Bolivia

— Supreme Decree to issue the Labour Code, dated 26 May 1939 (*Protección Social*, Vol. 2, No. 14, 1939), as amended up to Act No. 975, dated 2 March 1988 (*Gaceta Oficial*, No. 1541, 8 March 1988, p. 3) [LS 1939-Bol.1; 1942-Bol.1; 1952-Bol.1]. Sections 41-51.

Botswana

— Employment Act 1982, Act No. 29, dated 30 November 1982 (*Government Gazette*, Extraordinary, Supplement A, 9 December 1982, p. A135), as amended up to Act

No. 26, dated 29 September 1992 (*Government Gazette*, Vol. 30, No. 51, 9 October 1992, pp. A109-A113). Sections 2, 94-112 and Second Schedule.

— Declaration of Public Holiday Order 1992, Statutory Instrument No. 71, dated 12 August 1992 (*Government Gazette*, Supplement C, 21 August 1992, p. C469). Section 2.

Brazil

— Constitution of the Federal Republic of Brazil, dated 5 October 1988 (*Diario Oficial*, No. 191-A, 5 October 1988, pp. 1-32). Section 7(XIII), (XVI) and (XVIII).

— Legislative Decree No. 5452 to approve the consolidation of labour laws, dated 1 May 1943 (*Diario Oficial*, Vol. 82, No. 184, 9 August 1943, p. 11,937), as amended up to Act No. 9016, dated 30 March 1995 (*Diario Oficial*, No. 68, 31 March 1995, p. 4575) [LS 1943-Braz.1; 1945-Braz.2; 1949-Bra.2; 1951-Bra.1; 1952-Bra.1; 1955-Bra.1; 1957-Bra.1; 1967-Bra.2; 1970-Bra.1A-B; 1977-Bra.1; 1977-Bra.3; 1985-Bra.1]. Sections 58-71, 129-133, 382-386 and 473.

— See also country study in Part II for additional sources.

Bulgaria

— Labour Code, Decree No. 940, dated 4 March 1986 (*D'rjaven Vestnik*, Nos. 26-27, 1986), as amended up to Decree No. 292, dated 25 November 1992 (*D'rjaven Vestnik*, No. 100, 10 December 1992). Sections 136-171, 262 and 305.

Burkina Faso

— Act No. 11/92/ADP to establish the Labour Code, dated 22 December 1992 (*Journal Officiel*, No. 3, 7 January 1993). Sections 79-91.

— Information provided to the ILO by the Directorate of Labour, July 1995.

Burundi

— Act-Decree No. 1/037 to revise the Labour Code, dated 7 July 1993 (*Bulletin Officiel*, 1993) [DDS 1993-BDI1]. Sections 14 and 112-133.

Cambodia

— Labour Act 1992 (*Journal Officiel*, 1992). Sections 133-147 and 162-165.

Cameroon

— Act No. 92/007 to promulgate the Labour Code, dated 14 August 1992 (*Official Gazette*, 1992) [DDS 1992-CMR1].

— Act No. 73-5 to regulate public holidays in the United Kingdom of Cameroon, dated 7 December 1973 (*Official Gazette*, 15 December 1973, p. 426), as amended up to Act No. 76-9, dated 8 July 1976 (*Official Gazette*, 15 July 1976). Sections 2-3.

Canada

— CCH Canadian Limited: *1995 Canadian master labour guide*, 9th edition (North York, Ontario, 1995).

— See also country study in Part II for additional sources.

Cape Verde

— Decree No. 62/87 to approve a general legal scheme of labour relations, dated 30 June 1987 (*Boletim Oficial*, No. 26, First Supplement, 30 June 1989, p. 6), as amended up to Act No. 101/IV/93, dated 31 December 1993 (*Boletim Oficial*, No. 49, Third Supplement, 31 December 1993, pp. 2-9). Sections 42, 54, 91-99, 125-127 and 157-158.

— Information provided to the ILO by the Ministry of Labour, Youth and Social Development, June 1995.

Central African Republic

— Act No. 61/221 to promulgate the Labour Code, dated 2 June 1961 (*Journal Officiel*, Extraordinary, August 1961). Sections 118-119 and 127-128.

— Act No. 62-315 to prescribe legal public holidays in the Central African Republic, dated 21 May 1962 (*Journal Officiel*, No. 12, 15 June 1962, p. 412), as amended up to Ordinance No. 74/024, dated 21 February 1974 (*Journal Officiel*, No. 6, 15 March 1974, p. 192) [LS 1962-CAR1]. Section 1.

Chad

— Act No. 7/66 to establish a Labour and Social Welfare Code, dated 4 March 1966 (*Journal Officiel*, No. 7, Extraordinary, 24 March 1966, p. 353; errata: ibid., No. 13, 15 June 1966, p. 526) [LS 1966-Chad 1]. Sections 171-186.

— Decree No. 129/PR-MTJS-DTMOPS to prescribe hours of work and the exceptions and regulations for overtime for establishments working a 40-hour week, dated 6 May 1969 (*Journal Officiel*, 1969). Section 13.

— Decree No. 8/CSM to prescribe public holidays, dated 25 April 1975 (*Journal Officiel*, 1975), as amended up to Decree No. 231/FR/CSM, dated 22 September 1975 (*Journal Officiel*, 1975). Sections 1-2.

Chile

— Decree-Law No. 1 to consolidate, coordinate and systematize the Labour Code, dated 7 January 1994 (*Diario Oficial*, No. 34,772, 24 January 1994, p. 4), as amended up to Act No. 19,408, dated 22 August 1995 (*Diario Oficial*, No. 35,255, 29 August 1995, p. 2). Sections 22, 32, 35, 38 and 67-68.

China

— Decree No. 146 of the State Council on hours of work for workers and staff members, dated 3 February 1994 (*Gazette*, Vol. 752, No. 3, 17 March 1994, pp. 69-70), as amended up to Decree No. 174, dated 25 March 1995 (*Gazette*, 1995).

— Labour Act, dated 5 July 1994 (*China Daily*, 6 July 1994, p. 2) [LLD 1994-CHN1]. Sections 36-45.

— Provisions on annual festivals and days of commemoration, dated 23 December 1949.

— Regulations of the State Council on leave for personal reasons, dated 20 February 1980.

— Regulations of the State Council on home leave benefits for workers and employees, dated 14 March 1981.

Colombia

— Decree No. 2663 to promulgate the Labour Code, dated 5 August 1950 (*Diario Oficial*, No. 27,407, 9 September 1950, p. 929), as amended up to Act No. 50, dated 28 December 1990 (*Diario Oficial*, No. 39,618, 1 January 1991, pp. 1-13) [LS 1950-Col.3; 1951-Col.1; 1954-Col.1; 1956-Col.1; 1957-Col.1; 1961-Col.1; 1962-Col.1; 1965-Col.1; 1966-Col.2; 1967-Col.1A-B]. Sections 57 and 158-192.

Comoros

— Act No. 84-018/PR to promulgate the Labour Code, dated 18 February 1984 (*Journal Officiel*, 1984). Sections 117-129.

Congo

— Act No. 45-75 to promulgate a Labour Code, dated 15 March 1975 (*Journal Officiel*, Extraordinary, 17 March 1975, pp. 1-24). Sections 105-120.

— Information provided to the ILO by the Union patronale et interprofessionnelle du Congo (UPICONGO) (Employer and Interprofessional Union of the Congo), May 1995.

Costa Rica

—   Act No. 2 to promulgate the Labour Code, dated 27 August 1943 (*La Gaceta*, No. 192, 29 August 1943, p. 1169), as amended up to Act No. 7360, dated 4 November 1993 (*La Gaceta*, No. 217, 12 November 1993, pp. 1-13) [LS 1943-CR1; 1944-CR1; 1947-CR1; 1949-CR2; 1951-CR2; 1955-CR1; 1982-CR1; LLD 1990-CR1; DDS 1993-CR1]. Sections 136-153.

—   Information provided to the ILO by the Ministry of Labour and Social Affairs, May 1995.

Côte d'Ivoire

—   Act No. 95/15 to promulgate the Labour Code, dated 12 January 1995 (*Journal Officiel*, No. 8, 23 February 1995, pp. 153-177) [DDS 1994-CIV1]. Sections 1-2 and 21.2-25.2.

Croatia

—   Labour Act, Act No. 758, dated 17 May 1995 (*Narodne Novine*, No. 38, 8 June 1995, pp. 1176-1210). Sections 1, 14 and 30-49.

Cuba

—   Act No. 49 to promulgate the Labour Code, dated 28 December 1984 (*Gaceta Oficial*, No. 2, 23 February 1985, p. 17) [LS 1984-Cuba 1]. Sections 67-88 and 112.

—   Information provided to the ILO by the Comité Estatal de Trabajo y Seguridad Social (State Committee of Labour and Social Security), August 1995.

Cyprus

—   Information provided to the ILO by the Ministry of Labour and Social Insurance, September 1995.

Czech Republic

—   Labour Code, Act No. 65, dated 16 June 1965 (*Sbírka Zákonu*, No. 32, Text 65, 30 June 1965), as amended up to Act No. 264 of 1992 (*Legal Gazette*, No. 89, Text 451, 28 September 1992, p. 2550). Sections 1-7, 83-106 and 166.

Denmark

—   Act No. 681 respecting the working environment, dated 23 December 1975 (*Lovtidende A*, No. 65, 1975, p. 1951), as amended up to Act No. 177, dated 14 April 1993 (*Lovtidende A*, No. 39, 15 April 1993, p. 781) [LS 1975-Den.1]. Sections 50-61.

— Annual Leave Act, Act No. 273, dated 4 June 1970 (*Lovtidende A*, No. 17, 1970, p. 695), as amended up to Act No. 102, dated 3 March 1993 (*Lovtidende A*, No. 25, 16 March 1993, pp. 413-418) [LS 1970-Den.2; 1971-Den.2A; 1978-Den.1].

— Notification No. 526 respecting leave for training, sabbatical and child care, dated 20 June 1994 (*Lovtidende A*, No. 100, 20 June 1990, pp. 2726-2736).

— See also country study in Part II for additional sources.

Djibouti

— Act No. 52-1322 to establish a Labour Code in the Territories and Associated Territories under the Ministry for Overseas France, dated 15 December 1952 (*Journal Officiel*, No. 298, 15-16 December 1952, p. 11,541; errata: ibid., No. 25, 28 January 1953, p. 853), as amended up to Decision No. 296/7L, dated 19 December 1972 (*Journal Officiel*, No. 1, 10 January 1973, pp. 35-37) [LS 1952-Fr.5]. Sections 112-120.

— Order No. 73-1611/SG/T to amend the scheme of holidays with pay in the Territory, dated 3 November 1973 (*Journal Officiel*, No. 22, 26 November 1973, p. 367). Sections 2-5.

— Order No. 77-347-INT/AA to regulate public holidays with pay in the Republic of Djibouti, dated 4 October 1977 (*Journal Officiel*, No. 10, 24 October 1977, p. 89), as amended up to Order No. 77-609/PR/CAB, dated 17 December 1977 (*Journal Officiel*, No. 1, 9 January 1978, p. 7).

Dominica

— Labour Standards Act 1977, Act No. 2, dated 28 March 1977 (*Official Gazette*, 31 March 1977), as amended up to Act No. 6, dated 1 July 1991 (*Official Gazette*, 4 July 1991). Sections 2-3 and 10-12.

— Information provided to the ILO by the Ministry of Labour and Immigration, April 1995.

Dominican Republic

— Act No. 16-92 to promulgate the Labour Code, dated 29 May 1992 (*Gaceta Oficial*, 1992) [LLD 1992-DOM1a-b]. Sections 146-165, 177 and 203-205.

— Information provided to the ILO by the Confederación Patronal de la República Dominicana (COPARDOM) (Employers' Confederation of the Dominican Republic), May 1995.

Ecuador

— Labour Code, dated 30 June 1978 (*Registro Oficial*, No. 650, 16 August 1978, p. 6), as amended up to Act No. 55, dated 13 June 1994 (*Registro Oficial*, No. 462, 15 June 1994, pp. 2-3) [LS 1978-Ec.1]. Sections 41-68 and 136-137.

Egypt

— Act No. 137 to promulgate a Labour Code, dated 6 August 1981 (*Al-Jarida Al-Rasmiya*, No. 33, 13 August 1981) [LS 1981-Egypt 2]. Sections 1-3, 43-49 and 133-147.

El Salvador

— Decree No. 15 to promulgate the Labour Code, dated 23 June 1972 (*Diario Oficial*, No. 142, 31 July 1972, p. 7062), as amended up to Decree No. 859, dated 21 April 1994 (*Diario Oficial*, No. 87, 12 May 1994, pp. 3-13) [DDS 1994-SLV1]. Sections 116 and 161-194.

Equatorial Guinea

— Act No. 2 to promulgate the Labour Code, dated 4 January 1990 (*Boletin Oficial del Estado*, Extraordinary, 1990, pp. 1-38) [DDS 1990-GNQ1].

Ethiopia

— Labour Proclamation, Proclamation No. 42, dated 20 January 1993 (*Negarit Gazeta*, No. 27, 20 January 1993, pp. 268-328) [LLD 1993-ETH1]. Sections 2-3 and 61-91.

— Public Holidays and Rest Day Proclamation, Proclamation No. 16, dated 17 January 1975 (*Negarit Gazeta*, No. 13, 17 January 1975, pp. 54-56). Section 3.

Fiji

— Employment Regulations 1965, Legal Notice No. 59, dated 30 April 1965 (*Fiji Gazette*, No. 19, 21 May 1965, p. 101). Section 12.

— Wages Regulation (Building and Civil and Electrical Engineering Trades) Order 1990, Legal Notice No. 63, dated 8 February 1990 (*Fiji Gazette*, No. 18, Supplement, 21 May 1990, pp. 367-371). Section 6.

— Wages Regulation (Wholesale and Retail Trades) Order 1990, Legal Notice No. 62, dated 8 February 1990 (*Fiji Gazette*, No. 18, Supplement, 11 May 1990, pp. 363-366). Section 7 and Second Schedule.

— Wages Regulation (Garment Industry) Order 1993, Legal Notice No. 94, dated 29 October 1993 (*Fiji Gazette*, No. 37, Supplement, 5 November 1993, pp. 448-450). Sections 5 and 7.

Finland

— Act No. 604 respecting hours of work, dated 2 August 1946 (*Finlands författningssamling*, No. 604, 1946), as amended up to Act No. 1180, dated 17 December 1993 (*Finlands författningssamling*, No. 1180, 21 December 1993, p. 3228) [LS 1946-Fin.4; 1955-Fin.1; 1965-Fin.1A]. Sections 6, 11 and 16-17.

— Annual Leave Act, Act No. 272, dated 30 March 1973 (*Finlands författningssamling*, No. 272, 1973), as amended up to Act No. 1184, dated 17 December 1993 (*Finlands författningssamling*, No. 1184, 21 December 1993, p. 3232).

— Act No. 273 respecting study leave, dated 9 March 1979 (*Finlands författningssamling*, No. 273, 1979), as amended up to Act No. 1178, dated 17 December 1993 (*Finlands författningssamling*, No. 1178, 21 December 1993, p. 3226) [LS 1979-Fin.1].

France

— Labour Code, Act No. 73-4, dated 2 January 1973 (*Journal Officiel*, 1973), as amended up to 1994 [Dalloz: *Code du Travail* (Paris, 1994)].

— See also country study in Part II for additional sources.

Gabon

— Act No. 3/94 to establish a Labour Code, dated 21 November 1994 (*Journal Officiel*, No. 1, Extraordinary, 1995, pp. 1-36) [DDS 1994-GAB1]. Sections 1, 165, 169, 183 and 185.

Germany

— Hours of Work Act, dated 6 June 1994 (*Bundesgesetzblatt*, Part I, No. 33, 10 June 1994, pp. 1170-1177) [LLD 1994-DEU1]. Sections 3-7, 9 and 11.

— Young Persons Protection of Employment Act, dated 12 April 1976 (*Bundesgesetzblatt*, Part I, No. 42, 15 April 1976, p. 965), as amended up to Act, dated 31 May 1994 (*Bundesgesetzblatt*, Part I, No. 33, 10 June 1994, p. 1168) [LS 1976-Ger.FR2]. Sections 8-19.

— Act to provide for a minimum period of leave for workers, dated 8 January 1963 (*Bundesgesetzblatt*, Part I, No. 1, 12 January 1963, p. 2), as amended up to Act, dated 6 June 1994 (*Bundesgesetzblatt*, Part I, No. 33, 10 June 1994, p. 1170) [LS 1963-Ger.FR1]. Section 3.

— Information provided to the ILO by the Federal Ministry of Labour and Social Affairs, May 1995.

Ghana

— Labour Regulations 1969, Legislative Instrument No. 632, dated 15 September 1969 (*Ghana Gazette*, 1969) [LS 1969-Ghana 1]. Sections 42-59.

— Labour Decree 1967, Decree No. 157, dated 10 April 1967 (*Ghana Gazette*, 1967), as amended up to Decree No. 368, dated 8 July 1969 (*Ghana Gazette*, 1969) [LS 1967-Ghana 1; 1969-Ghana 1]. Sections 42 and 58-59.

— Public Holidays Law 1989, Act No. 220, dated 13 June 1989 (*Ghana Gazette*, 1989). Section 1 and Schedule.

Greece

— Decree to consolidate and supplement the provisions relating to the eight-hour working day, dated 27 June 1932 (*Efemeris tes Kyberneseos*, 30 June 1932), as amended up to Decree No. 327, dated 30 September 1992 (*Efemeris tes Kyberneseos*, No. 163, 1 October 1992) [LS 1932-Gr.2A; 1935-Gr.3A; 1936-Gr.1; 1959-Gr.1].

— I. Koukiadis: *Legal and contractual limitations to working-time: Greece* (Dublin, European Foundation for the Improvement of Living and Working Conditions, 1994).

— Act No. 1837 for the protection of young persons in employment, dated 22 March 1989 (*Efemeris tes Kyberneseos*, Part I, No. 85, 23 March 1989, p. 1105). Section 5.

— Act No. 539 respecting the granting of annual holidays with pay to employees, dated 5 September 1945 (*Efemeris tes Kyberneseos*, Part I, No. 229, 6 September 1945, p. 1096), as amended up to Act, dated 19 May 1982 (*Efemeris tes Kyberneseos*, Part I, No. 63, 26 May 1982, p. 511) [LS 1945-Gr.2]. Section 2.

— Act No. 1483 concerning protection and facilities for workers having family responsibilities, and amending and improving certain labour laws, dated 8 October 1984 (*Efemeris tes Kyberneseos*, No. 153, 8 October 1984, p. 1840) [LS 1984-Gr.2]. Section 7.

Guatemala

— Decree No. 1441 to promulgate the consolidated text of the Labour Code as amended, dated 5 May 1961 (*El Guatemalteco*, No. 14, 16 June 1961, p. 145), as amended up to September 1995 [LS 1961-Gua.1; DDS 1995-GTM1]. Sections 116, 127 and 130-131.

Guinea

— Ordinance No. 003/PRG/SGG/88 to issue the Labour Code, dated 28 January 1988 (*Journal Officiel*, 1988) [LS 1988-Gui.1]. Sections 139-160.

— Order No. 1391 to apply equivalent hours for certain professions, dated 15 May 1990 (*Journal Officiel*, 1990).

— Order No. 1389/MASW/DNTLS/90 respecting public holidays, dated 15 May 1990 (*Journal Officiel*, 1990).

Guinea Bissau

— General Labour Act, Act No. 2, dated 5 April 1986 (*Boletim Oficial*, Third Supplement, No. 14, 1986). Sections 43-44, 46, 54, 56, 60-61, 66-69, 72-76, 91 and 153.

— Information provided to the ILO by the Ministry of Labour, Youth and Social Promotion, August 1995.

Guyana

— Factories Act 1947, Act No. 30 of 1947 (*Official Gazette*, 1947), as amended up to Act No. 77 of 1974 (*Official Gazette*, Ch. 95:02, 1977). Sections 2 and 21-24.

— Factories (Health and Welfare) Regulations 1951, Regulation No. 16 of 1951 (*Official Gazette*, 1951), as amended up to Act No. 36 of 1953 (*Official Gazette*, 1953). Sections 5 and 16-17.

— Public Holidays Act 1919, Act No. 25, dated 13 September 1919 (*Official Gazette*, Ch. 19:07, 1919), as amended up to 1975 (*Official Gazette*, Legal Supplement, 8 March 1975). Section 3.

— Information provided to the ILO by the Ministry of Labour, Human Services and Social Security, May 1995.

Haiti

— Act to promulgate the Labour Code, dated 6 October 1961 (*Le Moniteur*, Extraordinary, Nos. 1-A to 1-D, 19 October 1961), as amended up to Decree, dated 24 February 1984 (*Le Moniteur*, No. 18A, 5 March 1984, p. 1) [LS 1961-Hai.1; 1984-Hai.1]. Sections 95-123.

Honduras

— Decree No. 189 to promulgate a Labour Code, dated 1 June 1959 (*La Gaceta*, Nos. 16,827-16,834, 15-23 July 1959) [LS 1959-Hon.1]. Sections 322-351.

— Information provided to the ILO by the Ministry of Labour and Social Security, August 1995.

Hungary

— Labour Code, Act No. 27, dated 30 March 1992 (*Magyar Közlöny*, No. 45, 4 May 1992, pp. 1613-1642) [LLD 1993-HUN1].

— See also country study in Part II for additional sources.

Iceland

— Act No. 88 on a forty-hour working week, dated 24 December 1971 (*Stjórnartídindi*, 1971), as amended up to Act No. 94, dated 31 December 1982 (*Stjórnartídindi*, 1982).

— Act No. 30 on paid leave, dated 27 March 1987 (*Stjórnartídindi*, 1987).

India

— Factories Act 1948, Act No. 63, dated 23 September 1948 (*Gazette of India*, Extraordinary, Part IV, 23 September 1948, p. 292), as amended up to Act No. 20, dated 1 December 1987 (*Gazette of India*, 1987) [LS 1948-Ind.4; 1954-Ind.1].

— Beedi and Cigar Workers (Conditions of Employment) Act 1966, Act No. 32, dated 30 November 1966 (*Gazette of India*, Extraordinary, Part I, No. 45, 1 December 1966).

— Mines Act 1952, Act No. 35, dated 15 March 1952 (*Gazette of India*, Part II, Extraordinary, No. 18, 17 March 1952, p. 155), as amended up to Act No. 42, dated 31 May 1983 (*Gazette of India*, Part II, Extraordinary, 1 June 1984) [LS 1952-Ind.3; 1959-Ind.2].

Indonesia

— Act No. 12 respecting labour, 20 April 1948 (*Lembaran Negara*, 1948), as amended up to Act No. 1, dated 6 January 1951 (*Lembaran Negara*, No. 2, 1951) [LS 1951-Indo.1].

— Decision No. KEP-72-MEN/84 of the Minister of Manpower on the basis for the calculation of overtime wages, dated 31 March 1981 (*Lembaran Negara*, 1981).

— Government Regulation No. 21 on annual leave for workers, dated 16 March 1954 (*Lembaran Negara*, No. 37, 1954), as amended up to Ministerial Decision No. 69, dated 10 May 1980 (*Lembaran Negara*, 1980).

— Presidential Decision No. 251 on public holidays, dated 16 December 1967 (*Lembaran Negara*, 1967), as amended up to Presidential Decree No. 148, dated 18 April 1968 (*Lembaran Negara*, 1968).

— Information provided to the ILO by the Department of Manpower, August 1995.

Iran, Islamic Republic of

— Labour Code, dated 20 November 1990 (*Rouznameh Rasmi*, No. 13,387, 17 February 1991, pp. 1-14) [LLD 1990-IRN1]. Sections 51-74 and 82.

Iraq

— Act No. 71 promulgating the Labour Code, dated 27 July 1987 (*Alwaqai Aliraqiya*, 1987) [LS 1987-Iraq 2]. Sections 54-68, 83 and 92-93.

Ireland

— Conditions of Employment Act 1936, Act No. 2, dated 14 February 1936 (*Public Statutes of the Oireachtas*, 1936), as amended up to Statutory Instrument No. 34, dated 19 March 1987 (*Iris Oifigiúil*, 31 March 1987) [LS 1936-IFS1; 1944-Ire.2].

— Protection of Young Persons (Employment) Act 1977, Act No. 9, dated 6 April 1977 (*Acts of the Oireachtas*, 1977, p. 7).

— Holidays (Employees) Act 1973, Act No. 25, dated 21 November 1973 (*Acts of the Oireachtas*, 1973), as amended up to Statutory Instrument No. 91, dated 2 April 1993 (*Statutory Instruments*, 1993) [LS 1973-Ire.3].

Israel

— Hours of Work and Rest Law, Act No. 47, dated 15 May 1951 (*Sefer Hakhukim*, No. 76, 22 May 1951, p. 204) [LS 1951-Isr.2]. Sections 2-4, 7, 10, 16-17 and 20-21.

— Annual Leave Law, Act No. 63, dated 4 July 1951 (*Sefer Hakhukim*, No. 81, 11 July 1951, p. 234) [LS 1951-Isr.3].

— Information provided to the ILO by the Ministry of Labour and Social Affairs, January 1996.

Italy

— Legislative Decree No. 692 concerning the limitation of the hours of work of wage-earning and salaried employees in industrial and commercial undertakings of all kinds, dated 15 March 1923 (*Gazzetta Ufficiale*, No. 84, 10 April 1923, p. 2893), as amended up to Act No. 1079, dated 30 October 1955 (*Gazzetta Ufficiale*, No. 269, 22 November 1955, p. 4039) [LS 1923-It.1; 1955-It.4]. Sections 1-5.

Jamaica

— National Minimum Wage Order 1975, Order No. 339, dated 22 October 1975 (*Jamaica Gazette*, Vol. 98, No. 105, Supplement, 30 October 1975, pp. 571-574), as amended up to Order No. 44, dated 29 June 1992 (*Jamaica Gazette*, Vol. 115, No. 24, 6 July 1992, pp. 127-129). Sections 2-5.

— Holidays with Pay Act 1973, Order No. 189, dated 22 May 1973 (*Jamaica Gazette*, No. 57, Supplement, 31 May 1973, p. 307), as amended up to Order No. 54B, dated 27 June 1991 (*Jamaica Gazette*, Vol. 114, No. 32B, Supplement, 27 June 1991, pp. 218C-218D). Section 3 and Schedule.

— Holidays (Public General) Act 1895, dated 27 April 1895, as amended up to Legal Notice No. 93S, dated 1 September 1985 (*Jamaica Gazette*, 1986). Section 2 and Schedule.

Japan

— Labour Standards Law, Act No. 49, dated 7 April 1947 (*Kampoo*, No. 303, 7 April 1947, p. 1), as amended up to Act No. 99, dated 26 September 1987 (*Kampoo*, 26 September 1987, pp. 9-11) [LS 1947-Jap.3; 1987-Jap.1].

— See also country study in Part II for additional sources.

Jordan

— Act No. 21 to promulgate the Labour Code, dated 14 May 1960 (*Al-jarida al-rasmiya*, No. 1491, 21 May 1960, p. 511), as amended up to Provisional Act No. 37, dated 5 November 1988 (*Al-jarida al-rasmiya*, No. 3582, 6 November 1988, pp. 2100-2101) [LS 1960-Jor.1; 1965-Jor.1]. Sections 2 and 37-48.

Kenya

— Regulation of Wages (General) Order 1982, Legal Notice No. 120, dated 12 August 1982 (*Kenya Gazette*, 1982), as amended up to Legal Notice No. 122, dated 30 April 1987 (*Kenya Gazette*, 1987). Sections 2 and 5-6.

— Regulation of Wages (Agricultural Industry) Order 1982, Legal Notice No. 121, dated 12 August 1982 (*Kenya Gazette*, 1982), as amended up to Legal Notice No. 92, dated 20 April 1993 (*Kenya Gazette*, No. 26, 30 April 1993, pp. 135-136). Sections 5-8 and Second Schedule.

— Information provided to the ILO by the Ministry of Labour and Manpower, June 1995.

Korea, Republic of

— Labour Standards Law, Act No. 286, dated 10 May 1953, as amended up to Act No. 4220, dated 13 January 1990 (*Labour Laws of Korea*, 1992, pp. 43-64). Sections 42-48 and 55-57.

— Industrial Safety and Health Act, Act No. 3532, dated 31 December 1981, as amended up to Act No. 4220, dated 13 January 1990 (*Labour Laws of Korea*, 1992, pp. 89-115). Section 46.

— See also country study in Part II for additional sources.

Kuwait

— Act No. 38 regulating conditions of work in the private sector, dated 1 January 1964 (*Al Koweit al-Yaum*, No. 489, 1964), as amended up to Act No. 28, dated 11 June 1969 (*Al Koweit al-Yaum*, 1969).

Kyrgyzstan

— Act No. 519-VIII respecting fundamental principles governing the labour legislation of the Krygyz SSR, dated 23 May 1972, as amended up to 1 December 1993 (*Ekonomika: Normativnyie Akty Kyrgyzskoi Respubliki*, December 1993, pp. 26-56). Sections 47-49, 59-82 and 103-104.

Lao People's Democratic Republic

— Decree No. 24/PR to promulgate the Labour Law, dated 21 April 1994 (*Official Journal*, 1994) [LLD 1994-LAO1]. Sections 25-30, 33, 37 and 42.

Latvia

— Labour Code of the Republic of Latvia, as amended up to Ministerial Regulations, dated 26 July 1994. Sections 5, 45-118, 170-171 and 186.

Lebanon

— Labour Code, dated 23 September 1946 (*Al-jarida al-rasmiya*, 1946), as amended up to 31 December 1993 (*Argus de la législation libanaise*, 1993) [LS 1946-Leb.1; DDS 1993-LBN1]. Sections 23 and 31-39.

Lesotho

— Labour Code Order 1992, Order No. 24 of 1992 (*Government Gazette*, Vol. 37, No. 118, Extraordinary, 12 November 1992, pp. 1195-1441). Sections 2 and 117-125.

— Public Holidays Act 1967, Act No. 3, dated 20 April 1967 (*Government Gazette*, Vol. 2, No. 11, 28 April 1967, pp. 96-97). Section 2 and Schedule.

Libyan Arab Jamahiriya

— Labour Code, Act No. 58-2970, dated 1 May 1970 (*Al-Jarida Al-Rasmiya*, 1 May 1970, Special supplement) [LS 1970-Libya 1]. Sections 1, 38, 41 and 85-96.

Lithuania

— Act No. I-924 on wages, dated 9 January 1991 (*Parliamentary Record of the Supreme Council of the Republic of Lithuania*, No. 12, 1992, pp. 5-7). Sections 7-8.

— Act No. I-2113 on holidays, dated 17 December 1991 (*Parliamentary Record of the Supreme Council of the Republic of Lithuania*, No. 12, 1992, pp. 22-27). Sections 6-7 and 23-24.

Luxembourg

— Consolidated text of the Acts respecting the legal regulation of the contracts of service of employees in private employment, dated 5 December 1989 (*Mémorial*, Series A, No. 74, 5 December 1989, pp. 1342-1346). Sections 3, 6 and 9.

— Act respecting the protection of children and young workers, dated 28 October 1969 (*Mémorial*, Series A, No. 55, 28 October 1969, p. 1263), as amended up to Act, dated 10 September 1981 (*Mémorial*, Series A, No. 76, 27 October 1981, pp. 1918-1924; errata: ibid., Series A, No. 83, 27 November 1981, p. 2044) [LS 1969-Lux.1; 1972-Lux.2A-B]. Sections 1, 9 and 12.

— Act respecting weekly rest of employees and workers, dated 1 August 1988 (*Mémorial*, Series A, No. 44, 17 August 1988, p. 858). Sections 6-7.

— Act to make uniform provision for the annual leave with pay of employees in the private sector, dated 22 April 1966 (*Mémorial*, Series A, No. 21, 28 April 1966, p. 403), as amended up to Act, dated 14 March 1988 (*Mémorial*, Series A, No. 12, 30 March 1988, p. 127) [LS 1979-Lux.2]. Sections 4, 6 and 16.

— Act to revise the provisions relating to statutory public holidays, dated 10 April 1976 (*Mémorial*, Series A, No. 16, 13 April 1976, p. 184). Section 2.

— Act respecting the institution of educational leave, dated 4 October 1973 (*Mémorial*, Series A, No. 57, 8 October 1973, p. 1349), as amended up to Act, dated 9 August 1989 (*Mémorial*, Series A, No. 54, 9 August 1989, p. 1004) [LS 1973-Lux.1]. Sections 1-3.

Madagascar

— Act No. 94-029 to promulgate a Labour Code, dated 25 August 1995 (*Journal Officiel*, No. 2324, 25 September 1995, pp. 2564-2577) [DDS 1995-MDG1]. Sections 85-116.

— Decree No. 68-172 to regulate overtime and to fix increases in wages for work performed at night, on Sunday and on public holidays, dated 18 April 1968 (*Journal Officiel*, 4 May 1968). Sections 1-3.

— Information provided to the ILO by the Government of Madagascar, August 1995.

Malaysia

— Employment Act 1955, Ordinance No. 38, dated 27 June 1955 (*Warta Kerajaan*, 1955), as amended up to Act No. A716 of 1989 (*Warta Kerajaan*, 1989) [LS 1955-Mal.2; 1966-Mal.1; 1982-Mal.2]. Sections 58-60.

— Children and Young Persons (Employment) Act 1966, Act No. 40, dated 28 April 1966 (*Warta Kerajaan*, No. 10, Act Supplement No. 4, 12 May 1966, p. 377) [LS 1966-Mal.1]. Sections 5-6 and 19.

— Holidays (Amendment of Schedules) Order 1986, Legal Notice No. S11, dated 8 May 1986 (*Warta Kerajaan*, No. S8, 22 May 1986, p. 23), as amended up to Order No. S5 of 1987 (*Warta Kerajaan*, Vol. 42, No. S4, 26 February 1987).

— Information provided to the ILO by the Ministry of Human Resources, September 1995.

Mali

— Act No. 92-020 concerning the Labour Code of the Republic of Mali, dated 18 August 1992 (*Journal Officiel*, Vol. 34, No. 8, 30 November 1992, pp. 1-32). Sections 131-154.

Malta

— Weekly Day of Rest and Annual Vacation Leave National Standard Order 1989, Legal Notice No. 38, dated 30 March 1989 (*Government Gazette*, No. 15,308, Supplement, 30 March 1989, pp. 147-148). Sections 3-4.

— National Day and Other Public Holidays Act 1975, Act No. 30, dated 23 June 1975 (*Government Gazette*, Supplement, 27 June 1975), as amended up to Legal Notice No. 40, dated 29 May 1987 (*Government Gazette*, No. 14,796, Supplement, 29 May 1987, p. B122). Section 2 and Schedule.

Mauritania

— Act No. 63-023 to establish a Labour Code, dated 23 January 1963 (*Journal Officiel*, No. 106, 20 February 1963, p. 53; errata: ibid., No. 112, 15 May 1963, p. 143), as amended up to Act No. 93-038, dated 20 July 1993 (*Journal Officiel*, No. 811, 30 July 1993, pp. 436-437) [LS 1963-Mau.1; 1970-Mau.1; 1974-Mau.1; 1976-Mau.1]. Sections 2-24 of Book II.

— Act No. 92-018 to regulate public holidays, dated 7 December 1992 (*Journal Officiel*, No. 797, 30 December 1992, p. 544). Section 1.

Mauritius

— Act No. 50 to amend and consolidate the law relating to labour, dated 24 December 1975 (*Government Gazette*, No. 90, Legal Supplement, 27 December 1975, p. 165), as amended up to Act No. 54, dated 5 December 1984 (*Government Gazette*, 1984) [LS 1975-Maur.1]. Sections 15-17 and 21.

Mexico

— Federal Labour Act, dated 2 December 1969 (*Diario Oficial*, No. 26, 1 April 1970, p. 1; ibid., No. 29, 5 June 1970, p. 16), as amended up to 16 December 1987 (*Diario Oficial*, No. 14, 21 January 1988, p. 19) [LS 1969-Mex.1; 1973-Mex.2; 1975-Mex.1; 1979-Mex.1]. Sections 58-81.

— See also country study in Part II for additional sources.

Moldova, Republic of

— Fundamental principles governing the labour legislation, dated 1 October 1973, as amended up to Act No. 1315-XII, dated 2 March 1993. Sections 47-95.

Mongolia

— Labour Code of the Republic of Mongolia, dated 14 February 1991 (*Turiin Medeelel*, No. 2, February 1991). Sections 25-36 and 86.

Morocco

— Decree to issue regulations respecting hours of work, dated 18 June 1936 (*Bulletin Officiel*, No. 1234, 19 June 1936, p. 736), as amended up to Decree, dated 16 October 1947 (*Bulletin Officiel*, No. 1831, 28 November 1947, p. 1214) [LS 1936-Mor.1; 1937-Mor.2; 1947-Mor.3]. Section 1.

— Decree respecting annual holidays with pay, dated 9 January 1946 (*Bulletin Officiel*, No. 1744, 29 March 1946, p. 222), as amended up to Decree No. 2-88-24, dated 9 January 1988 (*Bulletin Officiel*, No. 3925, 20 January 1988, p. 55) [LS 1946-Mor.1; 1952-Mor.(Fr.)1; 1961-Mor.1]. Section 3.

— Decree respecting weekly rest and public holidays, dated 21 July 1947 (*Bulletin Officiel*, No. 1825, 17 October 1947, p. 1034) [LS 1947-Mor.2]. Section 4.

— Decree No. 2-86-349 to grant payments for overtime and arduous work, as well as for work clothing for certain officials and agents of collectives, dated 2 December 1986 (*Bulletin Officiel*, No. 3914, 4 November 1987, p. 325). Sections 3-4.

— Decree No. 2-62-101 to prescribe the list of public holidays with pay in commercial and industrial undertakings, the liberal professions, and agricultural and forestry undertakings, dated 28 February 1962 (*Bulletin Officiel*, 1962), as amended up to Decree No. 2-88-24, dated 9 January 1988 (*Bulletin Officiel*, No. 3925, 20 January 1988, p. 55). Section 1.

Mozambique

— Act no. 8 to approve the Labour Act, dated 14 December 1985 (*Boletim da República*, No. 50, Fifth Supplement, 14 December 1985, pp. 15-37), as amended up to Act No. 12, dated 30 July 1991 (*Boletim da República*, No. 30, Supplement, 30 July 1991, p. 22) [LS 1985-Moz.1]. Sections 1, 50-72, 110 and 155-158.

Namibia

— Labour Act 1992, dated 13 March 1992 (*Government Gazette*, No. 338, 8 April 1992, pp. 1-151), as amended up to Act No. 134, dated 22 September 1992 (*Government Gazette*, No. 491, 30 September 1992, p. 1) [LLD 1992-NAM1]. Sections 1-2 and 27-39.

Nepal

— Labour Act 1992, dated 15 May 1992 (*Nepal Recorder*, Vol. 16, No. 19, 12 June 1992, pp. 220-253) [LLD 1992-NPL1]. Sections 16-19.

— Labour Rules 1993, dated 8 November 1993 (*Nepal Recorder*, Vol. 17, No. 39, 25 December 1993, pp. 414-442) [LLD 1993-NPL 1]. Sections 3 and 29-33.

— Children's Act 1992, dated 20 May 1992 (*Nepal Gazette*, Part II, Vol. 42, No. 8, 20 May 1992). Section 47.

Netherlands

— Labour Act 1919, dated 1 November 1919 (*Staatsblad*, No. 624, 1919), as amended up to Act, dated 5 March 1986 (*Staatsblad*, No. 147, 1986) [LS 1922-Neth.1; 1924-Neth.5; 1928-Neth.3; 1930-Neth.2; 1931-Neth.1; 1933-Neth.4; 1933-Neth.7; 1935-Neth.2; 1950-Neth.1; 1951-Neth.1; 1955-Neth.1; 1956-Neth.1; 1960-Neth.1; 1964-Neth.1; 1977-Neth.1]. Sections 9, 16 and 20.

— Information provided to the ILO by the Ministry of Labour and Social Affairs, June 1995.

New Zealand

— Minimum Wage Act 1983, Act No. 115, dated 16 December 1983 (*Statutes of New Zealand*, 1983), as amended up to Act No. 27, dated 7 May 1991 (*Reprinted Statutes of New Zealand*, Vol. 27, 1991, p. 701).

— Holidays Act 1981, Act No. 15, dated 23 July 1981 (*Statutes of New Zealand*, 1981), as amended up to Act No. 26, dated 7 May 1991 (*Reprinted Statutes of New Zealand*, Vol. 27, 1991, p. 611) [LS 1981-NZ1]. Section 7(A).

— R. Harbridge and A. Honeybone: *Working time and the application of penal rates of pay: A gender and industry analysis in the 1993/94 year*, paper presented to the Sixth Labour, Employment and Work Conference (Wellington, 24-25 November 1994).

— See also country study in Part II for additional sources.

Nicaragua

— Decree No. 336 to promulgate the Labour Code, dated 12 January 1945 (*La Gaceta*, 1945), as amended up to Act of 1986 (*La Gaceta*, 1986) [LS 1945-Nic.1; 1962-Nic.1; 1969-Nic.1]. Sections 47-74.

Niger

— Act No. 62-12 to establish a Labour Code, dated 13 July 1962 (*Journal Officiel*, No. 4, Extraordinary, 25 August 1962). Sections 110-120.

— Decree No. 67-126/MFP/T to issue regulations pursuant to the Labour Code, dated 7 September 1967 (*Journal Officiel*, No. 19, 1 October 1967, p. 693), as amended up to Decree No. 90-203/PRN/MFP/T, dated 24 October 1990 (*Journal Officiel*, No. 15, 15 November 1990, pp. 780-781). Sections 229-267.

Nigeria

— Labour Decree 1974, Decree No. 21, dated 29 May 1974 (*Official Gazette*, No. 28, Supplement, 6 June 1974, pp. A63-A108) [LS 1974-Nig.1]. Sections 12, 17, 58 and 90.

— Public Holidays Act 1979, Act No. 3 of 1979, as amended up to Decree No. 26, dated 28 August 1984 (*Official Gazette*, No. 52, Supplement, 30 August 1984, p. A551).

— Information provided to the ILO by the Federal Ministry of Labour and Productivity, June 1995.

— E.E. Uvieghara: "Labour law and industrial relations in Nigeria", in R. Blainpain (ed.): *Encyclopaedia for labour and industrial relations: Volume 9* (Deventer, Kluwer, 1986), pp. 81-82 and 132-134.

Norway

— Act No. 4 respecting workers' protection and the working environment, dated 4 February 1977 (*Norsk Lovtidend*, Part I, No. 4, 14 February 1977, p. 77), as amended up to Act No. 2, dated 6 January 1995 (*Norsk Lovtidend*, Part I, 1995) [LS 1977-Nor.1; LLD 1995-NOR1]. Sections 25 and 46-51.

— Act No. 21 on annual leave, dated 29 April 1988 (*Norsk Lovtidend*, Part I, No. 7, 11 May 1988, pp. 233-244), as amended up to Act No. 34, dated 15 June 1990 (*Norsk Lovtidend*, Part I, 1990) [LS 1988-Nor.1].

— Act No. 1 relating to Sundays and public holidays, dated 4 June 1965 (*Norsk Lovtidend*, Part I, No. 21, 8 July 1965, pp. 992-995).

— See also country study in Part II for additional sources.

Pakistan

— Factories Act 1934, Act No. 25, dated 20 August 1934 (*Gazette of India*, 1934), as amended up to Ordinance No. 9, dated 28 January 1977 (*Gazette of Pakistan*, 1977) [LS 1946-Ind.1; 1947-Ind.3]. Sections 34-37, 49 and 54.

— West Pakistan Shops and Establishments Ordinance 1969, Ordinance No. 8, dated 30 June 1969 (*Gazette of Pakistan*, Extraordinary, 3 July 1969, p. 1057), as amended up to Ordinance No. 4 of 1975 (*Gazette of Pakistan*, 1975) [LS 1969-Pak.1]. Sections 8-16.

— Tea Plantations Labour Ordinance 1962, Ordinance No. 39, dated 1 June 1962 (*Gazette of Pakistan*, Extraordinary, 4 June 1962, p. 864) [LS 1962-Pak.1]. Sections 18-28.

— Mines Act 1923, Act No. 4, dated 23 February 1923 (*Gazette of India*, 1923), as amended up to Ordinance No. 4, dated 28 July 1975 (*Gazette of Pakistan*, Part I, Extraordinary, 1 August 1975, p. 435) [LS 1923-Ind.3; 1928-Ind.3; 1936-Ind.2; 1937-Ind.6; 1946-Ind.3]. Sections 22A-28G.

— Road Transport Workers Ordinance 1961, Ordinance No. 28, dated 30 June 1961 (*Gazette of Pakistan*, Extraordinary, 4 July 1961, p. 1075), as amended up to Act No. 12, dated 25 January 1975 (*Gazette of Pakistan*, Part I, Extraordinary, 25 January 1975, p. 20) [LS 1961-Pak.1]. Sections 4-6.

Panama

— Ministerial Decree No. 252 to approve the Labour Code, dated 30 December 1971 (*Gaceta Oficial*, No. 17,040, Extraordinary, 18 February 1972), as amended up to Act No. 44, dated 12 August 1995 (*Gaceta Oficial*, No. 22,847, 14 August 1995, pp. 1-46) [LS 1971-Pan.1; 1981-Pan.1; DDS 1995-PAN1]. Sections 30-61.

Papua New Guinea

— Employment Act 1978, Act No. 54, dated 12 September 1978 (*National Gazette*, 1978), as amended up to Act No. 16, dated 30 July 1981 (*National Gazette*, 1981). Sections 47-52.

— Information provided to the ILO by the Employers' Federation of Papua New Guinea, May 1995.

Paraguay

— Act No. 213 to establish the Labour Code, dated 29 October 1993 (*Gaceta Oficial*, No. 105 bis, 29 October 1993, pp. 1-30) [DDS 1993-PRY1]. Sections 194-234.

— Information provided to the ILO by the Ministry of Justice and Labour, July 1995.

— Information provided to the ILO by the Federation of Production, Industry and Commerce (FEPRINCO), December 1995.

Peru

— Constitution of Peru, dated 12 July 1979 (*El Peruano*, 1979) [LS 1984-Peru 1].

— Ministerial Decree No. 1208-85-ED to authorize paid leave on the death of a spouse, parent or child to employees and officials covered by Legislative Decree No. 276, dated 6 November 1985 (*El Peruano*, No. 1779, 13 November 1985, p. 39,782).

— Information provided to the ILO by the Ministry of Labour and Social Promotion, June 1995.

Philippines

— Presidential Decree No. 442 instituting a Labor Code, dated 1 May 1974 (*Official Gazette*, Nos. 23-25, 10-24 June 1974), as amended up to Republic Act No. 6725, dated 12 May 1989 (*Official Gazette*, 1989) [LS 1974-Phi.1; LLD 1989-PHL3]. Sections 82-94.

— Executive Order No. 203 providing a list of regular holidays and special days to be observed throughout the Philippines and for other purposes, dated 30 June 1987 (*Official Gazette*, Vol. 83, No. 29, 20 July 1987, p. 3307).

— Department of Labor and Employment: *Handbook on workers' statutory monetary benefits* (Manila, 1994).

— Rules and Regulations implementing the Labour Code of the Philippines, dated 19 January 1975 (*Official Gazette*, 1975), as amended up to Rules and Regulations, dated 22 May 1989 (*Official Gazette*, 1989) [LLD 1989-PHL2].

Poland

— Labour Code, dated 26 June 1974 (*Dziennik Ustaw*, No. 24, Text 141, 5 July 1974), as amended up to Act, dated 28 December 1989 (*Dziennik Ustaw*, No. 4, Text 19, 27 January 1990, p. 37) [LS 1974-Pol.1; 1989-Pol.3]. Sections 128-134, 154 and Part IX.

— Information provided to the ILO by the Ministry of Labour and Social Policy, May 1995.

Portugal

— Legislative Decree No. 409/71 to establish new statutory provisions respecting hours of work, dated 27 September 1971 (*Diário do Governo*, No. 228, 27 September 1971, p. 1393), as amended up to Legislative Decree No. 398/91, dated 16 October 1991 (*Diário da República*, No. 238, 16 October 1991, p. 5373). Sections 5, 10, 29-30, 33 and 37-38.

— Ordinance to establish work rules for agriculture, dated 8 June 1979 (*Boletim do Trabalho e Emprego*, No. 21, 6 June 1979, p. 1538). Sections 18 and 24.

— Legislative Decree No. 49,408 to approve a new set of rules governing individual contracts of employment, dated 21 November 1969 (*Diário do Governo*, No. 275, 24 November 1969, p. 1670), as amended up to Legislative Decree No. 396/91, dated 16 October 1991 (*Diário da República*, No. 238, 16 October 1991, p. 5367). Sections 51, 122 and 124.

— Ministerial Ordinance No. 714/93 respecting the employment of young workers, dated 3 August 1993 (*Diário da República*, No. 180, 3 August 1993, p. 4172). Section 5.

— Legislative Decree No. 874/76 respecting leave, public holidays and absence from work, dated 28 December 1976 (*Diário da República*, No. 300, 28 December 1976, p. 2856), as amended up to Legislative Decree No. 397/91, dated 16 October 1991 (*Diário da República*, No. 238, 16 October 1991, p. 5370). Sections 2, 4, 6, 16, 18-19 and 23-24.

— Legislative Decree No. 421/83 respecting overtime, dated 2 December 1983 (*Diário da República*, No. 277, 2 December 1983, p. 3949), as amended up to Legislative Decree No. 398/91, dated 16 October 1991 (*Diário da República*, No. 238, 16 October 1991, p. 5373). Sections 5, 7 and 9.

— Act No. 4/84 respecting maternity and paternity protection, dated 5 April 1984 (*Diário da República*, No. 81, 5 April 1984, p. 1149), as amended up to Act No. 17/95, dated 9 June 1995 (*Diário da República*, No. 134, 9 June 1995, p. 3754). Sections 10 and 13.

— Information provided to the ILO by the Ministry of Employment and Social Security, November 1995.

Qatar

— Labour Law 1962, Act No. 3, dated 19 March 1962 (*Al-Jarida Al-Rasmiya*, 1962), as amended up to Act No. 2, dated 31 January 1981 (*Al-Jarida Al-Rasmiya*, No. 3, 11 March 1981). Sections 35-51.

— Information provided to the ILO by the Ministry of Labour, Social Affairs and Housing, May 1995.

Romania

— Constitution of Romania, dated 21 November 1991 (*Monitorul Oficial*, Part I, No. 233, 21 November 1991, pp. 1-24). Section 38.

— Act No. 31 on the establishment of the duration of the working time under eight hours a day for employees working under particular — harmful, difficult or dangerous — conditions, dated 22 March 1991 (*Monitorul Oficial*, Part I, No. 64, 27 March 1991). Section 1.

— Act No. 6 on the employees' paid holidays and other holidays, dated 5 February 1992 (*Monitorul Oficial*, Part I, No. 16, 10 February 1992). Sections 1-2, 6 and 10.

— ILO: "Statistical annex", in *World Labour Report 1995* (Geneva, 1995), p. 117.

Russian Federation

— Act to approve the Labour Code of the RSFSR, dated 9 December 1971 (*Vedomosti Verkhovnogo Soveta RSFSR*, No. 50, Text 1007, 16 December 1971), as amended up to Act, dated 1 March 1993 (*Vedomosti S'ezda narodnykh deputatov Rossijskoj Federacii I Verkhovnogo Soveta Rossijskoj Federacii*, 1993) [LS 1971-USSR1; 1974-USSR2; 1976-USSR2; 1980-USSR3; 1982-USSR1].

Rwanda

— Ministerial Order No. 641/06 to determine modes of applying the 45-hour week and to fix minimum rates payable for overtime, night work and work on non-working days, dated 13 August 1981 (*Journal Officiel*, No. 17, 1 September 1981, pp. 837-841). Sections 1, 7 and 15.

— Act to establish a Labour Code, dated 28 February 1967 (*Journal Officiel*, No. 5, 1 March 1967, p. 107), as amended up to Act No. 21, dated 13 November 1989 (*Journal Officiel*, No. 24, 15 December 1989, pp. 1827-1828) [LS 1967-Rwa.1]. Sections 122, 131 and 133.

— Presidential Order No. 268/06/2 to determine public holidays, dated 20 August 1973 (*Journal Officiel*, No. 24, 15 December 1973, pp. 303-304). Section 1.

— Presidential Order No. 442/06 to determine occasional leaves and to fix their duration, dated 10 May 1990 (*Journal Officiel*, No. 12, 15 June 1990, pp. 629-630). Section 1.

Saint Vincent and the Grenadines

— Wages Regulations (Industrial Workers) Order 1989, Statutory Rules and Orders No. 10, dated 31 March 1989 (*Statutory Rules and Orders*, 1989, pp. 19-21).

— Wages Regulations (Agricultural Workers) Order 1989, Statutory Rules and Orders No. 13, dated 31 March 1989 (*Statutory Rules and Orders*, 1989, pp. 29-30).

San Marino

— Act No. 7 respecting the protection of labour and workers, dated 17 February 1961 (*Bollettino Ufficiale*, No. 2, 16 March 1961, p. 11) [LS 1961-SM1]. Sections 16-18 and 21-22.

Sao Tome and Principe

— Act No. 6/92 to promulgate a legal system for individual working conditions, dated 21 February 1992 (*Diário da República*, No. 12, 11 June 1992, p. 45) [DDS 1992-STP1]. Sections 36-37, 39, 45, 47, 55-57, 59, 63 and 76.

Saudi Arabia

— Royal Decree No. M/21 to promulgate the Labour Code, dated 15 November 1969 (*Um-Al-Qura*, 1969) [LS 1969-Sau.Ar.1]. Sections 147-159 and 162.

Senegal

— Act No. 61-34 to establish a Labour Code, dated 15 June 1961 (*Journal Officiel*, No. 3462, 3 July 1961, p. 1015), as amended up to Act No. 87-29, dated 18 August 1987 (*Journal Officiel*, 1987) [LS 1962-Sen.2B; 1971-Sen.1; 1975-Sen.1; 1976-Sen.1; 1977-Sen.1; 1980-Sen.1; 1987-Sen.1]. Sections 134 and 142-145.

— Decree No. 70-184 to fix remuneration for overtime, dated 20 February 1970 (*Journal Officiel*, 9 March 1970, p. 259). Sections 2-4.

— Decree No. 74-1125 to fix the national holiday, 1 May and other public holidays, dated 19 November 1974 (*Journal Officiel*, 7 December 1974, p. 948), as amended up to Act No. 83-54, dated 18 February 1983 (*Journal Officiel*, No. 4939, 2 April 1983, p. 258). Section 2.

— J. Issa-Sayegh: *Droit du travail sénégalais: Tome 42* (Abidjan, Nouvelles Editions Africaines, 1987), pp. 495-496.

Seychelles

— Employment Act 1995, Act No. 2, dated 28 February 1995 (*Official Gazette*, Supplement, 13 March 1995, pp. 5-70). Sections 2-4.

— Conditions of Employment Regulations 1991, Statutory Instrument No. 34, dated 24 April 1994 (*Official Gazette*, Supplement, 29 April 1991, pp. 115-136), as amended up to Statutory Instrument No. 81, dated 3 July 1992 (*Official Gazette*, Supplement, 6 July 1992, p. 273). Sections 2-6, 9-11 and 20.

— Information provided to the ILO by the Ministry of Employment and Social Affairs, July 1995.

Singapore

— Employment Act 1968, Act No. 17, dated 6 August 1968 (*Government Gazette*, No. 18, Acts Supplement, 12 August 1968, p. 141), as amended up to Act No. 21, dated 10 August 1984 (*Government Gazette*, No. 24, Acts Supplement, 17 August 1984, p. 193) [LS 1968-Sin.1]. Sections 35-50.

— Employment of Children and Young Persons Regulations 1976, Regulations No. S3, dated 31 December 1975 (*Government Gazette*, No. 1, Subsidiary Legislation Supplement, 2 January 1976, p. 7), as amended up to Regulations No. S97, dated 25 April 1977 (*Government Gazette*, 1977). Sections 2-10.

— Holidays Act 1966, Act No. 54, dated 27 December 1966 (*Government Gazette*, No. 2, Acts Supplement, 6 January 1966, p. 3), as amended up to Act No. 24, dated 6 August 1968 (*Government Gazette*, No. 19, Acts Supplement, 12 August 1968, p. 209).

Slovenia

— Labour Relations Act, dated 29 March 1990 (*Uradni List Republike Slovenije*, No. 14, 16 April 1990, pp. 781-794), as amended up to Act, dated 20 December 1993 (*Uradni List Republike Slovenije*, No. 71, 30 December 1993, pp. 3691-3692). Sections 1 and 37-74.

Solomon Islands

— Labour Act 1969, Act No. 3, dated 1 June 1960 (*Official Gazette*, Ch. 75, 1960), as amended up to the Unfair Dismissal Act of 1982 (*Official Gazette*, 1982). Sections 10-12.

Somalia

— Act No. 65 to promulgate the Labour Code, dated 18 October 1972 (*Bollettino Ufficiale*, No. 10, Supplement No. 3, 25 October 1972, p. 1114) [LS 1972-Som.1].

South Africa

— Basic Conditions of Employment Act 1983, Act No. 3, dated 16 February 1983 (*Government Gazette*, No. 8558, 23 February 1983, p. 1), as amended up to Act No. 66, dated 29 November 1995 (*Government Gazette*, Vol. 366, No. 16,861, 13 December 1995, p. 1). Sections 2, 7 and 10-12.

— Public Holidays Act 1994, Act No. 36, dated 23 November 1994 (*Government Gazette*, Vol. 354, No. 16,136, 7 December 1994, p. 3).

— See also country study in Part II for additional sources.

Spain

— Act No. 8 to promulgate a Workers' Charter, dated 10 March 1980 (*Boletín Oficial del Estado*, No. 64, 14 March 1980, p. 5799), as amended up to Legislative Decree No. 1, dated 24 March 1995 (*Boletín Oficial del Estado*, No. 75, 29 March 1995, pp. 9654-9688). Sections 34-35 and 37.

Sri Lanka

— Wages Boards Ordinance 1941, Ordinance No. 27, dated 19 September 1941 (*Gazette*, 1941), as amended up to Act No. 36, dated 12 October 1982 (*Gazette*, Part II, Supplement, 15 October 1982). Sections 24-25 and 64.

— Shops and Office Employees (Regulation of Employment and Remuneration) Act 1954, dated 9 August 1954 (*Gazette*, No. 10,724, Supplement, 15 October 1954), as amended up to Act No. 44, dated 20 November 1985 (*Gazette*, Part II, Supplement, 22 November 1985) [LS 1954-Cey.1; 1957-Cey.2]. Sections 2-9.

— Holidays Act 1971, Act No. 29, dated 26 August 1971 (*Gazette*, 1971).

— Information provided to the ILO by the Department of Labour, July 1995.

The Sudan

— Individual Labour Relations Act 1981, Act No. 65, dated 20 June 1981 (*Sudan Gazette*, No. 1286, Supplement No. 1, 25 June 1981, p. 1). Sections 3-4 and 19-29.

Swaziland

— Employment Act 1980, Act No. 5, dated 26 September 1980 (*Government Gazette*, No. 55, Extraordinary, 10 October 1980), as amended up to Act No. 4, dated 14 January 1985 (*Government Gazette*, No. 388, 1985).

— Regulation of Wages (Manufacturing and Processing Industry) Order 1994, Legal Notice No. 60 of 1994 (*Government Gazette*, Vol. 32, No. 18, 15 April 1994, p. S47).

— Regulation of Wages (Agricultural Industry) Order 1994, Legal Notice No. 172 of 1994 (*Government Gazette*, Vol. 32, No. 48, 23 September 1994, p. S20).

Sweden

— Act No. 673 respecting hours of work, dated 24 June 1982 (*Svensk författningssamling*, No. 673, 1982), as amended up to Act No. 637, dated 11 June 1992 (*Svensk författningssamling*, No. 637, 1992) [LS 1982-Swe.2]. Sections 13-17.

— Annual Leave Act, Act No. 480, dated 9 June 1977 (*Svensk författningssamling*, No. 480, 1977), as amended up to Act No. 1329, dated 17 December 1992 (*Svensk författningssamling*, No. 1329, 1992) [LS 1977-Swe.2].

— Act No. 981 respecting the right of employees to time off for training purposes, dated 13 December 1974 (*Svensk författningssamling*, No. 981, 1974), as amended up to Act No. 89, dated 24 February 1982 (*Svensk författningssamling*, No. 89, 1982) [LS 1974-Swe.6].

— See also country study in Part II for additional sources.

Switzerland

— Federal Act respecting work in industry, handicrafts and commerce (Labour Act), dated 13 March 1964 (*Recueil des lois fédérales*, No. 4, 24 January 1966, p. 57), as amended up Act, dated 8 October 1993 (*Recueil des lois fédérales*, No. 16, 26 April 1993, pp. 1035-1036) [LS 1964-Swi.1]. Sections 9-20 and 34(1).

— Code of Obligations, dated 30 March 1911 (*Recueil des lois fédérales*, 1911), as amended up to Act, dated 17 December 1993 (*Recueil des lois fédérales*, No. 45, 15 November 1994, pp. 2386-2397) [LS 1971-Swi.1]. Section 329.

— Ordinance No. 1 respecting the Labour Act, dated 14 January 1966 (*Recueil des lois fédérales*, No. 4, 24 January 1966, p. 85). Section 62(1).

Syrian Arab Republic

— Act No. 91 to promulgate the Labour Code, dated 5 April 1959 (*Al-jarida al-rasmiya*, No. 71bis B, 7 April 1959, p. 1), as amended up to Act No. 132, dated 28 March 1960 (*Al-jarida al-rasmiya*, No. 80, 9 April 1960, p. 518) [LS 1959-UAR1; 1960-UAR2]. Sections 114-127 and 145.

— Presidential Decree No. 3309 to issue regulations for employment in the public sector, dated 22 August 1966 (*Al-jarida al-rasmiya*, No. 195, 28 August 1966) [LS 1966-UAR1B]. Sections 41-51.

Tanzania, United Republic of

— Regulations of Wages and Terms of Employment Order 1993, Government Notice No. 294, dated 22 December 1993 (*Gazette of the United Republic of Tanzania*, Subsidiary Legislation, Supplement No. 44, 31 December 1993, pp. 297-302). Sections 3, 6-7 and 10.

— Information provided to the ILO by the Ministry of Labour and Youth Development, June 1995.

Thailand

— Announcement of the Minister of the Interior respecting labour protection, dated 16 April 1972 (*Government Gazette*, No. 61, Special issue, 16 April 1972), as amended up to Notification No. 13, dated 28 April 1993 (*Government Gazette*, Vol. 110, Nos. 17-18, Special issue, 20-30 June 1993, p. 265) [LS 1972-Thai.2]. Sections 3-9 and 39-42.

Togo

— Ordinance No. 16 to promulgate a Labour Code, dated 8 May 1974 (*Journal Officiel*, Extraordinary, 10 May 1974). Sections 108, 110 and 116-118.

— Ordinance No. 79-10 to regulate public holidays, dated 2 March 1979 (*Journal Officiel*, No. 8, 1 April 1979, p. 178). Section 1.

Tunisia

— Act No. 66-27 to promulgate a Labour Code, dated 30 April 1966 (*Journal Officiel*, Nos. 20-22, 3-24 May 1966), as amended up to Act No. 94-29, dated 21 February 1994 (*Journal Officiel*, No. 15, 22 February 1994, pp. 318-325). Sections 79-115.

— Decree No. 95-1085 to fix public holidays giving leave for state officials, local collectives and public administrative establishments, dated 19 June 1995 (*Journal Officiel*, No. 51, 27 June 1995, p. 1357). Section 1.

Turkey

— Labour Act, Act No. 1475, dated 25 August 1971 (*Resmî Gazete*, No. 13,943, 1 September 1971), as amended up to Act No. 2869, dated 29 July 1983 (*Resmî Gazete*, No. 18,120, 30 July 1983) [LS 1983-Tur.3]. Sections 2, 5, 35-37, 41-49 and 61-67.

— Act No. 2739 respecting the national festival and public holidays and rest days, dated 25 May 1935 (*Resmî Gazete*, Part I, 1935, No. 3017, p. 5262), as amended up to Act No. 2429, dated 17 March 1981 (*Resmî Gazete*, No. 17,284, 19 March 1981, p. 2) [LS 1935-Tur.1]. Sections 1-2.

Uganda

— Employment Decree 1975, Decree No. 4, dated 2 June 1975 (*Uganda Gazette*, 1975) [LS 1975-Ug.1]. Sections 5, 38, 41-42 and 66.

— Information provided to the ILO by the National Organisation of Trade Unions (Uganda), May 1995.

Ukraine

— Fundamental principles governing the labour legislation of Ukraine, dated 10 December 1971, as amended up to 1 December 1992 [Direction of Labour and Social Questions: *Zbirnyk Materialiv z Pytan Trudovogo Zakonodavstva Ukrainy* (Vinnitsa, 1992), pp. 1-99]. Sections 50-51, 63-76, 84 and 106-107.

United Arab Emirates

— Federal Law No. 8 to regulate employment relationships, dated 20 April 1980 (*Al-Jarida Al-Rasmiya*, No. 79, April 1980, p. 26) [LS 1980-UAE1]. Sections 25-26 and 65-90.

United Kingdom

— See country study in Part II for sources.

United States

— Fair Labor Standards Act, 29 *United States Code* 201 et seq.

— See also country study in Part II for additional sources.

Uruguay

— Decree to make regulations under the labour laws respecting the limitation of the hours of work in industry, commerce and offices, dated 29 October 1957 (*Diario Oficial*, No. 15,258, 11 November 1957, p. 300-A) [LS 1957-Ur.1].

— Decree No. 287 to extend the system of a full working day to young persons between the ages of 16 and 18 years old, dated 21 May 1980 (*Diario Oficial*, No. 20,771, 30 June 1980, p. 647-A) [LS 1980-Ur.1].

— Act to amend and extend the system of annual leave with pay for salaried and wage-earning employees in the private sector, dated 23 December 1958 (*Diario Oficial*, No. 15,581, 5 January 1959, p. 14-A) [LS 1958-Ur.1].

— Act No. 15,996 respecting overtime in the private sector, dated 9 November 1988 (*Diario Oficial*, No. 22,752, 25 November 1988, pp. 427A-428A), as amended up to

Decree No. 550/989, dated 22 November 1989 (*Diario Oficial*, No. 23,005, 12 December 1989, p. 348A).

— H-H. Barbagelata: "Uruguay", in R. Blainpain (ed.): *International Encyclopaedia for Labour Laws and Industrial Relations*, Vol. 12, ELL-Supplement 128, October 1991 (Deventer, Kluwer, 1991), pp. 131-138.

Venezuela

— Organic Labour Act, dated 27 November 1990 (*Gaceta Oficial*, No. 4240, Extraordinary, 20 December 1990) [LLD 1990-VEN2]. Sections 154-155, 195-196, 205, 207, 212 and 219.

— Information provided to the ILO by the Ministry of Labour, July 1995.

— A. Llovera and L. Riera (eds.): *Ley orgánica del trabajo*, 2nd revised edition (Caracas, Centro de Investigaciones y Asesoría Jurídica del Trabajo, 1991).

Viet Nam

— Labour Code, dated 23 June 1994 [LLD 1994-VNM1]. Sections 68-79 and 119-127.

Yemen

— Decree-Law No. 5 concerning the promulgation of the Labour Code, dated 7 October 1970 (*Official Gazette*, No. 6, 15 October 1970). Sections 40-41, 54-57, 78 and 88-91.

Yugoslavia

— Decree No. 921 to promulgate the Act respecting the fundamental rights arising out of the employment relationship, dated 28 September 1989 (*Službeni List*, No. 60, 6 October 1989, p. 1469). Sections 24-46.

— ILO: "Statistical annex", in *World Labour Report 1995* (Geneva, 1995), p. 117.

Zaire

— Legislative Ordinance No. 67/310 to establish a Labour Code, dated 9 August 1967 (*Moniteur Congolais*, No. 16, 15 August 1967), as amended up to Act No. 73/008, dated 5 January 1973 (*Journal Officiel*, No. 5, 1 March 1973, p. 276) [LS 1967-Congo (Kin.)1; 1973-Zai.1; 1973-Zai.2]. Sections 100, 120 and 125.

— Order No. 68/11 to issue regulations respecting hours of work and payment for overtime, dated 17 May 1968 (*Moniteur Congolais*, 1968). Sections 5, 16, 19 and 21.

— Ordinance No. 72/363 to fix public holidays, dated 14 September 1972 (*Journal Officiel*, No. 22, 15 November 1972, p. 700). Section 1.

Zambia

— Minimum Wages and Conditions of Employment (General) Order 1990, Statutory Instrument No. 106, dated 9 August 1990 (*Government Gazette*, 17 August 1990, Supplement, pp. 299-301). Sections 4 and 8.

Zimbabwe

— Public Holidays and Prohibition of Business (Declaration and Notification of Public Holidays) Notice 1986, Statutory Instrument No. 177, dated 20 June 1986 (*Government Gazette*, No. 33, Supplement, 20 June 1986, p. 699).